World Class Schools

International perspectives on school effectiveness

Edited by David Reynolds, Bert Creemers, Sam Stringfield, Charles Teddlie and Gene Schaffer

with

Wynford Bellin
Shin-zen Chang
Yin Cheong Cheng
Wing Ming Cheung
John Clarke
Dympna Devine
Barbara Dundas
Astrid Eggen
Juanita Ross Epp
Walter Epp
Shaun Farrell
John Freeman
Barry Green

Marit Groterud
Henk Guldemond
Trond Eiliv Hauge
Chen-Jen Hwang
Peggy Kirby
Yong-yin Lee
Bjorn Nilsen
Hui-ling Pan
Mickey Pounders
Desmond Swan
Frans Swint
Wai Ming Tam
Dianne Taylor

London and New York

First published 2002 by RoutledgeFalmer
11 New Fetter Lane, London EC4P 4EE

Simultaneously published in the USA and Canada
by RoutledgeFalmer
29 West 35th Street, New York, NY 10001

RoutledgeFalmer is an imprint of the Taylor & Francis Group

Typeset in 10/12 pt Times New Roman
by Graphicraft Limited, Hong Kong
Printed and bound in Great Britain by TJ International Ltd, Padstow,
Cornwall

British Library Cataloguing in Publication Data
A catalogue record for this book is available from the British Library

Library of Congress Cataloging in Publication Data
World class schools : international perspectives on school effectiveness /
edited by David Reynolds . . . [*et al.*].
     p. cm.
     Includes bibliographical references and index.
     1. Schools – Evaluation – Cross-cultural studies.   2. School
improvement programs – Cross-cultural studies.   3. Educational
change – Cross-cultural studies.   I. Reynolds, David, 1949–

     LB2822.8.W67   2002
     389.1′58–dc21   2001048444

ISBN 0-415-25348-9

World Class Schools

This book reports on a unique study of school effectiveness in nine countries across the globe. The authors' aim was to design, conduct and analyse a study that would provide an insight into what may be universal, and what may be specific, factors producing effectiveness in schools and classrooms across nations. They use these findings to analyse educational policies and propose new ways of thinking about education and schools.

An ambitious project, the study combined quantitative and qualitative methods in a wide-ranging, multi-national and multi-year framework. In an attempt to define the factors that contribute to effective schooling, researchers studied schools, teachers and pupils in:

* Europe – the Netherlands, Norway, Republic of Ireland, the UK
* North America – the USA, Canada
* Australia and the Pacific Rim – Taiwan, Australia, Hong Kong

The results are fascinating. Not only do they offer valuable information for practical educational improvement, but it is hoped that they might encourage educationalists to look more deeply, and more often, at the rich educational world around them.

David Reynolds is Professor of Leadership and School Effectiveness at the University of Exeter, UK. **Bert Creemers** is Professor of Education and Research Director of GION at the University of Groningen, The Netherlands. **Sam Stringfield** is Principal Research Scientist at Johns Hopkins University, USA. **Charles Teddlie** is Distinguished Research Professor at Louisiana State University, USA. **Gene Schaffer** is a Professor at the University of Maryland, Baltimore County, USA.

To the children of the world – may they get the educational
science that they need

Contents

Preface

This book summarises findings from the International School Effectiveness Research Project (ISERP), which has been a multi-year study of differential school effects in nine countries on four continents, and uses them to analyse educational policies and to propose new ways of thinking about education and about schools.

The study arose from our dissatisfaction with the school effectiveness and international effectiveness research knowledge bases as they have existed. Within the school effects tradition, virtually every study has been conducted within a single nation. In the international effectiveness tradition, some effectiveness factors clearly have appeared to be travelling well and can be seen as universal, cross-nationally, and others have not. Yet there has been little research indicating why this might be so. Previous studies in the comparative education field have, by and large, been inadequate in not measuring such outcomes as student attendance and achievement. This is obviously limiting.

By contrast, the large, multi-national studies of student outcomes (such as the *Third International Maths and Science Study* of the late 1990s) have suffered on four counts. First, they have tended to use point-in-time measures, and this has offered little information on gain over time. Second, they have offered few practical prescriptions for educational improvement. Third, previous studies have tended to be purely quantitative or qualitative, yet much of modern educational research has moved to what is a more valuable mixed-method approach. Finally, previous international studies have often become bogged down in red tape and squabbles among scholars within and between countries as to how to progress, when to release reports and the like.

We wanted to design, conduct, analyse and publish a multi-year study that was intellectually and practically ahead of all others and this volume is the story of our efforts. In many ways, we have done this and ISERP has been a success, since it has enabled us to address many of the questions that have festered and still fester within our field. In some areas, though, we have received an education as to why multi-national studies have been so difficult to conduct.

For those of us who were the core team that planned ISERP, and we hope for the readers of this volume, the product has been well worth the effort. We hope that the school effectiveness, teacher effectiveness, international effectiveness and comparative education research communities will now walk more easily, and better informed, into the intellectually difficult areas of what may be universal, and what may be specific, factors producing effectiveness in schools and classrooms across nations. We also hope that educationalists in general will avert their eyes from their own cultures and look at the rich educational world around them more than they have managed to do historically.

David Reynolds
Bert Creemers
Sam Stringfield
Charles Teddlie
Gene Schaffer
July 2001

Note: we have used 'students' and 'pupils' to refer to young people interchangeably throughout the text, following the international traditions of different countries and different authors.

Part I

World class schools

ISERP, background, design and
quantitative findings

1 The intellectual and policy context

*David Reynolds, Sam Stringfield,
Charles Teddlie and Bert Creemers*

Introduction: the need for a cross-national approach

We live in a world which is becoming 'smaller' all the time. The influence of information technology has made it possible for productive processes to spread around the world in ways simply impossible before. The spread of mass communications, and particularly of satellite broadcasting, makes ideas that were formerly found only in isolated cultural 'niches' globally available. The enhanced interactions between citizens of different countries through visits, vacations, migration and electronic contact are clearly both breaking down cultural barriers and yet at the same time also leading to a reassertion of cultural distinctiveness amongst those exposed to increasing international globalisation.

The effects of globalisation have been the subject of much speculation. Friedman (1999) made one of the strongest and most detailed cases for the importance of understanding globalisation (which ended in his fourth grade daughter's classroom) and argues for many more people to become much more skilled at the gathering and integration of this kind of information. Similarly, David Gabbard's (2000), *Knowledge and Power in the Global Economy* repeatedly focuses on the need to see the economy, and education, in a global context. No less an authority than W. Edwards Deming (1993), speaking largely to a US audience, states 'Our problem is education and development of a culture that puts value on learning' (p. 6) and Friedman and Gabbard make clear that the same can be said within every nation wishing to succeed in the twenty-first century. For better or worse, each country's educational and economic systems are more tightly tied to each other today than at any time in history.

For all of us, as individual educators or as national educational institutions, to engage in 'best practice' we must find best practice, whether it is in Newcastle or New York or in New Orleans or in New Delhi or in Hong Kong's New Territories. Each nation must seek new ways to improve schooling by casting the broadest net possible. It only makes sense that nations do this together, so that scholars can learn together and nations grow together, and this process has in recent years been moving apace. In the United Kingdom, references to the superior achievements of 'Pacific Rim' economies or the 'Tiger' economies have historically peppered the speeches of Government and Opposition spokespersons, as has recognition of the possible educational reasons behind their success. In the United States, a similar debate about the implications of the low levels of performance of American schools in various international surveys continues to take place, with popular explanations including such things as the enhanced time that students from societies like Japan spend in school (e.g. Stedman, 1999) and their high levels of 'opportunity to learn' or supposed superior teaching methods (Stigler and Hiebert, 1999). Other societies too have been looking outside their own cultural and geographical boundaries in the search for factors they might add to their own educational systems to improve their 'blend' of practice, as in the case of the interest from the countries of the Pacific Rim in the so called 'progressive' technologies of education that have historically been the province of the Western European and particularly British educational traditions (Reynolds, 1997; Townsend and Cheng, 2000).

However, academic traditions of research and scholarship have run behind this increased internationalisation of education, and the field of school effectiveness which this study is located within has not historically been noted for particularly internationalised traditions. Indeed, in its early phases the field showed heavily ethnocentric tendencies. Literature referred to within books and articles had usually been almost exclusively based upon scholars and researchers within the country of origin of the writer (see Good and Brophy, 1986a, b for an American example, and Mortimore *et al.*, 1988 for one from Great Britain). Although there had been acknowledgements of the seminal North American studies of Edmonds (1979a, b), Brookover *et al.* (1979) and Coleman *et al.* (1966) and of the British studies of Rutter *et al.* (1979) and Mortimore *et al.* (1988) in virtually all school effectiveness publications from all countries, there had historically been no science of school effectiveness across countries as there has customarily been an international reach in the case of medicine, in most areas of psychology and in all of the 'applied' and 'pure' sciences. Only in the last few years has an international 'reach' in the field been obvious, shown in the literature reviews such as those of Scheerens and Bosker (1997) and Teddlie and Reynolds (2000), probably generated by the International Congress for School Effectiveness and Improvement (ICSEI) which now brings together researchers and others from over sixty countries to its annual meetings, and by the *School Effectiveness and School Improvement* journal.

The ethnocentric situation within which school effectiveness had been located is even more surprising given that its sister discipline of school improvement/school development shows considerable evidence of a historic internationally established community. The landmark review of literature by the Canadian Fullan (1991), for example, shows awareness of developments in school improvement practice and theory in probably a dozen societies outside North America, and the comparable review of improvement literature from Great Britain by Hopkins and colleagues shows considerable awareness of American, Canadian, Dutch, Norwegian, Australian and Swedish developments (Hopkins *et al.*, 1994).

One of the features of this historic absence of cross-national communication within the field is the lack of recognition of what the existing internationally based educational effectiveness studies can contribute to our understanding (for speculations on this theme see Reynolds *et al.*, 1994a, b, c). The cross-national studies of the International Association for the Evaluation of Educational Achievement (IEA) and of the International Assessment of Educational Progress (IAEP) all have fascinating descriptions of cross-national variation on achievement scores, together with limited, though useful, descriptions of classroom and school level processes that appear associated with the national differences. (IEA examples are Anderson, Ryan and Shapiro, 1989; Postlethwaite and Wiley, 1992; Robitaille and Garden, 1989. IAEP examples are Foxman, 1992; Keys and Foxman, 1989; Lapointe, Mead and Phillips, 1989.) The Third International Science and Mathematics Study (TIMSS) has also further aroused interest in the classical quantitative paradigm (Harris, Keys and Fernandes, 1997) and its more qualitative derivatives (Stigler and Hiebert, 1999).

However, these studies are rarely referenced or their insights utilised within the *national* research enterprises of the dozen or so countries where significant school effectiveness research has been in progress. Indeed, whilst there is synergy between school effectiveness research and such areas as educational policy, educational assessment and instructional concerns within most countries, there is no evidence within any country of engagement between school effectiveness and the comparative education discipline, or even with its concerns. Comparative education itself of course has a number of features that may make it less useful than it might have been to the wider educational research community, including the presence of theories drawn up without apparent empirical reference, the absence of 'hard' outcome measures and the very widespread assumption that policy interventions in the educational policies of societies have corresponding effects on the nature of educational processes and educational outcomes, a kind of 'for outcomes see policies' approach that is of very dubious validity. It should be admitted openly, therefore, that the lack of intellectual progress made by studies in the 'IEA tradition' and by comparative education in general may not have made those traditions attractive to other disciplines.

The benefits of a cross-national approach

The limited presence historically of cross-national perspectives and relationships within the field of school effectiveness, the neglect of the internationally based effectiveness research on educational achievement, and the lack of interaction between educational research communities within societies and the comparative education discipline, are all features of the present state of the school effectiveness discipline that must be seen as having been increasingly intellectually costly. Indeed, we have argued this extensively elsewhere (e.g. Reynolds *et al.*, 1994a, b, c, 1998; Reynolds and Teddlie, 2000a, b, c).

Firstly, the educational debates that are currently in evidence in many societies concerning the appropriate means of improving their educational standards (in the United Kingdom, United States, Germany, Norway and Sweden, to name but a few of the locations) are often based upon proposed simplistic 'transplants' of knowledge from one culture to another, without any detailed acknowledgement in the political or educational policy debate as to the possible context-specificity of the apparently 'effective' policies to the original societies utilising them.

A contemporary example of translation of findings from one culture to another is the current enthusiasm for whole-class direct and interactive instruction at Key Stage Two (ages seven to eleven) in British primary schools, clearly based upon an enthusiasm for the educational practices of the Pacific Rim and the making of a consequent association between their high levels of achievement and their classroom practices (Lynn, 1988; Reynolds and Farrell, 1996). The same enthusiasm has also been clear in the United States (Stevenson and Stigler, 1992). In a decade when educational policy prescriptions are travelling internationally with increasing frequency, it is unfortunate that school effectiveness researchers still seem locked into a mind-set that can handle only the patterns of intakes, processes and outcomes of their own cultures, rather than attempting to throw light on issues of possible context-specificity or universality. Although policy experimentation of this kind has not been harmful thus far, there is no guarantee this will continue.

Secondly, another reason for the usefulness of internationally based perspectives is that the school effectiveness discipline needs to understand much more about why some much-utilised variables 'travel' in explaining effectiveness across countries, whilst others do not. Assertive principal instructional leadership is perhaps one of the most well supported of all the American 'correlates' that lie within the 'five factor' model originally formulated by Edmonds (1979a and b) and subsequently developed into the 'seven factor' model by Lezotte (1989), yet in spite of the massive empirical support for the importance of this factor in the United States (e.g. Levine and Lezotte, 1990), Dutch researchers (e.g. Van de Grift, 1989, 1990) have been generally unable to validate its importance within the differing Dutch educational and social climate (apparently Dutch principals are often promoted out of the existing school staff and have a much more facilitative, group-based and 'democratic' attitude to their colleagues).

The third reason for the use of an internationally based perspective is that only international studies can tap the full range of variation in school and classroom quality, and therefore in potential school and classroom effects. *Within* any country the range in school factors in terms of 'quantity' variables (such as size, financial resources, quality of building, etc.) and in terms of 'quality' factors (such as teacher expectations, teacher experience, school culture, etc.) is likely to be much less than the range *across* countries. Put simply, it is likely that the existing estimates we have concerning the size of educational influences (schools and classrooms together) upon students, which have settled into a range of from 8 per cent to 14 per cent of variance explained in virtually all of the recent empirical studies (see Teddlie and Reynolds, 2000), are merely artefacts of these studies' lack of school and classroom variation within nations. The true power of school and classroom is, if this reasoning is correct, only likely to be shown by cross-cultural and comparative work on international samples.

The fourth reason why school effectiveness could gain considerable benefits if there was an enhanced internationalisation of the field is that international study is likely to generate more sensitive theoretical explanations than those offered at present. Today's situation within the field of school effectiveness displays an absence of more than a handful of theoretical explanations of even a 'middle range' variety (see Teddlie and Reynolds, 2000, ch. 10) and the reason why an international perspective may generate both intellectually interesting *and* practical middle-range theories is connected with the ways in which school and classroom factors 'travel' cross-culturally to a very varied degree, as noted earlier. Why is it that 'assertive principal instructional leadership' does not predict effective school status in the Netherlands? What is it in the local, regional or national ecology that might explain this finding? Answering this question inevitably involves the generation of more complex explanations that operate on a number of 'levels' of the educational system/society interaction, and is likely to be generative of more complex, sensitive and multilayered explanations than those generated by the simple *within* country research findings.

The international effectiveness studies

There *is* a pre-existing body of research that attempts to look at issues to do with possible differences in school effectiveness and school effectiveness factors between countries and the factors associated with them, which is that which has been generated by the IEA and by the IAEP which we noted earlier.

The studies themselves are of course numerous, as are commentaries, critiques and reviews of them – indeed, one of the more surprising strands running through the assessments of their work made by members of the IEA teams is their evident pleasure at the impact that their studies have had as measured by media interest, articles on their work in popular magazines and the like (see for example Noah, 1987). Briefly, the IEA conducted the First and Second Science Studies (Comber and Keeves, 1973; Rosier and Keeves, 1991; Postlethwaite and Wiley, 1992; Keeves, 1992); the First and Second Mathematics Studies (Husen, 1967; Travers and Westbury, 1989); the Study of Written Composition (Purves, 1992) and the Classroom Environment Study mentioned earlier (Anderson *et al.*, 1989). Recent published projects include the major TIMSS project (the Third International Mathematics and Science Study). The IAEP conducted two studies of science and mathematics achievement cross-culturally (Keys and Foxman, 1989; Lapointe *et al.*, 1989). The IEA also published the findings of the First Literacy Study (Elley, 1992; Postlethwaite and Ross, 1992). Reviews of the great majority of these studies are in Reynolds and Farrell (1996).

The results of these studies differ to an extent, according to the precise outcome measures being utilised, whether it be reading/literacy, numeracy, or science achievement. What is common, though, is a 'country against country' perspective, as in the recent TIMSS study (Harris, Keys and Fernandes, 1997).

However, all these studies have been conducted utilising a cross-sectional methodology in which achievement is measured at a point in time, and it is unclear the extent to which cultural, social, economic and educational factors are implicated in the country differences. Because of the difficulty of untangling these various influences, cohort studies are more useful, whereby the same children are studied over time, permitting an assessment of the effects of education with the other factors partially 'controlled out'. However, the expense of cohort studies has greatly limited their use in international research.

There are of course further problems that have placed severe limitations upon the capacity of these international effectiveness studies to generate valid knowledge about educational effectiveness. Some problems are present in all cross-national research, such as those of accurate translation of material, of ensuring reliability in the 'meaning' of factors (such as social class or status indicators, for example), of problems caused by Southern Hemisphere countries having their school years begin in January and of problems caused because of retrospective information being required.

In certain curriculum areas, the cross-national validity of the tests utilised gives cause for grave concern and, as an example, the IEA study of written composition failed in its attempt to compare the performance of groups of students in different national systems that used different languages. The latter study indeed concluded that 'The construct that we call written composition must be seen in a cultural context and not considered a general cognitive capacity or activity' (Purves, 1992, p. 199). Even the simple administration of an achievement test in the varying cultural contexts of different countries may pose problems, particularly in the case of England where the 'test mode' in which closed questions are asked in an examination-style format under time pressure may not approximate to students' general experience of school. By contrast, the use of this test mode within a society such as Taiwan, where these assessment methods are very frequently experienced, may facilitate Taiwanese scores, just as it may depress English achievement levels below their 'true' levels.

In addition to these basic problems that affect all large-scale international comparative research, there are specific problems concerning the IEA and IAEP international effectiveness studies that represent virtually the totality of this international research enterprise so far:

Research design

- The basic design of these studies, which are concerned to explain country against country variation, may itself have been responsible for problems. Generally a small number of schools each possessing a large number of students are selected, which makes it difficult to make valid comparisons between schools once factors such as school type, socio-economic status of students and catchment areas are taken into account. Statistics may also be unstable because of small numbers.
- Curriculum subjects have been studied separately, making an integrated picture of schools in different countries difficult.
- There has been considerable difficulty in designing tests which sample the curricula in all countries acceptably, although the TIMSS project expended considerable energy to ensure a geographical reach of items, and also published its results 'unadjusted' and 'adjusted' for the curriculum coverage of individual countries.

Sampling

- There have been very large variations in the response rates that make interpretation of scores difficult. In the IAEP, for example, school participation rates of those schools originally approached varied from 70 per cent to 100 per cent across countries, and student participation rates varied similarly from 73 per cent to 98 per cent. In the IEA Second Science Study, the student response rate varied from 99.05 per cent (in Japan) to 61.97 per cent (in England). Although all IEA and IAEP studies have been weighted to take account of differential response between strata, and although a comparison of responding and non-responding schools on public examinations in the above study showed little difference, the potential biases caused by variation in response rates have been a matter of considerable concern. As in many other areas, the TIMSS study made particular efforts to deal with variation in response rates.
- Sometimes samples of students used have not been representative of the country as a whole (e.g. one area of Italy was used as a surrogate for the whole country in one of the IAEP studies).
- Sometimes there have been variations as to when during the school year tests are administered, resulting in a sample of students of different mean ages in different countries.
- Choice of certain 'grades' or ages for sampling may not have generated similar populations for study from different countries. In the IEA Second Science Study, the mean ages of the country samples for the 'fourteen-year-old' students ranged from 13.9 to 15.1 years. Given the known relationships between age, length of time in school and achievement, this variation may have been responsible for some of the country differences.
- Policies in different countries concerning 'keeping children down' or 'putting children up a year' have generated difficulties of comparison, particularly affecting the ages of children in different countries.

- Variations between countries in the proportion of their children who could have taken part in the studies makes assessment of country differences difficult. Mislevy (1995) notes that, whilst 98 per cent of American children were in the sampling frame and eligible to take part in one study, the restriction of an Israeli sample to Hebrew-speaking public schools generated only 71 per cent of total children being in eligible schools.

An absence of needed data

- In many studies there has been a lack of information upon the non-school areas of children's lives (family and home environment) that might have explained achievement scores. Surrogates for social class utilised, such as 'number of books in the home', have not been adequate.
- Outcomes data has been collected mostly on the academic outcomes of schooling, yet social outcomes may be equally interesting. It is clear from the Stevenson (1992) studies that the 'superiority' of Japanese students over those of other societies may extend to areas such as children's perception of their control over their lives (locus of control), yet these 'affective' outcomes have been largely neglected. The explanation for this is clear (the problems of cross-cultural validity and reliability) but it is not clear why routinely available non-cognitive data (such as that on student attendance rates, for example) have not been used.
- The factors used to describe schools have often been overly resource-based (because of the greater perceived chance of obtaining reliability between observers in these areas across countries no doubt), in spite of the clearly limited explanatory power of such variables. At classroom level, only some studies (including TIMMS) have used any measures of processes, with the use of videotapes of classrooms by the TIMSS project being particularly interesting, although of course rare.
- Some of the most important educational effects are likely to lie in the areas of the 'moral messages' that the humanities subjects, like history, geography and civics, possess and which are integrated with their curriculum content. These differences, which formed the basis of the fascinating analysis by Bronfenbrenner (1972) of variations between the United States and the former Soviet Union in the propensity of their students to be 'pro-social' or 'anti-social', would probably repay study, but have not been studied because of the clear difficulties of investigation once one moves beyond subjects like mathematics where there are agreed 'right' answers across all countries.

An absence of needed analyses

- Only limited attempts have been made to analyse international samples differentially, by achievement say or by social class, with the exception of a limited amount of analysis by gender.

From all these points above, it will be clear that the large-scale international effectiveness surveys of international achievement of the IAEP and the IEA need to be subject to some caution. Not all studies possess the same design, analysis and methodological problems: no studies possess all the design, analysis and methodological problems in total. Enough studies possess enough of these problems, though, to make one cautious about interpretation. We should add at this point that of course our own study reported in this volume also has some of the same problems, whilst we hope making considerable progress in overcoming many of them.

The case for cross-national research

We have argued that there is more and more evidence that educational debate and discussion is becoming internationalised, in ways not seen before, in a world that is itself more and more internationalised. To resource this discussion, school effectiveness research has found considerable difficulty because it had been quite ethnocentric, with groups of scholars working in different countries pursuing isolated research agendas, largely uninfluenced by the agendas of other countries, although this is thankfully now changing. School effectiveness research has particularly found difficulty in addressing why some factors appear to travel across contexts, whilst others do not, which suggests a much more complex picture of the effective school 'technology' than the 'one size fits all' of the movement's earlier phases (see reviews of this in Levine and Lezotte, 1990; Sammons *et al.*, 1995). However, the international educational effectiveness research that has been undertaken thus far which attempts to look at 'what works' in different countries, and at related issues, has suffered from a number of design faults that have made it difficult to know how much relevance to attach to the findings.

The effect of all these factors means that at the moment we do not possess the kind of knowledge that is needed to address the issues which the increasingly internationalised world of education needs to address. In the absence of understanding about what 'travels' and why, and in the absence of understandings about the complex educational contexts of the world, the 'technology' of educational practices, processes and systems available to different countries will remain too limited for these countries to achieve the educational goals and targets that their politicians and policymakers are increasingly setting for them.

It is important to emphasise, though, that our aim in this study and this volume was to do considerably more than contribute to knowledge about what can be loosely called 'country differences', the tradition exemplified by the studies of the IEA discussed above. Our study indeed was planned to move beyond 'international horse races' of countries based on their achievement test scores by deliberately introducing contextual factors *within* countries as potentially important determinants of 'what worked'. With school effectiveness as a discipline showing evident difficulty in moving beyond 'steampress' models of effective schools of a 'one size fits all' variety, within countries let alone between them, we had wanted to intellectually advance the entire school effectiveness paradigm and research community as well as the rather moribund comparative education tradition. How school effectiveness has 'plateaued' in terms of advancing our knowledge, and our view of its related problems, form the remainder of this chapter.

The three generations of school effectiveness research

The first generation of research into school effectiveness started about twenty years ago. The Coleman Report (Coleman *et al.*, 1966), was widely interpreted as concluding that schools had little or no effect on student achievement when the effects of family-background variables have been taken into account, and generated a quite pessimistic view on the influence of education in general and more specifically on the influence of schools and teaching. In addition to methodological critiques of the report, there was a reaction against the report and studies were published that tried to prove that some schools did in fact do much better than could be expected of them on student achievement tests. Mostly these studies used a research design comparing positive and negative 'outlier' schools, selected from already existing data bases, and research was published in the United States in this tradition that got much attention in both the scholarly and the popular press. Ron Edmonds (1979a, b), a School Board superintendent, particularly addressed educational practitioners and Brookover *et al.* (1979) addressed the educational research community. These studies led to a 'movement' of school effectiveness research, and school improvement projects based on the findings of school effectiveness research, in the United States.

In the United Kingdom, school effectiveness research started with the work of Reynolds (1976) and the *Fifteen Thousand Hours* study (Rutter *et al.*, 1979). The important within-school factors determining high levels of school effectiveness in this latter study were the balance of intellectually able and less able children in a school, the reward system, the school's physical environment, the opportunities for children to take responsibility, the use of homework, the possession of academic goals, the teacher operating as a positive role model, good teacher management of the classroom and strong leadership combined with democratic decision-making from the headteacher. In British school effectiveness research, not only academic outcomes were measured. Other factors such as rates of attendance, rates of delinquency and levels of students' behavioural problems were also incorporated in the research designs.

The results of the early school effectiveness studies were that a number of factors appeared to be related to effectiveness, such as the American five factors that are often mentioned:

- strong educational leadership from the principal/headteacher;
- high expectations of student achievement;
- an emphasis on basic skills;
- a safe and orderly climate;
- frequent evaluation of pupil progress on achievement.

After the mid-1980s, a second generation of school effectiveness studies were carried out. These were rooted in school effectiveness research and school improvement experiences and projects, but took advantage of the criticisms of earlier school effectiveness research and the availability of new techniques for statistical analysis such as hierarchical linear modelling (HLM). Quite a lot of the research projects still used 'outlier' designs but the studies were carried out utilising more relevant methods such as classroom observation.

Major studies carried out or published after the mid-1980s were those by Mortimore *et al.* (1988) in the United Kingdom and by Teddlie and Stringfield (1993) in the United States. In the same period, school effectiveness studies also began in other countries like the Netherlands, Hong Kong and Norway (for an overview see Reynolds *et al.*, 1994). The majority of studies, as in the past, took place within primary education, because it was expected that educational effects in primary schools could contribute greatly to educational outcomes and to the future careers of students. In fact, most recent research and analyses support this viewpoint, since the results of students in secondary education are to a large part determined by the outcomes of their primary education (see the review in Reynolds *et al.*, 1996).

Mortimore's classic research was based upon fifty randomly selected London primary schools. Over a period of four years, the academic and social progress of 2,000 children were traced. Mortimore and his colleagues identified a number of schools which were effective in both academic and social areas. These schools possessed the following characteristics (Mortimore *et al.*, 1988):

- purposeful leadership of the staff by the headteacher;
- the involvement of the deputy head;
- the involvement of teachers;
- consistency amongst teachers;
- structured sessions;
- intellectually challenging teaching;
- a work-centred environment;
- a limited focus within sessions;
- maximum communication between teachers and students;
- good record-keeping;
- parental involvement;
- a positive climate.

The major comparable study carried out in the United States was the Louisiana School Effectiveness Study (Teddlie and Stringfield, 1993) which in fact was a programme of five studies, starting in 1980 with the first pilot study, and continuing through 1992 with the fourth study (the fifth study is currently being analysed and published). The study addressed both the 'meso' school level and the 'micro' classroom level, and used a combination of quantitative and qualitative techniques, with the data analysed at both the school and the classroom level. Differences between the more effective and the less effective elementary schools (selected as 'outliers') were found, with the classrooms of the more effective schools being different with respect to their pupils' higher time on task, the presentation of more new material, the encouragement of independent practice, the possession of high expectations, the use of positive reinforcement, and the presence of firm discipline, a friendly ambience, student work being displayed and a pleasant appearance of the classroom.

In addition to these two major studies, a lot of studies also looked into the specific characteristics of more effective schools and a review of those North American studies was provided by Levine and Lezotte (1990). Their summary confirmed the salience of the school effectiveness 'five-factor model', although additional effectiveness characteristics were included in this review from the teacher effectiveness area.

The research projects carried out in the second half of the eighties had more sophisticated research designs than earlier studies, and made use of more sophisticated techniques for data analysis. In some countries like the United States and the United Kingdom, the techniques for data collection often included school and classroom observation. In other countries, like the Netherlands, questionnaire-based surveys were used to collect data. Some studies, for example the Louisiana School Effectiveness studies, made a distinction between the school and the classroom levels, whereas other studies continued to mix classroom and school factors, which also held for most of the reviews of the research literature. Although research was improved over those years, the result was still a long list of correlates of school effectiveness that urgently needed regrouping and rethinking in order to generate better understanding, and Stringfield *et al.* (1992) rightly concluded a decade ago that the field needed to be developing sophisticated, practical, contextually sensitive models of effective schooling.

By the early to mid-1990s, many of the advances that were evident in the second phase of effectiveness research had largely run their course and a third phase began in which school effectiveness research largely plateaued intellectually. Contextual variation in 'what worked' was established in some of the studies that we noted at the beginning of this chapter, and in some within-United States work (Virgilio *et al.*, 1991; Wimpelberg *et al.*, 1989; Teddlie and Stringfield, 1993) on the effects of different socio-economic contexts, urban/rural differences and governance factors such as the private/public divide. If there was any unease at the extent to which these findings on the possible context-specificity of school effectiveness factors were intellectually invalidating the early material from the 'one size fits all' tradition within the school effectiveness research community, such unease rarely raised its head due to the increasing official sponsorship of the effectiveness community and the promotion of the simplistic five-, seven- or thirteen-factor models by governments and policymakers in some countries. With effectiveness researchers now enjoying considerable growth in the attention given them, in the research resources available to them and in the practitioner communities' willingness to buy their services, a group of people who had historically been distrusted by their professional peers and marginalised within their own professional research communities might have been excused for not rushing to complicate their knowledge bases with any notions of context-specificity that might have made their official acceptance more problematic.

Additionally, there was no sign that 'context' as a factor loomed any larger when researchers designed their research strategies, and the large-scale studies mounted in the United Kingdom, Australia and the Netherlands showed no desire to maximise contextual variation in order to possibly learn from it. In the United States, which had shown more sensitivity to context in the 1990s, the absence of further large-scale studies led to little further development. Whilst school improvement researchers were increasingly realising that effective school change initiatives might need to be of different contents in different contexts (e.g. Hopkins, 1996), governmental adoption in many countries like Britain of standardised improvement solutions for national contexts that were highly differentiated again had the effect of stultifying much movement in 'context-specific' directions.

All this is not to say that school effectiveness research did not continue to make valuable intellectual progress in the 1990s. Amongst the more useful 'cutting edge' areas were:

- the increased attention given to model-building or theoretical analyses, with some researchers erecting models that focused on the multiple levels of the classroom, the school, the district and the nation (e.g. Creemers, 1994; Stringfield, 1994), whilst others usefully bounced school effectiveness empirical findings off 'meta-theories', such as contingency theory, that had been historically utilised within other research fields (Scheerens and Bosker, 1997);
- a revival of interest in teacher or instructional effectiveness (e.g. Hill, 1997; Creemers, 1994; Reynolds, 1998), generated by the acknowledgement in some

reviews (e.g. Scheerens and Bosker, 1997; Teddlie and Reynolds, 2000) that class-room influence was much greater than that of the school. Merging together the school level and the classroom level to look at the 'interface' or interaction between the two levels was more rare, however (see Teddlie and Reynolds, 2000);

• the merging of traditions historically associated with school effectiveness together with some of those from the school improvement movement, in which philosoph-ical positions have been largely forsaken in favour of a pragmatic attention to 'what works', involving utilisation of a 'technology' of school improvement that 'pulls all levers' to generate change, that uses multiple methods to measure this and which utilises all relevant disciplinary bodies of knowledge to conceptualise and generate further progress (see for example Reynolds *et al.*, 1993; Hopkins *et al.*, 1994; Teddlie and Reynolds, 2000, ch. 7).

However, the emergence of a large volume of criticisms of the school effectiveness movement in the United Kingdom in the mid- to late 1990s had the effect of remind-ing the field, if it needed it, that maintaining the central position it had obtained in the policy and practitioner communities would require a greatly enhanced sophistication of approaches and of findings, since it was precisely the simplicity of the 'one size fits all' approaches that critics had latched upon (e.g. Elliott, 1996; Hamilton, 1996). Reaction against, and criticisms of, the international horse races that were the result of the 'country against country' studies in the IEA tradition (see Slee and Weiner, 1998) made the same general points about the international effectiveness commun-ity and its deficiencies. What school effectiveness research needed, we believed, was exactly what we had planned and undertook through the 1990s – the International School Effectiveness Research Project (ISERP).

Conclusions

Whilst there has been continuing useful work in the field of school effectiveness, in no sense has the limited progress noted in the areas above made up for some intellectual stagnation in the 'core' of the discipline, of intellectual and policy centrality, namely the issue of 'what works' to improve children's educational outcomes, and *why* certain effectiveness factors may or may not work in different educational contexts. To try to improve the quality of our knowledge and understanding of this 'core' was the task of this study, and we move on in the next chapter to concentrate upon how we designed our research to answer our key intellectual questions:

• *Which* school and teacher effectiveness factors are associated with schools/teachers being effective in different contexts?
• How many of these factors are *universals*, and how many are *specific* to certain contexts?
• What might explain *why* some were universal and some specific, and what are the implications of any findings for policy, for practice, and for the school effectiveness research base?

2   The methodological strategy
of ISERP

*Charles Teddlie, David Reynolds
and Sam Stringfield*

Introduction: the history of ISERP

The research programme evolved from a series of discussions among a group of four senior researchers from the Netherlands, the United Kingdom and the United States, and reflected the emergence of a number of reviews and models of educational effectiveness in the early to mid-1990s (Creemers, 1994; Reynolds *et al.*, 1994c; Scheerens, 1992; Scheerens and Creemers, 1989), which were noted in Chapter 1. These general reviews and beginning theories of educational effectiveness from different countries provided the intellectual foundations for the development and adoption of the overall methodology and specific instruments that were used in the study.

The organisational structure of the group evolved as more countries were added to the study. Table 2.1 summarises the order of entry of countries into the study and the phases in which they participated in data collection. While ISERP researchers attempted to generate a central source of funding for the project, this overall project funding was never realised and each country had to fund its own internal financial operations. As the study grew larger with the addition of more countries, there was a continuing debate among the ISERP members as to the value of adding more countries. Indeed, the participants grew from the original group of three countries and four researchers to one of nine countries and twenty-five plus researchers. Requirements for entry into the study included:

Table 2.1 Order of entry of countries into ISERP and their participation in rounds of data collection

Country	First round	Second round	Third round (optional)
Australia*	√	√	
Canada	√	√	
Hong Kong	√	√	
Republic of Ireland**	√	√	√
Netherlands	√	√	
Norway	√	√	
Taiwan	√	√	
United Kingdom	√	√	√
USA	√(pilot)	√(1st)	√(2nd)

*   Due to the different school year, Australia was one-half year behind the other countries in data collection.

** Due to late entry into the study, Ireland was two years behind the other countries in data collection.

- the country research team had to have at least one participant associated with a university in the country being studied;
- the country research team had to agree to utilise the basic design developed by the ISERP participants;
- the country research team had to send representatives to all ISERP meetings;
- the country research team had to be able to produce a sample of schools that agreed to participate in the study for two years.

There were several techniques that the core research team utilised to try to establish commonalities across all the country studies. These included:

- adherence to the four rules for entry into the study described above, which involved fidelity to the overall design of ISERP (see Table 2.2 below), which dictated the sample;
- the generation and distribution of common theoretical statements that guided the research (e.g. Creemers, 1994; Reynolds *et al.*, 1994a, b, c);
- the generation and distribution of a common set of goals for the study;
- the generation and distribution of a 'common core' of research instruments (tests, protocols, surveys, etc.), which each country team was expected to administer;
- the generation and distribution of a set of twelve predetermined dimensions, which were to guide the preparation of the case studies (see later in this chapter);
- the utilisation of 'intervisitations' in which senior research team members visited sites in other countries.

There were three major research questions of the study, as we noted in Chapter 1:

- *Which* school and teacher effectiveness factors are associated with schools/teachers being effective in different contexts?
- How many of these factors are *universals*, and how many *specific* to certain contexts?
- What might explain *why* some were universal and some specific, and what are the implications of any findings for policy, for practice, and for the school effectiveness research base?

Table 2.2 Overall design of ISERP (9 levels of country × 3 levels of effectiveness × 2 levels of SES)

Country	Lower-SES, more effective school	Lower-SES, typical school	Lower-SES, less effective school	Middle-SES, more effective school	Middle-SES, typical school	Middle-SES, less effective school
Australia						
Canada						
Hong Kong						
Republic of Ireland						
Netherlands						
Norway						
Taiwan						
United Kingdom						
USA						

ISERP therefore involved trying to understand the effects of societal (country) differences on the ways whereby schools became more effective. ISERP also investigated whether effective schools' characteristics varied within and across countries depending on the social class-contexts of the students' schools. Since the design involved extensive use of case studies, it was designed to generate a better understanding of 'why' any country and social class contextual differences in effective school characteristics may have existed.

The research design characteristics of ISERP

Reynolds *et al.* (1998) noted the following characteristics of the research design, which are now probably regarded as 'cutting edge' across the school effectiveness community internationally, in part due to this study itself:

- the decision to focus on elementary grades, since it is easier to separate 'school effects' from 'intake effects' at the lower-grade levels;
- the decision itself to look at context variables, since such variables had productively been included in 'cutting-edge' SER since the mid-1980s (Teddlie, 1994b);
- the decision to use mathematics as the outcome variable, since other basic skills (e.g. reading, written comprehension) had to be interpreted within specific cultural contexts;
- the decision to gather data at the multiple levels of the classroom and the school which has become axiomatic in SER over the past decade as both theory (e.g. Creemers, 1994; Scheerens, 1992; Scheerens and Creemers, 1989), and mathematical models capable of analysing multiple levels of data, have been developed (e.g. Aitkin and Longford, 1986; Bryk and Raudenbush, 1992; Goldstein, 1995);
- the decision to add affective and social outcomes, since the need for multiple outcome measures in SER has been stressed in every major review of the field since the early 1980s (e.g. Scheerens and Bosker, 1997; Good and Brophy, 1986; Rutter, 1983; Scheerens, 1992; Sammons *et al.*, 1995; Teddlie and Stringfield, 1993);
- the decision to sample 'outlier' and 'average' schools, since without the resources to generate large sample sizes, this technique (also used in the Louisiana School Effectiveness Study) allowed us to 'maximise our contrasts' (Reynolds *et al.*, 1998, p. 117).

ISERP employed the longitudinal case-study design, that utilised mixed methods both in terms of data collection and analysis, which was illustrated in Table 2.2. The design involved crossing country (nine levels) by effectiveness status (three levels) by social class (SES) of school student body (two levels), a design which was based on the Louisiana School Effectiveness Study (LSES), which had crossed the social class of student body by effectiveness status in one region of the USA (Teddlie and Stringfield, 1993). ISERP added the country dimension to the LSES design. The sampling scheme from each country was supposed to involve having either one or two schools per cell (i.e. six or twelve schools per country).

Since the design was longitudinal, it therefore avoided the methodological problems associated with cross-sectional studies, since a cohort of students was followed as they moved through their schools from ages seven to nine. ISERP was designed to be a 'contextually sensitive', longitudinal, international study of school effectiveness, emphasising the study of process variables through the utilisation of mixed methods (Tashakkori and Teddlie, 1998). The strength of the design was the generation of rich, context-specific case studies of differentially effective schools from different countries. The comparative analysis, as noted previously, was to assess which effective schools factors 'travel' across countries and social contexts.

Methodological issues

ISERP is a good example of what has been referred to elsewhere as a 'parallel mixed model design' (Tashakkori and Teddlie, 1998), which involves mixing simultaneously the qualitative and quantitative approaches at three different levels of the research process:

- the type of investigation (confirmatory and exploratory) – which involves drawing conclusions from previous research, developing a point of view, and formulating questions and hypotheses;
- the type of data collection and operations (quantitative and qualitative) – which involves designing the structure of the study and gathering the data;
- the type of analysis and inference (statistical and qualitative) – which involves summarising the data, determining the significance or importance of the results and drawing conclusions.

At each level of the research process, ISERP simultaneously used the qualitative and quantitative approaches. For example, our design included both questions and hypotheses. Based on previous research, we hypothesised that schools designated as 'more effective' would exhibit greater achievement gain than those designated as 'less effective'. We also expected that 'more effective' schools would be characterised by classroom teaching that was better than that found in 'less effective' schools, again based on previous research (e.g. Teddlie, 1994a). These hypotheses are based on the traditional quantitative approach to research, which is identified with the positivistic or post-positivistic research paradigms. At the same time as we were formulating these research hypotheses, we were also developing the three guiding research questions that were described earlier in this chapter. For these questions, which really were the focus of the study, we had no directional hypotheses, since these were exploratory issues that were to be examined through the case-study approach. These questions are based on the traditional qualitative approach to research, which is identified with the constructivist research paradigm.

Similarly, when we were gathering data in the field, we were simultaneously gathering quantitative (closed-ended) and qualitative (open-ended) data. All the types of data are described in detail later in this chapter, but a brief listing of the items include the following: student achievement and IQ data, principal interviews, teacher interviews, the 'child study', observations around the school, multiple classroom observation instruments and instruments based on the key case-study dimensions. These data-collection instruments run the gamut from the most quantitative to the most qualitative, with some capable of generating both types of data (e.g. the classroom observation instruments).

In ISERP, it was the research questions, and hypotheses, which determined the development of the study. Tashakkori and Teddlie (1998, pp. 20–1) labelled this 'the dictatorship of the research question', not of the paradigm or the method. This is important, because there are still many researchers working within the school effectiveness area who consider themselves to be primarily quantitatively or qualitatively orientated, as attested to in a recent survey (Teddlie and Reynolds, 2000, ch. 2).

Some of these 'scientists' (quantitatively orientated) or 'humanists' (qualitatively orientated) appear to still be involved in 'paradigm wars', in which the superiority of one or the other method is being debated (e.g. Denzin and Lincoln, 1994; Gage, 1989; Guba, 1990; Lincoln and Guba, 1985; Smith and Heshusius, 1986). In ISERP, we 'shut down' these paradigm wars, adopting a pragmatist orientation (e.g. Howe, 1988), and focused on providing the most complete answers to the research questions regardless of the type of data that were being collected.

There are four general characteristics of the ISERP case studies that require some further discussion:

- the country teams were asked to include both a positive and negative 'outlier school' in the case studies that they generated for this volume;
- a set of qualitatively orientated dimensions (Table 2.3) was developed to assist the country teams as they gathered open-ended data in the field and analysed those data to generate the case studies;
- the country teams were asked to include a whole school day of observation that focused on a single child (Stringfield, 1995) as part of their case studies;
- each country team was asked to attempt to include an intervisitation to another country as part of their participation; they were also expected to play host to other country teams visiting their country and to allow the visitors access to any of the schools in their sample. These intervisitations provided much useful analysis and are described as a methodology in more detail in Appendix Two of the Supplementary Information (see p. 302).

In keeping with the outlier design of the study (Stringfield, 1994), we were interested in the contrasts that existed within countries on the key design dimensions (effectiveness of the school, SES of the school). Some countries were unable to satisfactorily distinguish between low- and middle-SES schools in their countries but most countries were able to distinguish between two pairs of schools: one more effective and one less effective low-SES school, and one more effective and one less effective middle-SES school.

When completing qualitative data analyses, researchers have the choice of either developing their own themes (emerging) or of utilising themes that already existed based on previous studies or theory (a priori). Huberman and Miles (1994) stated that qualitative data can be analysed either inductively (emerging themes) or deductively (a priori) depending upon the stage of the research cycle in which researchers are working. While most researchers working within the constructivist paradigm prefer to inductively develop their own themes, there were reasons why the a priori theme method was better for the case studies. These reasons include the following:

- Several of the researchers in ISERP were novices to qualitative research methods and analysis. These researchers expressed a desire for 'something to hang on to'; that is, they preferred to have a framework within which to interpret their own data.

- Developing 'emerging themes' might have taken several weeks or months of observation. Without a central funding base, we did not have the resources to spend extensive amounts of time at each site.
- Given the diversity among the nine country teams, there was genuine concern that each team might develop a totally different set of dimensions, and the design of the study required some comparability at the end. Researchers were told that if a certain dimension made no sense within their country, it was to be eliminated but that themes emerging from a particular country context were very valuable and were to be included in the country case studies.

The twelve case-study dimensions emerged, to a large degree, from discussions among the team members about factors that were potentially distinguishing characteristics within and across countries during the periodic meetings of all countries (see Table 2.3). Most of the dimensions were expressed in deliberately 'broad' terms (e.g. the curriculum, the principal, expectations) so that hopefully each country team would be able to describe something about that dimension.

Input into the development of the 12 dimensions came from several sources:

- a review of the relevant SER literature, conducted by researchers who were asked to share that information with the larger group;
- from information gathered from discussion of the first visits to the case-study sites; each team was asked to work on ideas and themes as they visited their schools and to share these with the group;
- information gleaned from the initial intervisitations, in which team members from one country visited another;
- discussions of common themes among the team members as they held their periodic whole-team ISERP meetings.

Emerging themes were triangulated through intervisitations and whole-team discussion in an iterative process, somewhat similar to constant comparative analysis (Lincoln and Guba, 1985). Finally, one of the most experienced qualitative researchers on the team was asked to generate a set of dimensions. These dimensions were presented to the whole team, alterations were made, and the group agreed to use the twelve dimensions to further the analysis of the qualitative data. In many respects, the twelve dimensions served as an organiser for qualitative information as it was gathered. Once the data were categorised into the broad dimensions, then each country team had to make some sense out of the information in each category.

After the researchers had been working on their own country analyses, they were asked at a whole-team meeting to rank the dimensions in terms of their importance to schools in their countries. These rankings allowed the generation of some interesting cross-country comparisons, which are summarised in Chapter 13.

A unique aspect of the case studies was the use of the 'whole school day methodology' (WSD) or 'child study' (Brigham and Gamse, 1997; Schaffer, 1994). In this process, one 'typical' or median child from the study cohort at a school was selected, based on the intake test data. That child was then followed by a researcher for an entire school day. The process is also known as 'shadowing'. (Full details of this are available in Appendix Two of the Supplementary Information).

Table 2.3 Twelve ISERP case-study dimensions with prompts/anchors

Case-study dimension	Prompts/anchors/questions
(1) General characteristics of the school	Student body size Number of teachers and staff Description of school and catchment area Public/private organisation, etc.
(2) A day in the life of a child (whole-school day)	Events in the life of a typical student at the school on a typical day Does the school experience seem to make sense to the child? Etc.
(3) Teachers' teaching style	Teacher behaviours in classrooms. Techniques for teaching maths, etc.
(4) The curriculum	What is taught? When is it taught? Etc.
(5) The influence of parents	Contacts with the school How the parents participate, etc.
(6) The principal	Style of leadership Organisation of the school, etc.
(7) School expectations of pupils	Expectations for students Assessment system Discipline system, etc.
(8) School goals	Academic goals Social goals, etc.
(9) Interstaff relations	Contact between staff members How is information passed on about students? Etc.
(10) School resources	The source of the resources How many outside resources are there? How important are the outside resources? Etc.
(11) Relationship with local authorities	What type of contacts? How important are these contacts? Etc.
(12) School image	School presentation to the community Is an image necessary for the survival of the school? Etc.

Sampling issues

Sampling was a major problem for some of the countries involved, as will be seen in Chapter 3. Even if we had been able to generate data bases that perfectly matched the requirements of our study design, the ISERP project was never large enough in terms of absolute numbers to produce representative samples of schools, especially for the larger countries. That is a major reason why the focus was always on the development of longitudinal case studies, with data-rich descriptions of schools and classes.

It was important that each country do as good a job as possible in generating its sample, so that we could draw some tentative conclusions concerning how school effectiveness factors might 'travel' across contexts and countries. Difficulties encountered in sampling in Australia and Canada made such comparisons very difficult for these countries within the ISERP framework, and these two countries only have limited data included in Chapter 3, which summarises the quantitative analyses from the study. Despite this, these countries' researchers contributed case studies that generated some interesting conclusions regarding school effectiveness processes important within their countries.

Other countries, such as Taiwan and Hong Kong, were able to generate a sample more representative of the study design, but had at least one 'missing cell', which meant that at least one of the six conditions generated by the 2×3 design described earlier in this chapter was not found in their samples. Data from these countries were included in Chapter 3, and their case studies also generated interesting contrasts that can be compared with the other countries.

There were also problems in generating representative samples of schools for certain large countries in the study (e.g. Australia, Canada, the US). As an example, the initial design of the study included a sample from the US that included four states (California, Iowa, Louisiana, North Carolina) and by weighting samples from each of these four states, it would have been possible to generate a data set that would have approximated national averages in terms of SES, achievement and other important demographic variables in the US context (e.g. ethnicity, wealth of local communities).

When ISERP failed to receive central funding, the team had to accept schools from two districts in Louisiana as the US sample. The researchers from that state had ongoing school effectiveness research studies, plus a research team that could be put into the field at low cost. The researchers from California and Iowa were not involved in ongoing research, nor did they have research teams that could gather data as efficiently as the Louisiana team. North Carolina's public schools were undergoing substantial reorganisation and reform efforts such as through magnet schools, and it was not possible to establish a stable student population in any of the area's schools because of dramatic student population shifts.

Therefore, twelve schools from the two districts in Louisiana were accepted as the US sample for ISERP. Some of the difficulties of using the state as representative of the US include the following:

- it is a high-poverty state;
- its students traditionally score low on standardised tests;
- almost the entire minority population in the state is African-American;
- it represents only one region of the country (the South).

The manner in which the sample in Louisiana was drawn ameliorated some of these problems. While the state is high poverty, the twelve schools came from two primarily urban/suburban districts that are among the wealthiest in the state. It is true that Louisiana students score lower on standardised tests, but that typically does not start happening until the later elementary grades (fourth grade and above), therefore the students in the sample should have scored at about the national average for students their age. While there is an increasing number of different minority groups in the US, African-Americans represent one of the two largest such groups in the country, and probably the most important one from a historical point of view with regard to delivery of educational services. Thus, if one state from one region were the necessary sample for the US in ISERP, then the Louisiana sample, as constituted, would probably generate data as generalisable to the national averages in achievement and SES as any other.

The concerns regarding generalisability to the country level in the case of certain large countries are associated with quantitative results, while *transferability* considerations are important in the qualitative research in the case studies contained later in this volume. Specifically, it is important that the results from a particular case study (the sending context) are transferable to another setting (the receiving context). According to Lincoln and Guba, *transferability* may be described as follows:

> Naturalists make the opposite assumption: that at best only working hypotheses may be abstracted, the transferability of which is an empirical matter, depending on the degree of similarity between sending and receiving contexts . . . That is to say, in order to be sure of one's inferences, one will need to know about both sending and receiving contexts. We move then from a question of generalisability to a question of transferability. Transferability inferences cannot be made by an investigator who knows only the sending context.
>
> (Lincoln and Guba, 1985, p. 297)

In order to make the results from the case studies transferable, authors needed to describe their results in sufficient detail so that a reader can determine if the results from that case study (or case studies) are transferable to his/her specific school context. Such transferability comes about as a result of authors providing 'thick descriptions' (e.g. Geertz, 1973; Yin, 1994; Lincoln and Guba, 1985) of their case-study sites and of the contrasts that they found among them.

While we may never be able to conclude that our ISERP samples are representative of the schools in any given country, by providing 'thick' case-study descriptions we can establish the transferability of the results from the ISERP case-study sample to other contexts. In a case-study-driven research project, it may indeed be more important to be sure that descriptions of sites and events are as explicitly described as possible than it is to fret over whether or not the sample is representative of the country being studied.

Before turning to the issue of selection of differentially effective schools and schools from different SES contexts, some more considerations regarding the generalisability of the ISERP country samples should be made (see Table 2.4).

Of all the ISERP participants, the United Kingdom, Ireland and the Netherlands appear to have samples that are the most representative of their countries. The following statements summarise the representativeness of each of the country samples.

- In the UK, the sample comes from one LEA, an area described as 'Midshire', which contains a wide variety of schools from which to select a representative sample. The selected sample appears to be highly representative of the country.
- The Republic of Ireland and the Netherlands are relatively small European countries that have somewhat homogeneous schools. The researchers in these countries have apparently selected schools that are overall representative of the country.
- The US sample has been described in detail above. The conclusion is that this sample is as good as possible given the fact that only one state was involved.

Table 2.4 General characteristics of each country's complete ISERP sample

Country	Number of schools in study and in each cell of study design	Location of schools within country	Notable characteristics
Australia	8 Undetermined	Queensland	Sampling problems made assignment of schools to cells of study design difficult
Canada*	5 One per cell, with a missing cell (middle SES, less effective), where school withdrew from the study	Four in Ontario Province, one in Saskatchewan Province	Very diverse group of schools. The shools in Ontario are characterised as: one located on a 'reserve', one rural, one inner city, and one surburban
Hong Kong**	6 There were four low-SES and two middle-SES schools. There were an equal number of schools in each effectiveness category	The two case-study schools were from 'old districts' in Kowloon, which is on the opposite side of the Hong Kong island.	Only the Kowloon schools are described in the case studies. These were moderately low-SES schools in districts with 'declining young populations'
Republic of Ireland	6 One per cell	Dublin	Lower-SES schools were particularly well matched, with students coming from the same area, yet going to differentially effective schools. Little difference between the more or less effective middle-SES schools
Netherlands	6 One per cell	Throughout the Netherlands	The sample included both private and public schools, which was appropriate given the large number of private schools in the country
Norway***	9 This sample was categorised as six middle-SES and three low-SES schools, yet the SES data indicate that all schools are upper-SES. An equal number of schools in each effectiveness category	Six schools in Oslo; three schools in Trondheim	There were two separate country studies, with separate research teams. Researchers concluded that low-SES schools were not common in Norway, and included none in the sample. Oslo team was comfortable with the effectiveness designation of its schools; Trondheim team preferred to refer to 'degrees' of difference
Taiwan	7 All cells represented except mid-SES, less effective.	All case-study schools were in the Taipei area	There was little variance among the mean scores of schools on the CTBS pretest. This pretest was used to classify the schools as more or less effective
United Kingdom****	12 Two per cell	All from one LEA, 'Midshire'	The region from which the ISERP sample was drawn is highly representative of England
USA	12 Two per cell	Two primarily urban school districts in Louisiana	Louisiana is a high poverty state, with traditionally low performing schools. The two districts are wealthier, and therefore more representative of the USA than the state. There are fewer differences among the mid-SES schools than among the low-SES schools

*   Based on information found in the case-study chapter. This information is not in agreement with the data presented in Table 3.1 and 3.2, which ignored classification status of schools due to faulty sampling.

**   No additional information on characteristics of the sample was found in the case-study chapter.

***   While the schools were designated as low- and middle-SES, actual SES data presented in Table 3.1 indicate that all Norwegian schools were upper-SES.

**** Midshire is a pseudonym for a local education authority in England.

- The Australian and Canadian samples may not be entirely representative of their country's schools. While attempts were made to generate representative samples, the results were basically volunteer, or convenience, samples.
- The Norwegian sample appears to be representative of many of the schools that are found in the affluent areas of Oslo and Trondheim. Schools in rural areas were not included. Two of the nine schools were located in immigrant areas.
- It is difficult to determine how representative the Hong Kong and Taiwan samples are of their countries. It appears that most of the Taiwanese schools were from Taipei. If this is the case, then rural (and poorer) schools may be underrepresented. Hong Kong may also not have adequately sampled from rural poorer areas.

As noted above, schools were to be placed into one of three provisional effectiveness categories at the start of the study by their local research team: more effective, typical and less effective. It was planned to recategorise the schools after the two year study based on the gain scores that their students made on the CTBS tests, after controlling for initial achievement and SES. Due to missing data, and other considerations, the initial local research team classification was used throughout the quantitative analyses, which classification is mostly validated by how the schools 'played' over the two years (see Chapter 3).

While it is common practice to utilise 'value added' test scores to define a school's effectiveness level, several countries in ISERP did not have the data required (i.e. multiple years of achievement data, SES information) to do this. Therefore, two methods were used in ISERP to classify schools into effectiveness categories:

- when the data were available, schools were selected using some form of value added scores based on an analysis of existing data bases (Hong Kong, the Netherlands, the UK, the US);
- in other countries where data were not available, schools were selected on the basis of reputational criteria (Australia, Canada, Ireland, Norway, Taiwan) provided by key informants, such as members of the Inspectorate, the Educational Department, and the like.

The ISERP team was concerned about the use of these two types of criteria for assigning school effectiveness status, but the lack of appropriate data bases in some countries made it necessary. Reynolds *et al.* expressed concern about these differences:

> Whilst in the long term it was intended that schools' effectiveness classifications reflected their gain scores and performance over time rather than their initially assigned performance, there was a concern about the possible biases to the study introduced by some countries using clear value-added methods of school choice whilst other countries were probably inevitably using informants who might have found utilising value-added formulations rather difficult.
>
> (Reynolds *et al.*, 1998, p. 118)

These considerations point out the importance in a study like this of having large archived data bases with which to begin selection. Table 2.5 indicates that the UK researchers had access to a large data set from Midshire, which included free school meal information on schools and on pupil achievement tests (Key Stage Two tests).

Table 2.5 Criteria utilised in assigning initial effectiveness and socio-economic status to schools

Country	Criteria used for determining effectiveness status	Criteria used for determining socioeconomic status
Australia	No standardised test data available. Team attempted to use reputational criteria.	No test data available. Team used reputational criteria, then CTBS intake data.
Canada	There was no 'central registry of effectiveness ratings'. Reputational criteria was initially used in selecting schools from two provinces.	SES status determined by general characteristics of students attending schools. The inclusion of a school on a reserve added an extra dimension of variation.
Hong Kong	Effectiveness criteria based on survey of 90 schools using several criteria: student attitudes, student satisfaction with school, and student academic achievement.	SES status determined on basis of schools being located in middle-class or lower-class neighbourhoods.
Republic of Ireland	Reputational criteria as perceived by the Inspectorate of the Department of Education.	Lower SES schools came from one 'catchment' area. Middle SES schools came from different middle-class parts of Dublin.
Netherlands	National testing data collected for IQ, SES, and ethnicity.	SES status determined by a school score. The school score is based on student scores in a system in which low SES Dutch students receive a score (of 1.25), students whose parents work on a ship (1.4), migrants (1.7), and students from other ethnic backgrounds (1.9).
Norway	No official testing system at the elementary level. All schools selected on basis of assessments by local governments or ISERP team. Determination of effectiveness status made based on observations after ISERP started.	No lower-SES schools were included, because the team did not believe there were that many in Norway. All schools were middle-SES 'according to national SES standards'.
Taiwan	Initial sample of schools selected on reputation as 'strong' or 'weak' schools. Outlier schools picked for ISERP based on students' performance on CTBS pretest.	SES status determined on basis of schools being located in middle-class or lower-class neighbourhoods.
United Kingdom	Regression analysis using school free-meal rate to predict achievement scores (English, maths) for eleven-year-old students in Midshire	SES status determined by school free meal rate.
USA	Consistent performance (over a two-year period) that was above, at, or below average on standardised achievement tests, controlling for SES status of schools. Effectiveness status confirmed by local education officials using reputational criteria.	Lower-SES defined as school having 90 per cent or more of its students in free-lunch programme. Middle-SES defined as school having 35 per cent or less of its students in free-lunch programme.

Similarly, researchers from the US had access to complete data bases from two large urban/suburban districts, which contained a percentage of students on a free-lunch programme and student achievement over a two-year period. The Netherlands used a national data base that included achievement, IQ, ethnicity, and SES data. Details regarding the particular type of data analyses used to generate effectiveness status for these countries are located in Table 2.5.

Hong Kong also used a large data base to classify its schools, but the process was more complicated than generating achievement value-added scores. Effectiveness criteria in Hong Kong were based on a survey of ninety schools using several criteria, including: student attitudes, student satisfaction with school, and student academic achievement, all criteria other than achievement.

Particulars regarding the reputational criteria used in the other five countries are also contained in Table 2.5. The Republic of Ireland depended upon the Inspectorate of the Department of Education to assist them in classifying their schools by effectiveness status. Intervisitations and anecdotal evidence indicate that these classifications were accurate. Norway and Taiwan also used reputational criteria to initially select the sample of schools and determination of effectiveness status was made based on observations after ISERP started in Norway. In Taiwan and Australia, final classifications were based on students' performance on the CTBS intake test administered during the first year of ISERP. In Australia and Canada, reputational criteria alone were used. The Australian team found it difficult to assign effectiveness status to the schools due to 'conflicting evidence', but did generate case studies of more and less effective schools.

Confirmatory evidence for the initial classification comes from internal country comparisons of scores on the CTBS intake test. Data located in Chapter 3 (Tables 3.1 and 3.2) indicate that the schools 'played in position' for the most part, with less effective schools scoring lower than more effective schools after SES has been held constant.

The determination of SES status (middle or low) proved as challenging to the ISERP team as that of the effectiveness status. A few countries argued that the concept of low-SES and middle-SES did not travel well. For instance, the Norwegians argued that most schools in their society were of mixed SES and it proved difficult for the ISERP team to determine operational definitions of low-SES and middle-SES. At one point, in some frustration, one researcher stated: 'The middle class works with its head. The lower classes work with their hands.' This definition did not carry the day, although the later use of Prospects classifications from the United States (Puma *et al.*, 1997) to check SES classification approximated to this definition.

Only three countries (the Netherlands, the US, the UK) had data bases that could allow them to assign SES status to the students attending schools. Most other countries used 'type of neighbourhoods' the students came from to classify the schools. The Dutch used a data base that included information on individual students that allowed an SES measure to be constructed. As noted in Table 2.5, different weightings were given to students if they had different SES and ethnic backgrounds. In the UK, SES status was determined by school free-meal rate, as it was in the US. For Hong Kong, the Republic of Ireland and Taiwan, the SES status of schools were determined by the neighbourhoods from which the students came. This technique appeared to work well, as will be described later in this section.

There were problems of allocation of schools to categories in Australia and Canada. The Australian team argued that the students in all the schools in the sample came from 'mixed' neighbourhoods, and could not be labelled 'middle-SES' or 'low-SES'. The wide diversity among the Canadian schools, including one school on a reservation, made SES classification difficult. Looking at the total population of Norwegian schools, there were very few high- or low-SES schools, and most of the sampled schools were mixed SES, characterised as middle-SES schools in the Norwegian sense of the word. Two schools in the sample have a proportion of immigrant children.

Confirmatory evidence for the initial SES classification comes from internal country comparisons of scores using the Prospects classification noted above. These data resulted in average school-wide scores ranging from 1.0 (lowest SES) to 3.0 (highest SES), which were generated by teachers describing the category of work that best described the occupation of their students' fathers and mothers. Data located in Chapter 3 (Table 3.1) indicate that the schools' initial SES status was confirmed in most countries (Canada was not included). There was less variance between schools on SES in the Netherlands and Taiwan than there was in the US and the UK, which probably reflected real differences between more homogeneous societies (e.g. the Netherlands, Taiwan) and more heterogeneous societies (e.g. the US, the UK).

Instruments and protocols used in ISERP

Instrument development was a challenge for a diverse group of nine countries and over twenty-five researchers. The ISERP instruments were developed during four different meetings, each of which was attended by around fifteen researchers. Despite the occasionally chaotic nature of the meetings, there was an overall procedure for developing the ISERP instruments that was followed for the most part. This overall procedure involved three distinct processes:

1   It was determined at the onset that there would be some compulsory and some optional instruments. That is, some of the instruments would have to be administered by all countries, while others would only be administered by countries that were interested in them. Table 2.6 contains a list of the compulsory instruments, while Table 2.7 contains a list of the optional instruments. Therefore, the instrument development process involved the selection of a common core of data required from all countries, together with additional protocols for some countries. This strategy was necessary given the diverse opinions of the countries regarding what were important constructs and what were not. If a number of countries did not want to collect data using a certain instrument, the country putting that instrument forward, and any others who wanted to use it, could administer the instrument as part of their optional data base. Those countries could then use data generated from these instruments in writing their case studies, or for other purposes.

2   The general guide for developing the required instruments was to match an instrument protocol with each of the constructs from the theoretical model shown in Figure 2.1, a classic 'input–process–output' school effectiveness model.

3   The pressure to generate instruments in areas as diverse as school processes, teacher experiential and behavioural variables, classroom behaviours, principal factors, mathematics, student social attitudes, etc. all meant that there was a tendency to use pre-existing instruments in cases where team members had used them before. Thus there was a three-part decision-making process:

Table 2.6 List of instruments and protocols required for use in ISERP

Level	Theoretical construct	Operational definition	Strengths/weaknesses	Required/optional
Student	Intelligence	Dutch IQ Test	Reliability and validity indices available	Required
Student	Achievement	California Test of Basic Skills (Mathematics); the California Achievement Test was used in the US	Extensive reliability, validity indices available	Required
Student	Socio-economic status	'Prospects' definitions (Puma, 1997)	Reliability and validity indices available	Required
Student	Attendance	Number of days student attended/ Number of days in school year	Reliable and valid	Required
Student	Locus of control	Adaptation of Crandall, Katkovsky and Crandall instrument (1965) by Hong Kong Team	See Table 3.3	Required
Student	Self-concept mathematics	Designed by ISERP Research Team	See Table 3.3	Required
Student	Attitudes toward school	Designed by ISERP Research Team	See Table 3.3	Required
Student	Democratic attitudes	Designed by Norwegian Team	See Table 3.3	Required
Student	Qualitative descriptions of school days for students	Designed by ISERP Research Team	'Trustworthiness' established by intervisitations	Required
Teacher	Effectiveness of teaching	VTBI plus additional items	Reliability and validity ratings available for original VTBI items when used with five point scales) (Teddlie, Virgilio and Oescher, 1990)	Required
Teacher	Time-on-task for classroom	QAIT by Schaffer *et al.*, 1994	Reliability and validity ratings available	Required
Teacher	Qualitative descriptions of school days for teachers	Designed by ISERP Research Team	Qualitative data used in generating case studies	Required
School	Staff and principal variables	Designed by ISERP Research Team	Qualitative data used in generating case studies	Required
School	Curriculum/assessment factors	Designed by ISERP Research Team	Qualitative data used in generating case studies	Required
School	Reinforcers (school control mechanism)	Designed by ISERP Research Team	Qualitative data used in generating case studies	Required
School	Finance and resources	Designed by ISERP Research Team	Qualitative data used in generating case studies	Required
School	Parent/community factors	Designed by ISERP Research Team	Qualitative data used in generating case studies	Required
School	School goals	Designed by ISERP Research Team	Qualitative data used in generating case studies	Required
School	School organisation and management	Designed by ISERP Research Team	Qualitative data used in generating case studies	Required
School	Transitions	Designed by ISERP Research Team	Qualitative data used in generating case studies	Required

Table 2.7 List of instruments and protocols that were optionally used in ISERP

Level	Theoretical construct	Operational definition	Strengths/weaknesses	Required/optional
Student	Sociometry	Designed by researchers from two member countries	No reliability and validity	Optional
Student	Creativity	Designed by ISERP Research Team	No reliability on individual items	Optional
Student	Reading achievement	Various definitions, including CTBS	Different for each test involved	Optional
Teacher	Teacher locus of control	Designed by ISERP Research Team	No reliability and validity	Optional
Teacher	Teacher level expectations	Designed by ISERP Research Team	No reliability and validity	Optional
Teacher	Classroom resources	From Schaffer, 1994	Reliability and validity ratings available	Optional
Teacher	Opportunity to learn	Designed by ISERP Research Team	No reliability and validity	Optional
Teacher	Teacher background	Designed by ISERP Research Team	No reliability and validity	Optional
Teacher	Ability grouping	Designed by ISERP Research Team	No reliability and validity	Optional

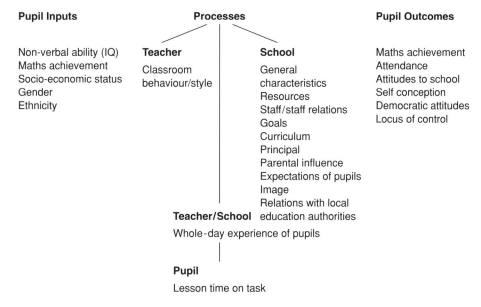

Pupil Inputs

Non-verbal ability (IQ)
Maths achievement
Socio-economic status
Gender
Ethnicity

Processes

Teacher

Classroom
behaviour/style

School

General
characteristics
Resources
Staff/staff relations
Goals
Curriculum
Principal
Parental influence
Expectations of pupils
Image
Relations with local
Teacher/School   education authorities

Whole-day experience of pupils

Pupil

Lesson time on task

Pupil Outcomes

Maths achievement
Attendance
Attitudes to school
Self conception
Democratic attitudes
Locus of control

Figure 2.1 Allocation of specific data to specific conceptual areas

(a) adopt pre-existing instrument as is;
(b) alter pre-existing instrument, making it more representative of the ISERP construct;
(c) make up a new instrument to assess the construct.

There were twenty instruments and protocols compulsory for participation in ISERP (see Table 2.6). Of these instruments nine were administered at the student level, three were administered at the teacher level, and eight were administered at the school level. These instruments and protocols were representative of a wide range of quantitative and qualitative data gathering techniques. They included:

- standardised achievement and IQ tests (the California Test of Basic Skills);
- SES data generated from a system with 'standardised' definitions of occupations (Puma *et al.*, 1997);
- attendance data;
- three different measures of students' attitudes and self-perceptions;
- two measures of teacher behaviour in the classroom based on established observational systems (Teddlie *et al.*, 1990; Schaffer, 1994);
- student and teacher twelve-dimensional observational protocols, designed by the ISERP team, to generate data for the case studies;
- eight instruments, developed by the ISERP team, to measure various components of the entire school (e.g. curriculum, school goals, school organisation and management).

The optional instruments and protocols are listed in Table 2.7. If a country decided to use that instrument in its case studies, then the instrument is described in more detail in that particular chapter (see Chapters 4–12).

All instruments, and material concerning their origins, construction and properties, are available in the supplementary information, Appendix Five.

Conclusions

It should be clear from this chapter that a wide range of approaches were adopted to gather data that would address our theme of possibly finding *universal* and *specific* effectiveness factors, and that a wide range of instruments and systems were utilised accordingly. In general, the study was conducted through use of multiple methods involving both rich qualitative data being collected on the case-study schools and quantitative data being collected from a sample of pupils from these and other schools, their progress over time and their attributes. In some cases, mixed methods of quant- itative and qualitative data were utilised within the same instrument (as in the case with the classroom observation system). Figure 2.1 shows how these data are related to the overarching dimensions of 'intake', 'outputs' and 'processes' that are customarily used to classify factors and instruments in school effectiveness and international effective- ness research.

In the next chapter, we move on to look at the whole sample of quantitative data that we collected, and then subsequently in other chapters to the case studies of schools of different levels of effectiveness in the different countries. The lessons we have learned in terms of substantive findings and understandings are then reviewed in our final two chapters.

3 The quantitative data

*Bert Creemers, Sam Stringfield
and Henk Guldemond*

Introduction

As we have outlined in Chapter 2, ISERP is a mixed-method study which draws heavily upon qualitative data to explain variance in effectiveness at different school levels, and additional qualitative data are used in the description of the different cases as well. In order to provide the reader with a base from which to interpret the following chapters, we provide here a general overview of the quantitative data collected across the nine ISERP countries. It was not the purpose of ISERP to compare results between countries with respect to outcomes to find the most 'effective' country, since we were not primarily interested in a 'horse race', although we did in fact look at country differences. However, we were very interested in finding out which, if any, school effectiveness factors 'travelled' between countries. Also, ISERP was designed to provide information on the factors and characteristics that might be taken into account in planning future studies.

To remind ourselves, the three research questions in the ISERP study are the following:

- *Which* school and teacher effectiveness factors are associated with schools/teachers being effective in different contexts?
- How many of these factors are *universals*, and how many are *specific* to certain contexts?
- What might explain *why* some were universal and some specific, and what are the implications of any findings for policy, for practice, and for the school effectiveness research base?

This chapter proceeds from a discussion of the strengths and the limitations of the data sets, through to a presentation of results of the research across the different countries. This provides a context for the global description of the factors at school and classroom level that 'travel' in explaining differences. Chapters 4 to 12 give the fine-grained case-study data that shed more light on the operation of the processes that are identified here.

Strengths and limitations of the data sets and procedures

The research teams from nine nations met several times to choose and discuss measures. Training on the administration of the various measures was extensive. After the common team-training, quantitative and qualitative data collection tasks were conducted by each country's research team. While efforts had been made to assure standardisation in each step of the process, it became clear over time that interpretation of instructions for instrument administration varied somewhat among countries. As quantitative data sets were gathered within countries, individual research teams forwarded data sets to a central location at the University of Groningen, in the Netherlands. There, data were checked for accuracy. Any evidence of incomplete data sets or data that appeared to be in an unexpected range caused a member of the quantitative team to initiate follow-up procedures. Individual nation's teams were asked to re-examine their data and, where appropriate, to provide additional information. This often resulted in months of extensive communications between the research teams and the central quantitative data team.

Where data could not be gathered or corrected, variables and/or data were excluded from that country's quantitative analyses. In some countries the sampling was substantially outside the intended 2×3 sampling frame, and therefore only some of their data sets are presented in this chapter. A further limitation was that Taiwan and Hong Kong were not able to provide data from schools in a full 2×3 design format. The effects of these sampling limitations have been noted in Chapter 2 and will be noted as appropriate throughout this chapter. Complete data was not available on Canada, so it was only partially included in the quantitative analysis, and data for Australia are presented in a subset of quantitative analyses.

In the remainder of this chapter, data will be presented in the following order:

1   Descriptive presentations of various data sets, by country and then broken down within country.
2   Relational data analyses, including limited between-country analyses, but focusing on within-country analyses. Of particular relevance to ISERP's overall research questions, the key one- and two-year within-country analyses will be presented in the following areas: the relationships between students' ability, their initial age seven achievement and their socio-economic status, and their end-of-first and -second-year achievements. Other analyses look at the variance explained by educational factors in different societies, and the educational factors themselves which appear from the quantitative data to be 'travelling'.

Student outcomes within and across countries

First we provide an overview of the descriptive characteristics (means and standard deviations) associated with the most important pupil variables at the time of intake. The data are presented separately for each category of design variables (three effectiveness categories and two school SES categories). This is followed by an overview with respect to the achievement levels for each separate country for three separate time points.

At the start of the project, within each country, student background data were collected. These included IQ/aptitude, socio-economic status of families; and the students' initial achievement levels. All students were in the first term of their age-seven year in school. Data from this initial data-gathering effort are presented in Table 3.1. Note that five countries have a full 3×2 design, with three levels of initial effectiveness classification and two levels of SES. Hong Kong's, Australia's and Taiwan's research teams perceived their six schools as falling into fewer than six cells. Both

Table 3.1 Demographic, background and mathematics achievement data at intake

Initial effectiveness rating	Rated socio-economic status [SES-R]	Observed SES	SES-SD	n of schools	n of classes	n of students	Non-verbal Ability	(S.D.)	Maths computation Mean	(S.D.)	Maths concepts and applications Mean	(S.D.)
USA												
Low	Low	1.5	(.51)	2	7	177	23	(5.4)	438	(87)	466	(89)
Low	Mid	1.9	(.46)	2	7	200	27	(5.7)	534	(50)	616	(48)
Mid	Low	1.6	(.49)	2	8	230	23	(5.8)	453	(91)	497	(96)
Mid	Mid	1.7	(.42)	2	8	218	27	(5.4)	539	(69)	617	(78)
High	Low	1.5	(.55)	2	6	154	24	(4.8)	491	(63)	514	(64)
High	Mid	1.9	(.54)	2	7	186	27	(5.2)	562	(41)	613	(61)
UK												
Low	Low	1.0	(.17)	2	4	78	18	(8.0)	462	(97)	525	(72)
Low	Mid	1.4	(.40)	2	3	71	22	(6.8)	497	(90)	592	(47)
Mid	Low	1.0	(.14)	2	6	83	21	(5.7)	489	(88)	545	(68)
Mid	Mid	1.4	(.37)	2	4	71	26	(5.3)	561	(77)	616	(67)
High	Low	1.1	(.26)	2	4	116	20	(6.0)	487	(81)	560	(80)
High	Mid	1.6	(.39)	2	3	90	26	(5.7)	542	(78)	608	(80)
Taiwan												
Low	Low	1.3	(.53)	2	4	139	26	(6.1)	620	(58)	648	(54)
Low	Mid	1.3	(.50)	1	2	71	27	(5.8)	627	(60)	653	(46)
Mid	Mid	1.6	(.56)	1	2	73	28	(6.1)	632	(70)	661	(59)
High	Low	1.5	(.54)	1	2	84	27	(6.7)	635	(50)	656	(40)
High	Mid	1.5	(.57)	2	4	149	30	(4.9)	635	(49)	668	(42)
Norway												
Low	Low	2.6	(.47)	1	2	35	24	(6.2)	402	(105)	480	(94)
Low	Mid	2.7	(.50)	2	4	89	23	(5.9)	435	(90)	518	(54)
Mid	Low	2.5	(.52)	1	3	71	22	(7.1)	384	(114)	462	(101)
Mid	Mid	2.5	(.49)	2	4	101	25	(6.2)	438	(87)	541	(88)
High	Low	2.4	(.46)	1	2	55	22	(7.7)	347	(140)	460	(106)
High	Mid	2.6	(.59)	2	4	103	26	(6.0)	458	(100)	548	(77)

Table 3.1 (cont'd)

Initial effectiveness rating	Rated socio-economic status [SES-R]	Observed SES	SES-SD	n of schools	n of classes	n of students	Non-verbal Ability	(S.D.)	Maths computation Mean	(S.D.)	Maths concepts and applications Mean	(S.D.)
Hong Kong												
Low	Low	1.7	(.59)	2	4	149	28	(5.3)	642	(38)	643	(41)
Mid	Low	1.7	(.59)	2	4	153	28	(6.4)	641	(45)	640	(57)
High	Mid	2.2	(.70)	2	4	154	27	(5.7)	627	(43)	649	(42)
The Netherlands												
Low	Low	1.7	(.40)	1	2	37	24	(5.3)	486	(73)	523	(54)
Low	Mid	1.7	(.40)	1	1	22	27	(4.8)	538	(51)	558	(37)
Mid	Low	1.7	(.38)	1	1	26	23	(7.3)	474	(63)	529	(39)
Mid	Mid	1.9	(.27)	1	2	42	28	(4.5)	560	(53)	572	(47)
High	Low			1	1	17	23	(7.3)	509	(128)	513	(61)
High	Mid	1.9	(.31)	1	1	25	30	(3.9)	515	(38)	586	(44)
Australia												
Low	Mixed	1.6	(.63)	3	8	133	28	(5.0)	534	(62)	607	(66)
High	Mixed	1.7	(.48)	3	10	130	27	(4.5)	549	(45)	621	(51)
Ireland												
Low	Low	1.0	(.14)	1	1	23	26	(4.9)	532	(66)	577	(45)
Low	Mid	2.3	(.69)	1	1	13	28	(4.5)	499	(95)	584	(111)
Mid	Low	1.0	(.23)	1	1	12	26	(4.2)	518	(51)	585	(48)
Mid	Mid	1.9	(.70)	1	1	38	30	(4.0)	556	(49)	646	(61)
High	Low	1.2	(.53)	1	2	46	26	(4.4)	530	(93)	572	(50)
High	Mid	2.2	(.62)	1	1	34	31	(4.4)	533	(94)	604	(60)

teams reported being unable to resample to fill the missing cells in time to participate in the study, and/or that local national circumstances made the 3×2 design conceptually untenable.

A second area revealed in Table 3.1 concerns the relationship between a priori categorisations of schools on the SES dimension, and measured levels of parental SES. In three of the countries, student-level SES data consistently supported the initial school classifications. Those three were the USA, Ireland and Great Britain. All three samples had substantial differentiations among schools regarding SES.

In the case of Taiwan, reported SES differences among schools were relatively modest, and the variance among students within schools was relatively large. Similarly, in Hong Kong, the schools' measured SES ratings match the classification schemes. In Hong Kong, as in Taiwan, the range of students' SES within schools was large relative to the US and UK, no doubt reflecting the heterogeneity of catchment areas.

The Dutch schools' measured SES was generally in line with their categorisation of schools, with one exception – the low effectiveness, middle-class school's measured SES was identical to those of two of the lower-SES schools. Note that the SES differentiations among schools were small, relative to the US and UK. The Dutch schools' levels of within-school variance were among the lowest in the sample, comparable to that in the UK, with the notable difference that the UK produced substantial between-schools mean differences in SES, and that in the Netherlands, the between-school differences were relatively modest. Typically, the within-nation mean school scores on the non-verbal ability test were correlated with schools' initial SES ratings. Differences among nations on this measure were consistently less than one standard deviation, and may have reflected the time of year at which the test was presented (in particular, it may be relevant that the test was administered relatively late in the year in Ireland).

Initial scores on the CTBS Mathematics Computation and Application subtests are presented in Table 3.1 and in a 'box and whiskers' plot in Figure 3.1. Data are presented as scale scores with high scores indicating greater mathematics skills. Initial mean levels on both subtests differed substantially within and among countries. Partly, these differences reflect national policies regarding the age at which students began receiving initial instruction in mathematics. Not surprisingly, the nation that began formal mathematics instruction at age seven had the lowest mean scores in the beginning of age-seven schooling (Norway); and the nation with the highest initial age-seven mean scores had begun mathematics instruction the earliest in this study (Hong Kong). Interestingly, the variation in the country means is similar to that reported in the TIMSS study mentioned earlier (Harris, Keys and Fernandes, 1997).

Within nations, between-schools variation in maths achievement scores in scores at the beginning of the study tended to reflect a combination of perceived initial effectiveness status and SES. With a few exceptions, schools 'played in position'. Lower-SES schools' mean initial performances tended to be below those of middle-SES schools, and schools that had been initially identified as less effective tended to have lower scores than those initially identified as more effective. Table 3.1 indicates that the range between the different categories of schools was small in the Taiwan and Hong Kong samples. Furthermore, the variance in those two countries was low, compared to the other countries. This indicates that these schools achieved relatively high results for a considerable group of students while keeping the students more or less together with respect to their achievement. The other countries show the opposite pattern: lower mean scores associated with more heterogeneity in achievement. We

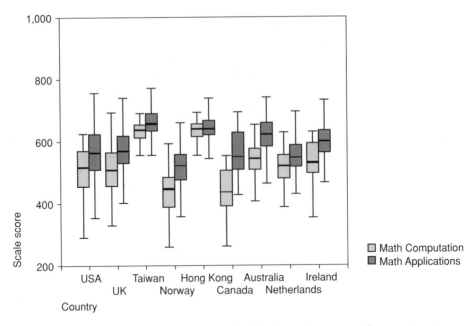

Figure 3.1 Mathematics Computation and Application subtest ranges by country at intake

speculate in our conclusions to this volume on the extent to which these kinds of results reflect upon the operation of systemic educational factors.

Achievement levels at intake, end of year 1 and end of year 2

In Table 3.1, the achievement levels at intake in computation and application on the CTBS were presented and similar data are now presented for the achievements at end of year 1 and end of year 2 in Table 3.2. As can be seen, students from Hong Kong and Taiwan did well on the test itself but the transformation into scale scores did not reflect the learning gains into a much higher scale score. In both countries, more

Table 3.2 Mathematics computation and application

National outlier status	SES	Maths computation			Maths concepts and applications		
		Intake	Year 1	Year 2	Intake	Year 1	Year 2
USA							
Low	Low	438	555	631	466	582	622
Low	Mid	534	571	628	616	624	642
Mid	Low	453	560	614	497	594	608
Mid	Mid	539	587	659	617	624	641
High	Low	491	578	634	514	591	626
High	Mid	562	591	634	613	639	667

Table 3.2 (*cont'd*)

National outlier status	SES	Maths computation			Maths concepts and applications		
		Intake	Year 1	Year 2	Intake	Year 1	Year 2
UK							
Low	Low	462	524	599	525	561	595
Low	Mid	497	559	643	592	596	625
Mid	Low	489	560	627	545	593	648
Mid	Mid	561	625	669	616	655	677
High	Low	487	571	638	560	604	636
High	Mid	542	629	681	608	662	674
Taiwan							
Low	Low	620	638	687	648	635	680
Mid	Low	627	634	679	653	628	672
Mid	Mid	632	642	687	661	638	690
High	Low	635	646	690	656	655	682
High	Mid	635	645	696	668	661	694
Norway							
Low	Low	402	513	611	480	589	612
Low	Mid	435	515	613	518	572	599
Mid	Low	384	469	587	462	552	554
Mid	Mid	438	540	602	541	600	609
High	Low	347	479	593	460	548	595
High	Mid	458	531	618	548	603	625
Hong Kong							
Low	Low	642	648	693	643	667	724
Mid	Low	641	654	691	640	656	713
High	Mid	627	654	688	649	671	723
Canada							
Low	Low	.	515	603	.	528	586
Mid	Low	.	577	635	.	678	631
Mid	Mid	.	579	654	.	644	678
High	Mid	440	506	651	544	614	672
Australia							
Low	Mixed	531	564	641	608	614	698
High	Mixed	545	578	671	618	643	706
The Netherlands							
Low	Low	486	564	645	523	567	664
Low	Mid	538	575	648	558	586	670
Mid	Low	474	562	653	529	578	651
Mid	Mid	560	629	681	572	625	699
High	Low	509	555	641	513	574	659
High	Mid	515	587	686	586	601	710
Ireland							
Low	Low	532	563	632	577	627	696
Low	Mid	499	544	639	584	629	700
Mid	Low	518	560	642	585	619	680
Mid	Mid	556	600	675	646	673	736
High	Low	530	591	637	572	625	695
High	Mid	533	595	650	604	704	731

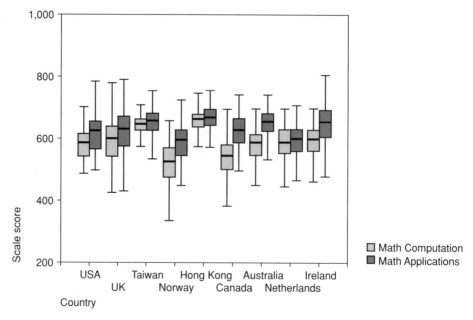

Figure 3.2 Mathematics Computation and Application subtest ranges by country – end of year 1

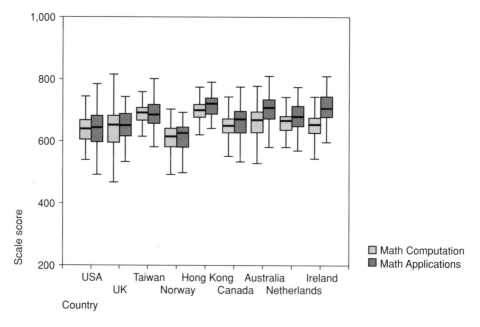

Figure 3.3 Mathematics Computation and Application subtest ranges by country – end of year 2

advanced levels of the test were used and apparently the transformation of raw scores into scale scores does not reflect this in a much higher scale score. Figures 3.1, 3.2 and 3.3 show country means and distributions at the beginning and at the end of the two years of the study and indicate that all Western countries have a considerable variance within countries, especially in the tail end of the distribution. The variance in Taiwan and Hong Kong is smaller but there is a slight increase over the two years.

Affective outcomes

Data were also collected on the students' attitudes and a series of questions were asked regarding the students' attitudes towards school, the teachers, mathematics and to fellow students. All items were administered using five-point scales. Also, questions were asked about the students' democratic attitudes. These items covered opinions about who made decisions in class and whether students were permitted to give their opinions on a variety of subjects. These latter items were given on a three-point rating scale. A fourth series of items measured the locus of control (LOC) of the students, involving items which described situations in which, for each situation, the student gave an opinion on which of two options had most likely caused the situation. For each item, one option described an internal LOC and one option described an external LOC (for further details see the Supplementary Material, Appendix Five).

In both years 1 and 2, factor analysis of the items concerning student attitudes resulted in a three-factor solution, found by an analysis across all students. The first factor can be interpreted as attitude towards school, the second factor as self-concept, and the third as attitude towards mathematics. This three-factor solution was found by separate factor analyses for most of the countries. In the rare within-country exceptions, factors were found which were interpreted as social behaviour towards teachers, classmates or both. However, there were few exceptions. The quantitative team decided to work with the following scales: attitude towards school, self-concept, attitude towards mathematics, democratic attitudes and locus of control. The number of items and the reliabilities for these scales are given in Table 3.3.

The correlation between the students' attitude towards school and the maths computation score in both years is 0.10 (with a higher score on attitudes meaning a more positive attitude towards school). The correlation of the attitude towards school and the maths application test was 0.07 in both years. For both years, the correlation between locus of control and each part of the mathematics test was about −0.27. Given that a more positive score on the scale means a more external locus of control, this finding suggests that students who explained events more by internal causes scored

Table 3.3 Characteristics of the attitude scales

Scale name	No. of scale points per item	No. of items	Reliability (Cronbechs alpha)
Attitude towards school	5	6	.71
Self-concept	5	5	.66
Mathematics attitude	5	2	.59
Democratic attitude	3	8	.61
Locus of control	2	10	.67

Table 3.4 Rotated factor solution of the attitude scales

	Factor 1	Factor 2	Factor 3	Factor 4
Att. y1	.14	.73	−.21	.06
Att. y2	.75	.21	−.10	.09
Locus y1	−.05	−.07	.83	−.16
Locus y2	−.02	−.08	.81	−.02
Self y1	.16	.74	.18	.19
Self y2	.77	.08	.13	.22
Maths y1	.20	.69	−.14	−.09
Maths y2	.72	.21	−.12	−.16
Democ. y1	−.09	.32	−.03	.78
Democ. y2	.25	−.17	−.20	.74

Note: Att. = attitude toward school, Locus = locus of control, Self = self-concept, Maths y1 = measured in year 1, Democ. = democratic attitude, Maths y2 = measured in year 2.

slightly higher on mathematics tests. The correlation between self-concept and the mathematics test was almost zero. The correlation between mathematics attitudes and the scores on the mathematics tests was about 0.14. The correlation between the democratic attitudes and computation score was about 0.10, and the correlation between democratic attitudes and application was about 0.07. All these correlations were computed over the entire sample and all correlations, except the self-concept ones, were significant. However, the values of the correlations were low, and the sizes of the correlations within each separate country decreased or approached zero. The results indicated a weak positive relationship between affective and academic outcomes, but also pointed to the possibility that attitudes are either not well established or well measured at the age that our sample of children were at.

As can be seen in Table 3.3, the correlations between the attitude measurements in year 1 and the measurements in year 2 were rather low. Because the correlations between the scales were higher, it was decided to carry out a factor analysis over all attitude scales as collected in both school years. A principal component analysis resulted in four factors with an eigenvalue larger than 1. These factors were varimax rotated. The rotated solution is presented in Table 3.4, which shows that the first component has primarily loadings from scales measured at the second year. The second component has scales measured at the first year. The third component covers the locus of control scales, the fourth the democratic attitude scales. We had not expected to find components which were so heavily influenced by the time of measurement. Also, one should notice that the scales which load on separate factors (locus of control and democratic attitudes) both had different types of items than the other scales. So, an interpretation that the factors are influenced by method and time artefacts cannot be excluded, which makes it unwise to consider any further possible analyses with these scales. These results suggest that the students, who were eight or nine years old during test-taking, do not yet have clearly formed attitudes or have attitudes that are changing over time.

Whilst we did not attempt further analyses of the affective and attitudinal data and their links with other factors, this is certainly an interesting area for future research. We join the existing international effectiveness literature in ending up in a somewhat perplexing situation with regards to the analysis of non-academic outcomes.

The relationship between achievement and student background in different countries

The next analyses present correlations between data on student background and the CTBS scale scores. As can be seen in Table 3.5, the information is provided by country.

The empty cells in Table 3.5 indicate that no information was available on this variable. For Australia no background data were available on ethnicity. In Canada, information was provided on gender and non-verbal ability for only eighteen students. In the samples from Hong Kong and Taiwan, there were no children who could be described as members of an 'ethnic minority'. As can be seen in Table 3.5, there was a rather low but significant relationship between SES and the maths scores in the USA, UK and Taiwan for all CTBS measurement points. This is less apparent in Norway and the Netherlands, and Ireland exhibits correlations that are difficult to understand. The correlation is the lowest in Hong Kong, perhaps an indication of the strong support of school education by parents across all social groups. The moderate correlations between non-verbal ability and the maths intake test is an indication that our non-verbal ability and mathematics tests measured somewhat different cognitive domains. There was a relatively consistent negative relationship between 'ethnicity' and outcomes, indicating that minority groups, however defined in the various countries, were academically at risk across nations.

The correlations between background variables and maths outcomes tended to decrease from initial testing to the end of year 1 and end of year 2 regardless of country, which appears to be an indication that the influence of background variables on mathematics achievement was declining over time in favour of the influence of schooling.

Multi-level analysis

Early in the design stages of ISERP, as outlined in Chapter 2, it was decided to move forward with a 2 × 3 schools within country design (yielding only six to twelve purposefully selected schools per country), so our potential for making strong cross-country

Table 3.5 Simple correlations between outcomes, SES, non-verbal ability and gender at different time points

Country	SES	n.v. ability	Ethn	Gender
USA				
Computation (pre)	.31**	.61**	−.37**	−.06
Computation (end year 1)	.30**	.38**	−.24**	.03
Computation (end year 2)	.29**	.39**	−.24**	.05
Concepts and applications (pre)	.36**	.60**	−.47**	−.13*
Concepts and applications (end year 1)	.36**	.52**	−.38**	−.02
Concepts and applications (end year 2)	.33**	.45**	−.36**	−.07
UK				
Computation (pre)	.29**	.50**	−.08	−.05
Computation (end year 1)	.28**	.45**	.06	.08
Computation (end year 2)	.26**	.46**	.08	.18**
Concepts and applications (pre)	.38**	.57**	−.01	.08
Concepts and applications (end year 1)	.27**	.41**	.03	.13**
Concepts and applications (end year 2)	.21**	.50**	.05	.09

Table 3.5 (cont'd)

Country	SES	n.v. ability	Ethn	Gender
Taiwan				
Computation (pre)	.15**	.37**	.	.05
Computation (end year 1)	.18**	.37**	.	−.02
Computation (end year 2)	.15**	.36**	.	−.02
Concepts and applications (pre)	.24**	.53**	.	.04
Concepts and applications (end year 1)	.21**	.46**	.	.06
Concepts and applications (end year 2)	.20**	.50**	.	.05
Norway				
Computation (pre)	.15**	.36**	−.28**	−.15**
Computation (end year 1)	.12*	.42**	−.32**	−.07
Computation (end year 2)	.09	.38**	−.09	−.10
Concepts and applications (pre)	.06	.37**	−.28**	−.02
Concepts and applications (end year 1)	.11*	.47**	−.25**	−.08
Concepts and applications (end year 2)	.10	.33**	−.34**	−.07
Hong Kong				
Computation (pre)	.00	.35**	.	−.01
Computation (end year 1)	.09	.44**	.	.03
Computation (end year 2)	.13*	.34**	.	.02
Concepts and applications (pre)	.06	.53**	.	.00
Concepts and applications (end year 1)	.11*	.49**	.	.00
Concepts and applications (end year 2)	.09	.44**	.	.01
Canada				
Computation (pre)	.	.39	.	−.27
Computation (end year 1)	.	.45	.	−.22
Computation (end year 2)	.	.42	.	−.26
Concepts and applications (pre)	.	.30	.	−.23
Concepts and applications (end year 1)	.	.45	.	−.38
Concepts and applications (end year 2)	.	.43	.	−.36
Australia				
Computation (pre)	.07	.42**	.	−.07
Computation (end year 1)	.10	.48**	.	−.07
Computation (end year 2)	.12*	.38**	.	−.08
Concepts and applications (pre)	.06	.47**	.	−.03
Concepts and applications (end year 1)	.14*	.49**	.	−.07
Concepts and applications (end year 2)	.08	.48**	.	−.05
The Netherlands				
Computation (pre)	.17	.41**	−.28**	−.11
Computation (end year 1)	.12	.33**	−.12	−.17*
Computation (end year 2)	.08	.45**	−.04	.08
Concepts and applications (pre)	.28**	.57**	−.21*	−.01
Concepts and applications (end year 1)	.11	.47**	−.20*	−.01
Concepts and applications (end year 2)	.15	.53**	−.15	.19*
Ireland				
Computation (pre)	−.12	.26**	.06	.02
Computation (end year 1)	−.06	.06	.02	.08
Computation (end year 2)	−.01	.29**	.17*	.02
Concepts and applications (pre)	−.04	.23**	−.00	−.01
Concepts and applications (end year 1)	.17	.23**	.16*	−.07
Concepts and applications (end year 2)	.06	.33**	.20*	−.05

* p < .05
** p < .01

Table 3.6 Percentages of variance to be explained at school level before and after correction for student background variables

	intake → end year 1 A1 unconditional model	intake → end year 1 B1 with background covariates	end year 1 → end year 2 A2 unconditional model	end year 1 → end year 2 B2 with background covariates	intake → end year 2 C
USA	.35	.29	.37	.20	.25
UK	.21	.11	.22	.07	.10
Taiwan	.03	.02	.07	.04	.04
Norway	.13	.04	.11	.06	.08
Hong Kong	.18	.10	.02	.02	.05
Netherlands	.16	.08	.17	.04	.15
Ireland	.09	.00	.11	.01	.12
Australia*	.18	.13	.22	.16	.04

* background covariates available for only six schools.
Note: in this final analysis (model C), the CTBS intake score was added as a final covariate.

inferential statistical analyses were limited. All of our multi-level analyses must therefore be examined with the greatest caution, obviously. One challenge clearly concerned the small 'N' at the school level (six in most countries). A second concern, in terms of the potential interpretation of results, was that schools were selected into ISERP quite purposefully to be outliers, not randomly so as to approximate representativeness.

Given the within country outlier design of the study, one might expect that schools within the countries would differ strongly in levels of achievement gain. These large differences in outcome might be reflected in a large between-school variance component. This should be the case in a statistically derived model which focuses on gains in achievements and therefore controls for differences in background characteristics of students. In Table 3.6 the magnitude of variance components at the school/class level is summarised per year from pretest to the end of year 1, and from the end of year 1 to the end of year 2. Finally, the analysis is carried out for a two-year period (intake–end of year 2). The first is using the unconditional model (model A). The second model (model B) takes the pupil covariates of gender, ethnicity, social background and non-verbal ability into account. The percentages reflect the relative magnitude of the residual variance component at school/class level as compared to the total variance in the unconditional model. The final model, in addition to student background characteristics, also takes the CTBS intake pre–post score as a covariate into account.

As can be seen in Table 3.6, there was substantial variance at school/classroom level between the schools in the USA. Thirty-five per cent of all student-level variances remained at higher levels; and 29 per cent after controlling for background variables. For Great Britain, Australia, Hong Kong and the Netherlands, that amount of school/classroom variance, after controlling for student background, was smaller but at least 18 per cent, between intake and the end of year 1. In Norway, Taiwan and Ireland, the variance between intake and end of year 1 was quite small. The school-level variance between end of year 1 and end of year 2 that remained after controlling for student background was quite small in most countries. However, the variance remaining to be explained at the school level between intake and end of year 2, for the US, UK, the Netherlands and Ireland was still considerable when the initial mathematics achievement score was added to the analysis, by contrast with that of Taiwan and Hong Kong.

Data from Hong Kong were particularly interesting, since Hong Kong had a substantial school/classroom variance component in the unconditional model at the time of intake which virtually vanished within a period of two years. This indicates that in the Hong Kong schools, school-level means were converging over time, and since Hong Kong's achievement means were the highest in the study, this appears to indicate that the Hong Kong schools in the sample were achieving both excellence and equity. We speculate in our final chapter as to the reasons why some Pacific Rim educational systems like Hong Kong manage to achieve goals which have consistently failed to be achieved in Anglo-Saxon countries.

The effect of student background factors – multi-level analyses

In Table 3.5 the simple correlations were presented between outcomes as measured by the CTBS computation and concepts/application tests at the different effectiveness levels and SES, non-verbal ability, ethnicity and gender. Note that the relationship between non-verbal ability and maths scores were consistently moderate to strong (.32 to .62). Between SES and maths, the student-level correlations were typically low to moderate (−.09 to +.38).

The analyses presented indicate that achievement correlations with gender were low throughout the nations (−.17 to +.18), with the exception of Canada which may well reflect data entry problems. Analyses across cycles of testing indicated that the non-verbal ability measure had a significant positive relationship with maths achievement in all countries for both years. It was previously noted that student samples from Taiwan and Hong Kong contained no 'ethnic minorities', and that data from Canada and Australia lacked coding for several demographic variables, therefore data on ethnicity were available only for the US, UK, Norway, the Netherlands and Ireland. In the UK, the Netherlands, and Irish samples, relationships between maths scores and ethnicity were almost always small (−.08 to −.34). The US was unique in having consistent and moderately large relationships between ethnicity and maths achievements (−.24 to −.47).

Table 3.7 gives a summary derived from multi-level analysis of the statistically significant student-level background variables for each country's gains separately between intake and end of year 1 and between end of year 1 and end of year 2. SES did not have a significant positive effect on gain, except for Hong Kong in the second year. This indicates that both within and among nations, while socio-economic status had an initial effect on student achievement, it had virtually no impact on students rates of *growth* in mathematics achievement.

In the first year gender had a significant effect in the USA and Great Britain samples, and in both years for Australia, where girls outperformed boys. Ethnic minority status had a negative effect in Norway in the first year and, surprisingly, a positive effect in the UK, both in year 1 and year 2.

Finally, in the multi-level analysis, initial (age seven) achievement was included. As can be seen in the right-hand column of Table 3.7, initial achievement was always positively associated with gain, with the exception of Australia where there had been some data difficulties. Initially high-achieving students consistently gained more than did initially low-achieving students. This finding replicated in every country, every year.

That SES rarely had a significant effect on achievement gain although the simple correlations were significant in Table 3.5 was caused by the fact that in the multi-level analysis the most powerful variable, in this case non-verbal ability, was introduced in

Table 3.7 Statistically significant relationships between student background variables and maths gain in years 1 and 2

	Year	Non-verbal	SES	Gender [girls higher]	Ethn. minority	Prior Achiev.
USA	1	Δ		Δ		Δ
	2	Δ				Δ
UK	1	Δ		Δ	Δ	Δ
	2	Δ			Δ	Δ
Taiwan	1	Δ				Δ
	2	Δ				Δ
Norway	1	Δ			∇	Δ
	2	Δ				Δ
Hong Kong	1	Δ				Δ
	2	Δ	Δ			Δ
Netherlands	1					Δ
	2	Δ				Δ
Australia	1	Δ		Δ		
	2	Δ		Δ		
Ireland	1	Δ				Δ
	2	Δ				Δ

Δ = positive effect (p < .05)
∇ = negative effect (p < .05)

the analysis first. That absorbs some variance from other variables that are collinear with non-verbal ability.

Which classroom factors travel cross-culturally?

We now move on from analysis of the effects of variation in student backgrounds on achievement to consider one of the 'core' factors that we wish to concentrate upon – what educational 'process' factors may be responsible for differences between students in their educational outcomes across contexts. We possessed a range of data on the classrooms and classroom processes of different countries' schools, derived from utilisation of a classroom observation rating scale based upon the Virgilio Teacher Inventory (VTBI), which subdivides into factors measuring classroom management, quality of instruction and classroom climate (data was missing for the United Kingdom, Taiwan and Australia for year two of the study).

Table 3.8 presents a summary of the significant effects of the three factors on gain in student outcomes over time, and shows a tendency for the three factors to operate similarly and be associated with gain in different contexts, with the two exceptions of management being negatively associated with gain in the Dutch schools and classroom climate being negatively associated with gain in the schools of Ireland. Whilst some countries did not find significant relationships between classroom factors and outcomes, the great majority of the significant differences are in the direction to be expected from existing research.

If these data show what travels to be relatively similar at classroom level, one further set of data further supports this. Table 3.9 shows those of the individual items from the VTBI that discriminate significantly at 0.05 level between schools of different levels of effectiveness across the entire sample of schools we had data on. Firstly, note

Table 3.8 Summary of multi-level analyses (classroom observation)

	Year	Management	Instruction/Teaching	Climate
USA	1			
	2	Δ**	Δ**	Δ**
UK	1	Δ*	Δ*	Δ*
	2	na	na	na
Taiwan	1	Δ+		
	2	na	na	na
Norway	1	Δ*	Δ*	Δ*
	2			
Hong Kong	1			
	2			Δ*
Netherlands	1			
	2	∇*		
Australia	1			
	2	na	na	na
Ireland	1			Δ*
	2			∇*

*   = significant at .05 level
** = significant at .01 level
Δ   = positive effect
∇   = negative effect

Table 3.9 Items on classroom observation rating scale: discriminations amongst the three ISERP effectiveness categories, combining all countries

Effectiveness category

Low v Middle	7, 18, 31, 45
Low v High	14, 19, 21, 32, 39
Low v Middle and High	8, 20, 24, 29, 30, 33, 38
Middle v High	[None]

Concept from classroom observation rating scale	*Overall Categorisation*
7 The teacher uses behaviour incentive systems to manage student behaviour	Management
8 The teacher gives positive academic feedback	Management
14 The teacher continuously monitors the entire classroom	Management
18 The teacher has a clear presentation	Instruction
19 The teacher presents detailed directions and explanations	Instruction
20 The teacher emphasises key points of the lesson	Instruction
21 The teacher has an academic focus	Instruction
24 The teacher checks for understanding	Instruction
29 The teacher uses a high frequency of questions	Instruction
30 The teacher asks academic questions	Instruction
31 The teacher asks open-ended questions	Instruction
32 The teacher probes further when responses are incorrect	Instruction
33 The teacher elaborates on answers	Climate
38 The teacher communicates high expectations for students	Climate
39 The teacher exhibits personal enthusiasm	Climate
45 The teacher prepares bulletin boards that are attractive, motivating and current	Climate

how it is easier to distinguish the teacher-level factors that discriminate between the low effectiveness schools and the other categories, a finding that parallels the experience of researchers who have undertaken within country work (Teddlie and Reynolds, 2000).

Secondly, note how the core teacher behaviours that discriminate between the low effectiveness schools and those of middle and high effectiveness are precisely those core factors that the world's teacher effectiveness researchers have identified historically as being associated with differential pupil gain *within* schools (see Teddlie and Reynolds, 2000 and Creemers, 1994), namely:

- positive feedback;
- good lesson structure through emphasising key points;
- checking for pupil understanding to establish the appropriateness of instruction;
- a high quantity of high-quality questioning;
- the use of academic-related questions;
- motivating students through probing and elaborating on their answers;
- showing high expectations of what children can achieve.

To emphasise a point which we will return to later, it is clear that there exist some teacher behaviours which across *all* contexts are associated with higher pupil gain on mathematics. These are the universals that our study set out to find. To emphasise again, these behaviours that are universals are not simply indicating that *conceptually* such factors as higher expectations affect pupil gain in different societies but that in terms of fine-grained behaviour the concept of high expectations is operationalised differently in different countries – *it is the fine-grained behaviours that are the same in different countries.* We return to further consideration of some of these issues in Chapter 13 (full details of all instruments and analyses are available in Supplementary Information, Appendices One and Five).

Differential effects of background factors

One of the major issues in educational effectiveness research concerns the effectiveness of classes and schools in relationship to pupils' background characteristics, especially the question whether schools and classes can do better than other schools and classes for the disadvantaged (Stringfield *et al.*, 1997). Indeed, we noted earlier that one of the starting points for educational effectiveness research was to better understand why some schools perform better for disadvantaged students than do other schools (Brookover *et al.*, 1979; Rutter *et al.*, 1979). Over the last twenty years many studies have been carried out to examine the characteristics of classes and schools that are more effective for disadvantaged students and gradually this question has been expanded into a more general question about the differential effectiveness exhibited by certain schools (Teddlie and Reynolds, 2000).

In ISERP we proceeded to analyse our data to gain a handle on these issues, and we asked within and across countries: what are the effects of various potentially disadvantaging variables on students' maths achievements, and do they vary cross-culturally? The global analysis we reported earlier in this chapter is supplemented by more detailed analyses here.

Tables 3.10 and 3.11 provide the results of this analysis for the two subscales of the CTBS, mathematics applications and mathematics computations, by various detailed

Table 3.10 Effects of diverse background characteristics on students' maths computational scores, by country

		USA#		UK		Taiwan		Norway		Netherlands	
		Difference	N	Difference	N	Difference	N	Difference	N	Difference	N
Non-native-born	Intake	1 N/s	344			N/a					
	year 2	3***	652			N/a					
	pre–post difference	-2									
Minority ethnic	Intake	23***	347			N/a		97***	383	46***	143
	year 2	10***	665			N/a		19***	365	12 N/s	122
	pre–post difference	13						78		34	
Father's education											
primary only	Intake	56***	152	31***	385	N/a		22*	385		
	year 2	18***	226	8***	398	N/a		19*	365		
	pre–post difference	38		23				3			
lower secondary only	Intake	49***	152	31***	385	15**	468	28*	385		
	year 2	8***	226	19***	398	8 N/s	414	20*	366		
	pre–post difference	41		12		7		8			
Father's SES (low)	Intake	22***	163	21***	344	7***	465	-5**	324		
	year 2	8 N/s	379	15***	356	4***	411	0 N/s	314		
	pre–post difference	14		6		3		-5			

	@	N	@	N	@	N	@	N	@	N
Minority language at home										
Intake	N/a		N/a		N/a		80***	382		
year 2	5*	262	N/a		N/a		16	364		
pre–post difference							64			
Mother's education										
primary only										
Intake	N/a		27***	383	14*	463	29**	383		
year 2	N/a		20***	403	18*	409	27**	364		
pre–post difference			9		–4		2			
lower secondary only										
Intake	11**	206			3*	463	49**	383		
year 2	7*	262			4*	409	20**	364		
pre–post difference	4				–1		29			
Mother's SES (low)										
Intake	15***	235	7***	380	5**	461	–22*	242	19*	117
year 2	3 N/s	436	5***	400	2**	407	–12**	239	14*	99
pre–post difference	12		2		3		–10		5	
Gender (female)										
Intake	5 N/s	456					14**	385		
year 2	–16***	468					4 N/s	366		
pre–post difference	21						10			

@   Difference between population with background characteristic and mean population score
*   p<.05
**   p<.01
*** p<.001
+   Difference between score differences at intake and year 2.
#   Six more schools were added to the USA study in year 2, doubling the size of the sample.
N/a Not enough data were available to determine differences.

Table 3.11 Effects of diverse background characteristics on students' maths application scores by country

		USA#		UK		Taiwan		Norway		Netherlands	
		Difference	N	Difference	N	Difference	N	Difference	N	Difference	N
Non-native-born	Intake					N/a					
	year 2					N/a					
	pre–post difference										
Minority ethnic	Intake	34***	347			N/a		85***	383	31***	143
	year 2	15***	665			N/a		87***	364	20	122
	pre–post difference	19						−2		11	
Father's education											
primary only	Intake	76***	152	6***	386	N/a		30*	385	13**	104
	year 2	27***	717	−2***	399	N/a		24***	365	5 N/s	89
	pre–post difference	49		8				6		8	
lower secondary only	Intake	23***	152	32***	386	17***	468	29*	385	1**	104
	year 2	−5***	717	21***	399	16***	413	41***	365	1 N/s	89
	pre–post difference	28		11		11		−12		0	
Father's SES (low)	Intake	29***	163	23***	345	11***	465	−37***	324	7	108
	year 2	15*	379	14***	357	10***	410	10***	314	−6 N/s	89
	pre–post difference	14		9		1		−47		13	

Characteristic	Difference@	N	Difference@	N	Difference@	N	Difference@	N	Difference@	N
Minority language at home										
Intake	17 N/s	108	78***	382	N/a		N/a		N/a	
year 2	12*	99	78***	363	N/a		N/a		N/a	
pre–post difference	5		0							
Mother's education: primary only										
Intake	−7 N/s	117	51***	383	16***	463	26***	384	43***	206
year 2	4*	99	54***	363	36***	408	17***	404	40***	717
pre–post difference	−11		−3		−20		9		3	
lower secondary only										
Intake	17**	117	58***	383	13***	463	8***	381	18***	235
year 2	13**	99	43***	363	11***	408	3***	401	7***	436
pre–post difference	4		24		2		5		11	
Mother's SES (low)										
Intake			−22 N/s	242	5***	461				
year 2			−11*	238	5***	406				
pre–post difference			−11		0					
Gender (female)										
Intake										
year 2										
pre–post difference										

@ Difference between population with background characteristic and mean population score
* p<.05
** p<.01
*** p<.001
+ Difference between score differences at intake and year 2.
# Six more schools were added to the USA study in year 2, doubling the size of the sample.
N/a Not enough data were available to determine differences.
N/s Differences were not significant at the 0.05 level.

socio-economic factors. The first score in each cell is a calculation of the difference at the beginning of the study between students with specific, particular background characteristics and the mean for the entire country sample.

In the USA and the UK, and to a lesser degree in Norway, the importance of different background factors can be found in relationship to student results, especially factors related to the socio-economic status of the family. Father's education, father's SES, mother's education and mother's SES seem to be important in certain countries. Also, to be a member of an ethnic minority is an important factor that contributes to lower achievement in several countries.

Whilst it is difficult to say much with confidence about our findings here, given the limited number of countries, and given the missing data in some 'cells' of the countries that we have, it is clear that it is Taiwan which exhibits the weakest relationship between parental disadvantage and student achievement. Interestingly in one of our earlier analyses on the effect of student general socio-economic status (not further elaborated as here) upon achievement, it was Hong Kong (but not Taiwan in this case) that recorded the least significant effect of background upon achievement. We speculate in Chapter 14 about the reasons for the findings concerning Hong Kong and Taiwan.

Conclusion

While the majority of data gathering for ISERP was richly qualitative, as will be shown from the next chapter onward, the quantitative data in this chapter set out a valuable frame for interpreting subsequent chapters. The quantitative data collected are of course restricted to the student and classroom levels. Much more school-level and national information is contained in the qualitative material collected in the study. The school sampling framework of the study, three levels of effectiveness and two levels in SES background of schools, was not met by all ISERP countries. This created an obvious limitation in the use of inferential quantitative analyses and this chapter cautiously concludes on its quantitative data, a caution magnified by the fact that sampling was purposive not random.

Regardless of country, background variables explained the majority of variance in student outcomes in ISERP. However, the influence of background factors was not completely systematic between and sometimes within countries. Across countries, non-verbal ability was the most stable student-level predictor of mathematics achievement. The percentage of variance accounted for by background variables decreased over time in every country, as students learned in school.

Taking into account background variables, a considerable amount of variance still could be explained at the class and school level across most countries. The proportion of variance was considerable in the USA sample (for learning gain over two years), in the UK and the Netherlands. Note that these were the three Western countries that were able to use previously existing quantitative data sets to guide initial sampling, although one is unsure as to the extent to which this was responsible for our findings. In other countries, the percentages of variance explainable were lower, a finding which partially replicates other national and international studies. Still, the finding was somewhat surprising, because one might expect larger interim school variance, given the outlier design, in all countries in which we researched.

The components of the educational processes in the classroom, like classroom climate, instructional behaviour and the management behaviour of the teacher, contributed to the explanation of student results. One or more components of classroom climate predicted student achievement in most countries. Individual, discrete teacher behaviours in certain core areas appeared to be associated with pupil gain across all the schools of the sample, when the schools were grouped together by effectiveness category.

Interestingly, the great majority of the significant findings were in the direction anticipated from the world's teacher effectiveness and school effectiveness research, and indeed the individual items of teacher behaviour that significantly link with the effectiveness status of schools amount to virtually a replication of the core findings on structure, questioning, expectations and class management that are regarded as the most important components of effective teaching *within* those societies that have researched in this area.

We now go on to explore which school-level factors may be universal, and which not, predictors of effectiveness, to add to the instructional-level factors we have identified here.

Part II

World class schools

Case studies of more effective and less effective schools in different countries

4 North America – the United States[1]

Charles Teddlie, Dianne Taylor,
Peggy Kirby, Sam Stringfield,
Mickey Pounders and John Freeman

Introduction/context

Any effort to describe US pre-college education must begin with the concept of variance. There are virtually no rules for which frequent exceptions are not the norm. The US population now exceeds 260 million people, and the geographic area in which our people live spans a continent plus islands in the mid-Pacific.

The low-socio-economic-status schools: general characteristics

Beauregard: the more effective school

Beauregard Elementary was a low-socio-economic-status (SES) elementary school serving 440 students in grades K–5,[2] and in a small pre-kindergarten programme. The thirty-one member professional staff included twenty teachers, 72 per cent of whom had taught at the school for more than five years. Beauregard was attended by students from low-SES homes; over 90 per cent of the students were eligible for free lunch.

Despite their poverty, these students scored well on district-administered standardised tests. For the various school years, the composite for Beauregard scored well above the composite score for DuBois Elementary (the less effective, low-SES school). In fact, Beauregard scored as well as some middle-SES schools on these tests.

Beauregard was located in one of the first suburbs built in the city after the Second World War. The neighbourhood was characterised by small- to medium-sized homes, originally built to house workers at an oil refinery. Thus these houses were now about fifty years old. The area surrounding the school was a mixture of well-maintained, modest, single-family dwellings, houses for sale or rent, and apartment complexes resembling public housing. Over the past thirty years, this area had declined from a solid middle-class neighbourhood, to an area of low income and poverty, where crime was common.

[1] Funding for the US team's intervisitation to other nation's schools was generously provided by the Danforth Foundation. Professor Stringfield's time spent in fieldwork, writing and editing was supported by a grant from the Office of Educational Research and Improvement, US Department of Education, to the Center for Research on the Education of Students Placed at Risk at Johns Hopkins and Howard Universities (Grant No. \$117D-40005). However, the opinions expressed by Dr Stringfield are his own, and do not represent the policies or positions of the US Department of Education.
[2] Kindergarten through to grade 5.

Despite the changes in the community, the principal, Ms Lamonico accurately described the school as one of the few neighbourhood elementary schools left in the city. During the years of decline, the neighbourhood had gradually become largely African-American, and parents almost 100 per cent working class. The fact that Beauregard still enrolled 12 per cent white students was a testament to its community reputation. Ms Lamonico, who had been principal for eighteen years, estimated that 20 per cent of the students were new to the school each year, indicating a greater student body stability than was found in many schools serving predominantly low-SES students.

The school was located on a dead-end street at the rear of several blocks of modest homes. The two main classroom buildings were completed forty and thirty-three years ago. There was also a small separate administration building and a gym-auditorium connected to the classroom buildings by covered walkways. Additionally, three temporary buildings accommodated over-enrolment. A large grassy playground and a large parking lot gave children room for 'sprints' and other athletic tests, which were supervised by the school's 'coach'.

DuBois: the less effective school

DuBois Elementary was quite similar to Beauregard in most general demographic characteristics. The school served 418 students in grades K–5. A professional staff of thirty-three included a core faculty of nineteen teachers, whose classrooms were clustered mostly by grade level. The principal, Mrs Jones, was new to the school and managed the school without an assistant principal. In contrast to Beauregard, principals at DuBois had changed frequently over the last twenty years; consequently, the secretary, who had a long tenure at the school, was invaluable.

Nearly all of the students at DuBois were African-American and more than 90 per cent were in the free-lunch programme. DuBois students scored among the lowest in the district on standardised tests. Located in a low-income area of rental doubles, triples and quads, the school stood out as a two-storey, brick building that was constructed in the 1920s as the first district school serving high school students exclusively.

Despite the poverty of the surrounding neighbourhood, the building was relatively free of graffiti and the grounds were usually neat and clean. Behind the school, students had a small grassy area and two black-topped areas for organised sports and outside recreation. Play equipment was limited to a few basketball goals. Students had physical education (PE) classes and daily recess periods during which these outdoor areas were used. Staff and visitor parking was on one side of the school. The other side contained two portable buildings which housed additional classrooms. The entire campus was set off by a four-foot chain-link fence.

Schoolwide, teachers placed emphasis on maintaining discipline in the hallways; thus students were observed walking single file without much interaction as they went to and from class. This behaviour contrasted with their activity in some classrooms and on the playground, which bordered on chaos for teachers who were weak disciplinarians.

DuBois had the feel of an urban, cramped environment, separated from its community by a fence. On the other hand, Beauregard had the open, slightly sprawling feel of a suburban campus that was closely tied to its surrounding community. These obvious physical differences helped to create the different educational and social psychological environments at the two schools.

A day in the life of a child

Beauregard: the more effective school

The student chosen for the 'child study' was named Skyleera, although everyone called her Skye. She was a nine-year-old, third-grade, African-American girl who was well behaved and well liked by the teacher and the other students. According to her teacher, Ms Snider, Skye was a typical child for this class. She had just turned nine, and lived with her mother and two younger sisters in a nearby apartment complex that resembled public housing. Skye walked to school with her friends and classmates, who also lived in the same complex.

Skye generally liked Beauregard and felt safe there, although she complained about some 'bad' students who misbehaved. She had liked all her teachers, including Ms Snider, and expressed excitement about going to fourth grade the next year. Although Skye's mother was unemployed, she was involved in her daughter's education, helping with her homework each night. Ms Snider attributed much of Skye's success and interest in school to her mother. Skye described the day of observation as a typical one for her because she 'learned, listened, and played'. Classrooms at Beauregard were mostly quiet, and students well behaved in the hallways. As for Ms Snider, she appeared to be genuinely liked by the class and received a gift from them on Teacher Appreciation day.

Skye was on task most of the time, and enjoyed the variety of activities that the teacher planned. Most of the students understood and completed their tasks, with the notable exception of two boys who were discipline problems. When a fight erupted between them, it was quickly quelled and they were banished to the office.

Ms Snider took the time to help students by offering tips to help them do well. For example, during a spelling lesson, she reminded the class that their 'biggest, biggest weakness is not reading instructions carefully'. The third grade in Louisiana is a year in which the students are given increasing responsibility for initiating and completing their own work; learning to pay attention to written directions is crucial for this development.

Skye was animated during the day and often volunteered to read aloud or to perform duties. Ms Snider allowed class discussions to stray from the immediate topic if the comments were relevant to the curriculum. On several occasions, she brought the class back on point by relating comments of a student to the main lesson. In one such instance a group of girls, including Skye, were asked to recite rhymes they sang while jumping rope. These rhymes were then linked by Ms Snider to the reading lesson.

In addition to using their daily experiences as learning tools, Ms Snider gave students an opportunity to think critically. In one instance, Ms Snider asked students to distinguish fact from opinion in a paragraph. A discussion about such statements ensued.

Ms Snider planned to return to Beauregard the next year. She had been at the school several years and had no plans to move. Skye was also looking forward to another year at a school where she was able to succeed.

DuBois: the less effective school

In contrast to the coordinated activities at Beauregard, at DuBois the day was fragmented. Activities were constantly interrupted for small groups of students to leave for, or return from, tutoring, for the class to go to recess, to lunch, to PE, to the library, or for special programmes (for which teachers sometimes had little advance notice). The lack of coordination was made worse by limited efforts to tie students' daily experiences to textbook information.

The child study at DuBois involved a nine-year-old, third-grade, African-American girl named Shaneal. Shaneal's slender build and dreadlocks made her look taller and older than she actually was. She was a relatively quiet child who intermittently attended to the work assigned, and alternatively engaged in other activities such as talking or entertaining herself with projects of her own making. For example, when the teacher, Ms Powell, read a story to the class about Martin Luther King, Shaneal cut strips of paper and glued them on as fake fingernails. Although many of Shaneal's fellow students were disruptive and the room often fell into chaos, Shaneal did not engage in such behaviour. As a result, she was rarely reprimanded.

Unlike Beauregard, where Ms Snider often engaged the class in discussions, Ms Powell started mornings with a list of assignments written on the board which students were to complete on their own. These assignments were seldom checked with the class, so neither correct nor incorrect answers were discussed. Rarely did Ms Powell *teach* a lesson, engaging in active instruction only thirty to sixty minutes a day. When she did teach, she allowed extraneous student questions to subvert any importance that might have been attached to the lesson. As students tired towards the end of the day, misbehaviour in the room often worsened.

Despite the dull routine, Shaneal said she liked school and felt she could learn from her teacher. Nonetheless, she complained that the older kids picked on her, and felt the school was not a pleasant place to work because 'students fight too much', and the cafeteria and bathrooms were dirty. Still, Shaneal liked Ms Powell and said she liked going to school.

Ms Powell described Shaneal as a cooperative student whose progress in class was acceptable, but not noteworthy. Shaneal's mother was pleased with her progress in school and made sure that homework was done when it was assigned. Like Shaneal, her mother complained about Shaneal getting harassed. She instructed Shaneal to tell the teacher when this occurred; however, when nothing changed as a result, she felt she had no recourse. Shaneal's mother knew of no efforts to involve parents at the school, though this was an explicit goal of the principal.

Both the teacher and Shaneal affirmed that this was a typical day. Ms Powell would not be returning to DuBois the following year, and hoped instead to get a placement in a gifted class. Otherwise, she thought she might quit teaching. As for Shaneal, she would be returning to a school which actually impeded her progress towards meeting her academic potential.

Teachers' teaching style

Beauregard: the more effective school

Ms Lamonico was keenly aware of the strengths and weaknesses of the teaching staff, and said she wished there were more time for observations. Her knowledge of the staff probably came from her long tenure at the school and the fact that she had hired virtually all of them. She described the third-grade teachers, whom she considered a 'weak' group, in accurate, diagnostic detail. She felt that the lower-grade-level teachers

(K, 1st, 2nd) were more open to innovation. There were more centre-based activities and small-group instruction at the lower grades, while the upper-grade teachers, by contrast, were more traditional, according to Ms Lamonico.

Staff development at Beauregard over the past two years emphasised innovative techniques, including whole-language development, mathematics manipulables, problem-solving techniques across curricula and the independent student use of the library for research projects. In this vein, Ms Lamonico allowed some autonomy for experimentation with different instructional techniques. Second-grade teachers took this opportunity to implement a semi-departmentalisation scheme for one academic hour per day.

The three third-grade teachers, on the other hand, were more conservative and represented a range of ability and experience. Two had over twenty years of experience, while the third was just beginning. Skye's teacher, Ms Snider, was one of the more experienced teachers. She emphasised cooperative learning and would allow dyads of students to leave the classroom to find a spot on campus where they could work together on practice and review. She explained that weaker students encountered problems in a classroom setting where they felt embarrassed. Consequently, she encouraged 'private' cooperative learning. Ms Snider appeared confident that the students would attend to the assigned task and the observer did not see any evidence of problems with the implementation of the technique.

Unfortunately, the other third-grade teachers were not so successful. Ms LeBlanc, also an experienced teacher, had poor control of her students. Though Ms Lamonico worked with Ms LeBlanc on keeping the noise down, real success was not achieved. Ms Lamonico placed a premium on quiet hallways and classrooms, saying that she wanted school to be an orderly, peaceful place for students, many of whom came from chaotic environments. Classroom noise was less problematic for Ms LeBlanc, who said she encouraged cooperative learning and tolerated the noise level as a necessary side-effect.

The new teacher, Ms Wheat, was still 'learning the ropes'. She had some discipline problems and tried early on to compensate for them by yelling. Ms Lamonico suggested that she observe other teachers who used more successful student-management practices. Earlier in the year, Ms Wheat indicated that she might not return next year, but was more optimistic at the year's end. She said she had learned a lot and pointed out that she had done well on the state-mandated evaluation for intern teachers.

DuBois: the less effective school

There was little in the way of inventive teaching at DuBois. Most classes were taught either using whole-group instruction or written assignments. Kindergarten was the only grade where small centre-based learning was used extensively. It seemed that pre-service preparation and district policy encouraged the use of innovative techniques at this level.

Students in the two third-grade classes were seated in groups; however, group work was infrequent. In Shaneal's class, Ms Powell did *not* use group work during any of the days that she was observed. Group work would probably have not been effective had she tried it, given the level of chaos in the class.

Ms Drake, the other third-grade teacher, primarily used teacher-directed, whole-class instruction, but occasionally had students work in groups. Ms Drake had better classroom-management skills and, unlike some other teachers at the school, was able to keep students seated without being mean. Ms Drake occasionally spent class time helping students learn ways to deal with their feelings. Nonetheless, most of the activities which students did in her room were traditional, and seldom required students to think critically.

The description in the previous section of a child's day at DuBois is of Shaneal's teacher (Ms Powell). Morning work consisted of students completing assignments written on the board. The afternoon typically involved some type of teacher-directed instruction. Neither seemed effective, but some students (it varied who they were) were always working on an assignment regardless of the chaos around them. By the end of the year, the class in unison could give answers to various multiplication items. It was difficult to assess the children's reading ability since they seldom read aloud.

Ms Jones, the principal at DuBois, gave no indication that she knew what occurred in the classrooms or anything about the instructional style of the teachers. She was observed in the classrooms only once, and then for a state-mandated observation.

The curriculum

Beauregard: the more effective school

Variance on this dimension is limited given the fact that teachers received curriculum guidelines from both state and district. Many details regarding the mathematics curriculum at Beauregard and DuBois were similar: the students studied approximately the same topics in approximately the same sequence. Ms Lamonico at Beauregard, however, had much more to say about curriculum delivery than did Ms Jones at DuBois. For instance, Ms Lamonico indicated that she encouraged extensive use of 'hands on' problem-solving techniques in maths. She indicated that instructional emphasis previously centred on the textbook, but that now teachers were encouraged to add relevant information from varied sources.

Ms Lamonico further stated her opinion that it was 'more humane' to integrate the curriculum. Therefore, she allowed the teachers to alter the specific number of hours per day devoted to the various subjects, saying that the concept of assigning 'a set number of hours each day to each topic is ancient'. As a part of her more humane orientation to curricular matters, Ms Lamonico had a school rule that homework should take no more than one hour per day. In a newsletter to parents, she stated that violations of this rule should be reported to her directly.

A final point with regard to curricular issues concerned multiculturalism in the textbooks and in the district guidelines. Ms Lamonico saw this as a significant change that had occurred over the past five years. Ms Jones at DuBois made no such comment.

DuBois: the less effective school

In contrast to Ms Lamonico, Ms Jones did not seem especially interested in curriculum issues, explaining that these issues were a matter of district and state policy. In the third grade, students reviewed addition and subtraction in the fall and moved to multiplication by mid-year. At Dubois, maths instruction was typically whole-class, with blackboard demonstrations by the teacher. Teachers in both third-grade classes worked with students on recognising that 7×9 was the same as 9×7, and that $63 - 7$ was similarly related to $56 + 7$.

Both third-grade teachers taught maths in a traditional way: students worked problems and the teacher demonstrated lessons on the board. Ms Powell taught maths in the afternoon, but she did not teach the subject every day. The other third-grade teacher placed an emphasis on maths and taught it in the morning. She made a great effort to include it every day, even if the morning was interrupted by some school activity. In addition, she tried to give real-world examples for the concepts taught. Ms Powell did not do this during the observations.

The influence of parents

Beauregard: the more effective school

In an interview, Ms Lamonico indicated that 50 per cent of the parents belonged to the parent–teacher organisation and that 15 per cent of the parents served as helpers in the classrooms. A monthly newsletter kept parents informed about school events and other important information. Ms Lamonico also indicated that a *required* parent–teacher conference was held each nine-weeks period and that 90 per cent of the children had parent(s) who attended.

DuBois: the less effective school

By contrast, Ms Jones asserted that increasing parental involvement was a main priority; however, parents were rarely seen at school, except for discipline problems. She offered no indication that her emphasis on parent involvement had resulted in increased parent visits to the school to volunteer or attend meetings. Therefore, at Dubois, parents who were involved seemed to be more like Shaneal's mother, who expressed an interest in the child's work and ensured that homework was done.

The headteacher/principal

Beauregard: the more effective school

For Ms Lamonico, Beauregard was her 'mission' in life. A devout Catholic who had never married, Ms Lamonico had intended to be a nun, but had devoted her life to education instead, and particularly to Beauregard. Several district administrators, along with others from the educational community, agreed that Ms Lamonico did an exceptional job at Beauregard. When the head of the district research unit was asked to confirm the effectiveness status of potential ISERP schools, he said of Ms Lamonico: 'I don't know how she does what she's done. It's been an exceptional school for a number of years.'

Indeed, Beauregard's success always seemed to come back to Ms Lamonico. Over her eighteen years at the school, she had developed a philosophy of education and an idiosyncratic leadership style that worked. She stated very matter of factly that she 'pretty much ran things here'. She did form the site-based council mandated by the district reform programme, but continued to make the important decisions at the school herself. The council was used mainly to get information to the faculty as quickly as possible.

Still, Ms Lamonico was not autocratic and she consciously attempted to give the faculty limited autonomy in organisational planning and curricular issues. As noted, she encouraged instructional innovation and allowed one grade level to semi-departmentalise at the teachers' request.

In one interesting story about her administrative style, Ms Lamonico discussed a laminating machine which she had purchased with her personal funds. She made a rule that only she could use the laminator; therefore, she came to school daily at 6.30 a.m., two hours before school started, to run the machine. Her early arrival and the positioning of the laminator in the school office created the opportunity for her to greet teachers, chat with them informally about classes and to overhear conversations that gave her an overall sense of teacher morale. In this way, she got to hear about much of what was happening schoolwide without having to ask or take additional time during her busy day.

Through observations and interviews, an image of Ms Lamonico emerged that was consistent with her description of Beauregard as her 'mission'. She was devoted to her students and faculty in ways that went beyond the normal caring of an administrator. One got the impression that she would be a very difficult person to replace.

DuBois: the less effective school

There had been four principals at Dubois during the past seven years. The first of these was there for sometime, but was terminated for 'embezzling' funds from a school account, which damaged the school's image considerably. While the district would deny it, Dubois had become a kind of 'dumping ground' for ineffective elementary principals and could be characterised as having 'absentee' leadership.

Ms Jones, the current principal, was autocratic and rude when she thought outsiders were not present. She frequently interrupted classes over the intercom to reprimand the student body or the faculty. Despite this, she could be charming when the situation called for it, as during interviews with the research team.

When dealing with students, she was often insulting. Near the beginning of the year, one observer heard her reprimand two students who had been fighting. She admonished one, saying, 'You just as mean and hateful and low-down as you can be.' Then later, when trying to get both students' side of the story, she said to one: 'Now, you shut up, you had yo' turn. An' take yo' han' away from yo' nose; there ain't nuthin' wrong with yo' nose.' As noted, with talking to outsiders, she was polite and used standard grammar with ease.

School expectations of pupils

Beauregard: the more effective school

While there were some complaints from faculty about the family backgrounds of students, the overall expectation level for students was high at Beauregard. For example, Ms Wheat stated explicitly that she maintained high expectations for her students because 'children are capable of living up to your expectations'. These high expectations for students at Beauregard appeared to be associated with their activities at the school, not with longer-term educational goals. For instance, while it was clear that she expected students to do well while they were at Beauregard, Ms Lamonico stated that she expected only 5 per cent would go to college.

The success of Beauregard students was known in the broader education community, leading the major research university in the state to select Beauregard as a 'professional development school'. As a result, teaching majors went to the school to observe and act as aides. Interviews with both university faculty and students in the university programme confirmed the high expectation levels for Beauregard students.

To assess student progress, teachers in the lower grades at Beauregard experimented with various forms of authentic assessment, such as portfolios. Schoolwide, assessment consisted primarily of teacher observation and teacher testing. Like all public school students in the state, Beauregard students took state-mandated standardised tests each spring.

High expectations also applied to discipline, an area in which Ms Lamonico was also directly involved, although she complained that this took time that she could have devoted to classroom observations. It was not unusual to see a number of children sitting outside her office waiting their turn to report their offences. Teachers seemed to value Ms Lamonico's willingness to act as the major disciplinarian.

DuBois: the less effective school

Expectation for students was still another area of contrast between these two low-SES schools. Students were not expected to do well academically or socially at DuBois. Expectations were highest with regard to hallway decorum. While students were almost always orderly in the halls, there were numerous playground fights, leading to the frequent cancellation of recess.

Further, students in both third-grade classes seemed to be 'on edge'. Also, as noted, students in Ms Powell's room often fell into chaos and fights occurred frequently. However, students were seldom hurt and were almost never sent to the office. At worst, misbehaving students were sent to another teacher's class for a period of time where he/she sat idly until returned to class.

Ms Drake's class was more similar to others at Dubois in terms of overt behaviour. Generally, students seemed to be on the verge of fighting and often made insulting comments to each other. As noted, Ms Drake had better management skills and was able to keep the anger just below the surface. Most teachers at Dubois, including the third-grade teachers, posted five to seven classroom rules, in keeping with the letter, though not the spirit, of good classroom management. Most often, however, these were negative rules stated 'without the negative', such as 'Keep your hands to yourself', rather than 'Respect yourself and others'.

School goals

Beauregard: the more effective school

Ms Lamonico chose *not* to participate in the 'academic enhancement' aspect of the district reform programme, which she perceived as 'gimmicky'. She was pleased with the schoolwide goals that she and the faculty had developed over the past several years and did not believe that an enhancement would do anything constructive for the school. The administration and faculty at Beauregard developed their school goals over a period of time, and without the assistance of an external change agent.

Ms Lamonico listed three main goals for the school: (1) continued instructional improvement; (2) more parental involvement and interest; and (3) discipline improvement. Instructional improvement was the school's number-one goal and was operationally defined in terms of improved teaching in the classroom, and schoolwide adoption of more inventive methods of instruction and assessment. It is important to emphasise that improved scores on standardised tests was *not* the criterion.

As for parental involvement, Ms Lamonico said that the school was striving to change its image in the community from that of a 'kind of glorified baby-sitter'. The school actively solicited parents to participate in their children's education at home and at school. Part of her rule that homework could take only one hour per night was so that parents would have more time to interact with their children in 'fun ways'.

DuBois: the less effective school

Ms Jones was less able to articulate goals for Dubois. In her defence, she had been at the school less than one year when asked this question. Still, she boasted having thirty years' experience in education, which should have led to the development of achievable goals for the school. Her main goal, firmly asserted, was increased parental involvement. As noted, by the year's end, little in the way of parent participation was evident. Although the school had developed goals for the district enhancement programme, no effort was expended by either the principal or the faculty to meet these goals.

Academically, Dubois students were expected to muddle through. Ms Drake, the third-grade teacher with better classroom order, expressed concern about the standardised testing of her class. Her concern, however, had more do to with the reflection on her as a teacher than on the importance of student learning. Shaneal's teacher, Ms Powell, had an unspoken goal of just getting through the day. For her, learning was ancillary to maintaining control. Ms Powell was troubled by the lack of discipline in her class, but unlike Ms Wheat or Ms LeBlanc at Beauregard, Ms Powell received no assistance from the principal.

Inter-staff relations

Beauregard: the more effective school

The three third-grade teachers at Beauregard were different from one another in terms of teaching styles; nevertheless, they often discussed their lessons, the techniques and resources they used, how particular students were doing, and the like. One of the experienced teachers took the new teacher 'under her wing', giving her advice on various academic and personal issues.

There seemed to be some tension among the second-grade teachers on a personal level, but much of this was attributed to a teacher described by the researchers as a bit of a malcontent. Indeed, Ms Lamonico appeared to command the respect of the faculty as a whole. Teachers seemed to appreciate that she went out of her way to handle discipline problems and to give the teachers autonomy in a limited sense.

Ironically, offers of greater autonomy were rejected by teachers at some grade levels. In particular, when Ms Lamonico gave each grade level the authority to assign students to classes, the kindergarten and third-grade teachers opted to have her continue making the assignments. For those who took the opportunity to compose the classes, all the students' records were accessible so that informed decisions could be made about which children would go into each classroom.

DuBois: the less effective school

Despite close proximity to their grade-level colleagues and mandated weekly meetings, Dubois teachers did not collaborate, other than to share some materials and keep each other aware of the concepts they expected to teach. Attempts by a new teacher to establish functioning planning groups were politely rebuffed and this teacher turned to friends at other schools for professional collaboration.

Each spring, teachers provided written information on students, noting reading level, which skills had been developed and which ones still needed development. Although teachers had access to this information, little thought was put into assigning students to classes. Because of limits on class size, there were three second-grade classes when the school was first studied. When the students moved to the third grade, the classes were not reorganised, but went as a block, with the extra class split between the two teachers. This again contrasted with Beauregard, where most teachers took the interest to place students in groups that held the most promise for success.

School resources

Beauregard: the more effective school

One of Ms Lamonico's strengths was her ability to bring extra resources into Beauregard. Her school was sponsored by the largest milk company in the area. Each year, the company sent employees and cows to the school for educational and publicity purposes. Students really liked these events, as they otherwise had little contact with farm animals.

Through Ms Lamonico's fund-raising efforts, each teacher received $150–170 each year to purchase materials for their classrooms, a fact of which Ms Lamonico was proud. She claimed that she had the 'best equipped [low-SES] school in the city', and indicated that other principals were jealous. The observers at her school agreed, noting that each classroom had at least one computer and a video-cassette player together with a television.

In addition to classroom supplies, money was also spent on air-conditioning the cafeteria – no perk in south Louisiana, where temperatures can soar into the low nineties (the low thirties Celsius) in September and May. Ms Lamonico could provide these funds because she raised about $10,000 per year through school-sponsored events.

DuBois: the less effective school

Teachers at Dubois did not complain about inadequate resources, but the school had fewer resources than others in the district. Every room did have an overhead projector and appeared to have sufficient textbooks. Record and cassette players were also readily available. On the other hand, no classroom had its own video, and cassette tape players and computers were not available outside the library.

DuBois was designated as a 'maths/science/performing arts academy' under the district's academic enhancement programme, and described itself as 'The school where all children can learn'. Students were supposed to be instructed in the use of computers so that they could work at their own pace using maths and science software programmes. However, none of the second- or third-grade classrooms had a single computer, let alone the number required for this kind of enhanced programme.

The observers were aware of *no* tangible outside resources, although DuBois had been adopted by several businesses. It was not clear what these adopters supplied, as was often the case in this district. Business sponsorships often turned out to be publicity ploys, unless the school cajoled resources from the sponsors. Such work, required patience and persistence, usually from the principal, and was not characteristic of the 'absentee' leadership style at DuBois.

One programme implemented at Dubois, and used to great advantage at *other* schools, was 'Library Power'. This district-sponsored programme brought extra funds into the school to enhance library services, which included the purchase of additional books and the development of lofts and reading areas where students could 'flop' and read silently. This programme was intended to teach students to use the library as a resource when needed throughout the day. During the two years of observations, it was not evident that students used the library outside of regularly scheduled library classes.

On a more positive note, Dubois did provide a symphonic quartet performance for lower-grade students which seemed to be well received. In addition, a programme was begun concerning anger management. Each week a woman from the community met with whole classes to encourage children to learn alternatives to physical confrontation.

Relationship with local authorities

Beauregard: the more effective school

Ms Lamonico said that she seldom saw anyone from the central office, in part because the staff had been cut so severely, especially in the area of supervisors of instruction. This arrangement seemed to suit Ms Lamonico; she liked running the school with minimum outside interference.

DuBois: the less effective school

Contact with district administrators was limited for Dubois as well. However, in this case, it seemed that DuBois was one of those schools that the district would rather forget. As noted above, a former principal had caused the district embarrassment over embezzlement charges, and subsequently the school appeared to have become a dumping ground for ineffective principals.

School image

Beauregard: the more effective school

As can be discerned from the above, Beauregard enjoyed a positive image in the community. Much of this should be attributed to Ms Lamonico's 'missionary' work over the past eighteen years. Newspaper articles extolling Beauregard's high scores on state-mandated tests were proudly placed outside the principal's office, and the annual programme by the milk company never failed to generate positive newspaper or television stories. Even a negative news story about a gun incident did not appear to seriously damage the reputation of the school, partially because the principal handled it promptly and downplayed the incident as unusual for the school, which it was. Ms Lamonico never had trouble recruiting teachers to her school, even though it was a low-SES school. The extra classroom equipment, the supply money and the continued academic emphasis at Beauregard 'set it apart from other schools from poor areas', according to Ms Lamonico. Since she had an adequate teacher pool, she was able to make good personnel decisions.

DuBois: the less effective school

Unfortunately for the students and teachers at Dubois, the schools' community image was poor. The incident that received the most publicity over the past several years was the embezzlement case. Complicating the situation, the series of temporary principals had little chance to change the community's image of the school, even if these principals had had the desire. Further, the constant outflow of disgruntled teachers from the school confirmed perceptions in the educational community that Dubois was a place to avoid.

Conclusions

Table 4.1 contains a summary of the differences between the two lower-SES schools across the twelve predetermined ISERP dimensions of contrast, which as we noted in Chapter 2 were established by the ISERP research team based on their knowledge of the SER literature and on the impressions that were gleaned from the initial fieldwork.

The middle-SES schools: general characteristics

Kennedy: the more effective school

Kennedy Elementary was a middle-SES, more effective school with 519 students in grades K–5. Kennedy was located in a quiet, middle-class suburban neighbourhood. The typical home in the surrounding area was thirty years old, small to average in size, with well-manicured lawns and gardens. Although the neighbourhood is almost exclusively white, the student body at Kennedy is about 45 per cent African-American. These children were bused five to eight miles to school from low-income apartment buildings and houses. Approximately 30 per cent of the students received free or reduced-price lunch.

Thirty-four teachers comprised the professional staff. The school experienced very little teacher turnover, and was a popular site for student teachers from local universities. On average, teachers had eighteen years of experience at Kennedy. The principal was on sabbatical the year we visited, but maintained a reputation as a no-nonsense manager with a strong academic focus.

Like Jackson District educators, Kennedy's principal and teachers placed great emphasis on test scores. Although Kennedy teachers spent less time teaching test-taking skills and administering practice tests than other schools in Jackson, there was nevertheless an obvious bustle about standardised testing during the spring semester. Not surprisingly, 98 per cent of Kennedy students met the state standard on the state's criterion-referenced test.

Table 4.1 Summary of differences between the two lower-SES schools across the twelve dimensions

Dimension of contrast	More effective lower-SES (Beauregard)	Less effective lower-SES (DuBois)
General characteristics of the school	90 per cent free lunch High test scores Attractive campus in decaying neighbourhood.	90 per cent free lunch. Low test scores Well maintained but cramped campus in poverty-ridden area
A day in the life of a child	Teacher attempted to link student's experiences to academic content	No attempt to link student's experiences to academic content
Teachers' teaching style	Some teachers inclined toward innovative practice	Traditional teaching techniques
The curriculum	State/district curriculum with some teacher input in certain subjects and grades	State/district curriculum implemented as mandated
The influence of parents	50 per cent PTO involvement High parent participation for lower-SES school	Little or no parent involvement Little or no effort by school to involve parents
The principal	Principal of 18 years saw success of students as her 'mission' in life	Four principals in seven years
		District 'dumping ground' for ineffective principals
School expectations of pupils	Consistently high for both achievement and behaviour at school	Consistently low for achievement
		Some expectation of hallway decorum
School goals	Three overall goals well articulated and pursued	Goals not articulated nor pursued
Inter-staff relations	Professional relations centred around grade levels	Friendships formed along racial lines. No planning for student assignment
	Considerable planning for student assignment	
School resources	Best-equipped inner-city school in district	No tangible outside resources Noticeable dearth of technology in classrooms
Relationship with local authorities	Minimum outside involvement	District office personnel avoided school
School image	Generally good as fostered by the veteran principal	Negative, with residue from previous school scandals

The Kennedy student body enjoyed a large play area, with both grass and asphalt surfaces. Play equipment included brightly painted elevated chutes, into which students tossed balls in their own version of basketball. The school was located adjacent to a playground and recreational facility, which could be used for physical education and student assemblies.

Zachary Taylor: the less effective school

Zachary Taylor Elementary was also a kindergarten–grade-five school with over 800 students, served by approximately forty-five faculty members. Administrative duties were carried out by a principal, who had been at the school for fourteen years, and a full-time assistant principal, in her second year. Each grade level had four to six teachers and two aides, who assisted teachers with clerical duties, but not student instruction.

At one time, this school had only white students and was located in a remote area of the district. The school is now surrounded by middle-class subdivisions, with one area of noticeably newer and more expensive homes. Less than half of the students' population was African-American, and all of these students were bused in from other areas of town. Like Kennedy, about 30 per cent of the students received free or reduced-price lunch. Approximately 89 per cent of Zachary Taylor students met the state standard on its criterion-referenced test, which was well below the 98 per cent passing rate for Kennedy. Kennedy also outscored Zachary Taylor on the state-administered norm-referenced test each year.

Most of the classroom aides and a new PE teacher were hired with money made available through site-based budgeting. In this district, individual schools may choose to utilise budgeted salary in creative ways if district approval is received. At Zachary Taylor, the teachers had agreed to increase their class sizes in order to hire more support staff (e.g. aides, PE teachers). There were thirty to thirty-two students in each regular classroom.

The school was built in the late 1960s and was in very good repair. Nevertheless, classrooms were crowded, and none of the facilities were adequate for the number of students enrolled. The school-building layout was shaped somewhat like a large E with four separate buildings connected by large covered walkways. There were also twelve portable buildings clustered behind and between the classroom buildings. While the main buildings and grounds were very clean and well kept, some portables were in need of major repair. It appeared that these portables had simply been 'let go' and that teachers with the least experience were placed in them.

The playground was very large, yet equipment was limited to a few old climbing bars, except for the one section for kindergarten students. This area had new swings, ladders and climbing bars that were visible from the main street leading to the school.

A day in the life of a child

Kennedy: the more effective school

The student chosen for the 'child study' was Jeremy, a third-grade, white male, described as a precocious and flirtatious eight-year-old. He was outgoing and talkative, sometimes too talkative for his teachers' preference. Teachers constantly but gently prodded Jeremy to remain on task and 'stay still'. Jeremy had twenty-one classmates, which contrasted with the thirty to thirty-two students in the typical Zachary Taylor third-grade classroom.

Jeremy had four (sometimes five) teachers during the day in this departmentalised Jackson School District elementary school. All of his classes contained one or two computers and an overhead projector, and two had a television and VCR. Walls of bookshelves were lined with textbooks and story books. The rooms were cluttered, but with useful supplies and equipment. Most classes had desks in rows, but these were occasionally pushed aside for 'on-the-floor' story-time or arranged in circles.

Jeremy's day began with fifty-five minutes of homeroom and cultural arts (with PE substituted for cultural arts two days per week). Second period followed, with fifty-five minutes of English, then ten minutes of recess. After recess, Jeremy went to his third teacher of the day for maths (fifty-five minutes), then on to the fourth for reading. Although reading instruction lasted one and a half hours, it was interrupted by a thirty-five-minute lunch period. His day ended with fifty-five minutes of social studies or science. One striking aspect of Jeremy's day was the amount of moving about, each time necessitating the packing and unpacking of books and supplies.

Jeremy enjoyed the social aspects of schooling ('I like lunch-time and recess and when I go to computer'), but accepted the academic rigour that characterised life at Kennedy. Students arrived at class on time, quickly settled in and generally attended to the teacher. Embedded routines for distributing and collecting papers, for traffic flow and where to sit, and for appropriate protocol during class, were apparent in all third-grade classes. Accompanying the rules and routines, however, was a complacence about learning that pervaded the classroom. (Researchers administering tests at Kennedy lamented that 'no one smiled' and wondered if smiling was against the rules. They also noted that visitor rules – signing in, wearing name badges, etc. – were much stricter than at other US schools in the study.)

Zachary Taylor: the less effective school

Seth, an eight-year-old white male, was the subject of the child study at Zachary Taylor. Seth's day was disjointed and characterised by a lack of emphasis on learning. Class activities were frequently interrupted for recess, lunch, PE and 'enrichment' activities, such as computer lab and music.

The fragmentation was exacerbated by a lack of coordination among subject areas, even though students were in self-contained classes. Unlike Kennedy, where Ms Brown integrated language arts into a science lesson, subject-area assignments at Zachary Taylor were completely unrelated to each other. Moreover, science was not taught on any of the days that researchers visited the school.

According to the teacher, Seth worked more diligently than usual during the day he was observed. While other students were often inattentive to assignments, Seth applied himself. However, much of the work planned by Ms Cline, his teacher, involved worksheets and rote question-and-answer activities. At no time was Seth engaged in critical thinking through the design of a lesson.

Generally, students did not seem to be the central focus at Zachary Taylor. More importance was placed on teachers' completing paperwork, than on engaging students academically. Often Seth and his classmates worked by themselves while Ms Cline attended to work at her desk. Even during PE, students were given free play time so the teacher could complete required forms. A lack of emphasis on students was also evident when students were at recess. Duty teachers typically stood together some distance from the children. Although they knew that fights would erupt during the last recess of the day, they made no effort to circulate among the children as a preventative measure.

While Seth seemed to like school, commenting that the 'good teachers and the good principal' were the things he liked best, he did not express excitement and, in fact, seemed a little apprehensive during his interview with the researcher. When asked if the day he was observed were typical, Seth said that it was.

Teachers' teaching style

Kennedy: the more effective school

Because Kennedy practised both departmentalisation and tracking, the student's day was characterised by frequent movement and adjustments to multiple teachers in multiple classrooms. Although students had a homeroom, they spent no more time in that room than in others. Each transition created extended non-instructional time and a need to readjust to a new context with its new rules. Students were assigned to classes by ability, and all were aware of whether they were in Level 1 or 2 classes.

Despite the schedule, time-on-task was quite high (90 per cent) during classroom observations. However, time lost between classes was not entered into the estimation, and we calculated that loss to be as much as thirty minutes a day.

Instruction at Kennedy was almost always directed to the whole class. Cooperative learning techniques were seldom used. Teachers did engage students in discussions about the lessons, but these discussions were seldom animated. Nevertheless, teachers averaged high scores (4.5 on 5.0 scales) on indicators of effective teaching practices (Virgilio, Teddlie and Oescher, 1991) during classroom observations. Teachers were uniformly skilled in lesson presentation, beginning with an overview of what was to be accomplished, presenting in a variety of manners, soliciting and answering questions and providing opportunities for guided and individual practice.

Zachary Taylor: the less effective school

The scores on time-on-task and on indicators of effective teaching practices at Zachary Taylor for the classroom observations were much lower than those at Kennedy. Instruction was very traditional, with students usually seated in rows (except in one class where students were grouped by arrangement of table desks with four to six students in each group). Teachers followed lesson plans/teachers guides that addressed each subject separately. There was very little integration of subject matter (maths is maths, reading is reading, etc.).

Any type of group work was minimal, while lecture was the most common mode of instructional delivery, with a high reliance on printed worksheets and practice pages. Most classrooms had 'centres' located in various places, but these areas seemed to be more display-orientated than actual work stations. A high priority was placed on students 'finishing' their work, even though most of this 'work' was not very productive and usually consisted of repetitive worksheets.

The curriculum

Kennedy: the more effective school

The curriculum was very traditional with a strong emphasis on academic goals. Teachers followed state and district curriculum guides with strict guidelines about what content to cover on what day. The extent to which teachers adhered to the guidelines or adapted to their students' needs varied from school to school in the Jackson District. Teachers at Kennedy mentioned the curriculum guides in their discussions, but they did not feel as constrained by the guidelines as peers at other schools. (In some other schools, administrators actually monitored curriculum progress to be sure that material was being covered as prescribed.)

The cultural arts period at Kennedy served a variety or purposes. Students participated in 'Values Education Programme' as well as more traditional arts and crafts projects during this time. Students had PE two times per week.

Testing was emphasised in the curriculum. Teachers taught test-taking skills and administered practice tests routinely just prior to standardised testing. A moderate level of anxiety about testing was apparent during this time. Test scores were published in the local newspaper (by school and district). In a community that must compete for enrolments and tax revenues with non-public interests, test scores were an important point of comparison. For example, a principal of another Jackson school had been removed from her position under suspicion that she had altered student responses on the state tests. The curriculum in Jackson schools emphasised what is tested: primarily maths and language arts.

Zachary Taylor: the less effective school

There were no special techniques observed for the teaching of maths. During the teacher interviews, no one identified any special training or workshops they had received in maths. Most teachers responded that they followed the state content guide.

There was not much innovation within this school, even though it had adequate resources. The teachers were comfortable with their current procedures and saw no need for change. The weekly grade-level meetings could have been used to address curriculum, but were not.

Schedules were not followed closely: more emphasis was placed on daily activities than on academics. The schedule could have been easily modified to place more activities back to back, thus reducing the loss of class time. As at Kennedy, transitions took their toll on the academic atmosphere of this school.

The influence of parents

Kennedy: the more effective school

Parent participation at school functions was very strong, but was associated with student success in school. At open house, the gifted and talented teachers attracted the

UNIVERSITY OF WOLVERHA...
Walsall Learning Centre

ITEMS ISSUED:

Customer ID: WPP6131241X

Title: excellence of play
ID: 7624846775
Due: 21/04/2015 23:59

Title: World class schools : international
perspectives on school effectiveness
ID: 7622691359
Due: 05/05/2015 23:59

Total items: 2
Total fines: £2.80
14/04/2015 20:56
Issued: 10
Overdue: 0

Thank you for using Self Service.
Please keep your receipt.

Overdue books are fined at 40p per day for
1 week loans, 10p per day for long loans.

largest parent group. Teachers indicated that a small group of parents never attended parent conferences or activities. Teachers associated children's success in school with the values parents placed on education.

Parents at Kennedy ran the library and helped in the school office. Few were used in classrooms but many assisted with special schoolwide projects. There were always enough volunteers to chaperone field trips or supply refreshments for school parties.

Two parent conference days were held each year. Parents might attend on either of the days; additionally, parents or teachers might request conferences at any time. School activities were held three to four nights during the year; attendance was very high, with parents filling the school cafeteria for each event. Parents received newsletters about events once each month and a separate district newsletter with parenting tips each month.

Zachary Taylor: the less effective school

Very few parents were involved in daily activities at the school. Most teachers responded that parent participation was low, with the exception of the first 'parent conference day' and the Open House at the beginning of the year. The teachers focused on discipline problems and the lack of parent support. They all mentioned that parents helped with parties, field trips, etc. but, 'that's all'. One reason for this may be that each grade level had two aides who performed much of the clerical work. Based on conversations in the community, parents were supportive of the school and felt it was doing an adequate job.

The headteacher/principal

Kennedy: the more effective school

The principal had a reputation in the district as a well-respected, no-nonsense administrator. She saw to it that the school kept on track with its rather complicated departmentalisation scheme and academic schedule, yet she allowed the teachers as much freedom as possible within that overall framework.

Zachary Taylor: the less effective school

The principal's style was very 'laissez-faire'. He was visible around the office area/ front of the school, but was rarely seen in the classroom areas or the back of the campus. Most of the daily administrative duties had been delegated to the assistant principal (field trips, bus monitoring, material and supply ordering, teacher evaluation, etc.). Each grade level had a chairman and grade levels met weekly to plan and review their schedules for the week. As a result, the principal had most of his activities covered by other employees. Two full-time secretaries 'ran' the office and most communication with teachers.

The principal was very vague on hiring practices, but seemed to be proud of most of the faculty. Observation of his actions and conduct within the school suggested that his delegation of authority and responsibility created a situation where if something negative happened, someone else was responsible. The principal then could step in and 'fix it'.

School expectations of pupils

Kennedy: the more effective school

School expectations appeared to be related to students' prior academic achievement. Students were assigned to levels on the basis of prior achievement (on standardised tests and teacher grades), and they rarely changed level. Teachers covered the curriculum in more depth and faster for Level 1 students than for Level 2 students, but the quality of instruction did not differ by level. Teachers commented that parent involvement in their children's education was a direct indicator of student success. Thus expectations were a reflection of their teachers' perceptions of the degree to which parents valued education.

Discipline was strictly, yet fairly enforced. Students uniformly observed posted and spoken rules of conduct, including: seating assignments in every class, methods for distributing and collecting materials, protocol for class discussions and proper hallway traffic. If there was any criticism to be raised about Kennedy, it would involve the oppressive environment created by the rules. While academic press was complemented by the task-orientated atmosphere, social climate suffered from its rigidity.

Zachary Taylor: the less effective school

Student expectations were very low. Three of the four teachers interviewed expressed the feeling that 'we can't do as much as we used to do' regarding their students and their potential academic performance. Teachers in this school taught to the median child, with the better students not getting much and the slower students getting less. Teachers seemed to accept the fact that several students would not be able to do much, so little was expected. Even though there had been no recent influx of low-SES students, these lower expectations persisted. A partial explanation lay in the teachers' perceptions of the lack of parent involvement.

Teachers also complained about discipline problems, reiterating that many students and most parents 'just don't care'. Our observation, on the other hand, was that the students in this school were generally very well behaved.

School goals

Kennedy: the more effective school

The school appeared to focus on immediate academic goals for students, rather than long-term goals. Indeed, scores on the state-mandated tests were the most obvious priority. Both testing and the curriculum strongly reflected basic academic skills in language arts and mathematics. Embedded in a philosophy of idealism, the district's (and state's) curriculum expressed the belief that there was an enduring body of truth that all educated people should learn. Although teachers talked about individual differences and multiculturalism, these were not profoundly integrated into the curriculum.

Zachary Taylor: the less effective school

Academic goals for students were rather generic and standard, and they had little meaning or relevance for the students or most teachers. All of the staff members could recite proper educational goals for students, but any real meaning for students in this school was absent. A higher priority was placed on order and following rules.

Discipline goals were posted in most classrooms in the fashion of rules and consequences. A few of the classes had behaviour charts, where accumulated stickers entitled one to special privileges or prizes.

Inter-staff relations

Kennedy: the more effective school

Kennedy faculty planned together at least once per week by grade level. Teachers within grade level cooperated occasionally to produce thematic units, but more regularly to organise schedules and plan activities such as parent conferences. Since all teachers at each grade level taught all students in that grade, teachers were able to collaboratively discuss students' needs. Third-grade teachers agreed that their team worked well together because they respected one another's strengths.

Zachary Taylor: the less effective school

Regarding promotion from grade to grade, teachers indicated that very little information was passed on to one grade level from the previous one. Class lists were received the day before school started, and the only preparation that could possibly be made was name tags on desks or bulletin boards.

Communication between grade levels was limited because of the size of the school. The location of student folders in the counsellor's office limited teacher access. State and local testing programmes were planned such that results were returned in the summer or at the end of the year. Teachers rarely took the time to refer to student performance measured the previous year.

These teachers did seem to get along well with each other, and many socialised together after school hours. The lounge was a fun place to talk and visit during recess and lunch. Teachers enjoyed each other's company, but there was little professional conversation. Talk about school programmes or student performance was rare.

School resources

Kennedy: the more effective school

Although state and district funding were the primary revenue sources in Jackson, two extra sources of funding differentiate schools within the system: Title I and community support. Kennedy did not qualify for schoolwide Title I, but did benefit significantly from community support. Perhaps the greatest support was in the form of volunteer assistance. For instance, parents staffed the school library. Since the district had cut funding for librarians in elementary schools, this gave Kennedy students an advantage that many other elementary students in Jackson did not have. Most parents supported the parent–teacher organisation through dues and donations. This was an important revenue source for the school, supplementing the limited equipment/supply budget. Monetary support from school–business partnerships allowed the staff to purchase token incentives for student performance and supplemental supplies.

Zachary Taylor: the less effective school

This school was primarily dependent on district resources. The principal was able to secure donations for funding the construction of a 'little red schoolhouse' in the middle of the classroom area. This started out as a historical/enrichment project, but in reality the principal needed another classroom and the district (due to a federal court order) did not allow any new portable classrooms to be purchased. The principal stated that the 'little red schoolhouse' was *not* a portable classroom, since there was no way to move it from its position between the two classroom buildings.

Resources appeared adequate for this school. The classrooms were well equipped, students had current textbooks and the workroom was well stocked with paper goods. None of the teachers ever mentioned the need for more materials or any lack of supplies. The principal controlled the budget and seemed to find access to funds when needed. The school sold ice cream daily, which supplied some 'in-house' funds for special projects.

Relationship with local authorities

Kennedy: the more effective school

Teachers and administrators appeared to be only moderately affected by the agendas of the central office. Test scores were a high priority throughout the district. Kennedy scores were consistently at or near the top for the district; thus little pressure for change was exerted from above. Further, Jackson had a relatively small central office staff for a district of its size; hence, district personnel spent little time in any one school.

Zachary Taylor: the less effective school

Very positive relationships existed between this school and the community, except with the fire marshall who would not approve the 'little red schoolhouse' for several weeks. Apparently no local building permit was issued, and the building was not cleared for fire code reasons at first and then not cleared because of the width of the treads on the steps leading to the door. The building was finally approved and was in use.

School image

Kennedy: the more effective school

Although Kennedy only partially recruited from a defined neighbourhood, this was the image that it presented to the community. One reason for this was that the largest group of supporters were neighbourhood parents. While this image was comfortable, it excluded a group of mainly African-American parents whose children were bused to Kennedy from less affluent areas. The proportion of non-majority students had grown significantly over the last twenty years. The teacher population had not changed dramatically; most teachers had nearly twenty years' experience. The low rate of teacher turnover, coupled with the need to compete for resources, may account for the desire to retain the original 'neighbourhood school' image.

Zachary Taylor: the less effective school

The image of the school was a relic from the past. Most of the elements of the school's image were no longer relevant or realistic for contemporary students. The parents of many current students once attended this school, and they remembered their positive experiences there. During one visit, we felt as if we had walked into a typical American school of the 1950s or 1960s. The school was comfortable, it was orderly and it was clean. Teachers were carrying out their duties, and students were sitting in straight rows. Classrooms were quiet and everyone assumed learning was taking place. It was not immediately apparent that students were not working to their potential. Everyone seemed to be caught in complacency with no internal or external pressure for change.

Conclusions

Table 4.2 contains a summary of the differences between the two middle-SES schools across the twelve predetermined ISERP dimensions.

Kennedy Elementary was classified as the more effective school on the basis of its standardised test scores, adjusted for SES variations. Its strengths lay in (1) an experienced and skilled teaching staff; (2) moderate community support, especially from parents; and (3) a strong academic focus. An emphasis on testing and rigid codes of conduct, however, weakened the social climate of the school, and in our opinion, reduced student motivation. Further, a significant portion of the school appeared to be less represented in the school's mission and in its activities. The school's strengths in terms of its seasoned professionals and academic press might also render it less adaptable to change. Nevertheless, in terms of its *academic* record, it had much to offer other middle-SES schools attempting to improve overall student achievement.

Conclusions for United States schools

Table 4.3 presents a comparison of the power of the ISERP dimensions of contrast to differentiate effectiveness status, in lower- and middle-SES schools and indicates that the dimensions of contrast are more clearly drawn between the lower-SES schools than they are between the middle-SES schools. Differentially effective lower-SES schools contrast with one another more distinctly, and on more of the ISERP contrast dimensions, than do differentially effective middle-SES schools. If these results are correct, then differentially effective lower-SES schools are more different from one another than are their counterparts in middle-SES environments. In other words, lower-SES schools vary more widely on the twelve ISERP dimensions of contrast than do middle-SES schools.

There is, indeed, some evidence from other contextually sensitive SER that this is the case. Recent studies (e.g. Evans and Teddlie, 1995; Hebert, 1994) indicate that differentially effective middle-SES schools have principals who are more like one another than do differentially effective low-SES schools, where more effective and less effective principals have very distinct 'leadership styles'.

The reduction in variance among differentially effective middle-SES schools may derive from the tendency for less effective middle-SES schools to adhere to some minimal baseline level of community ordained behaviour and achievement. This may be due to factors such as the state of initial 'preparedness' of middle-SES students to

Table 4.2 Summary of differences between the two middle-SES schools across the twelve dimensions

Dimension of contrast	More effective mid-SES (Kennedy)	Less effective mid-SES (Zachary Taylor)
General characteristics of the school	98 per cent pass rate on State test Located in middle/upper-middle-class suburban area Substantial busing of minority students	89 per cent pass rate on state test Large school (800+) Overcrowded classes Local in rural/suburb area Most white student body with substantial ethnic minority
A day in the life of a child	Fragmented day due to departmentalisation High time-on-task in classroom	Fragmented day due to scheduling problems Moderate level of time-on-task in classrooms
Teachers' teaching style	Technically skilled teachers Disappointing classroom climate	Very traditional teacher-centred whole-class instruction
The curriculum	Teachers did *not* feel constrained by State curriculum dictates Fairly traditional approach	Staff comfortable with traditional procedures in teaching state curriculum
The influence of parents	Very strong for non-teaching activities Minority parents not encouraged to participate	Weak parental involvement for a middle-SES school

The principal	Well-respected no-nonsense principal who encouraged staff participation in some decisions	Laissez-faire leadership style Principal was a delegator
School expectations of pupils	Attention paid to how the school looked in community Expectations based on child's previous achievement	Faculty expectations more like that for a lower-SES school
School goals	Emphasised testing Focus on immediate, not long-term, goals	More emphasis on maintaining order than on academic goals
Inter-staff relations	Departmentalisation encouraged professional interaction	Interaction limited due to school size and poor school climate
School resources	Resource-rich environment	Adequate resources
Relationship with local authorities	Independent due to small district office staff	Independent due to small district office staff and geographical isolation
School image	Effective 'neighbourhood' school Little acknowledgement of cultural diversity in student body	Portrayed as 'Neighbourhood' school, but this was a relic from the school's past

Table 4.3 Comparison of dimensions of contrast between differentially effective lower- and middle-SES schools

Dimension of contrast	Contrast between lower-SES schools	Contrast between middle-SES schools
General characteristics of the school	Medium	Medium
A day in the life of a child	High	Medium
Teachers' teaching style	Medium	Low
The curriculum	Medium	Medium
The influence of parents	High	Medium
The principal	High	High
School expectations of pupils	High	High
School goals	High	Medium
Inter-staff relations	High	High
School resources	High	Medium
Relationship with local authorities	Low	Low
School image	High	Low

learn and external community pressure (Slater and Teddlie, 1992). In the words of Ron Edmonds (Brandt, 1982), middle-class parents will intervene in any school in which a significant portion of the students aren't doing well. This reduction in variance among middle-SES schools appears to be a phenomenon found in other ISERP countries, as we outline in Part III.

The explanation for this may be that certain behaviour is not tolerated in middle-SES schools, regardless of their effectiveness level. Looking at Table 4.3, one can see that there is less variance among differentially effective middle-SES schools (as compared to lower-SES schools) on six dimensions: the child study; instructional style of teachers, influence of parents, school goals, school resources and school 'image'. Less effective middle-SES schools appear to provide a minimally acceptable school experience for children, hire teachers who are at least minimally competent, have a minimal level of parental support, are able to articulate some broadly acceptable school goals, have adequate resources and project a somewhat positive image in the community. If they do not, then severe problems will arise between the school, the district and the community.

5 North America – Canada

Walter Epp and Juanita Ross Epp

Introduction/context

The eclectic nature of Canadian education makes diversity a hallmark of the Canadian system. There is no 'typical' schooling in Canada. Education is the responsibility of the provinces and territories and each has its own set of regulations and its own peculiarities. In British Columbia and Ontario, school principals are not included in the teachers' unions. In the other provinces, teachers and principals belong to the same union. Most provinces have one public school system, but in three of them (Alberta, Ontario and Saskatchewan) there are publicly funded, separate schools for Roman Catholic students. In Quebec there are four publicly funded school systems based on language and religion (English Catholic, French Protestant, English Protestant and French Catholic). The geographic and political diversity of the country is recreated in its school system.

The low-ses schools: general characteristics

Inner-City: the more effective school

The Inner-City School was situated on the corner of two main intersections in a residential/business area in a city of 113,000. Approximately one-half of the students were of Caucasian extraction. Several students were of First Nations ancestry or came from mixed ethnic backgrounds. Many students at the school came from single-parent families. About half of the students arrived on buses from other parts of the city. Extra-curricular activities usually occurred at lunch-time, so as not to interfere with busing schedules.

The two-storey building was one of the first schools constructed in the city. It was very old and was starting to show its age. The school yard was fenced in to keep children from running into traffic. The hallways inside were decorated with student art work.

The First Nations people who had left the reserve, sent their children to inner-city schools such as the one in our study. The Inner-City School was attended by about 300 students between the ages of four and twelve. There were two classes of each of grades 1 through 6, with an average pupil–teacher ratio of 23:1. There was a staff of sixteen including the principal and vice-principal. One-third of the teachers had been on the staff for more than five years.

Fly-In: the less effective school

The remote Fly-In reserve in Northern Ontario was accessible only by air, for the majority of the year. For three months (January to March) the community could only be reached on a winter road built over the ice. Vehicles were brought up to the community on the winter road and were used for local transportation along with snowmobiles and all-terrain vehicles. There was a nursing station, a Northern Store (the contemporary Hudson Bay post), a modern school, a community centre, and a scattering of houses. Sixteen hundred people lived in this community, 90 per cent were unemployed. The school was the main employer and others worked at the Band administration office, the nursing station and the store.

The word 'Band' is used here to describe a group of people, the First Nations population of the community as well as the administrative unit, consisting of a chief and a group of elected councillors charged with running the reserve. Until recently, the community was under the control of the federal government and the affairs of the community were taken care of by a white 'First Nations Agent'. In more recent years, the running of the community had become the responsibility of the 'Band Council' – the chief and the councillors.

The loss of traditional lifestyle and decades of intervention – learned dependency, residential schools and loss of opportunity for economic self-sufficiency – had resulted in a lifestyle characterised by *ennui*, lack of hope and a proliferation of social problems. The reserve had been 'dry' for approximately ten years, which meant that alcohol was forbidden and, therefore, only available on the black market. Even so, half of the residents suffered from severe alcohol problems and other drug-related problems, and diseases were rampant. Officials were particularly concerned about the number of violent deaths on reserves, especially the incidence of accidents and suicides.

In spite of these problems, the local people had made great strides in taking control of the issues and seeking improvement. Education had become the vehicle for change. The school had been controlled by the Band since 1988, and the Band Council received money from the federal government on a yearly basis based on the number of students enrolled. The Band Council, after receiving a budget from the Education Director of the local education authority, gave the money to the school through its financial officer. This increased autonomy and encouraged site-based decision-making.

The school was a modern building with a gymnasium and a library, and looked very like any other school except for the First Nations art work, some by local artists and some by the children themselves, that was displayed in the halls and classrooms. There were about 500 students enrolled and the education authority employed eighty-two people – administrators, teachers, teacher aides, bus drivers, support personnel, janitors, etc. There were twenty-eight teachers, which translated into a pupil–teacher ratio of about 18:1. Nearly half of the teachers were First Nation, mostly local people who had been able to get their teaching certificates through a university programme which allowed them to study in the community. It was not uncommon to find local people who lacked official qualifications, but who had gained the confidence of the education authority, in charge of classrooms. The non-First Nations teachers were mostly from Newfoundland.

The 'Newfoundlanders' were a potential source of information on the clash between the two cultures. They seemed to stay in the community for extended periods of time, perhaps because Newfoundland is quite similar to the region in harshness of climate, size of population and feeling of community. These 'outsider' teachers stayed long enough to grasp some of the difficulties and differences between First Nations and non-First Nations cultures. They felt, for example, that the standards at the school were different from those in other communities and were especially concerned about attitudes toward attendance.

Students attended this school from pre-kindergarten to grade 11. There were two classes of each grade and most classrooms had a teacher as well as a teacher aide. Students wishing to finish their senior matriculation had to leave the community to attend school at a First Nations-run residential school or in the nearest city, both of which were at least 400 kilometres away.

These two schools both had large numbers of First Nations students. The statistics comparing these two schools would suggest that the Inner-City School was more effective. The average grade score for the CTBS test scores in mathematics, for example, showed the Inner-City School to be more effective by an entire grade. But, as we examined the two schools using more qualitative processes, we found that, at least for the education of First Nations students, things were not as simple as they seemed.

A day in the life of a child

At both schools, children started to arrive by bus and on foot at about 8.40 a.m. The Fly-In students played outside until the bell rang to indicate the beginning of classes at 9.00. In Inner-City, there was a bell to permit entry to the school at 8.40, although if it was really cold students could wait in the entry. Another bell rang at 8.55 and the students lined up at the outside doors to proceed in an orderly fashion to their classrooms. A third bell rang to indicate the beginning of classes at 9.00. These bells were indicative of the differences in philosophy which marked these two schools. At Fly-In, time and order were of lesser importance than was encouraging attendance. Children often came late and there was some coming and going throughout the school day since students did not require permission to visit the bathroom. Inner-City was more regimented and student behaviour was monitored more carefully.

In both schools there were morning exercises. At Inner-City the exercises were broadcasted over the intercom. The principal's message was followed by the national anthem and a minute of silence. Prayer was no longer allowed in Ontario schools because it might infringe on the rights of non-Christian students. At Fly-In, the exercises took place in each individual room under the direction of the teacher.

It was perhaps ironic that there was prayer here. There were seven missionary churches in this community and although Christianity had caused deep divisions among the local people, overall it was a strong presence. Technically, education at this school was the responsibility of the Canadian federal government, which made this school immune to the province's regulations forbidding the use of prayer. Expressions of First Nations' spirituality were evident in the art work on the walls but not in the daily observance of Christian ritual.

Inner-City: the more effective school

There was a formal schoolwide discipline plan, based on both rewards and punishments. For example, if a teacher saw a student behaving in a positive manner, the student received a 'ticket'. This ticket was placed in a drum and at the end of each month, the principal drew several tickets and winning students were rewarded with small prizes. Baseball caps, books, tickets to local sporting events and other treasured items were among the prizes. When students were seen behaving in an unacceptable manner, they lost tickets. This reduced their chances of winning a prize. At the end of each month, the principal announced the winners to the rest of the school. A student who behaved well and was rewarded many times in a month had a greater chance of winning.

Fly-In: the less effective school

There were general school rules and expectations, but discipline in the school had been left to individual teachers. The principal placed less emphasis on instructional or disciplinary leadership than did her counterpart at Inner-City. She focused mainly on liaison work with government-funding agencies and educational consultants.

Teachers' teaching style

Inner-City: the more effective school

The grade 2 teacher was anxious to succeed and believed in firm discipline. He was kind and careful with the children, but was given to sudden explosions in which he raised his voice to students who had broken the rules or had failed to grasp his meaning. His lessons were well planned, although they were generally continuations of textbook materials – twenty minutes of instruction, followed by seatwork. The day was divided equally between mathematics and language arts, which were taught every day, and other courses such as art, music, physical education, and social skills.

Cooperative learning methods were expected by the local board, so he did, therefore, use group work on occasion. However, the processes were often variations on teacher-led instruction. Students were given worksheets and instructions and were asked to sit together in groups to do the work. This allowed for some interaction among the students, but they could as easily have done the work alone at their seats. The teacher was not pleased when groups communicated too much and engaged in off-task behaviours. He spent the time admonishing groups who were getting too loud and explained the work to groups who did not understand the assignment. He felt that these students were not good at cooperative learning because they could not remain focused.

Fly-In: the less effective school

The teacher at Fly-In was a First Nations woman who loved to teach. She was well organised, firm, and confident. She was well planned and, although her techniques were similar, in that she taught the lesson and used seatwork to follow it up, there was a sense that she was exceedingly interested in the subject at hand and eager to help the children to understand it. She used both lecture and small-group methods. The students did get loud, especially when they were working in a group but she appeared to control the students by her 'presence' – she did not yell, and displayed a confident and consistent approach.

The curriculum

Inner-City: the more effective school

At Inner-City, the curriculum was a standard provincial curriculum of language arts, mathematics, sciences, etc. However, they too had implemented an additional course which was intended to teach students social skills. Its delivery was divided among the teachers at the various grade levels and everyone felt that it had improved relationships among everyone at the school and had had a positive effect on safety both in class and on the playground.

Fly-In: the less effective school

At Fly-In the provincial curriculum had been modified somewhat to make it more relevant to the needs of the students. The stated goals for the school at Fly-In were excellence in education, openness to new and innovative ideas and maintenance of some of the traditions of the people.

The school had a mandatory First Nations languages programme for all grades from kindergarten through grade 11 and there were two full-time First Nations language teachers on staff. Most of the students who came to the school for the first time were bilingual in English and Ojicree. The language programme was one way to ensure that the young people maintained their Ojicree language skills and maintained communication between generations.

A recently introduced programme, 'The Journey Within', emphasised self-awareness and self-esteem for First Nations children. The programme was an attempt 'to enhance the child's sense of physical, mental, emotional, and spiritual well-being'. The course included units on personal awareness, family, community, culture and environment. This programme had been credited with helping the community to maintain a much lower rate of teen suicides than some other reserves. Another programme was the 'Artists in the School' programme. Local artists and crafts people came into the classrooms to give children instruction, guidance and inspiration in art as there was a healthy and vibrant artistic community.

Ontario law forbids the teaching of religion in public schools, but, as mentioned earlier, this school was not bound by Ontario law. It had a Bible studies programme which was taught weekly to all grades in the school – a non-denominational programme with its main focus on the Bible. This was a contentious issue as there were several different denominations of Christians on the reserve and some of the local people would have preferred an emphasis on traditional First Nations spirituality.

The influence of parents

Inner-City: the more effective school

There was an active parent–teacher association and parent volunteers were common. They helped out on field trips and one volunteer came into this particular class for one afternoon per week. School newsletters were sent out to parents at least once a month to inform the parents of special events or student successes. Parents were notified of their child's progress seven to ten times per year. This included the use of 'meet the teacher' evenings, private phone calls or in-class meetings at the end of the day.

Fly-In: the less effective school

Parents were less often seen at Fly-In. These parents had a healthy respect for professionals as they were regularly attended to by social workers and health officials. They trusted the teachers to do a good job and saw no need for input into daily life at the school. Distances precluded many trips out of the community, although there were some wilderness field trips which parents participated in. School newsletters were sent out to parents occasionally, and parent–teacher interviews were held three times a year.

The headteacher/principal

Inner-City: the more effective school

The principal described his management style as interactive. He included teachers in many decision-making processes, especially since this style of management was mandated by the local school board. The principal was available if students wished to talk to him. Many students stopped at the office to let the principal know of their successes or concerns. The vice-principal dealt with discipline problems. It was not uncommon for both the principal and the vice-principal to be working over the lunch hour.

The principal said that although he set the goals for the school, he attempted to be flexible; to change the goals to meet the changing needs of the school. The emphasis at the time of this study was on developing a curriculum to promote cooperative learning and provide a safe environment for all students. A school-growth team, composed of the principal, vice-principal, support teacher and teacher representatives, met regularly to discuss issues arising at this particular school. This team was examining issues pertaining to school improvement.

Fly-In: the less effective school

The principal and vice-principal were both local people. This served both to enhance and undermine their status. The administrators allowed teachers full autonomy in the day-to-day running of their classrooms and concerned themselves more with liaisons with the Band Council and negotiating funding. They tried to be available during breaks in the staffroom in order to keep in touch with what was going on in the school.

The principal carried out teacher evaluations twice a year, based on a classroom visit. These evaluations were extremely important for teachers, as those in Band-controlled schools had no job security. They were working from yearly contracts and a bad evaluation could mean not being rehired the following year. The goals for the school were set by the education authority and staff were expected to carry them out.

Inter-staff relations

Inner-City: the more effective school

Staff relations may have been a bit strained due to outside issues which had in the mid-1990s affected all schools in Ontario. As a part of budget constraints, the provincial government imposed legislation which negated standing board/teacher contracts. Each school board was forced to cut costs and, in some places, this was done by scheduling unpaid days off for teachers and cutting school programmes. In this city, the cuts forced teachers to forgo the nine days of teacher development that they would have received during an ordinary school year. Salary freezes and hiring limitations were also put in place. This 'social contract' had a negative effect on teacher development, morale and job security.

The teachers had little to do with each other as each teacher usually did his or her work at a desk in the homeroom. Even though each teacher received a certain amount of planning time per week, the teachers' schedules were not conducive to group planning. They met at staff meetings approximately once a month.

Fly-In: the less effective school

There was much more inter-staff visiting because staff members were all a part of an isolated community. However, there appeared to be two separate staffs – the First Nations and the non-First Nations – and each group was critical of the other. The non-First Nations teachers felt that First Nations teachers were allowed to 'get away with' too much – that they took too much time off, that they set a poor example by a higher level of absenteeism and by allowing students to 'run wild'. The First Nations teachers felt that the non-First Nations were too controlling and interventionist and were lacking in understanding of First Nations culture.

Resources

Inner-City: the more effective school

At Inner-City the budget was decentralised, in that some decisions on spending were made at the school level. However, the cost of teachers and the selection of new personnel was taken care of by the board. Schools were encouraged to order their supplies through the school board office because of the economies of scale.

Teachers at Inner-City had access to resources at the Instructional Material Centre located at the board office. Audio-visual material, curriculum textbooks and supplementary material were available there, along with resource kits for a variety of subjects. Teachers from all over the city had access to this material at no charge, but they must have reserved the material they wished to use approximately two weeks in advance.

Teaching material could also be obtained from other school boards at a cost. Teachers also had access to materials through the local university and local public libraries.

Fly-In: the less effective school

Fly-In was funded by the federal government but the budget was locally controlled. Budget decisions were made by the local education authority in consultation with the administration. The school was very well equipped and there were no shortages in supplies and personnel. However, there were no supporting community resources and there were complications of time and travel in order to bring in resources from outside.

Relationship with local authorities

Inner-City: the more effective school

Inner-City was a local entity which was generally free from political interference, although it was very susceptible to funding issues. There was ongoing contact with police because the police were automatically summoned if there was violence, and any issues pertaining to the illegal use of drugs had to be reported to the local authorities. The local police force employed officers responsible for delivering educational programmes to a variety of city organisations. Once a year, officers came into the classroom to teach bicycle, street safety, or drug and alcohol awareness.

Local health nurses administered fluoride treatments to the children on a regular basis. Hearing and vision checks were conducted in most grades. Students in each class were regularly checked for head lice (once or twice yearly) by parent volunteers and school personnel. This check usually coincided with a visit from the local health nurse.

Fly-In: the less effective school

At Fly-In, the relationship with the local authorities was very much an aspect of tribal politics. There were allegations that jobs and job security were based on nepotism. A Band Council resolution could bar anyone from the reserve, so teachers had to be careful not to offend. For example, teachers caught with alcohol could expect to be dismissed. This made teachers, especially the non-First Nations teachers, nervous about job security and their futures. The local teachers would always be local whether they taught in the community or not. The non-First Nations teachers were there only to teach and as such were never regarded as permanent members of the community.

School image

Inner-City: the more effective school

For Inner-City, their reputation and image was of little concern. The schools in this city were not in competition with each other for students. Students were assigned by the residence of their parents. The only other option was to switch to the separate school system, which some parents could do, but this was not a major concern. The school did keep in touch with parents, through parent organisations but there was little effort to be high profile with the community in general.

Fly-In: the less effective school

Fly-In had a positive image in the community and was considered to be innovative and provided leadership for other Band-controlled schools. Parents appeared to be quite confident that the school was providing quality education for their students and were pleased with the growing number of First Nations teachers in the school and the school's stated eventual goal of educating for a self-governing future for aboriginal people.

Conclusions

A walk through Inner-City showed the orderliness and control which allowed this school to function effectively. Teachers treated the students with respect, especially if they were complying with the school rules and guidelines. It was perhaps this adherence to routine and personal interaction which made this school work for most students. The consequences of misbehaviour were known, the expectations were made clear and the teachers and principals were committed to their work. Traditional attributes of standard school practice allowed this school to produce quiet hallways and positive academic outcomes.

The central problem of examining for effectiveness lies in the criteria to be used to indicate effectiveness. The First Nations students in these two schools served as representative evidence of this difficulty. At Inner-City, students were learning the useful skills of listening, understanding expectations and carrying out orders. The people who did well in this school would be prepared for the job market in the traditional sense. However, there were students at this school who did not respond well to the strong structure, routine and control. Among those students were many children of aboriginal ancestry. Insistence on control and routine could cause these students to withdraw from school as soon as possible, in order to avoid it. There were, in other words, issues of differential school effectiveness (see Teddlie and Reynolds, 2000).

At Fly-In, on the other hand, there was a very different approach to student performance. The entire community was plagued with the problems of violence, abuse and poverty, and the school attempted to make allowance for these difficulties. Individuals, both students and staff, were recognised and special circumstances were understood and accepted. In spite of the community problems and organisational challenges, the educational initiatives at this school had been remarkable. The First Nations artist programme, the self-esteem initiatives and the community-based teacher education programmes all spoke of a hope for a more positive future – a future which included these students. The community-based teacher education programme, for example, was intended to integrate local people into the school system. They studied on the reserve, then were employed by the local school authority, team teaching with existing teachers or taking over classrooms which were previously staffed by non-First Nations teachers. The process symbolised a community hoping to take charge of its own future, which means that the social outcomes of this school may have been substantial in ways that the academic outcomes were not. Differences between the two schools are summarised in Table 5.1.

The middle-SES schools

The remaining ISERP schools have been given the pseudonyms Rooted, Suburban and Village. Rooted was selected as a low effectiveness school. It was in a rural area where the parents farmed or worked in the lumber industry. These families had been in the area for years, and everyone in Rooted therefore knew everyone else. Suburban was chosen as the 'typical' middle-class school. There was more transience here but most of the parents had professional jobs in the community. Village, selected as the effective middle-class school, was located in a small 'bedroom' community close to a big city. We will examine the three schools using only some of the twelve dimensions

Table 5.1 Summary of differences between the two low-SES schools across twelve dimensions

Dimension of contrast	More effective low-SES (Inner-City)	Less effective low-SES (Fly-In)
General characteristics of the school	CTBS scores ahead of low effectiveness Low-SES school	Low CTBS scores Geographically isolated, on a reserve
	Situated in inner city Good reputation built up over time 50 per cent white 50, per cent ethnic minority 300 students Pupil/teacher ratio 23/1 Old building	Building a reputation First Nations population 500 students Pupil/teacher ratio 18/1 New building, good facilities
A day in the life of a child	Time well managed	Low attendance rate (60 per cent) Tolerance of lateness
Teachers' teaching style	Firm discipline, some shaming of troublesome students Mostly whole-class interactive instruction	Well organised Use of small-group methods as well as whole-class instruction
The curriculum	Commitment to basic skills Standard provincial curriculum	Emphasis upon First Nations culture in art work etc. First Nations language programme Modified provincial curriculum Native language programmes

The influence of parents	Active involvement in PTA Use of newsletters to parents Regular meeting of parents with their child's teacher	No PTA-teachers left alone Infrequent newsletters Rare parent/teacher interaction
The principal	Committed to 'order', instructional leader Involving teachers in decision-making; Available to all students Strong sense of 'mission' inculcated to all	Entangled in outside commitments Involvement in staff social relationships
School expectations of pupils	Firm discipline, generated by reward system with schoolwide orientation	Emphasis on teacher autonomy Discipline left to individual teachers
School goals	Strong social control Importance of routine Respect for students	Building strong, distinctive social identity Social outcomes emphasised because of community disintegration
Inter-staff relations	Business-like; slightly strained because of budget constraints	Cliques, with a split between 'non-First Nations' and 'First Nations' teachers
School resources	Good quality of audio-visual material; curriculum textbooks and learning material	Good quality of audio-visual material; curriculum textbooks and learning material
Relationship with local authorities	Conventional relationship with educational district; close links with health, welfare and police agencies	Complex relationships with local authorities
School image	Little concern with image because of an absence of competition between schools	Positive image in the community

of contrast, since, as in the case of the United States schools, many of the dimensions did not seem able to discriminate between schools.

Teacher–student relationships

Student–teacher relationships were important in all three schools. At Rooted the teachers knew all the students well and had taught their brothers and sisters. Relationships were community- rather than school-based, in that everyone saw each other in other roles, as well as at school. The teachers at Suburban and Village had less lasting relationships with their students, but knew them well and interacted with students outside of their own classrooms and in extra-curricular activities.

For example, at Village (the exceptional school), the teacher arranged the desks in groupings and encouraged students to talk to each other about their work. She frequently used humour in her instruction and joked with the students. Students knew their responsibilities and the atmosphere in the room was one of peaceful productivity.

Processes used to control student behaviour

Control and discipline were important issues in all the schools. Some schools used a schoolwide system of rewards, such as the one at Inner-City which we described earlier. In these schools the discipline was teacher-based, with various forms of 'backup' from the principal. The process depended on the individual teacher as well as on the situation and style of the principal.

The principals in all three schools knew every student by name and were a presence in the hallways and on the playground. Students in all three schools were delighted when the principal noticed them and congratulated them for things they had done.

When students were caught misbehaving, the principal at Suburban selected out culprits for detention. The other two, coincidentally both women, tended to take the child aside and to talk to him or her, explaining why the behaviour was inappropriate and asking the student to take responsibility for changing it.

Meanwhile, classroom discipline was mainly up to the teacher. In all three schools, the teachers observed had few discipline problems. Teachers treated students like friends. They smiled at the students and spoke to them in a conversational manner. Students were encouraged to talk about their own lives and out-of-school activities. Excessive noise was admonished with a quiet reminder or, in the case of Suburban, with a song. Here the teacher would start to sing a very quiet song. Students near to her would join in and before long the whole class would be singing with her. When the song was completed, they gave themselves a round of applause, then all students would return to their work.

Teaching strategies

Cooperative learning and group work were used in all three schools, but not exclusively. Teachers used various teaching strategies, such as lectures, seatwork, and projects. At Village the emphasis was on resource-based learning programmes in which students were encouraged to interact with a wide range of print, non-print and human resources. The students, with the help of the teacher and librarian, learnt how to evaluate and analyse this information. The Learning Resource Centre, which used to be called a library, was a vital part of the programme intended to help students and staff to become more effective users of information and ideas. The teacher–librarian assisted teachers in planning units of study, and helped students to acquire a variety of skills for location of information.

Intervention programmes

All of these schools were using special programming ideas to supplement the student learning, to provide additional learning in an extra-curricular context or to enhance life skills. The academic aspect of the school, although of primary importance, was certainly not the only aspect of learning which the schools attempted to facilitate. At each school there were some extra-curricular programmes running, even though the length of the school day was circumscribed by the arrival and departure times of school buses. Participation was voluntary, which meant that not all children were participating in the additional programming.

In the schools that were not effective, Suburban and Rooted, the extra-curricular programmes and interventions ran over the noon-hour and usually involved sports, with some art and drama. The extra-curricular emphasis was especially noticeable in Village, which had been identified reputationally as an effective school. Perhaps it was these special programmes which gave the school the high profile which earned it this reputation. It was, indeed, a busy school.

At Village there were 'add-ons', both during class and after school hours. These programmes were considered co-curricular rather than extra-curricular, as they were directly related to, and ran alongside, the academic programme. These included clubs (Earth Club, Chess Club, Junior and Senior Choir, and Drama Club), School Patrol, Care Partners, Circle of Friends, Awards, Athletics, Intramural and Student Representative Council. The school patrol consisted of volunteers who assisted other students in safely crossing streets. In the Care Partners programme, classes of older students were matched with younger classes to promote interaction across the grade levels. They would do joint activities such as cooking, crafts, skating and storytelling. The Circle of Friends consisted of grade 4 to 8 students who volunteered to help other students who needed assistance at recess time. Noon-hour sports programmes were based on participation with little emphasis on winning. There were a number of special days throughout the year to contribute to school spirit.

The special programmes were also a part of the school day. There were special classes in computers and all students learned keyboarding and computer applications. An optional Band programme was available for students from grade 6 upwards. Students could also take core French, industrial arts and home economics. Although core French was still available in the other two schools, these other options were not available until the students reached high school.

Conclusions

As Table 5.2 shows, it proved much more difficult to discriminate between the middle-class schools in terms of their effectiveness processes than the two low-SES, a finding which parallels the American situation reported in Chapter 4. We analysed the three schools (low effectiveness, typical effectiveness and high effectiveness) together to try

Table 5.2 Summary of differences between the mid-SES schools across twelve dimensions

Dimension of contrast	More effective mid-SES (Village)	Less effective mid-SES (Suburban and Rooted)
General characteristics of the school	Situated in a progressive middle-class suburban community	Situated in an out-of-town community, middle-class commuters
A day in the life of a child	Close relations between teachers and children Cooperative learning emphasis Used whole-class instruction, project work with individualised work	Close relations between teachers and children Cooperative learning emphasis
Teachers' teaching style	Student interaction encouraged Use of group work Highly productive	
The curriculum	Heavy use of additional programmes to supplement student learning	Use of additional programmes to supplement student learning
The influence of parents	Closely involved in the wide range of clubs Involved in school patrol as volunteers	
The principal	Very close to the children	Very close to the children
School expectations of pupils		
School goals	Emphasis upon control and discipline using pupil involvement additionally	Emphasis upon control and discipline using pupil involvement additionally
Inter-staff relations		
School resources		
Relationship with local authorities		
School image	Had used pupil involvement in clubs and societies to promote image	

to make sense of the situation, with pooled ratings for Suburban and Rooted schools together.

Conclusions for Canadian schools

Analysis began with an examination of the two low-SES schools on the opposite ends of the 'reputationally effective' continuum. Here we encountered issues which complicated the diverse Canadian approach to education even further. Both of these schools served some aboriginal peoples, one in a First Nations community and the other in a more mixed context where dominant non-First Nations values were favoured. This situation made a 'ruling' on effectiveness even less possible, because of the need to be informed and interpreted by examining the background issues surrounding the lives of the children before they reached the schoolhouse door, and the conflicting values which they encountered in the school itself. However, there did appear to be school factors within these two schools which might be important for an understanding of school effectiveness. These factors were teacher–student relationships, processes used to control student behaviour, teaching strategies, intervention programmes and student attendance.

The effectiveness of schooling, in the low-SES contexts in which we observed, appeared to be based on positive teacher–student relationships which were supported by schoolwide policy and which contributed to effective control, based on personal commitment to maintaining positive relationships. This context allowed teachers to effectively use a variety of teaching strategies. These strategies were often augmented by special programmes which focused on other aspects of the students' lives, in addition to academic subjects. All of this created a positive environment which encouraged students to attend regularly. These elements are possible in all low-SES schools throughout Canada, in spite of the diversity of provincial and local contexts. For the middle-SES contexts, we are unsure of the applicability of these findings.

6 The Pacific Rim and Australia – Taiwan

Eugene C. Schaffer, Chen-jen Hwang, Yong-yin Lee, Shin-zen Chang and Hui-ling Pan

Introduction/context

Chinese education spans thousands of years of using Confucian beliefs and tenets to organise its educational processes and programmes. Based on honour, respect and relationships, this tradition requires a high level of esteem for teachers and the school, and the pursuit of educational excellence. Even today, ancient Chinese stories and poems form a basis of shared beliefs related to language, literature and civics and underscore the educational system in Taiwan. On the other hand, mathematics, with the exception of the training on the abacus, uses Western content, curriculum sequence and presentation. Taiwan is a culture which increasingly represents a blend of different influences, both historical and contemporary.

The low-socio-economic-status schools

YUAN: the more effective school

Located near Sun Shan Airport, Yuan Elementary School was easily overlooked by casual passers-by, unless the 3,000 plus students who attended the school were streaming across the broad street toward the alley that served as its entrance road. Their way across this six-lane road was protected by older students. Every six- to twelve-year-old student carried a backpack, and most had the school colours and logo emblazoned on their jogging suits. At the school gate where younger students said goodbye to their mothers, the older ones ran into the school yard to jog on the oval track in front of the school or to race to the classroom where they talked, completed an assignment, or cleaned the classroom and teacher's desk. This scene repeated itself over and over, beginning at 7.30 a.m. and continuing until the morning announcements at 8.20 a.m. when late students, arrived in their parents' cars and in taxis, waved and dashed in the front entrance and up the stairs to their class.

In the neighbourhood served by Yuan there are new ten- or fifteen-storey buildings covered with tile and stainless steel in the main street that represent the affluence and tremendous material progress made by the Chinese in Taiwan over the last ten years. In the alley that leads to the school from the main street a previous period in Taiwan's fortunes presents itself, when in the early 1950s, the Nationalist government left the mainland and established itself on the island. The housing constructed at that time was two- or three-storeys tall, concrete and brick, later covered with tile when money was available and fashion rather than survival was considered important. Much of the housing around the school is of this period and unlike other parts of Taipei, has not been modified, enlarged, or modernised with the improving fortunes of the population. Walking around the school's wall, even older construction is evident. Wooden buildings, built from the 1890s through the 1940s under Japanese rule, back up to the school and in some cases have been attached to the school wall. Trash, old cars, and motorcycle tyres lean up against these buildings. These dwellings represent the lowest standards of housing in a city where land is a high-priced commodity.

Having circled the school ground, you enter the main gate into a much quieter and greener environment where palm trees line the walkway and the inside of the green, painted brick wall that surrounds the school and the school yard. There are morning ceremonies and the red, blue and white flag of the Republic of China waves in the breeze behind a bandstand at the end of the running track. The entrance is a poorly lit area that leads down three steps to a large, well-lit auditorium-like room with row after row of office desks facing one another. From one desk placed off to the side, the dean of instruction can survey the entire room.

Walking out of the office you cross a large interior courtyard where students are playing and sweeping the ground. The students greet teachers, talk to one another and run into their rooms when the jobs are done. The school is in the shape of a large square around the courtyard. Each side is three or four storeys high, made of cement and painted green or covered with tiles. It currently holds around 3,500 students. Each classroom is accessed from a balcony on the courtyard side of the school with balconies on each of the four levels that connect all of the classrooms. The classrooms have windows on both sides permitting the air to flow freely all year round. This is a necessity in a country where temperatures reach more than 35 degrees centigrade while school is in session and fans supply the only movement of air.

The school is similar in the quality of the facilities and level of repair of dozens of elementary schools throughout Taipei and many other of the cities in Taiwan. All of the basic elements of schools and classrooms – desks, textbooks and instructional materials – are available for students. At the same time none of these is either particularly sophisticated nor, save the text material, particularly new. Twenty or thirty years before, the current teachers may have sat in similar desks as students. The lighting is adequate neon lights that, since the 1960s, have reduced a number of students to wearing glasses. The walls could stand a new coat of paint. The bulletin boards display student work as well as materials developed by the teacher. As in many of the classrooms in Taiwan, the desks are arranged in double rows of seven or eight so that students can work in pairs when appropriate. There are seats for an average class of thirty-five students, which is a marked reduction from ten years ago when over forty-five students were assigned to each class.

If we look at a day in the life of a child, sitting in the second row from the outside window, Mei-hwa Hwang looks at her teacher, who has been talking to two boys at the front of the class. Most of the children are excited and turn around to look at the foreign visitor in the back of the room.

Class begins with the class leader calling everyone to stand and bow to the teacher in unison, wishing the teacher well. The class leader asks the students to sit, and Mei-hwa settles in for a fifty-minute class on the calculation of area, a mandated topic for the fourth grade.

The teacher begins the lesson by asking a question about the homework – an area problem. The students answer chorally, a common response pattern in Chinese schools. At the blackboard, the teacher begins to draw a rectangle on the board with a ruler, explaining the exercise in their mathematics books. She marks each of the centimetres on the board as she draws a rectangle 7 centimetres long and 3 centimetres wide.

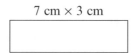

7 cm × 3 cm

Apparently reviewing, the teacher asks the children how to calculate the area in square centimetres. One boy answers the question, standing beside his desk, and the teacher asks if the other students have got the correct answer. Except for one student in the back of the room, all of the students appear to understand the answer, and raise their hands to show that they got 21 centimetres. Mei-hwa seems to understand as she measures the rectangle in her text, calculates the answer, and writes her response in the textbook that also serves as a workbook. During this time, all of the students' eyes are on the teacher, with the exception of those of the one student who did not answer the question. This student appears to be more interested in the visitor in the back of the room than in the instruction taking place at the front.

Moving on to a new problem, the teacher uses a square that is 5 centimetres on each side. 'Measure the sides', she says. 'What is the area?' The teacher begins to review each step of the process, asking questions that will lead to the answer. A boy is asked to respond to the teacher's step-by-step questions. When he makes an error, another male student is asked to continue. This student works through the problem correctly and everyone looks at the book to complete his or her own problem. In four minutes, everyone has completed the problem, with only one student's attention drawn away from the classroom work, since he is playing with a key chain.

When the problem is finished the teacher says, 'No problems, right! Easy, wasn't it?' As a boy reads the next problem, students bring out rulers to measure the next square in the book. One student comes to the front of the class to complete the problem. The teacher reads the problem and helps a student, she goes to the next student and helps her, and then breaks into the work to give directions, commenting that if it is really a square, then the sides will all be the same length. One student calls out that he has finished the problem. 'That is', she says, 'any one side they measure will be the same length as the other three sides.' After going over each student's problem, the teacher goes to the front of the board to explain the possibility of conversion between centimetres and metres. Mei-hwa has followed all of the discussion, but has not asked for assistance or volunteered to work at the board.

Given the figure 120 cm, the students are to convert it to metres. When they finish a boy responds that it is 1 metre and 20 centimetres. The students applaud after the teacher says, 'correct'. The next problem involves a rectangle, 120 centimetres long and 30 centimetres wide. Again, one student works at the board while the others work at their seats. The student at the board gets the problem correct. Many of the students seated are finished and apparently correct as well. Mei-hwa, who has completed this part of the day's work, is leaning back on the two back legs of the chair and rocking slowly. The teacher goes from student to student to correct their work, appears satisfied with their performance, and begins the next part of the lesson by putting the next three problems from the text on the board. While she does this, the students take a break and talk to one another.

The teacher draws three more rectangles on the board. When she is finished three or four minutes later, students raise their hands to go to the front of the room. One boy and two girls go to the front of the room to begin working on the problems. As they finish, the teacher goes over each one of the problems with the people at the board. When all of the students at the board have the questions correct, it is now almost 9.20 and the teacher begins to wrap up the lesson. She asks if everyone has the correct answers for the three problems on the board. One boy raises his hand and says he has one answer wrong, explaining when the teacher asks why this happened that he had not calculated the answers correctly. She says, 'You must be more careful'. The bell rings, but the students do not move. The teacher tells them, 'Next time we will begin to measure long distances'.

After students stand up, bow to the teacher, and thank her for teaching them in this hour, they rush from the room for the ten-minutes recess before music class. Mei-hwa turns to a friend and they go out of the door arm in arm to play.

JING: the typical effectiveness school

Jing is located on a busy, four-lane road south of Taipei. The area is located beyond a series of low hills covered with graves of generations of Chinese and, until recently, was considered to be very much in the country. A local joke, given the area's distance from the city and the nearness to the grave site, is that after going past the dead this must be Hell. In reality, this bustling area shows signs of being drawn into the urban sprawl of Taiwan's capital. Although a great deal of older and substandard housing remains, there is an infusion of new high-rise buildings as well.

A quick walk around the school wall permits an exploration of this wildly diverse housing. To the right of the school wall, a small alley winds through old single-storey housing with roofs that extend over the narrow paths. In some cases these paths are less than two feet wide, forcing pedestrians to slide sideways through the narrow alleys. Chickens and pigs reside in some narrow paths next to washing-machines. The other side of the school is less appealing with car parts, plastic barriers, and trash in front of the homes. An elevated highway directly behind the school cuts the school off from the neighbourhood on that side.

Across the street from the school is a newly constructed store with steel framing and girders. Directly behind the building is a market that sells, in the day-time, vegetables, fruits, meats and spices from open-air stalls. At night, these stalls are replaced by clothing and video rental stalls. Other stores in the immediate area open at 10.00 a.m. with a vast array of electronic goods and the latest fashions from Japan. This side of the street has a small family-run temple, rice stores that date from the turn of the century, and buildings over ten storeys high to be completed in a year's time. Areas such as this show their history, and the slow change reflects their distance from downtown and the scarcity of land and resources needed to upgrade the area. Many of the neighbours like this rural living, as it has been their way for fifty years or more. Change will come, but here unlike in more urban or open areas of Taipei, it will come slowly.

Jing Elementary School was founded in 1896 and was rebuilt in the 1960s. All students enter by a gate next to a guard box similar to those at every school in the country. The school forms a square around a running track and playground; it is three storeys high with classrooms around the square on each level. The teachers share a large room with their desks pulled together while the principal has an office with a table desk and two sofas. This is a typical arrangement in elementary schools.

The stone floors of the classrooms are cold on this January day, and students wear jogging suits and heavy overcoats, with a few sporting gloves as well. Though the doors and windows are closed to reduce the wind, none of the rooms have heat, so the students shiver as the day goes on. The teacher stands at the front of the room on a platform with a podium to hold materials. Most of the work she does is on a blackboard at the front of the room and poster boards she places on the board. There is no overhead, video projector, or computer in the room. The twenty-seven desks do not fill the room that originally had over fifty, ten years ago. This basic school description is similar to Yuan Chuan and is repeated over and over in many locations throughout Taiwan. The similarity in resources is determined by the allocations of the provincial government.

After thirty years of teaching, the principal, Mr Hong, began his service as a principal in Hwa School two years before the interviews. He noted that humanism was at the core of his educational philosophy and that all that he did in the school was predicated on what was best for the teachers and students. There is an anecdote, which may indicate the principal's sincerity about his role in the leadership of the school. According to one teacher's report, the principal did not air-condition his office because the teachers' office was not air conditioned. While this might not seem a sacrifice to some, in a climate of 35 plus degrees Celsius (95 degrees Fahrenheit) from May through September it is considered a significant sacrifice by the teachers.

After his arrival two years ago, the principal had worked to instil pride and to broaden the interests of children. He advocated the use of folk music in the school, involved community resource persons for school activities, developed a choir and invited well-known singers to the school. He also organised remedial teaching after school, and in summer he assigned every school administrator, including himself, and selected teachers to counsel children who had exhibited behavioural problems during the year. To set the tone for school relations, the principal emphasised life education in the school. There are six goals for the school. The goals are to love the country, to emphasise ethics, to enrich life skills, to promote morality, to have physical health, and to foster cooperation. In addition to promoting student learning, Mr Hong develops teacher's professional knowledge and skills each year through teaching seminars. Topics undertaken by the faculty include mathematics and social studies. Professors from local colleges take the main responsibility for teaching these inservice programmes. This effort was in addition to the Wednesday afternoon sessions nationally arranged for teacher training, when videotapes, discussions of homework and strategies to improve teaching are topics. During the year, the principal attends each teacher's classes to understand how teachers interact with students. Good staff relations were kept in the school through these strategies, but the principal felt that the busy school day decreased the occasions for teachers to discuss the school beyond the formal periods noted above.

If we look at a day in the life of a child Fang Tang-fang is a small boy, with clothes that are similar to others in his class. Fang is considered able but average by his teacher. When it is announced that he will be the student observed during the day he receives an unmerciful teasing and his clothes are pulled at by the other students. This reaction on the part of other students does go away, but the apparent effect of a foreign observer takes time to overcome. After standing and saying hello to the teacher and then turning and saying hello to the observer, the students settle down. In the first class of the day, mathematics, the topic is 'How can we determine the perimeter of objects?'

Beginning with sample rectangles, the class will proceed to measuring more complex shapes. Their teacher creates a rectangle out of eight pieces of paper on the board.

As she finishes, three students quietly walk into the room and take their seats. The teacher turns, asking: 'Why aren't you all sitting correctly?' The students squirm to an upright position. 'How many squares are across the top of the paper?' she asks, 'and how many are on the side?' She calls up a female student to determine the perimeter of this shape. The student writes '8 × 2 × 2' and stands and waits without going any further, so the teacher calls a second girl to the board. After she writes '4 × 2 = 8', the teacher asks which is correct. Students shout out that the second girl is correct, and the first student is asked to sit down. The teacher says, 'I don't understand exactly what she had in mind, but this is incorrect. Who got it correct?'

She then places another rectangle on the board. Four students come to the board; each writes '6 × 2 = 12' and then write a description of 'perimeter'. 'The correct answer', says the teacher, and she asks the class to applaud. Fang has not gone to the board, but he is attentive and does seem to understand the work based on his answers.

Saying 'Let's see if you forgot this', the teacher places another rectangle on the board and calls up a student. The class calls out the answer before the student can finish the problem; there are no errors now and they seem to understand the problems, so the teacher begins to ask longer problems with greater areas. 'Do you understand that the size doesn't matter?' she asks. 'Do you know what I mean?' Now, thirty minutes into the class period, a student states that the class should be able to work problems without assistance.

Introducing an alternative method, the teacher indicates that each of the rectangles can be measured on two sides and that this will help to understand the concept of the perimeter. 'What do you think of this one?' she asks a student, who appears puzzled, and asks what the teacher means. He doesn't seem to have a sense of what to do with this problem. The students do propose an alternative, but it is not in fact new. A new form placed on the board make the students gasp in unison; one says, 'I'm dead' in dialect. Asked to find the perimeter of this new one, five students go to the board.

7 cm

3 cm

It is late in the period, but the students are intent on getting this problem done and begin to talk to one another. 'You don't need to talk to do the problem', says the teacher, 'even if you are not at the board. You need to use your heart to get this correct.' Clearly, none of the students at the board have understood the concept at this point. Fang has not understood either. He looks perplexed and listens to the teacher. The teacher begins to clear up the problem, asking five new students to come to the board. After she says, 'This is easy now', the bell rings and the students stand and bow. The teacher says they will continue tomorrow and the students leave the class for a physical education lesson.

After lunch, the students take a nap until 1.10 when the Westminster Chimes wake them and they begin the afternoon class, a lesson in colour and art. Previously introduced to the complementary colours, they are now beginning to develop a drawing that repeats a series of colours – in this case, apples. The teacher introduces the concept and begins to hand out paper, which the students cut into eight sections. Using coloured chalk, the teacher introduces the complementary colours, and shows them on the board the different complementary colours they might use to create their painting. Apparently the teacher is trying to teach complementary colours rather than drawing per se. One student calls out that another student has taken his crayon and he can't write; the teacher does not respond. She begins to help students to fold the paper into eight equal areas for their paintings.

A fair amount of discussion goes on while the students set up their painting and begin to work. They are concerned that they need to draw something, and the teacher says the shape does not have to be an apple, but should be simple, so that they can spend time on the colours. In ten minutes, the students are settled and using their paper and crayons. The teacher asks the class to quieten down: 'People who are painting don't need to talk.' She explains the colour system, circulates around the room and pushes the students to complete their work.

Moving to one student, the teacher takes the student's paper, and suggests that a dog must have worked on it. She gets another sheet and begins to fold it into eighths so that the student can do the work. Other students, concerned for his performance, want to give him a piece of paper. The teacher tells the class she will take care of him, and gives him a new sheet, folded correctly. After folding another sheet of paper for another student, she begins to circle the room again.

She compliments a few students on how lovely their paintings are, comments on others, then sits at her desk and begins to work. Students like to see what she is doing, which also lets them see what the observer is doing. The students have formed two small groups, one around the teacher and the other around the observer. When the teacher chases them away from the observer, most go to see her work or go back to their seats. As the period winds down, most of the students have drawn the pictures they are going to use to paint, but they have not yet started to colour. The students spend more time around the teacher than continuing to work in what they were asked to complete. Fang is working on his painting, but does turn around to talk to friends and to get paint and water for the colours he needs to complete the work.

Paint brushes at the ready, Fang stands over his painting. Thanks to brush painting in schools, and the daily use of chopsticks for eating, he seems quite at ease with the paintbrush and paints, as is true for most of the students. At this point in the lesson, the teacher quietens the students down by asking which row is the best behaved. She begins calling and naming rows and the behaviour that identifies them as well behaved. Most students settle down immediately. Fang has begun to paint, having collected a paint tray from the front of the room.

'Remember the way to do this: if the foreground is light, the background should be dark, and if the foreground is dark, the background should be light,' says the teacher. She continues to sit at the back of the room, grading students' papers as the students work on their own work, discuss what they are doing, and report on the behaviours of others. 'Whose time is this to talk? Everyone get to work', says the teacher. Students settle down again. It is clear they like this class and the opportunity to talk and move around. Working on student papers and grading their morning work, the teacher calls students to her desk to discuss their work. To one, she says: 'Why have you done such a messy job?' The student is right in front of the teacher and appears quite intimidated. She tells him to work on this, and that she will write something in her weekly report to his parents. The teacher says, 'Who is running in and out of class?' Another student comes in and she says, 'You are the representative . . . Why are you outside?' The student responds and she sends him to his seat. Picking up a picture with one error, the teacher shows it to the class, corrects the error and goes on. At the back of the room, she talks to a student who is using his neighbour's paint. The teacher says: 'You have forgotten your materials again. How can you do this? How can your family let this happen?'

After going around the room, she begins calling students up about their work, complimenting those who have done the work correctly and criticising those with problems. Most exchanges are public and easy for others to hear. Many do stop and listen if there is a real issue. When two students threaten to paint one another with the brushes, the teacher does not notice this immediately, but she does seem very aware of the overall performance of the students. After a break, she gets up and walks around again to see how they are doing.

Fang has taken somewhat of a different approach from the other students by beginning to paint all of the background pieces first. Most of the others are painting the individual paintings, foreground and background. Fang is on target and appears to be working with reasonable speed. When the bell rings, students continue to work, but move in and out of the class at will. Fang is working and talking to his friend.

Students pour by on their way to the playground, or just run on the balconies. The pattern of the teacher giving suggestions and directions to the students and correcting them continues. At the end of the day, some students have begun to clean up while others are working on their painting. The teacher brings four of the better paintings to the board and discusses them. Finally, she gives out the work she has corrected. The students bow to her, and then begin to leave the school.

Moving on to look at other classes in Jing, the teachers displayed somewhat different instructional styles in the classrooms. In comparing the classes at Jing, Fang

Tan-fang experiences a less democratic atmosphere in his class than was observed in another class in the same school. In the other class, instruction included grouping strategies and an emphasis on student-developed examples becoming the foundation for learning mathematics, this describes the more democratic style. In brief, the tone of the other class is as described below.

When the bell sounds, the teacher enters the classroom, and interacts with individual pupils concerning their learning of specific maths problems. After completion of this discussion with the students, the teacher explains the characteristics of division. The teacher asks, 'How many pupils are in the class?' 'Thirty-one!' the students respond in unison. The teacher asks, 'What can we do if we want to divide the thirty-one pupils into five groups?' Some students work at the board, while others work the problem at their seat. When one pupil at the blackboard answers correctly, she is given a big round of applause by her classmates – called 'love encouragement'. This example of the teacher's instructional strategy illustrates both the concepts of division – devisor, dividend and quotient – and the teacher's willingness to support the student's performance and involve other students in the teaching and learning.

Most parents of Jing School are encouraged to play active roles in the school's affairs. They keep contact with school through the 'home correspondence book', written by the teacher every day and through phone calls from the Parents Committee. Usually parents were formally invited to the school twice a year, once for the PTA and again for the Day of School Sports Competition. In order to strengthen the ties with parents, the school sends a newsletter to parents twice a year. At the classroom level, parents do not volunteer to be teacher's aides and teacher–parent contacts are usually initiated by the teacher.

Every school in Taiwan creates a Parent Committee which donates funds to support the school's operation. However, in the current liberalised environment in Taiwan, the Parent Committees of some middle-class schools have become more involved in the decision-making processes of the schools and insist on a voice in decisions about school policy.

HWA: the less effective school

Hwa is located just inside the north-west border of Taipei. It has 3,461 pupils, 97 classes, 138 teachers, and 25 non-teaching staff. The school buildings are typical for Taiwan: built in the shape of a square surrounding an open field, with each wing three or four storeys high. An extra wing has been added recently near the main gate. The total land size is 35,082 square metres. In addition to the first through sixth grades, the school has three classes for slow learners with seventeen pupils in each class, and one twenty-student class for students with athletic talents. The school contains a publicly supported kindergarten programme with four classes of five-year-old children. While kindergartens in public schools are rare in comparison to US schools, a decline in enrolment made it feasible at this school. Over one thousand pupils have left over the last four years, with many of the pupils moving across the river to new developments, after a new bridge was built near the old community.

The head of guidance explained that the school is in an old, resource-deprived community. Most parents are immigrants from other parts of the island who have come to Taipei to work as labourers, hoping for better living standards and educational opportunities for their children. A large proportion are single-parent families.

The children usually live with their fathers and are cared for by other relatives. Weekly schedules are the same as those in other elementary schools in Taiwan, with the exception of permitting first and second graders to participate in 'song and motion' activities rather than the morning ceremonies.

If we look at a class, class 3.1 is one of the highest-achieving classes in the third grade at the school. On mathematics performance the class has been as strong as the higher-grade classes. The forty-four pupils are taught by a teacher in her early fifties, in a classroom of 90 square metres, with twenty-eight tables in seven rows. Each table sits two pupils. The teacher's desk is at the back corner of the classroom so that she faces the blackboard as the pupils do. A big bulletin board on the back wall of the classroom exhibits outstanding student work and maths instructional messages, including terms of division and a plastic milk bottle with a slip showing its weight. Several out-of-date children's newspapers are posted under the blackboard.

Today, the class starts a language lesson. In the first twenty minutes, the teacher asks three pupils to speak about a pre-prepared topic, 'A trip', in front of the class, one after another. After they have all finished, the teacher gives them feedback about the lack of feeling in their fact-orientated narration. Moving to Lesson Nine in the textbook, the teacher asks each pupil to read a small portion of two to three sentences. Each student has an opportunity to read from the text. Learning from the other students' complaints that they cannot hear each other reading, the teacher asks the class to tell her which students read loud enough. Two pupils are pointed out.

Next, the teacher discusses with the students the characteristics of a diary and what would make up a good diary selection. She writes 'date', 'day of the week' and 'weather' on the board, and proceeds with an in-depth review of the lesson. After the whole class finishes reading one paragraph, she asks the class questions on this paragraph. Getting no response from the students, she chooses some terms and asks students either to make sentences or to describe their meanings. The first term is 'a series of'. One student makes a sentence with the first term and gets feedback from the teacher, who then makes two more sentences on her own. The same student responds again with a strange sentence and the whole class laughs.

The teacher shifts to a new term 'turning clear (weather)'. Two students try to explain the meaning of the term. A contrasting term, 'turning cloudy', is introduced by the teacher. The teacher begins new words that describe human feelings such as 'pleasant' and 'happy'. One student makes a sentence during this time. As the activity continues, the teacher explains the serial relationship of 'road', 'street', 'lane' and 'alley'. One student initiates a question about the confusion between 'street' and 'road' which the teacher answers. Only about two to three pupils are inattentive during the entire lesson. Finally, the class is dismissed after being extended by three or four minutes past the bell.

If we look at another class, class 3.7 with thirty-four pupils, led by a woman in her twenties, falls in the middle of the lower half of maths achievement of the school's entire third grade. The classroom is set up so that the teacher's desk is at the right-back corner, parallel to the last two rows of pupils' tables. A bulletin board on the back wall posts lists of pupils' quiz scores, with a rank for each name. There are also some how-to-calculate examples of addition, subtraction, multiplication and division maths problems, and big cards of new Chinese vocabulary words.

In the afternoon, the class works on Chinese calligraphy, a new curriculum area for the third grade. The class already had four morning periods of instruction, including maths, Chinese, natural science, and physical education; and one afternoon period of Chinese. Before the individual seatwork, the teacher spends twelve minutes teaching students how to draw a perpendicular line of a specific character with a traditional Chinese brush. Drawing with a chalk on the blackboard, she does not give a direct demonstration in using Chinese brushes. She frequently asks questions about the differences between writing the character 'right' and the character 'palace' in hand-writing, and which stroke to start on writing 'palace' in Chinese brush. Only a few students visibly react to her questions.

As students are preparing their workbooks, inks and brushes to practise Chinese calligraphy, the teacher suddenly asks about a class taught by another teacher that morning. She notes that a pupil is using his pen improperly and mentions the problem to the student. He is puzzled and the teacher explains herself.

As the teacher patrols the classroom, students write from twenty-two to twenty-four characters each. She makes a few comments about individual performance. One student finishes his work earlier than the others but his strokes are out of proportion and the teacher takes away the worksheet and asks him to write all of the characters again. She uses metaphors to remind students of one of the techniques of writing Chinese calligraphy: 'If you modify the finished stroke with an extra stroke on the same line, it will just look like your face is covered with dust.' She tells one student, 'the strokes of your character are too thin.'

Most of the pupils are not in the habit of studying the examples on top of the worksheet while copying each character four times. These behaviours are important for good calligraphy. Accordingly, most of the pupils' products are not impressive. A majority of the students do not finish the assignment during the allotted time and the class continues after the bell. The teacher announces that the Chinese character practice will continue into the next period. The pupils work for twenty minutes of clean-up and then stay thirty minutes longer to complete their homework in the classroom under the supervision of their teacher.

The middle-socio-economic-status school

LIN: the more effective school

Located in the northern area of Taipei City, Lin Elementary School has 20,060 square feet of land, 1,663 pupils, 49 classes, 74 teachers and 16 non-teaching staff. It is considered a medium-size school. The school buildings, built as a hollow square, includes three wings for instructional operations and one wing for a teachers' boarding-house. Unusually, Lin Elementary includes a kindergarten programme with three classes of age-five children. Four elementary schools are within a block of each other in this old community where Lin is located. All the schools are losing pupils as the younger generation moves out of the community.

About three hundred of the pupils attracted to Lin Elementary School are scheduled to be studying at other schools in the neighbouring school districts. The school has been cited by the Taipei Board of Education as an outstanding school in three categories: appropriate pupil behaviour, beautification of the school, and environmental protection. Among the attractions of the school, are two large and well-lit pottery classrooms and an open-stack room of teaching aids, with plentiful material and equipment. Special-needs children are integrated into the regular classroom.

Today, at the teachers' morning meeting from 7.45 to 8.00 a.m., the principal presents money awards to two teachers for their successful coaching of pupils who won outstanding-performance awards in composition and physical education in inter-school competitions. The principal has been serving at this school for more than six years. Extremely active, she involves her staff in many school-orientated activities, and runs the school through a 'walk around' management style. To assure this, she has set up schedule sheets in boxes at certain spots in school buildings for herself and other administrative heads to write down the times that they walk by. Expressive and outgoing, she explains how she had the plant arrangement modified and the school buildings repainted in recent years.

If we look at a class, class 3.2 is taken from the eight classes in grade 3 at the Lin Elementary School. The achievement level of language and maths for seven of the eight classes is both very high and homogeneous. This observed class 3.2 is a model class for high achievement in the third grade. In this high-achieving class, thirty-four pupils are taught by a female teacher in her twenties. The classroom is about 90 square metres, a standard size in Taiwan. The pupils' desks are arranged in six differ-ent groups of five or six individual desks for each group. Pupils face each other, so cooperative learning teams can form. The teacher's desk is in one corner beside the blackboard, so that she can face her pupils while seated. Class rules such as keeping quiet in the classroom, respecting your teachers and elders, are written on long slips, and posted on the other side of the blackboard. A big bulletin board hanging at the back of the classroom exhibits examples of good art work of the pupils, and some outstanding group reports of social and natural science are posted on the side-wall of the classroom. A 'the term of today' with its explanation, and a description of the 'healthy family' were also displayed on one side of the blackboard.

After art and music, composition, physical education and social science have been studied on this day, the class has a lesson on the subject of three cards on New Year Greetings, a lesson from the textbook. At first, the teacher asks the class to read the whole lesson silently for three minutes, and reminds the students to pay attention to the main ideas of the lesson while they read. Next she asks the class to read the entire lesson aloud. Noting that one student circled the main idea of the lesson in his text, she praises him. 'This shows strong study skills.'

With new vocabulary cards posted on the blackboard, a pupil who prepared the cards becomes a student teacher, coming to the front of the room to lead the class. After read-ing the word once, the student demonstrates the line series of this character and asks all his classmates to raise their right hands and write the word in the air. To test them, he reads the meaning of the word and turns the card over. More than half of the stu-dents raise their hands to ask him to repeat the word's meaning. The class moves on to new terms, reciting the terms loudly in unison after the student teacher. Students make new terms out of the vocabulary they have already learned and read the terms aloud.

The above activities are repeated eleven times with different cards and different student teachers with the teacher intervening when students are learning each new word. She uses different ways to extend or develop new meanings of the character, reminding the students of the similarity and difference between the new word and a familiar word, or asking students to describe an object the word describes. For the word 'lotus', the teacher demonstrates the 'lotus step' in folk dance. For the word 'neighbour', the teacher asks, 'What countries can be called as our neighbours?' For the word 'fox', she asks students to describe the animal. Although one student shows a picture of a fox from a big dictionary, the rest of the students are requested by the teacher to find a picture for their homework. In the last five minutes of the period, the students recite the messages on the eleven cards all over again.

If we look at another class, class 3.7, the maths achievement level of this class of thirty-four students is similar to that of class 3.2 but the school administration identifies class 3.7 as the lower-achieving. The lead teacher here is also a young lady in her twenties, and the pupils and teacher's desk are arranged just as in class 3.2. The classroom rules on one side of the blackboard differ slightly from those of class 3.2 and the bulletin board at the back of the classroom has a section called 'Little Scientist' as well as maths-related problems and pupils' outstanding art work. On the blackboard 'the term of today' is explained on one side; special messages list pupils' ID numbers under the following categories: 'Fail to pass on language', 'Fail to memorise the lesson', 'Fail to correct on language', 'Fail to correct composition', and 'Fail to memorise the poem'. Records on two sides of the classroom walls include 'Neatness of the desk', 'Failure to hand in assignment', 'Good performance for clean-up', 'Good performance for morning study time', 'Good performance for environmental recycling', and 'Good performance in class'.

An afternoon Chinese calligraphy class follows the study of two periods of natural science, social science, language, physical education, and speech. The lesson teaches three basic strokes for Chinese calligraphy. A poster showing how to hold a Chinese brush appropriately is put up on the blackboard, and before the lesson starts, the teacher draws three basic strokes on the blackboard, with the steps for each stroke broken down under each picture. The first basic stroke in calligraphy is the dot. The teacher asks her pupils to point to words with dots in them, gets responses from three students, and then demonstrates how to write a dot.

As the students begin to work at their seats, the teacher patrols the classroom, encouraging students to work for good calligraphy. Finding that most of the groups are not able to complete the work, she demonstrates for each group, either writing a dot herself on a student worksheet or holding a student's hand while he or she writes. When the class makes noise, a pupil is sent by the teacher to make an 'X', a bad record for the group, on the blackboard. Three students are praised and one student's work is shown to the class. After twenty minutes, the teacher demonstrates a second basic stroke, writing the stroke on the blackboard. Asking students to write the second stroke eight times on their practice sheets, she walks among the groups.

During the last three minutes of this period, the teacher asks students to do extra practice on the second basic stroke and shows that the stroke was written inappropriately by most of the students. She assigns homework before the class is dismissed, giving a lesson she planned by herself because she thinks the worksheets provided by the school are not good enough. Most students show a visible lack of confidence in their Chinese writing, practising strokes on scrap newspaper before writing on the worksheet. Their products are not as impressive as those shown in the high-performance classroom.

Conclusions

It is clear from the summary of findings in Table 6.1 that a number of the ISERP dimensions were not contributing a great deal to explaining the level of effectiveness

Table 6.1 Summary of differences between the low and middle-SES schools across eight dimensions

Dimension of contrast	Less effective lower-SES (Hwa)	Typical effectiveness lower-SES (Jing)	More effective lower-SES (Yuan)	More effective middle-SES (Lin)
A day in the life of a child	A limited number of curriculum objectives are the focus of students and the teacher. Instructional practices may differ in areas such as the inclusion of manipulatives, but the pace, coverage and quality of the curriculum remain consistent across schools			
Teachers' teaching style	Whole-class lecture and response with little focus on student interaction were the norm. Criticism was more common. Pace, involvement and feedback are similar to other schools		Classes tended to have more interactive small groups, less criticism and more interactive teaching generally	
The curriculum	All schools follow a national curriculum designed by specialists under the guidance of the Ministry of Education. Examinations at the end of middle school and high school are designed and graded at the national level and determine high school and college placement respectively. The local elementary schools can incorporate elements in the school curriculum such as pottery or Taiwanese literature to give the school an individual quality			
The influence of parents	Low-SES school parents spend less time in schools and their involvement is more prescribed than mid-SES school parents. Contact is teacher initiated and tends to be one-way communication through newsletters		Parents work in a number of school jobs, including volunteering as school guards or tutors. Parents are beginning to demand an increase in their decision-making	
The principal	Principal behaviours did not yield substantial differences. The principals although they are faced with many central office mandates and regulations. The principals appear to place their own stamp on the schools and in some cases appear very proactive. All can describe the behaviour of their teachers and have visited their classes			
School expectations of pupils	Whole low-SES schools had families with less education than others, school officials never showed and lower expectations for these children			
School goals	Schools share goals based on national curriculum and limited options for training. The concept of local control or local variance in goals has little currency in the schools. Individual school goals can only relate to life studies or the arts			
School resources	School size varies greatly among schools in urban settings and across the country. Resources and staffing are similar in all schools regardless of location because the funding is regulated at the national level. High performance schools differ from low performance schools in lower leaving rates of teachers and transfer rates of students			

Eight areas of the school deserve more discussion.

of the schools. These characteristics may explain the variance between Taiwan and other countries, but they may contribute little to the understanding of limited variance of Taiwan's schools. An obvious explanation is that the culture permits much less variance among schools than what might be expected or even accepted from schools in other countries. If there is less variance in the vision of what comprises the elements and purposes of schools, then it follows that the behaviours exhibited in the schools would vary less. All of this is also borne out in the limited variance of performance of the schools (see Chapter three).

Eight areas of the school deserve more discussion.

1   *Teaching styles*

In many ways, the teachers observed are normal for classrooms in Taiwan. The classes are taught through whole-class-directed instruction with a series of short lectures and student participation at the board and in their seats. Academic content knowledge, skills, and the development of thinking are the major goals of classroom activities while the more social outcomes of cooperation, physical activity, and life skills are more likely to be taught through tasks assigned to students outside classrooms and discussed in assemblies.

While some schools are beginning to use more child-to-child interaction and grouping during instruction, what is common to Taiwan's classes is the intensity of instruction. To reach academic goals, the high level of interaction between students and teachers, the quality and quantity of feedback to students, and the characteristics of the language used between teachers and students create an intensity of instruction that is a result of the combination of the pace and the focused nature of instruction. The entire time in the classroom is spent in interactive instruction with almost all students involved both listening and often doing an activity. Rarely is time spent working individually in seatwork or doing homework. For a number of reasons, this intensity appears to be present regardless of the designation of a school as a positive or negative outlier. First, the school, community and students expect learning to be an essential part of school and children's efforts. For most children, this pervasive atmosphere is basic to school. The pace, the effort of teachers and classmates, and the seriousness of the task, all contribute to this momentum in the classes. The focused nature of the classes is also maintained by ten-minute breaks every forty minutes, when students are given time to talk or run around.

Many opportunities are available for students to respond in groups, at the board or in their seats, to the teacher's questions and instruction. Little time is spent off-task or waiting for the teacher to start the next activity. Feedback, likewise, is direct, immediate and decisive. In an elementary classroom, if you speak, you stand. If you are wrong, you must sit down. Teachers tend to cajole, comment on and direct students at every turn. However, if there is an identifiable difference between schools it is the increased criticism observed in the low-SES less effective schools over other classrooms. This finding is similar to many other studies of the impact of criticism on student learning (Good and Brophy, 1986a, b). Also, it is clear that the more effective schools tended to have more interactive teaching. However, the pace, involvement and feedback in different classrooms seemed similar. Limited variance among the classrooms and high-level school performance may be most likely attributable to the powerful, motivating classroom environment observed in Taiwan's classrooms.

2   The curriculum

The curriculum did not differentiate between schools, since Taiwan's curriculum is determined nationally, with supplementary teaching materials developed by educational consultants or teachers. Each grade has a set of objectives for each subject that all students must master. The standards are essential, particularly in mathematics, and all students are expected to meet them regardless of their intellectual background, economic background or family education. The number of objectives is limited and teachers make a great effort to ensure all students attain them. The schools adhere to these national guidelines with diligence. Individual classrooms, schools and school units expend a great deal of effort to move through the objectives and materials within each semester. The classes observed in this study worked from the national text materials and often chose to use the nationally approved supplementary books and activities. The activities chosen in these supplemental texts tended to be practise text materials rather than curriculum enrichment materials. In some cases these might be manipulatives, but in most cases they were word problems or problem-solving activities that reinforced the overall concept or objective. The curriculum materials used to teach these objectives in the classes were often adapted from abroad, especially from the United States, and had added examples and photos from Taiwan. Materials are prepared in semester rather than year-long units, many in an expendable form so that students can write on the materials. In summary, it can be said that the opportunity to learn in all schools remains consistent in pace, content and quality.

3   The influence of parents

Parents in Taiwan are considered important to schooling and are often seen as supportive of the teachers, but in general, they do not play the volunteer role common in the United States and in other countries. However, in recent years, parent involvement has been increasing. Teachers continue to be the experts in education and, until the current generation, have been better educated than the general population. In lower-SES schools, most parents play less active roles in school affairs. They keep in contact with the school through the 'home correspondence book', written by the teacher every day, by phone calls, or through the Parent Committee. Usually parents are formally invited to school twice a year, once for the PTA meeting and again for the Day of Sports Competitions. To strengthen the ties with parents, one school sent a newsletter to parents twice a year.

In the classroom, parents in the less effective low-SES schools rarely volunteer to be teaching aides. Teacher–parent contacts were usually initiated by the teacher. Parents in the more effective schools, low- and middle-SES, play a more active role, including working as crossing-guards, library clerks and one-to-one tutors. Close contact occurs in these schools with the school holding a number of seminars and lectures based on the parents' interests. Attendance at these seminars is traditionally fairly high.

Parents in Taiwan clearly care about the schools their children attend and, as noted in the discussion of the changes of school fortune, are aware of the rise and fall of the school's place in informal achievement rankings. In schools, as in many parts of Taiwan's political and social life, citizens are gaining more of a voice and more control over the decisions that affect them. Every school in Taiwan has a Parent Committee whose main function has been the support of school operation through donations. Recently, the function of the Parent Committee has been changing, as parents demand more involvement in school decisions.

4   *The headteacher or principal*

It is clear from discussions with all of the principals that they are all controlled by the central administration. The principal has substantial freedom to distinguish his or her school from other schools only in peripheral areas, so some of these have created environments or activities that set them apart from other schools. Pottery, folk dancing, environmental activities and peer and volunteer tutoring are some of these variations. It is clear that parents and their communities recognise these actions on the part of the schools and identify the role of the principal as critical in the development of the school.

5   *School goals*

School goals could be stated by every principal and teacher. Most would sound something like the following:

> Education for Life is emphasised in the school. The six goals are to love country, to emphasise ethics, to enrich life skills, to promote morality, to have physical health, and to foster cooperation.
>
> > (Less effective low-SES principal)

The less-effective principal, interestingly, would give the same goals as the more effective. There is a clarity about the purpose of education that pervades all schools.

6   *Inter-staff relations*

Good inter-staff relations are generally maintained in all of the schools. The school days are busy for teachers with few occasions existing for teachers to chat. The main topics of the teachers are exchanges related to school matters and teaching ideas. In addition to the short breaks that might lead to teachers talking with each other, the weekly school teaching seminar is an occasion for the exchange of teaching techniques and educational ideology.

7   *School resources*

The school finances are supported by the City Bureau of Education in Taipei. Schools are given the same fund base by head counts. Each individual school also receives categorical funds for the improvement of facilities and special programmes. Local school and parent groups give donations to the schools for their work, but these are not often large sums of money. The political environment is such that many political groups support schools in order to gain the vote of the general population. Education receives strong support among the community and the political parties.

8   *Image*

Images of the schools are based on their public face. Some parents may choose schools based on their perceived academic quality, but the access to the school and proximity to home remain the critical factors. Parents may be concerned about quality, but they usually choose and support the local school.

Conclusions for Taiwan schools

Lack of variance in performance and processes among schools and children in Taipei's schools can be attributed to a limited number of factors. Part of this is the limited variance in terms of language, culture, money, background and family structure among the students. Eighty per cent of students in Taiwan speak Taiwanese at home, while most of the communications in the public are in Mandarin, the official language. While Taipei's population has a higher number of native Mandarin speakers than the average community in Taiwan, many students need to learn Mandarin when they enter school. Language learning does not play a significant role in differentiating learning levels. Basic cultural beliefs are shared by a great number of the Chinese population, including beliefs concerning education and the role of the family. Financial strength varies among the community, but the variance is less than in many communities in the world. With few zoning regulations and little control over neighbourhoods and population movements, however, differences between the communities are not as great as might be found in other countries with more significant class or racial distinctions.

Teachers have similar cultural backgrounds to their students. They received training from a limited number of institutions before the reformed policy in teacher education after 1994. Teachers from this comparatively small community share views on the goals of teaching, and teaching methods are similar for similar topics. Teachers' competencies tend to be quite standard across schools within Taipei, since their academic performance on college entrance examinations is in the upper 10–12 per cent of the population. While there may be small differences among the performance of teachers, the overall distinction in effectiveness may be more between urban and rural teachers rather than among teachers in Taipei. In addition, because of shared beliefs, the performance of teachers in Taiwan may be significantly more alike than those in other countries. In support of this strong community of education is the distribution of financial resources. Set by the central government, the per pupil funding is similar for most schools regardless of community resources. Before 1996, textbooks and curriculum were also standard in all schools but more freedom of choice has been recently allowed.

Despite all of the similarities in culture, language, curriculum and resources, there are a few elements that reveal differences among schools. At a school level, criticism of children in the less effective schools is endemic which suggests a more pervasive, and perhaps unspoken, view that the children will not be as successful as others in the society. A second factor is the involvement of parents, which is greater in the more effective schools.

What can be learned from the study of Taipei's schools relates to their uniformity, their relentless pace, high opportunity to learn, and their equity of resources, against a background of similar cultural values, language and experience. These dimensions give level foundations for student learning. The constant forward driving of the class-room and its focus on the essential learning of content, concepts and skills, secures for all students regardless of background support for learning to perform in society. The classroom also provides for all students the same level of involvement through group response, equal opportunity to respond, and continuous, if not always positive, feed-back. Finally, all of these dimensions occur on level foundations where not only the school resources are similar, but the levels of achievement of teachers are substantially higher than in other societies. We return to the lessons of the Taiwanese model of education in our conclusions in Chapter 14.

7 The Pacific Rim and Australia – Australia

Barry Green, Barbara Dundas and John Clarke

Introduction/context

The Commonwealth of Australia is a federation of six states and two territories. Each state and territory has its own government and concomitant instrumentalities, such as a public service, police force and education department, while the federal government retains control of such things as the armed forces, external and diplomatic affairs and the national economy. The Minister for Education in each state is responsible, through a Department of Education or an equivalent, for the provision of appropriate education for all children of eligible age. While each state has a system of local government in the form of urban and rural councils, these councils have no responsibility for education.

The mixed-SES schools: general characteristics

School One: the more effective school

Data indicated that the community from which this school drew the majority of its students consisted of people with a wide range of occupations, as well as a number who were unemployed. Occupations included manual workers, tradesmen, service-industry workers and company managers. Approximately 50 per cent of the community had lived in this geographic area for the previous five years. The median age of the population was thirty-two years, most residents owned or were purchasing their own home and the average annual family income was between 30,000 and 35,000 Australian dollars. More than 60 per cent of the adult population had no post-school qualifications, while almost 10 per cent had university-level qualifications. About 25 per cent of primary school students from this catchment area attended a private school, which was about the state average.

School Two: the less effective school

Data indicated that the community from which this school drew the majority of its students was of similar composition to that of School One, with a similar range of occupations represented. The population of the associated area was slightly more stable, with approximately 60 per cent of residents having lived in the geographic area for more than five years. The population was, on average, also slightly older than that of School One, with a median age of thirty-five years, and had a slightly higher annual income of between 35,000 and 40,000 Australian dollars. The statistics on home owner-ship were similar to those of the catchment area for School One. Compared to School One, slightly more (12 per cent) of the population in this catchment area had university-level qualifications and slightly less (58 per cent) had no post-school qualifications. Approximately 30 per cent of the primary-school-aged students who lived in this area attended private schools, which was a little above the state average.

A day in the life of a child

School One: the more effective school

The student central to the case study at School One, whom we shall call Ruth, appeared to be a normal, happy, lively, rather outgoing and social nine-year-old. She was described by her teacher, Mrs A, as being a good average student who tried hard. She was well groomed and dressed, as were all the students, in a freshly laun-dered and ironed school uniform. The classroom in which Ruth spent her days was bright and cheerful with every available space covered in either student's work or materials designed to assist the learning process. The students' desks all faced the front of the room but were arranged in a series of nested U-shapes rather than in formal rows.

Ruth, accompanied by two friends, arrived in the classroom some fifteen minutes before actual start-time and as soon as she completed some minor preparatory tasks, she sat at her desk and read a book. Other students were undertaking preparatory tasks, reading or completing worksheets on various topics. There was a low level of conversation occasionally punctuated by bursts of excited chatter which quickly sub-sided. Mrs A talked quietly with a number of students while completing her own preparations for the day. More than half the class was already present when Ruth arrived and the whole class was present before the official commencement time. In common with most state schools in Queensland, there was no daily assembly at School One, but a whole-school assembly occurred once a week.

Ruth's formal school day began with an hour and twenty-five minutes of English language. It was noticeable that academic activity began immediately and routine administration tasks, such as roll-marking, were completed while the students worked. The first activity consisted of a series of ability-graded comprehension exercises. Dur-ing this activity Mrs A continually circulated around the room assisting individual students, while a parent helper took a small group for reading practice. This was followed by a whole-class exercise in which the students worked their way through a series of progressively more difficult worksheets relating to the classification of vari-ous items. Ruth appeared to take her academic work very seriously, as did most of the students, and was wholly engaged in her task. Students who finished all the worksheets, worked on further-ability graded comprehension exercises for whatever remained of the session. The third and final English activity was an extended teacher-led dis-cussion about travelling and what might be needed to undertake a journey overseas. The pace at which this discussion was conducted was possibly a little slow and the concentration and interest level of some students lapsed at times.

Three boys misbehaved during the early stages of this activity in that they sat at the back of the group where they whispered to one another, giggled, and paid no atten-tion at all to the discussion. After a quiet warning Mrs A moved one of them apart from the main group and separated the other two. Her raised voice and angry tone indicated that she was not pleased. At the conclusion of the discussion Mrs A escorted the class to the library, where the teacher–librarian gave them a lesson on note-taking skills which lasted until morning break.

The session after morning break began with twenty minutes of silent reading, during which relaxation music was played very quietly. By the time Mrs A arrived back in the room a student had started the music and more than three-quarters of the class was already reading. Each student had his or her own special 'reading place' and Ruth spent this session curled up on a large cushion in a corner, totally absorbed in her book. The students were completely silent throughout.

Silent reading was followed by approximately seventy minutes of mathematics. The class first completed a set of exercises based on multiples of four, then divided into predetermined ability groups and undertook group-specific work. This work had been written on the blackboard by Mrs A prior to the start of school. Students were encouraged to attempt work up to two levels above their own, while students in the top group had ongoing extension work available. Ruth successfully completed her own work and most of that assigned to the group above hers. Everyone was expected to complete their tasks individually, rather than cooperatively, although conferring with other students undertaking the same task was allowed if it became necessary. Mrs A circulated around the class generally monitoring progress and giving help and encouragement where necessary. A very high level of engagement was observed during this activity. This session lasted until lunch-time, but students did not leave the classroom until they had been seen individually by Mrs A and she had marked their work.

The afternoon session began with an animated discussion between Mrs A and the class about how animals might be classified. The classification methods used in the exercise undertaken earlier in the day were discussed at length. This discussion concluded with an activity which required the application of classification processes, in which the students participated enthusiastically. The three boys who were disruptive earlier in the day were very subdued, having been spoken to by Mrs A during the lunch break. The activity was followed by art, which lasted until the end of the day. Mrs A spent the whole of the art activity listening to individual students read to her.

Mrs A said that the day had been completely typical and the students no better or worse behaved than usual. In fact, almost all the students were, like Ruth, very well behaved. The class contained one boy with some behavioural problems but Mrs A was obviously very aware of his potential to disrupt proceedings and kept a close eye on him. She rarely raised her voice or created a fuss and generally managed this student's behaviour in a manner which caused the least disturbance and disruption to the rest of the class. It was more than coincidence that she often happened to be standing right beside him when he appeared to be about to misbehave.

For the rest of the students, however, teacher expectation was so inculcated that behavioural considerations were a non-issue. Mrs A rarely needed to exercise overt control measures but when she did they were of a high order. She would, for instance, stop talking and simply wait for complete silence and attention, look at or stand beside students whose attention had wandered, deliberately involve such students in the current activity or, as a last resort, very quietly name the student concerned.

There was much evidence to suggest that a strong organisational/behavioural infrastructure existed in this classroom. The students knew what was expected of them in any given situation and performed accordingly. For example, set tasks were under-taken immediately and work was done in silence unless assistance was needed, at which point it became permissible to ask a neighbour for information. Social con-versation was far from forbidden in the room, but it was clear that the students not only knew when it was inappropriate, but were also too committed to task to have time for it.

It was also evident that a certain amount of flexibility had been incorporated into the infrastructure. Most students, for example, raised their hand when wishing to ask or answer a question or make a comment but this was not a hard-and-fast rule. It was also perfectly acceptable during discussions, less formal activities, or even during lessons if necessary, to make a comment without raising a hand. This appeared to encourage more reticent students to make a contribution without having to worry about being the centre of attention.

The level of engagement on-task during the academic activities was very high. Ruth, for example, who was only an 'average' student, was on-task for over 90 per cent of total academic learning time. There were, in fact, only three students in the class who engaged in deliberate off-task behaviour, and only one who did so to any great extent. Mrs A expected her students to work hard and set high academic and behavioural standards for them. She challenged them academically and deliberately tested the limits of their knowledge and abilities whenever possible. The predominant feeling in the classroom was one of purpose and Mrs A and her students appeared to share a common understanding of why they were there.

Mrs A's class was interrupted a number of times during the course of the day. For example, a parent came to the classroom door while Mrs A was actively teaching, and engaged her in a conversation which went on long enough for the students to become restless. Mrs A was obviously very uncomfortable and tried to terminate the con-versation several times without success. Similarly, Mrs A was twice interrupted by students from other classrooms bringing her notes which required some response. The intercom system installed in the classroom was another cause of interruptions to Mrs A's class. She was twice asked to provide information via the system and on neither occasion did the required information appear to be particularly urgent. Mrs A said that the intercom system was a major frustration for her.

School Two: the less effective school

The student central to the case study at School Two, whom we shall call Emily, appeared to be a normal happy, gregarious nine-year-old. She was described by her classteacher, Mrs B, as an academically average student. She was well groomed and neatly dressed, as were all the students, in school uniform. The classroom in which Emily spent her days was bright, attractive and remarkably tidy. There was a lot of very recent student work on display, as well as a variety of instructional charts and posters. The students' desks were arranged in a series of nested U-shapes, rather than in formal rows, and all faced the front of the room. Mrs B's desk was in a corner at the front.

Emily arrived in the classroom with a group of friends soon after it was opened by Mrs B. She engaged in a number of preparatory activities, while talking quietly with other students who were either similarly engaged or were playing board games or reading. The students appeared to be happy and relaxed and several stood around

Mrs B's desk and laughed and chatted with her. The entire class was present in the room before the official starting time. As at School One, there was no daily assembly at School Two, but a weekly whole-school assembly was held.

Emily's formal school day began with the students sitting on the carpet at the front of the room for roll-marking and 'Show and Tell'. The students then returned to their desks and embarked upon fifty minutes of mathematics. The first session consisted of a variety of ability-based activities and exercises, which the students undertook individually, in pairs, or in small groups. Some of the students undertook cooperative, experimental mathematics activities which generated a certain amount of noise and movement. Emily's task, in which she did not appear to be particularly interested, was to complete an activity sheet concerned with the subtraction of whole numbers greater than one hundred. Mrs B worked with a small group of low-achieving students, while at the same time attending to the needs of other students who came to her for assistance. The room was well organised during these activities and the students well behaved.

The second session consisted of the revision of the year's work to date by way of a series of activity sheets. The class was much quieter during this activity and the majority of students were on-task most of the time. However, some students continued to engage in quiet social conversations. Some time was spent by Mrs B at the end of the session in correcting the activity sheets with the class and the students responded enthusiastically to the skilful questioning techniques she used to elicit the correct answers.

Mathematics was followed by half an hour in the school library, during which time the teacher–librarian informed the class about a number of new fiction titles which had recently arrived. This was an interesting and quite dynamic presentation and the students were absolutely silent and attentive throughout. Emily and her classmates went straight from the library to morning break.

The session after morning break began with an hour and forty minutes of English language. Mrs B read a story to the class after which the students moved to pre-designated ability-based small groups and undertook a variety of language activities. Emily was part of a group of less able readers who were working on an activity sheet relating to a story which they had read. Although she had appeared to be engrossed in the story which Mrs B had just read to the class, Emily appeared to be reluctant to begin work on her language activity. Instead she coloured in a picture which formed part of the activity and engaged in quiet conversation with the girl next to her. When Mrs B noticed this digression and instructed Emily to begin work, she briefly complied then got up and joined the queue of students seeking Mrs B's assistance. This exercise took several minutes, but once back at her desk she completed her task quite quickly. When she had completed her activity sheet, Emily collected a comprehension worksheet from Mrs B's desk and worked on it in a somewhat desultory fashion for the rest of the session. During these activities Mrs B assisted the steady stream of students who came to her for help.

The last twenty-five minutes of the morning was spent in silent reading which was a daily occurrence at this time. Emily and her classmates appeared to consider this activity to be one of the highlights of their day. All the students were on-task and the room remained completely silent throughout. Mrs B marked work which the students had completed earlier.

The afternoon session was divided into three periods, each of about thirty minutes duration. The first period was spent in writing a Daily Diary, an activity which the students appeared to take very seriously and during which the room was once again completely silent. This was followed by a session in which the comprehension activity sheets which the students had begun during the morning were finished and presented to Mrs B for marking. The final activity of the day consisted of oral presentations by three groups of students on a variety of topics. Emily took a small part in one of these presentations which were, for the most part, very polished performances to which the rest of the class paid close attention. When the bell went to signal the end of the day, Mrs B dismissed the students and Emily left, as she arrived, surrounded by friends.

Apart from the journey to the library, and the very noisy exit of some boys to remediation and their equally noisy return, the day was entirely free from interruptions. Mrs B said that the day had been fairly typical and that the students' behaviour had been average. In fact, Emily and her classmates got along well together and were very well behaved. Mrs B did not have to exercise overt control over the class at any time during the day other than occasionally to request that the noise level be moderated or that an individual or group pay more attention to their work.

However, the level of application to task on the part of some students was a little inconsistent. For example, at different times during the day, a number of students appeared to avoid work by simply delaying compliance with Mrs B's instruction to the class to begin a particular task. Whenever Mrs B noticed this inactivity and directly instructed them to begin work they complied immediately but were sometimes off-task again shortly afterwards. A small number of students also occasionally employed what appeared to be deliberate avoidance strategies during some academic activities. Such strategies included continually sharpening pencils, conducting a prolonged search for some vital 'lost' item and crossing the room to borrow something from a friend. Group activities provided the greatest opportunity for students to avoid set tasks, although at times, some did not appear to address tasks with any serious intent even when engaged in formal seatwork. These students did not misbehave in any normal sense, but indulged in social chatter while undertaking academic tasks and appeared to treat such tasks somewhat casually. Their actual level of engagement was difficult to assess. The students who talked did so quietly and whenever Mrs B requested silence the class complied immediately.

Emily, an average student, was actively engaged on-task for about 75 per cent of academic learning time overall, but during some maths and language activities her level of engagement was somewhat lower. She was, for example, off-task for almost half of the first academic activity of the day.

Regular lack of application to task was not, however, common to the majority of the students and most of the class was on-task most of the time. Whilst the level of interest and engagement on-task of individual students varied throughout the day, only three students were regularly off-task or less than fully engaged, with a further three occasionally off-task or less than fully engaged. Furthermore, there were times when the entire class was wholly engaged on-task for extended periods and the students were sometimes so interested in an activity that they were reluctant to move on to the next. Mrs B was able to command complete and prolonged silence and/or attention whenever she wished. For example, the class was completely silent throughout student presentations, while writing daily journals and during reading. The atmosphere in this classroom was very pleasant and relaxed and Mrs B was obviously very popular with her students.

Teachers' teaching style

School One: the more effective school

Mrs A had no preferred method of teaching mathematics and used direct teaching, interactive discussion, group work and individual seatwork as and when necessary. Concrete materials and 'hands-on' activity-based learning were used when appropriate, and students occasionally worked cooperatively in mixed-ability groups. However, most mathematical work was undertaken on the basis of an ability-based grouping system. The word 'group', in this case, meaning a number of students working individually on the same task, with no connotation of cooperative work. This system enabled students to work at a level appropriate to their attainment but neither restricted them to that level nor imposed an artificial ceiling on their learning. In fact, students were actively encouraged to attempt work well above their supposed ability level. It should be noted, also, that mathematical tables were practised every day.

Language was taught by way of integrated cross-curricular units using much the same organisational structures as for mathematics. Silent reading and creative writing were important aspects of the daily programme, as were interactive teacher/student discussions and student presentations.

An analysis of a day's activity in Mrs A's class reveals that her students received over 70 minutes of interactive instruction and undertook over 130 minutes of closely supervised individual seatwork. In addition there were twenty minutes of small-group instruction and twenty-five minutes of student presentations of one form or another. The students were rarely given a single task but rather tasks were 'nested' so that as soon as one task was finished, the next task was there to be undertaken, as was the task after that if necessary. All such tasks were curriculum-related. Even when engaged in whole-class activities or in interactive sessions with Mrs A, students were expected to use 'waiting time' productively and to this end a number of predesignated tasks existed to be undertaken as appropriate.

As well as ensuring that no student was ever without productive work, Mrs A employed several other strategies in order to optimise the use of available time. One such strategy was hearing individual students read to her during art and craft activities. She had also devised a system which prevented long queues of inactive students forming at her desk. Similarly, no students were required to sit and listen to instructions or directions which did not apply to them. Once they had the information they needed they quietly removed themselves from the main group and began their allotted task. This common-sense approach to basic organisational problems meant that, on average, students lost only nineteen minutes per day in transitions from activity to activity and no student was ever without a pre-planned curriculum-related task.

Mrs A insisted that her students looked at her and were silent whenever she was talking to them, and moved around the classroom most of the time that she was not actively teaching the whole class or working with a small group. She further insisted that work was begun immediately, that every student engaged in task and that rules governing behaviour during academic activity were strictly adhered to. Mrs A also had very high expectations of the students and assigned the highest possible status to academic activity. In other words, a strong academic press was evident in this classroom along with a deliberately fostered sense that what was being undertaken was important.

School Two: the less effective school

Mrs B preferred to teach mathematics by way of small-group instruction utilising hands-on, activity-based learning whenever possible, with whole-class instruction being undertaken as necessary. Some mathematics topics were covered by way of a 'whole language thematic approach'. In the course of a day's mathematics activities a student might experience a number of learning modes, depending on the combination of activities undertaken.

Most language-related concepts and skills were taught through 'cross-curricular integrated units' commonly called theme work. During language instruction the students worked in streamed or mixed-ability groups, in pairs, individually or in some combination of these alternatives. Whole-class instruction was undertaken as necessary, such as when beginning a new unit of work or when introducing a new concept. Both silent reading and creative writing were undertaken every day, as was some form of student presentation and teacher/student discussion.

Mrs B engaged in small-group and/or individualised instruction for most subjects and went to a great deal of trouble to prepare workbooks and activity sheets for her students. She was also a very effective 'whole-class' teacher.

An analysis of the day's activity in Mrs B's classroom reveals that her students received about thirty minutes of direct teaching, another thirty minutes of small-group instruction, spent twenty-six minutes on student presentations, and undertook about 150 minutes of seatwork. Individual seatwork in maths and language was based mainly on workbooks and activity sheets.

Mrs B was very organised, her classroom ran very smoothly and a strong organisational/behavioural infrastructure was evident. Groups were predesignated, tasks clearly identified and further work was always available. Like Mrs A, Mrs B insisted that her students were silent and looking at her whenever she spoke to them.

The curriculum

School One: the more effective school

School One had developed implementation documents for a number of curriculum areas, as well as documentation detailing the recommended content coverage for each year level. There was scope for an overlap in the coverage of content between year levels, to allow for individual circumstances. Planning occurred between teachers at each year level to ensure consistency of implementation, assessment and reporting, as well as to minimise time spent on planning and the development of resources.

In implementing the mathematics and English curriculum at the classroom level, Mrs A consistently tested the limits of the students' 'comfort zone' in terms of academic complexity. When appropriate, she extended the curriculum covered for individual students and appeared unconcerned that some students might cover content recommended for the following year.

Mrs A reported that her class received, on average, 5.2 hours of mathematics instruction and 7.5 hours of English language instruction per week. They also received approximately one hour of mathematics homework and one hour of English homework each week.

School Two: the less effective school

School Two had also developed an implementation policy for a number of curriculum areas which specified the content coverage for each year level. Provision was made within this policy for an overlap in the coverage of content between year levels to allow for individual circumstances. Curriculum planning occurred between teachers at each year level to ensure consistency of implementation, assessment and reporting, as well as to minimise time spent on planning and resource development.

Mrs B reported that her class received, on average, 4.5 hours of mathematics instruction and 5.0 hours of English language instruction per week. No specific amount of homework was assigned in either subject, although homework was given.

The influence of parents

School One: the more effective school

There were a number of ways in which parents of students attending School One could be involved with the school. These included providing voluntary assistance in classrooms, helping to run the school tuckshop, membership of the Parents and Citizens Association and participation in a range of advisory committees. The function of these joint parent/staff committees was to make recommendations concerning various aspects of the school's operations to the principal. The Parents and Citizens Association was very active in the area of fund-raising, although a perennial issue was that most of the work was undertaken by a committed minority.

Mrs A described her level of contact with parents as 'only average', since both parents of most students in her class were in paid employment and therefore only came to the classroom when requested. She had on average, three contacts per year with the parents of most students, usually at her initiative, and wrote notes to parents once a term. There were two meetings a year to which all the parents of students in the class were invited, and a school newsletter was sent home each week.

Parents undertook volunteer work in Mrs A's classroom for about three hours per week. These parents undertook a range of classroom tasks, the majority of which involved working directly with students, and they accompanied the class on field trips and during extra-curricular activities. Mrs A had a very positive perception of the effect that the parents of her students had on their child's learning. She felt that almost all of the parents of the students in her class showed interest in their child's academic activity and gave positive reinforcement to the school's expectations.

School Two: the less effective school

The range of parental contact at School Two was similar to that at School One, although greater emphasis was placed on parents being an integral part of the decision-making process. The opinion of the parental body was regularly sought on a wide range of matters and parent/staff committees had actual decision-making power. The Parents and Citizens Association was very active in the area of fund-raising and was considered to play a crucial role in the provision of sufficient funds for the effective resourcing of the school.

Mrs B reported that, in general, her contact with parents was good and that she spoke to the parents of a typical student approximately four times per year. These contacts were usually initiated by her. In addition, there were two meetings per year to which all the parents of the students in the class were invited and Mrs B wrote notes to parents once a term.

Parental volunteers worked in Mrs B's classroom for approximately three hours per week and undertook tasks which involved working directly with students, as well as tasks which required no student contact. They also accompanied the class on field trips and assisted with extra-curricular activities. Mrs B felt that more than 80 per cent of the parents of students in her class had a positive influence on their child's learning by displaying interest, being involved and helping them at home.

The headteacher/principal

School One: the more effective school

The principal at School One viewed himself as a career educator and teacher, put student welfare at the forefront of all decision-making and was school-orientated in his outlook rather than system-orientated. The needs and welfare of students and staff were his first consideration in the formulation and implementation of all policy, including mandated systemic initiatives. In fact, the implementation of some mandated systemic policy seemed to be something of a token gesture.

The principal had very high expectations of his staff in terms of commitment to teaching and to the school in general. Staff performance was monitored informally but constantly. If the principal felt that a teacher was not performing at an appropriate level, and no explanation for this diminished performance was forthcoming, regular visits were made to that teacher's classroom and specific expectations were outlined. However, the principal was very aware of the difficulties and stresses currently associated with classroom teaching and was protective and supportive of his staff. He gave every possible assistance and all possible support to any teacher who made a genuine effort to overcome classroom problems, or whose performance was temporarily affected by such things as ill health or personal problems.

The principal viewed his management style as being consultative whenever possible, but autocratic as and when required. While the emphasis was on consultation with staff, parents and students, the principal stressed that the ultimate responsibility for decision-making rested with him. If it became necessary to disregard other people's opinions in order to implement a decision which he perceived to be in the best interests of the students and staff he was willing to do so.

The principal had what he described as an open-door policy for staff, parents and students, although he encouraged the making of appointments if an issue needed to be discussed at length. A range of consultative mechanisms existed throughout the school, which facilitated collaboration and communication.

School Two: the less effective school

The principal at School Two also viewed himself as a career educator and teacher, and put staff and student welfare at the forefront of his decision-making. He worked slightly longer hours than the principal of School One and was usually the first to arrive at the school and the last to leave. He deliberately involved parents in the decision-making process and gave them a genuine decision-making role. He attempted to implement mandated systemic initiatives and to comply, so far as was possible, with departmental directives.

The principal of School Two held his staff in high regard and was very supportive of them. He had a very democratic and egalitarian management style and teachers were strong participants in the decision-making process. He was firm but diplomatic in his dealings with staff, parents and the education authority and was held in high regard by staff, students and parents.

A range of consultative mechanisms existed throughout the school which facilitated collaborative decision-making and which enhanced communication. The principal was always available to parents, staff or students. If he was unable to see someone when they approached him, he made arrangements to see them as soon as possible.

School expectations of pupils

School One: the more effective school

At School One the overall expectations for students were high, in terms of both academic and social outcomes. These expectations related to longer-term educational goals, as well as to activities within the school.

All teachers were expected to implement a range of assessment processes to evaluate student progress. Decisions regarding common assessment and reporting procedures were made at year-level teacher meetings, although each teacher was able to undertake additional assessment and reporting to parents and students. The compilation of folios of student work samples, the recording of teacher observations and the administration of teacher-designed tests was common to all classes. Parent–teacher interviews were held to discuss student achievement and a written report card was issued.

Mrs A used a wide range of assessment strategies to measure student achievement. She placed particular emphasis on 'authentic' assessment such as the periodic gathering of student work samples and the systematic checking of student work as well as the use of techniques such as pre- and post-instructional testing and the administration of other teacher-designed assessment instruments. She also used class discussions to assess student development and sometimes utilised standardised tests. Mrs A usually determined achievement by relating attainment to defined goals, but she also, at times, did so by comparing individual attainment with objective standards, previous results or overall class achievement. Assessment results were used by Mrs A to give feedback to students, to provide extra content for high-performing students, to work individually with high- or low-performing students, to plan further instruction, to adjust curriculum and teaching methods, and to check the effectiveness of her teaching.

It was mandatory for all schools to have a Supportive School Environment Policy which, in part, outlined the reward and sanction system in operation. Schools were required to ensure that such systems emphasised a consistent 'whole-school' approach to managing student behaviour as opposed to simply reacting to extreme behaviours in isolation. The emphasis at School One was on a proactive teacher-centred system of control strategies, which incorporated a clear sequence of rewards and sanctions, while at the same time seeking to develop an internal locus of control in students. Behaviour problems within the school appeared to be minimal and when they did arise they were dealt with in a systematic manner.

School Two: the less effective school

Expectations, in terms of academic and social outcomes, were equally high at School Two. However, these expectations may have been moderated to some extent by a perception, on the part of some teachers, that certain students would have difficulties with academic achievement and/or behaviour, because of their 'home background'.

School policy relating to assessment and the reporting of assessment results to students and teachers, was similar to that of School One. Year-level teacher meetings were held to determine common assessment and reporting procedures. Assessment features common across all classes and year levels were the same as for School One and included the development of folios containing student work samples, the recording of teacher observations and the administration of teacher-designed tests. Parent–teacher interviews were held to discuss student achievement and a written report card was issued.

Mrs B used a range of assessment strategies similar to those utilised by Mrs A. In order to determine student achievement levels, Mrs B usually compared results to a student's previous work, to overall class results or to those of students of similar ability. Results were not usually compared to those of a normative group external to the school.

Results of assessment were used to give feedback to students on their progress, to provide extra work to low-performing students, to work individually with such students, to plan further instruction, to adjust instruction and teaching methods and to check the effectiveness of the teaching process. These results were also used to provide extra work for high-performing students, or to work individually with such students.

School Two had a Supportive School Environment Policy which was similar to that of School One and which focused on the rights and responsibilities of students. The school sought to develop an internal locus of control in students through the application of a collaborative problem-solving approach, which treated each incident independently and sought logical consequences and solutions. Behaviour problems within the school were observed to be minimal and those that did occur were routinely handled by the teaching staff.

School goals

School One: the more effective school

Students' academic and social achievement was the main focus of School One. The prime goal was to ensure optimum individual academic achievement, while at the same time developing social and cooperative behaviour. The aim of the majority of activities at the school was to promote staff and parent commitment to school philosophy and policies. While a corporate ethos had been maintained throughout the tenure of the then current principal, he stressed that maintaining philosophy and ethos was, at times, extremely difficult, since he was unable to choose his own teaching staff or even, in many cases, his ancillary staff.

School Two: the less effective school

The focus at School Two was also on the achievement of optimum academic and social outcomes. The maintenance of a supportive school environment was a priority and some emphasis was placed on the social and emotional development of students. Social justice perspectives appeared to have been integrated into all school policies and practices, and all departmental initiatives were in an advanced stage of implementation. A strong corporate ethos had been developed and maintained.

Inter-staff relations

School One: the more effective school

While some teachers had made stronger links with their colleagues than others, the atmosphere within the staffroom at School One was generally one of collegial support. Conversation was wide-ranging but school- and student-related topics figured prominently. The staff seemed generally to work as a cohesive unit and to have student learning, both academic and social, as their main focus. Curriculum planning meetings were convened and conducted by staff members and any decisions made were reported at whole-school staff meetings, and/or other forums, as appropriate. It should be noted that some teachers believed that too many committees had been established in the school and that the time thus spent could be more productively applied to classroom preparation.

There were a range of procedures in place within the school to ensure the effective transition of students between year levels. Syllabus documents, school programmes and student work folders were given to teachers at the start of the school year. While it was generally assumed that all the set work for the previous year had been covered, this was confirmed through discussion with the teacher from the previous year or by examining the student's individual work folders which contained samples of work and records of assessment. If children had been evaluated as having special needs, specific ascertainment records were also forwarded to the new teacher. In general, information on teaching strategies and student grouping were not passed on to the next teacher unless it was directly relevant to a child's specific educational needs.

When a new student was enrolled, it was normal school procedure for the child and his or her parents to be taken to the relevant classroom and introduced to the teacher before the child was due to be admitted, or on the first day of attendance. Parents of new students were asked to provide information relating to any special needs which their child might have. If further information concerning a new student was needed, the previous school was contacted by telephone or in writing.

The teachers at School One were generally happy with the support they received from both management and colleagues, were very willing to seek and/or accept such support, and had a very positive view of life within the school. They believed that swift and effective action would be taken by management if the need arose.

School Two: the less effective school

Staff at School Two were observed to have established warm and friendly collegial relationships, and a very strong feeling of mutual support and of working as a cohesive team was evident. Teachers of each year level participated in common curriculum planning meetings and work was shared between all teachers. Specialist visiting teachers were very obviously treated as equal members of staff and their expertise was highly valued. The overall feeling was of a whole staff working together.

The process used to ensure the effective transition of students from year level to year level at School Two was very similar to that in place at School One. Evaluation folders, which contained samples of student work and an assessment record, were provided by the teacher from the previous year. Copies of student record cards, which contained essential student information and an outline of major interactions with individual parents, were also maintained. For students with special needs, an outline of ascertainment recommendations and any specialist teacher reports were provided for the new teacher. Discussion with the teacher from the previous year was undertaken when necessary. As at School One, it was unusual for any information on teaching strategies or student grouping to be passed on to the next teacher.

When a new student was enrolled, it was standard admission procedure to introduce the student and his or her parents to the classteacher and to determine if the student had any special educational needs. Student workbooks were checked to confirm the level of achievement the student had reached prior to enrolment.

Both Mrs A and Mrs B had a positive view of the support given to students with learning difficulties and special needs, and of steps taken by their respective schools to address social justice issues relating to disability and the socio-economic status of students. Both also had positive perceptions of the way in which their schools addressed social justice issues relating to gender and race.

Both teachers felt that they were able to deal with new developments and challenges associated with their work, although they also felt that it was sometimes difficult to cope with everything they were now required to do. They both strongly believed that teachers carried a disproportionately heavy workload and both sometimes found it difficult to find as much time as they would have liked to prepare for teaching, supposedly their main task. Also, unfortunately, they both occasionally wished that they were doing another job.

School resources

Both schools received the majority of their funding through government grants, parental contributions and funds raised by the Parents and Citizens Association. The schools were relatively well resourced, with both having communal science and mathematics materials available, along with a variety of reading materials which included reading schemes and class sets of general fiction. All teachers interviewed in both schools reported that their classrooms were well stocked and that requests for resources were usually favourably considered by the school resource committee, within the context of whole-school requirements. Teachers in both schools had similar positive perceptions about the availability of adequate resources to undertake the task of teaching.

School image

The principals of *both* schools strongly believed that image, in terms of how their school was perceived by the community, was important to the welfare of their schools. The provision of funding and resources to the schools by the government was dependent on student numbers and, since parents in Queensland are not constrained by any zoning or catchment rules, they may send their children to the school of their choice. Student numbers in any particular school, therefore, are to some extent dependent on the public perception of that school and the consequent willingness, or otherwise, of parents to enrol their children.

Conclusions

If we look at Table 7.1, which summarises the information collected on the two schools, it is perhaps important to note, first of all, that the two schools and two classrooms described here were in many ways very similar. For example, the schools were physically alike, had much the same student population, and served communities of comparable compositions. Both had relatively low staff turnover, supportive parental bodies, similar levels of resources, good inter-staff relations and taught the same prescribed curriculum. Furthermore, the principals of both schools worked long hours, considered themselves to be 'career' educationalists and were committed to their respective schools. Both valued and protected their teachers, had established a range of communication and consultative mechanisms within their schools and were deliberately accessible to students, parents and staff.

Similarly, the case-study classrooms in both schools were very tidy and well organised and had large amounts of recent students' work carefully displayed. Both classrooms were relatively 'formal' in that all desks faced the front of the room, all student activity was teacher-controlled, and the teacher was central to the learning process. Both teachers were hard working and committed, popular with their students, very well prepared for their teaching day and saw themselves as career teachers. The students in both classrooms arrived early, appeared to be happy and relaxed, and were, in general, very well behaved.

Despite these similarities, however, the two schools and classrooms proved to be quite different in certain respects.

For instance, while the expressed goals for both institutions were similarly concerned with academic and social achievement, the interpretation and actualisation of these goals was perhaps a little different. School One (the more effective school) appeared to have a very specific and focused view of the purpose of schooling, which put student academic and social improvement as the prime goal and considered appropriate behaviour to be essential to, and an integral part of, this prime goal. School Two (the less effective school), on the other hand, appeared to have a broader view of the purpose of schooling which emphasised the growth of the whole person. It should be noted, however, that no difference in attitude to students was discernible between the two schools and that the principal and teachers in both establishments appeared to be equally caring and supportive in their treatment of, and relationships with, their students.

Another area of variance between the two schools was in their respective control mechanisms. While both had similar behavioural expectations of their students, they employed different mechanisms to achieve compliance with these expectations. In general, School One relied on a proactive teacher-centred system of control strategies, while at the same time seeking to gradually develop in students an internal locus of control. On the other hand, the development of an internal locus of control was central to the philosophy of School Two where a collaborative problem-solving approach

Table 7.1 Summary of differences between two mixed-SES schools across the twelve dimensions

Dimension of contrast	More effective mixed-SES (School One)	Less effective mixed-SES (School Two)
General characteristics of the school	Stable population, owner occupied Cross section of all occupations	Stable population, owner occupied Cross section of all occupations
A day in the life of a child	Formal classroom; high levels of time on-task Routines well established, no need for administrative or behavioural instruction High expectations of what children were capable of	Formal classroom; moderate levels of time on-task Routines well established, but some disobedience
Teachers' teaching style	Mixed methods, whole-class group and individual work Approximately 1/3 whole-class Differentiated groups plus always having work available to maximise coverage	Mostly group work Approximately 1/10 whole-class Considerable use of individual work with worksheets
The curriculum	Considerable planning for effective delivery of state mandated curriculum 12.7 hours of maths/English weekly 2 hours of homework in maths/English per child per week	Considerable planning for effective delivery of state mandated curriculum 9.5 hours of maths/English weekly No specific English/maths homework
The influence of parents	Considerable use of parents in classrooms, societies, etc., plus fund-raising	Considerable use of parents in classrooms, societies, etc.

The principal	Strong commitment to instruction and student welfare more generally High expectations of staff – open-door style Autocratic when necessary	Strong commitment to school welfare Supportive of staff – democratic management style
School expectations of pupils	High expectations academically and socially Staff commitment to frequent assessment	High expectations academically and socially, but moderated by the perception that some students may have limits caused by home background Staff commitment to use of assessment data
School goals	Optimisation of individual achievement academically and development of social and effective behaviour Very specific goals	Optimisation of individual achievement academically and development of social and effective behaviour Cooperative behaviour Emphasis on social justice Broad range of goals
Inter-staff relations	Generally supportive	
School resources	Classrooms well stocked with audio-visual material and textbooks	Classrooms well stocked with audio-visual material and textbooks
Relationship with local authorities	No information collected	No information collected
School image	Active attempt to improve image because of competition between schools	Active attempt to improve image because of competition between schools

was employed. Despite this difference in emphasis, the great majority of students at both schools appeared to be very well behaved.

The respective management styles and philosophies of the two principals also appeared to be somewhat different. The principal of School One, although generally consultative and democratic, was both autocratic and directive when he considered it necessary. He also had a limited number of very specific goals, evaluated everything in terms of achieving those goals, and allowed as little as possible to interfere with progress towards them, including, on occasions, regional requirements and mandated systemic imperatives. The principal of School Two on the other hand, seemed to be invariably democratic and egalitarian in both philosophy and style regardless of the situation. He also had a broader range of goals and tried, so far as was possible, to incorporate and provide for a wide range of needs and opinions. He may also have been a little more understanding of diminished teacher performance than the principal of School One.

A number of differences between the case-study classrooms were also apparent. For example, the students in the School One classroom (the effective environment) appeared to experience considerably more direct and interactive teaching than those in the School Two classroom, and much less individual work involving workbooks or activity sheets. Furthermore, while ability/attainment-related groups were integral to the teaching of core academic subjects in both classrooms, their effect may have been different. While ability-related grouping facilitates the provision of work of an appropriate level, it can also be restrictive in that it may limit students' academic activity to a narrow band of tasks which may or may not test the boundaries of their academic 'comfort zones'. The structure of the streamed grouping system in the School One classroom facilitated and encouraged the extension of students beyond supposed attainment levels and to some extent reduced the possible 'ceiling effect' of such groups.

There was also a difference between the two schools in the allocation of available time. For example, Mrs A reported that she devoted five hours and twenty minutes per week to mathematics, and allocated an hour of homework, while Mrs B reported that she devoted four and a half hours per week to this subject with no specific allocation of homework. Similarly, Mrs A reported that she allocated seven and a half hours per week to English, plus an hour of homework, while Mrs B reported that she allocated five hours per week to this subject and gave no specific amount of homework. It should be noted that variation between classrooms in the amount of time allocated to specific subjects occurred throughout the research sample.

It was also noticeable that the attitude of the respective groups of students to academic tasks was somewhat different. While the students in School One tended to treat all such tasks seriously, the attitude of some students in School Two appeared to vary from task to task. It should be noted that while the targeted average student in the School One classroom was on-task for over 90 per cent of academic learning time, the targeted average student in the School Two classroom was on-task for less than 75 per cent of academic learning time. The School One classroom also appeared to have a corporate sense of purpose and direction about it and a strong academic pressure. The School Two classroom, on the other hand, seemed to be slightly less pressured and a little more informal.

The two schools also appeared to differ somewhat in the way in which the marking of work was undertaken. While both teachers were equally insistent that all work be checked by them, this checking was, to some extent, undertaken in different ways.

While the marking procedures used by both teachers varied from day to day and from lesson to lesson, the teacher at School One appeared to do most checking as either a group- or whole-class activity during which concept and process were reinforced as well as errors being identified. The teacher at School Two, on the other hand, appeared to do most marking on an individual basis – that is, seeing each student in turn to check their work – or by collecting completed work and returning it marked.

8 The Pacific Rim and Australia – Hong Kong[1]

Yin Cheong Cheng, Wing Ming Cheung and Wai Ming Tam

Introduction/context

Currently, Hong Kong is rapidly developing in nearly every aspect of its society including economic, political, cultural and social aspects. The drastic impacts of the economic downturn since 1997, rapid globalisation, political transformation and information technology have further accelerated the changes and developments of education in Hong Kong (Cheng, 2000). During the past decade, a number of education policies have been issued to improve school education to meet the challenges from a changing education environment (Education Commission, 1982–97; Cheng, 1999). The understanding of the characteristics of the more effective and less effective schools in such a changing background may make an important contribution to the ongoing policy discussions and reforms in both local and international contexts.

In this chapter a more effective school (ABC) and a less effective school (XYZ) are compared.

ABC School

Academic achievement

As shown in Table 8.1, the average academic achievements of students in ABC School were very high, with school means of 69.88 on Chinese language, 57.29 on English language, and 25.39 on mathematics. They are considerably higher than the Hong Kong means (i.e. 65.10, 48.28 and 22.13) and much higher than those of XYZ School. In particular, the students' English language achievement was outstandingly good.

Table 8.1 Student academic achievement of ABC School and XYZ School

Subject	Hong Kong Means	ABC School Means	XYZ School Means
Chinese language	65.10	69.88	51.19
English language	48.28	57.29	30.93
Mathematics	22.13	25.39	14.30

[1] This chapter is based on the findings of a research project previously sponsored by the funding from the Epson Foundation and the Mainline Research Scheme of the Chinese University of Hong Kong to Dr Y. C. Cheng. The authors acknowledge their kind support.

According to the principal, the results of the academic attainment tests of their primary six students were always above the Hong Kong means. On top of this, the overall academic achievement of their graduates stayed always at the top 40 per cent of the whole population of primary six graduates in Hong Kong.

Students' attitude and satisfaction

From the findings of a questionnaire survey of all grade 6 students, students in ABC School seemed to have a positive self-concept, possess good attitudes to peers, be respectful to teachers, and love their school and learning. Generally, they perceived themselves as competent and optimistic. They believed that they could achieve their own standards in work, as well as those set by their teachers. They had harmonious relationships with classmates. Most of them worked together cooperatively and shared with each other their resources, such as books and pencils. During recess, students played happily with peers and very few students were lonely. Many of them also crowded around teachers who were on duty during play time. Many of the students reported that they loved the school and their teachers. Another phenomenon observed was that students loved reading. This validated the general impression that students had a positive attitude towards learning.

Regarding students' satisfactions, the views collected from students suggested that they were satisfied with the arrangement of the school, the relationship with members of the school, and the available opportunities for them to exhibit their talents. When asked if they would quit schooling, they answered 'no'. Although, some students held relatively negative views concerning homework overload, the overall impression of student attitudes was rather positive.

XYZ School

Academic achievements

As shown in Table 8.1, the average academic achievements of grade 6 students in XYZ School were very low (51.19 on Chinese language, 30.93 on English language and 14.30 on mathematics). They were much lower than the Hong Kong means and extremely low compared to those of ABC School.

Students' attitudes and satisfaction

According to their own report, students in XYZ School tended to have attitudes towards self, peers, teachers, school and learning which were less positive than those in ABC School. Some students had a rather negative conception of themselves. A few even viewed themselves as 'useless' and 'unhappy'. They reported having good relationships with classmates. Cheerful play relationships between peers, especially during recess were clear. Students indicated that they treasured their recess. They played with peers and felt relaxed after 'boring' lessons. Their attitudes to teachers and school were two areas found to be rather negative. General observations suggested that students did not approach teachers actively; some students even had a fear of their teachers. In their eyes, teachers were serious and would easily become annoyed. Teacher–student relationships were generally distant. Moreover, quite a number of the school's arrangements did not satisfy students. These included school facilities like playground, washrooms, recess time and plantations. Classroom environment was another source of dissatisfaction. They complained that the ventilation was not good; the chairs and desks were rather old and worn out; and that the learning environment was not comfortable in summer, due to the lack of air conditioning. These complaints and dissatisfaction with the physical environment of classroom and school were also shared by teachers.

As found in the study, the physical environment of the more effective school, ABC, was even worse than XYZ School. However, it was noted that complaints of the same kind was not so acute in ABC School. We found that students of ABC School had a generally more positive attitude to school arrangements and environment, and were more satisfied than students in XYZ School. This difference, according to observations, may come from the schools' effort to maintain existing equipment and facilities. ABC School's equipment and facilities, though old, were in good condition; while some of XYZ School's were not. This maintenance effort minimised the detrimental effect of out-dated facilities; and would thus provide a more favourable learning environment for students. This practice is exceedingly critical for schools which have been established for a long time as these two have been.

Curriculum

The curriculum taught in ABC School and XYZ School was basically the same. In Hong Kong, primary schools follow a common core curriculum. The subjects taught are normally English language, Chinese language, mathematics, science, social studies, health education, art and crafts, music and physical education. Religious education is also offered in religious schools. Variations in curriculum among schools are small. In view of this, the discussion on this area will not be dealt with separately.

In Hong Kong, teaching is generally conducted conventionally in a classroom. Teachers talking or a teacher-centred approach is the main feature of classroom teaching. This phenomenon was evident in both schools. Due to physical and resource constraints (e.g. class size, teacher–student ratio), an ideal form of activity-based learning environment is normally not possible. XYZ School in the present study adopted exactly this form of teaching. At its junior level, 'Activity Approach' was employed, while at the senior level (grades 5 and 6) conventional teaching was adopted. On the other hand, ABC School used conventional classroom teaching at all levels.

Another characteristic of curriculum delivery in Hong Kong is that a considerable portion of classroom teaching time at grades 5 and 6 (the last two years of elementary schooling) in many schools is allocated to training students in verbal and numerical reasoning. These two areas of students' capability are tested by the central education authority for the purpose of secondary school place allocation. Curriculum delivered in this way has a general feature of allocating insufficient time for cultural subjects like art and crafts, music and physical education. This phenomenon was also observed in ABC School and XYZ School.

Extra-curricular activities were also organised for students in the two schools. However, there was a great difference in terms of student participation. ABC School organised twenty different types of extra-curricular activities for students yearly. The school principal revealed that 80 per cent of students participated. In XYZ School, fourteen types were offered, in which 60 per cent of students participated. Participation of the two schools in inter-school competitions/functions was also different. The students of ABC School participated in twenty different competitions/functions and won 102 prizes. However, XYZ School sent students to participate in only nine events and won five prizes.

From the above we see that the delivery of the formal curriculum in the two schools was rather uniform in terms of subjects and methodology. However, where extra-curricular activities were concerned, the quality and quantity of student participation of ABC School was far better than that of XYZ School. In other words, students in ABC School might have had a better opportunity to experience quality education in extra-curricular activities. Also, students of ABC School reported that they were proud of the school and themselves. This might validate the previously described students' attitudes and satisfactions in school.

Classroom climate

School is a social system including different types of social interactions that can influence the performance of the principal, teachers and students (Halpin and Croft, 1963; Cheng, 1991). Inside the school, the classroom is a crucial social environment that affects student performance and, therefore, educational outcomes (Fraser and Walberg, 1991; Cheng, 1994a). The study of classroom climate is therefore essential to our understanding of effective school practice.

According to Moos and Tricket (1974), Bass (1981), French and Raven (1968) and Cheng (1994a), the major aspects of classroom climate examined in this research included the social interactions among students and teachers and also the power bases that the teacher used to influence student compliance in the classroom. Social interactions in classroom refers to affiliation, involvement, task orientation, competition, order and organisation, rule clarity, teaching innovation, teacher support and teacher control (Moos and Tricket, 1974). Power base refers to the use of reward power, coercive power, position power, personal power or professional power in class (French and Raven, 1968; Cheng, 1994a). In these two case studies, only classrooms of grade 6 students were observed.

ABC: the more effective school

Climate among students

Affiliation of students was close. Students reported that they had a good understanding of each other and close relationships both in classes and after lessons. Cooperation and mutual help in classes were evident. This validated the observations of their positive attitudes towards each other and their high level of social satisfaction reported in the last section. Apart from this good affiliation, the academic competition and involvement in class learning were also healthy. Students reported that they experienced a moderate competitive pressure for good academic achievement. Although they were keen to obtain higher grades in their studies, they did not want to damage the good relationship with their peers. This explained why competitiveness was not acutely high. Tied to this, they also did not have the high level of concentration in class, that one might expect from high academic achievers. Undesirable behaviours in classes, though not frequent, were also reported. However, this did not interfere with their normal learning. Such behaviours in the researcher's eyes were acceptable and normal. After all, the students were all around the age of eleven. One could not expect them to remain sitting in a traditional classroom for hours without signs of 'side-track behaviour'. In general, the classroom climate among grade 6 students in this school was considered to be positive and in harmony.

Climate between teacher and student

Teacher support was strong in the interaction between teacher and students in classes. Students reported that teachers were helpful and sympathetic. Teachers were sensitive to their needs and were ready to render help when approached. It was inferred that the good affiliation and relationship among students might be modelled on teachers' supportive behaviour. Although teachers were helpful and sympathetic, they did not give way easily when there was a chance for students to violate classroom rules. Strong teacher control was also exhibited. Moreover according to reports from students, rules and regulations were very clear. Whenever students were punished, the teacher explained clearly why they deserved punishment. Due to the large class sizes of around forty, teachers in Hong Kong are generally inclined to have very strict rules and regulations in the classroom. Without rules and regulations, with a class of forty it might otherwise be difficult to create a positive learning environment for all.

Regarding the lessons, students indicated that they normally found them quite interesting and were stimulated by new ideas and arrangements from teachers. Teachers also gave out instructions step by step, which were easy to follow. In short, the classroom climate between teachers and students was good for learning in the Hong Kong context. First, discipline problems were minimised by clear rules and strong teacher control. Further, the design and conduct of learning activities were systematic and interesting. Working in parallel with these, was the strong teacher support and sympathetic guidance in classes. This combination of rules and support create a nurturing environment for students to learn productively and teachers to teach effectively.

Teacher power base

The students saw themselves as complying with their teachers because they frequently helped them to solve problems in studies and greatly improved their academic achievement, as well as the fact that, as teachers, they were their superiors. This might be a result of the teachers' exercise of strict control and enforcement of rules in class. In this sense, teachers had successfully built their position of power. However, when asked more specifically, students said that they respected their teachers because they were their role models. Judging from this, their personal qualities as teachers and adults worthy of respect were also crucial. Thus, in addition to professional power and position power, personal power was the third source of teacher power in class. Since teachers were supportive and sympathetic, it would be natural to see the teachers in this school as exercising their coercive power less frequently. Students reported that teachers did not punish them often. If punishments were administered, students normally understood and accepted the reasons. It is interesting to note that students did not report that they complied with their teachers mainly in the expectation of extrinsic rewards.

XYZ: the less effective school

Observations indicated that students and teachers in XYZ School were generally not satisfied with the physical environment of their classroom. Besides this, the noise level and the ventilation problem in summer were more or less the same as ABC School. With both students and teachers not satisfied, it would not be difficult to estimate the probable negative impacts on students' learning.

Climate among students

Compared to ABC School, affiliation of students seemed to be relatively distant, even though grade 6 students in XYZ School still indicated that they had fairly good relationships. There was also only a little academic competition among students in class. Students reported that they did not have high levels of concentration and involvement in class learning. Undesirable behavioural problems in class happened frequently. When compared to ABC School, the frequency of student behaviour problems was relatively high. Teachers at ABC School indicated that, on average, around 75 per cent of class time was used for normal teaching and less than 25 per cent for handling student behaviour problems and other non-teaching activities. On the other hand, 25 per cent to 50 per cent of class time for handling student behaviour was reported by teachers of XYZ School. Of course, this had a negative impact on normal learning in the classroom. In short, we see that in XYZ School, the classroom climate among students lacked the kind of atmosphere conducive to academic excellence.

Climate between teacher and students

Students did not perceive their teachers as very helpful and supportive, as compared to those in ABC School. Teachers in XYZ School, at times, gave way when students violated classroom rules. Further, as reported by students, rules and regulations were sometimes unclear. Teachers occasionally gave inadequate explanations to students when they were punished for undesirable behaviour. In addition, students reported that lessons often lacked interest. Teachers' instructions were perceived by students as difficult to follow and sometimes unsystematic, and new ideas and designs for learning activities were not evident. To sum up, the classroom climate between teachers and students was poorer than at ABC School. First, discipline problems occurred rather frequently, and without clear rules and strong teacher control, a good learning atmosphere could not be achieved. Coupled with the lack of innovation and organisation of lessons, this had a considerable negative impact on students' learning in classes. This might explain why students were often not concentrating in classes.

Teacher power base

In the students' eyes, teachers had a supreme power, inherent in their position. Students complied with their teachers mainly because they were their superiors, rather than because they could facilitate their learning. This was markedly different from ABC School. In the students' perception, teachers in XYZ School exercised coercive power relatively more than reported of those in ABC School. It is perhaps not surprising to observe this in a negative learning environment, as teachers under such circumstances may tend to resort to punishments, to maintain peace and order in the classroom.

The above observations suggest that the classroom climate in the more effective school, ABC, was, in general, more positive than that in the less effective school, XYZ.

Teacher satisfactions and attitudes

Teachers' work performance was defined in these two case studies by observation of their job satisfaction and job attitudes/feelings (Cammann, 1983 and Cheng, 1994b). Specifically job satisfactions included social satisfaction (related to the social relationship with colleagues), extrinsic satisfaction (related to the salary or benefits provided by school), intrinsic satisfaction (related to the opportunities to develop and learn) and influence satisfaction (related to the opportunities to participate in decision-making and be autonomous). Job attitudes or feelings included the commitment to the job, feelings of job challenge, job meaningfulness and job responsibility.

ABC: the more effective school

In ABC School, teachers generally said that they were satisfied with the social relationships with colleagues. Teachers also showed high levels of intrinsic satisfaction, and reported that they had chances to work on meaningful tasks and develop themselves professionally. They showed moderate satisfaction with the opportunities to participate in school decision-making and to have autonomy in professional matters. The promotional prospects and extrinsic rewards for teachers in Hong Kong were generally fixed, as the salary of teachers was fixed to a standard scale and the number of promotion posts fixed at a ratio of around four teachers to one senior teacher. In this well-established school, the senior posts were all filled and the only possible extrinsic reward would be salary. Furthermore, as described previously, the physical environment of this school was quite unfavourable. This might explain why there was not such a high level of extrinsic satisfaction amongst teachers, as compared to other satisfactions in ABC School.

The level of job commitment was not as high as we might have expected. Some teachers reported that they did not have the drive to maximise their work output. A few teachers indicated that they might choose to work in another school. This might be due to the high work tension in this school, due to the emphasis placed on students' success in learning. Even so, the majority of the teachers still said that they found the work challenging and meaningful. They also felt that they had a responsibility to provide a good education service to students. Generally, they reported that they had already put great effort into their work.

From the above, we can see that teachers in ABC School were generally rather positive in their work. Their intrinsic satisfaction might be due to the good students' educational outcomes. They could easily see their effort rewarded through the development of high-quality students. That might explain why they found their job meaningful and challenging. Indeed, when teachers have these attitudes and satisfactions, they would have a positive influence on students' learning. In turn, positive students' educational outcomes would encourage teachers to work even harder and to be more satisfied. In this way, this 'mutual positive influence' between teachers and students would continue and the school could then be expected to move towards real excellence.

XYZ: the less effective school

Compared with the more effective school, ABC, teachers in the less effective school, XYZ, reported very low job satisfaction in nearly every aspect. In general, they were not satisfied with the social relationships amongst their colleagues. They did not enjoy the nature of their teaching job and so were not satisfied with the very limited opportunities for professional development. As would be expected, their intrinsic satisfaction was poor. Compared with ABC School, teachers in this school were dissatisfied with the few opportunities to participate in school decision-making and external benefits and awards available in school. Teachers reported that they did not have the spirit to invest more effort in their work. Cases of intended resignation from the job were also observed. However, the researchers also observed that some teachers still viewed their work as moderately challenging and as bearing responsibility. Generally, they reported that they had already put great effort into their work, but without effect. This showed that teachers felt a certain degree of helplessness in their work.

From the above, we could see that, in contrast to the teachers in ABC School, teachers in XYZ School were generally not satisfied with their work. The lack of satisfaction and sense of helplessness felt by teachers, inevitably had a negative impact on students' learning. In turn, the discouraging students' educational outcomes would reinforce teachers' sense of helplessness and dissatisfaction, leading to an even lower work input. Thus this 'mutual negative influence' between teachers and students would continue and the school become even less effective.

Inter-staff relationships

Based on the conceptions of Halpin and Croft (1963), Cheng (1992, 1994b), and Chan *et al.* (1991), staff relationships in the two schools were studied in terms of intimacy, *esprit*, disengagement and hindrance among staff and in the principal–teachers relationship. Intimacy refers to the extent to which teachers are closely related in school. *Esprit* is the morale developed through accomplishment and satisfaction in work. Hindrance is the extent to which teachers are burdened by unnecessary work, rules and regulations. Disengagement is the extent to which teachers feel that other teachers are annoying, irritating and disengaged in school activities. Principal–teacher relationship refers to the degree of teachers' satisfaction with the social and working relationship with the principal.

ABC: the more effective school

The observed level of intimacy and *esprit* among teachers was high in ABC School. Teachers generally treated colleagues as close friends and not merely as work partners in school. Different informal groups were found in this school. As reported by teachers, the relationships between these groups was 'peaceful'. Conflicting views were not aired. In social gatherings, teachers from different informal groups interacted cheerfully with members from the other groups, as well as with their own close colleagues. Disengagement among teachers was not common, although a few teachers said that they experienced the feeling of being disengaged. Their work morale was generally perceived to be very high and observations also supported this. Teachers felt that their teaching was full of energy. Discussions in staff meetings were normally focused on how to provide good-quality education to students. In short, a working atmosphere of high *esprit* and close relationships was evident.

Another interesting observation in this school was that teachers generally experienced a moderate level of hindrance. Tracing the causes, teachers said that they sometimes felt overburdened by clerical work. In Hong Kong, teachers are expected to take care of quite a lot of administrative work regarding student admissions, students' applications for public transportation subsides, reporting students' demographic data to the central education authority, and the like. These would inevitably create considerable clerical work which teachers might consider unnecessary. Moreover, what was specific to this school was that the principal exhibited a strong structural leadership. For example, he required records to be complete and systematic, which might require more clerical input from teachers. This may explain why teachers experienced the feeling of being hindered in teaching. Fortunately, the level of hindrance was not very high.

The relationship between teachers and the principal was rather good. Teachers were satisfied with the present established administrative structure and related operational procedures. Although they wanted to have more participation in school-policy decision-making, they considered that the present practice was acceptable. They were generally cooperative in carrying out policies and plans directed from the principal. In sum, both the principal and teachers were satisfied with the social and working relationship.

XYZ: the less effective school

In contrast to the observation in ABC School, the degree of intimacy and *esprit* was moderately low. Teachers treated colleagues as close friends only in their informal groups. Other colleagues were treated as work colleagues in school. The relationships among teachers were more related to their official capacities. At times, distant relations between teachers were also evident, as were competition and conflicting views between different informal groups. To a certain extent, this had a rather negative impact on the working environment. It was not surprising that a sense of disengagement was felt amongst teachers.

Morale of teachers was observed to be low, as compared to that of ABC School. This may be attributed to a number of factors. The first set of factors is related to the unfavourable working environment, in terms of intimacy and disengagement, as well as to the physical environment. The next factor was the quality of students' educational outcomes. With the present poor students' achievement, their sense of accomplishment and satisfaction would be low. Thus a relatively low level of *esprit* amongst teachers was expected.

It was observed that teachers generally experienced a rather high level of work hindrance. This may be caused by two main factors. The first was the system-wide hindrance, as outlined in the description of ABC School, imposed by the central education authority and not easily reduced at the school level. Another factor might be related to the weak structural and educational leadership of the principal. In the teachers' view, the whole school was poorly structured. Rules and work procedures, as well as the responsibilities of staff members (including support staff) were neither clear, nor known to everyone in the school. This inevitably generated hindrance to work among staff members as a whole. On the other hand, teachers would easily feel that they were being hindered when their ideas for improving teaching could not be implemented, simply because of the indifferent attitude of their principal. Working in a school like this, teachers would certainly experience a high level of hindrance at work, especially if they were ambitious.

Because of the weak leadership of the principal, teachers generally indicated that he would not interfere with their normal teaching and work, even though new ideas were often not endorsed by the head. This provided a rather good base for building up a soft social relationship between the head and his staff. Teachers reported that they had learnt not to be ambitious and were able to work peacefully with the head. The work life in this school was reported to be easy and without pressure. In general, the relationship between the principal and teachers was good, since the principal had no rigorous work demands on them and they were used to his present laissez-faire work relationship. In sum, this relationship was based on the 'easy work life' in the school.

We see that ABC School had better staff relationships than XYZ School. However, we should be cautious in interpreting the similarly reported good relationships between teachers and principal at the two schools. It should also be noted that the good relationships in both schools were basically built on different grounds as outlined above. Basically, the good relationship in ABC School was developed from the positive and healthy working environment. In contrast, the 'good' relationship in XYZ School was generated by the relatively 'easy work life' environment in the school. Tying the observations to students' achievement in both schools, it seemed that this identified variation in staff relationship might be one of the factors that had an impact on the effectiveness of schools.

The principal

Following the leadership conceptions of Bolman and Deal (1991), Sergiovanni (1984) and Cheng (1994b), this section describes the characteristics, and their potential influences, on a school principal's leadership. The leadership dimensions studied include human leadership, structural leadership, political leadership, symbolic leadership and educational leadership. Human leadership relates to the extent the principal is supportive and fosters participation. Structural leadership refers to the extent the principal develops clear goals, policies and organisational structure and holds people accountable for results. Political leadership is the extent to which the principal is persuasive and effective at building alliances and solving conflicts. Symbolic leadership is the extent to which the principal is inspirational and charismatic; and educational leadership refers to the principal's emphasis and encouragement of professional development and teaching improvement.

ABC: the more effective school

The principal of ABC School, Mr Brown, has been working in this school for twenty-one years. Prior to his present appointment as head four years ago, he worked as deputy head and teacher. He received his professional training from teacher college. He also did a certificate in organisational management, which he viewed as being very helpful in his role as principal.

Mr Brown reported that in daily work he invested a lot of effort in building up clear task goals, policies and organisational structure that held staff members accountable for results. Teachers also indicated that he was very careful and sensitive to possible design faults in school programmes. Moreover, he emphasised formal organisational structure. Observations indicated that the school had quite a number of rules and regulations, work procedures and records of meetings.

Apart from the above-identified strong structural leadership, the principal also demonstrated dominant educational leadership. He encouraged teachers to attend courses or training programmes that were good for professional development. He also focused his attention on teaching methodology, programme design and any other ideas that might enhance the quality of the education service provided by the school.

He focused less attention on human leadership and symbolic leadership, although, at times, he tried to understand the needs of staff members and listen to teachers' proposal and ideas. However, he did not often invite teachers to participate in the making of school policies. On the other hand, he did not seem to have invested substantial effort in sustaining school missions and culture. Teachers reported that they were not clear about the school goals and mission, but they were committed to the ongoing education tasks. They also expressed the view that Mr Brown did not attempt to resolve conflicts among members of the staff, nor build up alliances in the school.

To sum up, Mr Brown was a strong structural and educational leader. His efforts in structural aspects of management may have had a modelling effect on his teachers. Observations and reports from students indicated that teachers were clear in setting up rules, and systematic in organising learning activities. Moreover, his structural leadership might, to a certain extent, have influenced the schools' general good structure. This in turn provided students with a high level of extrinsic satisfaction. The effect of his educational leadership was fairly obvious. Firstly, we could not deny that his educational leadership had given teachers the opportunity to develop and experiment with innovative ideas. This might be validated by the observation that teachers under his leadership had a strong sense of challenge, meaningfulness and responsibility in their job. Last but not least were the students' sound educational outcomes.

XYZ: the less effective school

Mr Green, the principal, was an experienced school leader. He had been working in this school for thirty-three years with twenty-eight years as principal. He had a masters degree and a diploma in education, but he had not received any management training.

According to observations, Mr Green was a principal who did not demonstrate strong leadership. He did not focus on organisational structure. He did not have the established processes to define clear goals and structure, or to hold teachers accountable for outcomes. Teachers indicated that, as far as rules and regulations were concerned, he was a rather carefree principal. Educational leadership was also not prominent. Although he sometimes encouraged teachers to attend professional development programmes, his effort was not persistent. He seldom took an active role in leading teachers to improve teaching and programme design. However, he did endorse those teachers' proposals which engaged him.

According to teachers, he treasured human relationship and needs of staff members. He also invited teachers to participate in the decision-making process. Yet he did not demonstrate himself to be consistent and persistent. He was also not a good negotiator nor effective in resolving conflicts among staff members. This school had no clear school goals or mission made known to the teachers. They were basically ignorant of the concept of school missions. In fact, Mr Green reported that even he himself did not have a specific mission for the school.

To summarise, Mr Green was not a strong leader in either structural, educational, human, symbolic or political respects. His weak leadership might, to a certain extent, make his school unpopular and less effective. Let us take structural leadership and educational leadership as two examples. His weak structural leadership to a certain degree had a negative impact on the general school arrangements, which did not meet the needs of either teachers or students. Weak educational leadership might be one of the many causes that pushed teachers to a state of helplessness. This state of professional helplessness is, in turn, likely to have a negative effect on students' learning. Thus unfavourable students' educational outcomes might be expected.

Mr Brown of ABC School was obviously a strong leader in two aspects: structural and educational, while Mr Green of XYZ School was a rather weak leader. The difference in their leadership abilities, not to mention the managerial training of the principals, might be one of the many factors that make the two schools so different.

The influence of parents

Parental influence on students' performance and the actual parental participation in school activities are the two foci of investigation in this section. Hong Kong is a highly competitive society, academic attainment is the crucial factor when people compete for a job. This has directed the Hong Kong education system to be achievement-orientated. Thus, parental expectations on students' academic achievements are very dominant in Hong Kong, and the variation in parental expectations are very small, particularly in primary schools.

Students of the two schools generally said that their parents loved them and they were happy to live with their families. It was noted that some students of XYZ School had a rather negative view of their families and parents. However, this was not a general pattern. Regarding parental expectations, the observations were in line with the general expectations of the mass of the people in Hong Kong. The majority of the students reported that their parents expected them to be competent in studies and to go on to study at university. This was evident in both schools. However, some students in XYZ School also reported that their parents only expected them to complete secondary education. This is logical, since the academic achievements of XYZ School's students were clearly far lower than those of ABC School, and if parents were realistic they would certainly readjust their expectations.

Parents' association or parent–teacher associations in Hong Kong are not common. Many schools do not establish such associations, despite the persistent promotion of home–school cooperation by the central education authority. According to the researchers' general observations, one of the many reasons is that the school administration does not want parents to 'interfere' in the school's 'own' management. In the present study, we found that ABC School had founded a parents association, while XYZ School had not. One of the reasons for this difference might be the leadership of the principal. It was mentioned above that XYZ School seemed to operate as if it was virtually 'headless' (Cheng, 1991). The principal of XYZ School may not have the determination and competence to start up a parents' association in which the school could meet challenges from parents. However, this was not confirmed by the principal.

Communications between teachers and parents in both schools were more or less 'one-way' and normally took the form of students' handbooks, school notices and letters to parents, parents' day, open day, and teacher interviews with parents. These were basically initiated either by the school or the teacher. It should be noted that teachers would normally initiate an interview with parents when serious academic or behavioural problems of students were identified. Interviews with parents to inform them of the good work of their children were rarely arranged. Teachers from both schools had a largely convergent view that informing parents of students' problems was useful, in the sense that parents were generally eager to help rectify the 'problems'.

The observations of parental influence suggested that variations were small. However, concerning teacher–parent collaboration, the work of ABC School was more encouraging. Apart from the normal channels of communicating with parents, the school also collaborated with parents in the parents' association. We have reason to believe that the comparatively greater teacher–parent collaborations might, to a certain extent, aid the development of students. Thus this variation in home–school cooperation practice may also give us grounds to compare the effectiveness of the two schools.

School organisational characteristics

The school organisational characteristics, such as formalisation, participation in decision-making, strength of organisation culture and external relations are often believed to be important to school effectiveness. According to Olden and Hackman (1981), Hage and Aiken (1967) and Cheng (1994b), formalisation refers to the level of school functioning being formalised with clear written policies, procedures and records. Participation is the level of teacher participation in school decision-making and planning. Organisation culture is the extent to which staff share values, beliefs and assumptions about school mission, teaching, learning and management (Price and Mueller, 1986; Cheng, 1993b). In this section, these organisational characteristics of ABC School and XYZ School are compared and discussed.

ABC: the more effective school

Formalisation

Formalisation characteristics of ABC School were very obvious. The school had a good collection of clear written policies, procedures and records. Staff members were expected to work according to these rules and procedures. It was not surprising to have these clear formalisation characteristics for ABC School, since the school head possessed a strong structural leadership.

Participation in decision-making

The level of teacher participation in school planning and decision-making was low. Decision-making concerning school policies and plans was only done by a few senior teachers and the school head. Normally, extensive consultation of school policies and plans were not available and teachers were only given the chance to voice their opinion at panel meetings. Staff meetings seemed to be an occasion for the management to announce the decided policies.

Organisational culture

Organisational culture was not very strong. In fact, the school principal did not demonstrate strong cultural leadership. However, under his strong educational leadership, teachers were able to accomplish their goals in teaching and other related activities, to provide quality education services for students. Thus teachers, as the main force of culture development, had successfully built up a moderate culture in which an environment of nurturing collegiality was evident. Observations supported the above inference. Within the school environment, discussions on teaching methodology were observed. Stories of outstanding students and graduates were told frequently to students. Traditions of winning prizes in inter-school competitions, such as music festivals, speech contests and ball games were embedded in the minds of students and teachers.

External relations

External relations of the school were built mainly by the school principal. He participated in a number of community services and related working groups. They included the advisory committee of district affairs, the joint school association and the church. Students also participated in activities, such as the inter-school competitions, social services activities, and fund-raising activities for the aged.

XYZ: the less effective school

Formalisation

As mentioned in the previous section, the structural leadership of the principal of XYZ School was weak. It was therefore not unexpected to find that formalisation characteristics of this school were not clear. Written policies, procedures and records were not always available. Sometimes, rules and procedures were not clear or explicitly written, and staff members very often did not have rules and procedures to follow. They drew on their experience. Thus new staff members were often confused in this school.

Participation in decision-making

As with ABC School, the level of teacher participation was rather low. Decision-making concerning school policies and plans was done only by the senior teachers and the principal. Extensive consultation was not available. Staff meetings and panel meetings were occasions for the management to announce the decided policies. Variations between the two schools were limited.

Organisational culture

According to our observation, there was a culture of helplessness and 'headlessness' in XYZ School. We noted previously that the school principal did not demonstrate strong leadership and teachers felt helpless in their work. This helpless feeling was intensified by the 'mutual negative influence' between teachers and students. Teachers generally felt that they could do nothing to improve students' achievement. Moreover, many low-achieving students also had feelings of helplessness about their own academic competence. Stories of graduates who did extremely poorly were often told among teachers. Whenever they lost in an inter-school competition, excuses would be made that it was their tradition to lose.

External relations

External relations of the school were built mainly by the school principal. In relative terms, his participation in community services and related working groups was less active than that of ABC School. He only participated in the joint school association and the church. Students participated also in the activities previously mentioned, such as inter-school competitions, social services activities, and fund-raising activities for the aged. However, this was not very frequent.

From the above, we can see that the major differences between ABC School and XYZ School lie in the areas of formalization, school culture and external relations. These variations provide a sound basis for us to infer how ABC School was different from XYZ School in school functioning and outcomes.

Conclusion

Demographically, ABC School and XYZ School were very similar. They were located in old districts with students from a moderately low social-economic-status background. Both schools have standard resource inputs (e.g. financial support, salary, human resources, school buildings and facilities, etc.) from the Hong Kong government. XYZ School was more favourable in terms of location, class size and physical environments, but unfortunately, did not promise better performance than ABC School, in terms of students' academic achievements, attitudes and satisfactions in school. Surprisingly, the physical environment of XYZ School was even perceived as poor by students and teachers, while that of ABC was perceived as satisfactory (despite being less good). This finding supports the belief that the physical conditions of a school may not be the main factor in its effectiveness, particularly when compared with the effects of internal school processes.

In the analysis presented above, we found that there were differences between the more effective school, ABC, and the less effective school, XYZ, in terms of student performance, classroom climate, extra-curricular activity, teacher work performance, principal leadership, staff relationship and school organisational characteristics, as summarised in Table 8.2. In the more effective school, ABC, students had positive attitudes towards themselves, their peers, teachers, the school, and learning, and were more satisfied with the social relationships with peers and teachers, the opportunities to learn, perform and develop and with the school's arrangements and facilities. They also had very good academic achievements in Chinese language, English language, and mathematics.

Even though the curriculum content was standard, and the teaching methods were teacher-centred in both the more effective and the less effective schools, the quantity and quality of student participation in extra-curricular activities are very different in

Table 8.2 Summary of characteristics, Low-socio-economic-status schools

	The more effective school (ABC)	The less effective school (XYZ)
Student performance		
Attitude to self	positive	less positive
Attitude to peers	positive	positive
Attitude to teachers	positive	less positive
Attitude to school	positive	less positive
Attitude to learning	positive	less positive
Social satisfaction	satisfied	less satisfied
Intrinsic satisfaction	satisfied	less satisfied
Extrinsic satisfaction	satisfied	not satisfied
Chinese-language achievement	high	low
English-language achievement	high	low
Mathematics achievement	high	low
Curriculum delivery		
Curriculum content	standard/same	standard/same
Teaching methods	teacher-centred	teacher-centred
Extra-curricular activities		
Types of activities	20	14
per cent of students participated	80 per cent	60 per cent
Participation in outside events	20 occasions, 102 prizes	9 occasions, 5 prizes
Classroom climate		
Perceived physical environment	moderately good	poor
Affiliation	close	relatively distant
Competition	moderate	moderate
Involvement	moderate	barely involved
Teacher support	good	moderate
Teacher control	strong	moderate
Rule clarity	clear	moderate
Order and organisation	good	rather weak
Task orientation	good	rather weak
Innovation	good	rather weak
per cent of class time for teaching	around 75 per cent	around 50 per cent
per cent of class time for handling student behavioural problems	less 25 per cent	25 per cent to 49 per cent
Teachers' professional power	dominant	moderate
Teachers' position power	dominant	dominant
Teachers' reward power	weakly displayed	weakly displayed
Teachers' coercive power	weak	relatively stronger
Teachers' personal power	moderate	moderate
Teacher satisfactions and attitudes		
Social satisfaction	moderate	very low
Extrinsic satisfaction	moderate	low
Intrinsic satisfaction	moderately high	very low
Influence satisfaction	moderate	very low
Job commitment	slightly low	low
Feeling of job challenge	moderate	moderate
Feeling of job meaning	moderate	low
Feeling of job responsibility	moderate	moderate

Table 8.2 (cont'd)

	The more effective school (ABC)	The less effective school (XYZ)
Staff relationship		
Intimacy	high	low
Esprit	high	moderately low
Disengagement	low	moderately low
Hindrance	moderately low	high
Principal-teacher relationship	good	good
Principal performance		
Human leadership	moderate	weak
Structural leadership	strong	weak
Political leadership	weak	weak
Symbolic leadership	moderate	weak
Educational leadership	strong	weak
Parental influence		
Parent expectations	slightly high	moderate
Parents association	yes	no
School organisational characteristics		
Formalisation	good	weak
Participation	low	low
Organisation culture	positive-nurturing	negative-helpless
External relations	active	less active
School physical conditions		
Resource inputs from the government	standard, same	standard, same
Location, class size, external environment	unfavourable	favourable
Perceived school environment	satisfactory	poor

these schools. If we believe that extra-curricular activities are also a core part of school education, we can see that the extra-curricular activities in ABC School made a very important contribution but in XYZ School they did not.

In the classrooms of ABC School, the social climate was good, facilitating effective instruction and learning activities. Students had close affiliation and positive competition in learning; showed involvement in learning activities; and felt well supported by their teachers. In the classroom, the teachers had a good command of instructional activities and student concentration; established clear classroom rules for students; and maintained good order and organisation. They were also innovative in their teaching and effective in using class time. They had more professional power, but less coercive power to influence students. The profile of classroom in ABC School was very positive, while that in XYZ School was weak. Consistent with the past studies of classroom climate and impacts, the findings support the importance of classroom climate to educational effectiveness (Knight, 1990; Waxman *et al.*, 1990, 1992; Cheng, 1994a).

Undoubtedly, teachers are the major actors directly influencing the students' learning in school. Their satisfactions and attitudes in school can affect their teaching performance, and thus students' educational outcomes. In the more effective school, ABC, teachers were moderately satisfied with the social relationships with colleagues, the opportunities for professional development and participation in school decision-making, and the school arrangements and fringe benefits. But in XYZ School, teachers were, in general, dissatisfied in nearly every respect. In terms of job attitudes, teachers in ABC School seemed to have a greater sense of meaning in their job than those in XYZ School. The pattern of staff relationships in the two schools was also different. In ABC School, teachers had closer relationships with colleagues and their team spirit was higher. They felt less disengaged and less burdened by unnecessary work. In contrast, the social relationships in XYZ School were poor and teachers' team morale was low. Teachers felt strongly burdened by a meaningless workload. The findings support the importance of staff satisfaction, job attitudes and social relationships to school performance.

The principal's leadership in the more effective school, ABC, was clearly stronger, particularly in the structural and educational aspects, when compared with that in the less effective school, XYZ. In general, the findings are consistent with the leadership literature (Sergiovanni, 1994; Bolman and Deal, 1991; Cheng, 1994b; Hallinger and Murphy, 1987; Chan and Cheng, 1993). However, the political leadership of both more effective and less effective schools was weak. This might be different from the findings obtained in the Western countries. In Hong Kong, principals, in general, traditionally have a very strong formal authority to suppress potential conflicts and different opinions from staff; in addition, teachers tend to be more patient and compliant. It is perhaps not surprising that the principals of these two schools may not need to build any coalitions and exercise political tactics to handle school conflicts and diverse interests. The popular belief of the critical contribution of strong leadership to school effectiveness has been supported in this study.

Parallel to the findings about the principal's structural leadership, the functioning of the more effective school, ABC, was formalised with clear school policies, procedures and working plans. This helped the school members to know clearly what they should do, and how it should be done. ABC School also had a stronger school culture that could shape and maintain school members' working morale, values and beliefs about education. But the less effective school, XYZ, lacked systematic policies and plans to guide school members' work, and the school has developed an atmosphere of helplessness. This phenomenon was probably due to the very weak leadership of the school principal. It is interesting to note that teacher participation in school decision-making was low in both the more effective and less effective school. It seems that teacher participation in decision-making might not be as important in predicting school effectiveness in the Hong Kong context. This may need further exploration.

These two case studies suggest that schools can make a significant difference in student performance. Even though the input resources or the physical environments may be similar, or even less favourable, a school can produce better educational outcomes through the appropriate internal school processes and efforts of school members. The profiles of the more effective and the less effective schools identified in this study can provide an useful pattern to aid understanding of school processes and improve practice. Hopefully, these findings can contribute to the further research on school effectiveness and school improvement, in both local and international contexts.

9 Europe – the Netherlands

Frans Swint and Bert Creemers

Introduction/context

The Netherlands is a small European country, with an economy historically based mostly on agriculture and trade. The agricultural tradition has given way to an economy which is now based largely on service industries. The affluent status of the country created a well-resourced educational system, which currently takes about 15 per cent of the annual government budget.

Historically, the main religious groups in the Netherlands lived peacefully alongside each other. Although the population consists of substantial Catholic, Protestant and non-denominational groups, these groups hardly interacted. Each group had its own social circle of clubs, political parties, schools and broadcasting organisations. This division in social circles, or pillars as they are called, created a stable society. The pillarisation has been in place for centuries, and only began to decline from the 1960s onwards. Together with the philosophy that schools have to be in the neighbourhood where the child lives, it sets a background for an educational system with comparatively small schools. Since every denominational group in a community or neighbourhood needed its own schools, one would find a few small schools in most villages, instead of one big one.

We analyse the schools in this Netherlands case study looking at all of the relevant dimensions for each school, rather than looking at the schools grouped under each dimension as in the case studies so far reported.

The low-socio-economic-status schools

Winter: the more effective school

General characteristics

The neighbourhood in which the school was located consisted of mostly three-storey buildings, built in times when efficiency was given priority over aesthetics. This neighbourhood predominantly housed people working as labourers in factories and members of ethnic minorities. The school was across the street from a small shopping centre. It looked quite small from the outside as it was only one-storey high. Having crossed the street, one came to the metal fence surrounding the playground, with the paved playground surrounding the school. The part at the front was for the higher grades, and the part to the left of the school was for the lower grades, with the entire playground surrounded by a fence.

When one entered the school during the morning hours one noticed the silence in the entire building. Walking around the corridors, there was barely a sound. Glimpsing through the high windows which separated the corridors from the classrooms, one saw the students bent over their desks, doing some silent seatwork. Below the windows were the hooks on which the students hung their jackets, with the shoes of the students in a perfect line below the jackets. The narrow corridors filled with cheerful sounds at the start of breaks, or when the school day ended.

Next to the entrance was a small office for the principal. This office provided room for a desk and two chairs, with about two square metres left over. The staffroom was in the centre of the school, with the classrooms around it. It held a rectangular meeting table which could seat all nine teachers during team meetings. One corner had a seating arrangement of two sofas in the style of a Dutch living room in the 1950s.

In addition, the school had eight classrooms and an auditorium about twice the size of a classroom. The auditorium doubled as the school library with the collection of books showing signs of use. In one corridor, some tables were set aside, this corner served as the place for the students who stayed over during the lunch hour.

The school served about 165 students, which was slightly below the Dutch average (the average being 175). About 35 per cent of the students belonged to ethnic minorities, originating from a huge variety of nations. The principal described the students as coming from families with many problems. As a consequence 'the school had a difficult population'. The school had a teaching staff of eight teachers, a principal and two part-time teachers for teaching native languages to Turkish and Spanish students.

A day in the life of a child

The school opened for the pupils at 8.25. The children were expected to walk to their classrooms as soon as they entered the school grounds. In the corridor they took off their coats and shoes and put their slippers on. These slippers reduced the noise when students walked around. After entering the classroom, students picked up some assignment to fill the time until the lessons actually started, this could be silent reading or doing work on individual projects. Teachers walked around and urged students to start doing something.

Actual teaching started at 8.30. Mrs Wils, the teacher of the grade 5 class, gathered the students into a circle at the side of the classroom and said 'Good morning'. The class responded in unison. Next, Mrs Wils read the names of the students one by one. When Rachel, a girl of average height with long black hair, was called she said 'Good morning, Mrs Wils', as all her classmates did. A student tried to say 'Good morning, Señorita' in Spanish and smiled when he succeeded. Later on, in the interview, Mrs Wils revealed that she did not like this routine, but found it important that the students should learn some politeness.

The teacher then started with reading a story about an island inhabited by witches, pausing to ask questions. The students were engrossed by the story. Rachel listened, but did not know the answers to the questions. She asked a question about the story, to which Mrs Wils responded when no other student could answer. After this reading, the students quietly returned to their desks.

Then started a Dutch-language lesson. Mrs Wils read a sound and the students then had to make words which had these sounds in them. Rachel raised her hand with every sound as a sign that she knew an answer. Like most students, she was called a few times. The next exercise followed at high speed, in which students had to make words plural. During this whole-class teaching Mrs Wils handed out workbooks. The second part of the lesson was devoted to individual seatwork. The students completed the exercises which were performed orally in their workbooks. The class was silent during this part of the lesson.

During this period of individual work, Mrs Wils walked around to check on individual students' work. She occasionally made a remark for students to be silent or to work on. When Rachel finished her work, she picked up an extra task without needing instruction to do so. A classmate sat at a table in the back of the classroom listening to a tape, while reading along in a book. This was the listening corner of the class and all students were expected to do this one by one.

Mrs Wils in the meantime helped Amin. He had recently come from Turkey and did not speak Dutch yet. Up until then, he had only copied the movements of the class. When the class sat in a circle, he sat with them. When the class moved to their desks, he too went back to his place. He did not show understanding of what was said or explained, although he was supposed to try. His exercises were from a special workbook, aimed at quickly learning Dutch words which were important in class, like desk, chair, pen, workbook and teacher. Mrs Wils explained what she wanted him to do, occasionally using another student as interpreter. That week, she would go easy to give him time to adapt to his new environment. The following week the demands would be made firmer, and the week after that more would be asked. Amin worked on and his face brightened when he was allowed to play a game on the computer at the end of the day.

The next lesson was a mathematics lesson. Mrs Wils again did some exercises with the whole class. Next, the students worked for themselves. This pattern continued during the other lessons, as with the first. All lessons started with a few exercises with the whole class or discussion based on new information from a textbook, followed by a period of silent individual work. During whole-class teaching periods, the students were attentive and eager to give answers. They raised their hands to indicate that they wanted to respond, some even when they did not know the answers. During seatwork they were quiet and continued working without much help or prompting from their teacher.

At 10.05 the students sat in a circle again and had a sandwich, some fruit and drinks that they had brought from home. This eating together, which could be found in many primary schools, was partly to ensure that all students had something to eat during the morning. At about 10.15, the students went outside to play. A colleague of Mrs Wils was outside on guard duty today, thus Mrs Wils went to the staffroom to have coffee with her colleagues. The outside guard kept an eye on her class during the break.

After the twenty-minute break, the teachers gathered their classes on the playground to make sure that they walked in an orderly way to the classrooms. The class continued with a writing lesson. Mrs Wils directed the class through a series of words which had to be written. The final lesson of the morning was a reading lesson. The students read two pages for themselves, after which Mrs Wils asked questions. Then, Rachel had a turn to read aloud. When her classmates heard mistakes in her reading, they raised their hands. This kept everyone involved during an activity which would otherwise have involved only one student. After a few other reading turns, the students again read two pages for themselves. They then had to ask Mrs Wils questions about the text and say whether she had answered them correctly. Again, turns were given for reading and Mrs Wils noted the progress of the readers. To close the lesson, the students read the entire text aloud, with each student reading one sentence. The order in which the students had to read was routine: no one was unsure when to read or at which point in the text the class was at. At 12.00, the children went home for lunch. Of the entire school, about ten students stayed during the lunch break, eating lunches which they had brought from home.

The school opened again at 13.15. The students walked straight to their classes when they entered the school grounds. Mr Berends, the teacher of the adjourning classroom monitored whether the students started doing assignments instead of talking. Most days, the majority of students were indeed doing some task. Mrs Wils helped students to cross the street in front of the school. At 13.30 the lessons started again.

During the afternoon, three Spanish students were not present as they had a Spanish lesson. In the afternoon, the rest of the class moved to the auditorium where they watched a videoed episode from a series about nature. Rachel watched silently. Once she whispered something to Mrs Wils, who answered. After returning to the classroom, Mrs Wils asked questions about the episode. The geography lesson followed, in the same pattern as morning lessons: whole-class discussion based on an episode read in the textbook, followed by individual exercises. The last lesson of the day was a drawing lesson. During this lesson, Mrs Wils rearranged the places the students had in class. She called the names of the students who had to change places and these two students quietly took their belongings and swapped seats. This change of layout was performed every six weeks, to promote the integration of the various groups and races in class. Although not aware of the reason, the students liked to sit next to a variety of classmates, and when the time for changes came, they reminded Mrs Wils to make them. The day ended with the students sitting in a circle again, where they had an opportunity to tell the class about hobbies or things they did at home. On this day a girl played on a flute that she had brought from home. This lasted about ten minutes. At 15.30 the students went home.

Teachers' teaching style

Mrs Wils had a highly academic, focused style of teaching. Most teaching was whole-class orientated, with all students working on the same subject at the same time. Exercises were the same for the whole class. The exception was cases such as Amin's, whose Dutch knowledge was not as yet sufficient to keep up with the class.

One other exception occurred during a mathematics lesson. In the previous lesson, some students had not mastered the material covered. Mrs Wils gathered these students into one group and set the other students on other mathematics exercises. In the extra instruction group, she did examples of sums where ones had to be substituted by tens, like adding $25 + 28$. The first sum, she counted aloud with the students. Next, she had the students count aloud. When one girl continued counting after 53 when the others had already stopped, Mrs Wils repeated the sum with her. By doing more examples in this small group, she hoped that these students would catch up with their classmates.

Because the routines were so well known, no statement of rules was made during academic time. Some mornings when the class sat in a circle, Mrs Wils reminded the students about what went wrong the day before, and repeated how she liked the class to work. Sometimes, remarks like 'Did I give permission to talk?' were made during seatwork or transitions between tasks. Academic time was devoted to the subject assigned to it and side-tracking was never allowed. Mrs Wils was friendly to the students. When students asked more socially orientated questions, she gave a friendly and appropriate answer.

The teaching pattern found in this class could be found in all other classes in the school. Teaching was traditional and whole-class orientated. In Mr Berends's class, the routine was also clearly evident. Like Mrs Wils, he mostly taught the whole class and took care that students kept up with the work. During one school day, he was especially busy walking around and putting students whose attention wandered back to work. Later on he explained that the students had just had their annual school trip, which had been a very nice day, but he was now trying to get some work done in the small amount of time which was still left until the holidays.

Although the teachers experimented with other forms of teaching, for example small-group work, the staff seemed to be most comfortable with the traditional way of teaching. All staff members observed showed a proficiency in asking questions in such a way that all students remained involved during the lesson. During these periods, students seemed eager to respond. Lessons promoted involvement of all students.

The curriculum

The subjects taught in grade 5 were mathematics, geography, reading, writing, Dutch language, traffic, physical exercise, drawing, handicrafts and singing. In the higher grades, history, biology and English were added to the curriculum. Because of the 'freedom of education' described earlier, no method was prescribed for the school. The school had bought its methods from commercial publishers. These subject fields are the subjects taught in all primary schools.

In this school each subject was taught separately. All teaching followed the same general lines: some new content was presented to the students, either by explanation by the teacher or by reading a part from the textbook. Content was presented interactively, with the teacher frequently asking questions and the students responding. After the presentation, assignments were given. Everyone had to work individually on the assignments and there were extra tasks for fast-working students. The students did not get homework.

In grade 3 mathematics involved counting and doing sums with numbers up to 20; in grade 4, mathematics involved addition and subtraction with numbers up to 100 and the multiplication tables 1–5 and 10; grade 5 covered addition and subtraction with numbers up to 1,000, multiplication tables 1–10, and division. Clock reading and computing with money started in grade 4. In the higher grades the applications were covered in more detail and students learnt to work with decimal numbers (grade 6), long division, fractions (grade 6), percentages and measures (grade 7), and interest and rounding (grade 8). Most mathematics was taught whole-class. Although different mathematics methods made different nuances in their presentation, most covered the material in approximately this order in these grades.

The headteacher/principal

The principal of the school was Mrs Zandstra, who has been at the school for about forty years. During this time, she had seen the school change from a purely Dutch boys' school, to a primary school serving students of both sexes and many different nationalities. She had been principal for the last eleven years. Her basic attitude towards the school could be illustrated by her statements that 'Children do not come here to have fun' and 'Playing is allowed, but work comes first'. This seemed to set a culture that ran through the entire school.

A central aspect of this culture was an emphasis on quietness in the school building during academic time. To achieve this, the children came in one by one before school time and were always accompanied by the teachers when the whole class walked to other rooms. Strict rules for silence during work were maintained by all teachers.

Dutch teachers occasionally had a day off. During these days, Mrs Zandstra covered the class. This way, she was able to teach every class a few times a year. She thus knew all of the students at the school, and she also knew where the weak points of her teaching staff were, by checking unsatisfactory student progress, and could thus make suggestions for improvement.

Like most Dutch schools the important decisions were made by the entire team. Decisions about new methods, curriculum and the organisation of the school were prepared by a few teachers and then discussed in the staff meetings. The staff decided together about what was to be done. The management functions of the principal were primarily in coordinating the team and the school, guarding the budget and doing administration ('paperwork and those stupid plans we have to make for the government').

School expectations of pupils

All expectations of the school were implicit. Although no statements of expectations were made to students, they were clearly expected to work as hard as they could. Being lazy during the school day was forbidden; the teachers promptly put them back to work. During festivities, the students sang in their school song: 'It is learning, working and sweating', and 'The school is strong, by training and work'.

Decisions on rewards and sanctions were made by the classroom teachers. There was no school-based reward system. Rewards were mostly the feedback a student gets about the quality of the school work. There were no tokens or other material rewards for good work. Sanctions were given only when misbehaviour occurred, which was very infrequent. The kind of sanction depended on the teacher, though physical punishment is illegal in the Netherlands. Most commonly used sanctions included keeping the students for a short period after school time, making discipline speeches or assigning some mundane, additional work.

Student work was checked by the teacher every day. The school also had a school-wide assessment system. All students from grade 3 upwards were tested three times a year on mathematics and Dutch language. The results were compared with national norms. In the lower grades, students who were falling behind were given extra lessons. These lessons took place for half an hour at the end of the morning period. In the classroom there were about four students during this time, each busy with his or her own task. The supervising teacher read aloud with a student who had reading difficulties or guided a student through some difficult mathematics exercises.

Spring: the less effective school

General characteristics

This school was located in a low socio-economic-status neighbourhood. The houses around the school were small and old. Many had the front door opening directly on to the pavement, instead of the small garden which usually separated the pavement from the windows of the living room. The neighbourhood housed many people who were unemployed and many ethnic minorities. Stories about the students' families were regularly heard around school. These were stories about violence, fights in bars, police arrests of acquaintances and family problems. While students in other schools rushed home when the day was over, students here hung around before going home. According to one of the teachers, 'They do not have anything there to go back to'.

From a distance the school looked beautiful. It was located next to a wide green field and had a paved school yard all around it. From the outside all classrooms looked like small houses on their own. In the middle these classrooms were linked by a central hall, which had a small stage and an area for handicrafts. Windows marked the division between the classrooms and the central hall. There was a separate wing for the classrooms of the lower grades. In addition, the school had some small rooms which served as an office for the principal, for teaching native languages to Turkish students and for counselling of individual students. The building was in a good condition and looked quite attractive.

The school served about 240 students. This number created a funding allowance for eleven teaching jobs, which were shared by eighteen people. The work schedule of these teachers was divided according to clock hours rather than subject-matter hours. Thus the person assigned to a class at a certain time would teach whichever subject the class had timetabled for that period. During one writing lesson this resulted in a teacher whose time was up, going home, saying to the students: 'Tell Mrs Bergsma to continue with the word cat.' There was one part-time teacher responsible for teaching Turkish language. The school also had some support staff from a local unemployment project. These people worked on the maintenance of the building and assisted with the administration of the school.

A day in the life of a child

When one entered the school ground at 8.10, it was not unusual to see the first few students hanging around and waiting outside for school to start. Inside the building, staff members gathered around the tables set in a circle in the central hall. It was time for the first coffee and social chat about what they did the previous day. At 8.30 the school bell rang and the students streamed into the hall. The teachers stood up and urged students to enter their classrooms.

The school day in the lower grades started, as in most schools in the country, with a period during which students were allowed to tell what they had done the day before. The stories varied from talking about new toys, to fights in the neighbourhood. During these stories, the students sat, uninterested, in their chairs.

When Mrs Terlet, the grade 4 teacher, decided that she wanted to start the first lesson, some students shouted suggestions through the classroom. Some liked to do language, others preferred writing. A girl shouted that she had been bitten by a horse. The first lesson was mathematics, and Mrs Terlet began by doing an exercise with the whole class. There were two machines. One machine does + 4, the other does + 2. What would be the total result of these machines? A girl shouted 12 a few times, due to the fact that the teacher has just written + 2, + 4 and + 6 on the blackboard. Mrs Terlet explained the principle. Next question: at one bus stop 2 people enter the bus, at the next stop 1 leaves. Are there now more or less people in the bus than at the beginning? A girl suggested more, but does not know why. Mrs Terlet started a game in which she played the bus driver. She walked through the classroom and the students played the passengers. The number of students entering and leaving the bus served as a basis to demonstrate the assignments. Suggestions for answers were shouted through the classroom. For the next task, a girl was allowed to play bus driver. This led to + 4 and − 2 passengers. A student suggested + 6, because this was the answer to the previous question. Next, comparable sums had to be made in the student workbooks. A few students shouted 'easy', across the classroom. In response to the question asking what the net result would be of + 2 and − 3, a boy shouted 'very easy'. He had a turn and suggested zero. The lesson continued in this way. Some students seemed to understand the concepts which were being taught, while others continued to make mistakes in their work.

Next, there was a short language lesson. The students had to copy words, which they did silently. Just before the break, Mrs Terlet gave a warning not to walk on the ice during the break because it was too thin.

After the break, the first problem to be dealt with was students with wet socks and trousers. The morning lessons continued with another language exercise. Most students worked quietly. Mrs Terlet walked around to check and to make remarks about messy handwriting. At the end of the morning, the class played a game in which a pair of students had to solve a mathematics problem. The student who first answered correctly could then compete against another student.

The pattern of work seemed to vary. In Mrs Wierden's grade 5 class, the students had not appeared eager to start with their mathematics assignments, but during the writing lesson in the previous hour, everything had run smoothly. During mathematics some students just sat behind their desks doing nothing. Mrs Wierden tried to get them to work. Mary, a blond girl, suddenly started to cry. She did not want to do the mathematics assignment because it was too difficult. By the end of the lesson, many students had not done any of the assignments. After the break, the history lesson started with reading an extract from the textbook. Few students were interested. According to Mrs Wierden this was because the subject matter bore no relevance to their daily lives. Some students contributed by name-calling to classmates. Throughout the day, in a corner of the classroom, four students sat together and did the work assigned, unnoticed by their classmates or their teacher.

Teachers' teaching style

There was large variation between and even within teachers, in the ability to get classes started or to get the class moving on through the curriculum. Most of this variation seems to be due to discipline problems. During one day, Mrs Terlet stopped the mathematics lesson. It 'did not go well' on that day, and so there was deemed no point in continuing; however, 'Last Thursday and Friday went well'.

Later in the school year Mrs Wierden repeated rules before every new assignment started. Work was interrupted every now and then because some remarks had to be made about how to behave. Despite these speeches, order was maintained for only very brief periods of time. One could almost wait for the next interruption to occur.

One could hypothesise that the progress of the classes through the curriculum depended, to a great extent, on the students' willingness to comply with the teachers' wishes. This did not mean that the school did not try to create good working conditions. For Mrs Wierden's class, three different programmes to establish order were reported in one school year. One was strict discipline, sending students to the principal after disruptive behaviour, one was a behaviour training project and the other a rewards-based project. Mrs Wierden reported that each programme worked for a few days. When the new element became known to the students, the effect faded away and the programme was discontinued. During the observations, no programme-related teacher behaviour was seen. A complicating factor was that this disruptive class had two teachers, each teaching for a few days a week.

The teaching staff seemed to share the opinion that many of the difficulties in getting academic results were caused by the fact that the students came from deprived families. During the day teachers put great effort into their teaching. There was additional effort in giving extra attention after school time to students who fell behind in the lower grades. All teachers tried to move their classes through the curriculum. On the other hand, during some lessons it was observed that students refused to do academic work, or did not complete all work assigned. This performance did not seem to have any consequences. Probably the situation can be described best by a quotation from Mrs Terlet, who said: 'We do the best we can and see what results come out of the students.' Mrs Wierden remarked: 'The students do not achieve much. That is not surprising when you see where they come from.'

The actual teaching followed the same pattern as the one described within the other schools. A period of interactive whole-class instruction followed by a period of working alone. During teaching time, the teachers showed satisfactory teaching skills. Appropriate questions were asked of the students, effort was spent in posing questions so that new content was made clear and the teachers spent time during individual work on monitoring the students and giving individual feedback. The staff expended effort to create extra learning experiences for the students. During one project year there was a schoolwide food project, with a complete model supermarket built in the school that was used for a lot of activities. The last visit, a hot day in the summer, ended in a water party where teachers soaked the students with the fire equipment.

The curriculum

The school taught the same subjects as the other schools. However, it had brought other methods for teaching these subjects. The school seemed to have made a mistake with the method chosen for teaching mathematics: it did not seem to work for this student population. During observations there were lessons when the students did not appear to master the concepts taught. During a lunch break a teacher was correcting mathematics material – one student with all questions answered wrongly, followed the next student with all questions answered wrongly. Although teachers signalled difficulties with the method, the team was still enthusiastic about the realistic and self-discovering opportunities which the method promised to offer.

During a grade 3 lesson, students were supposed to master the concepts of more than, less than and equal to, as related to >, < and =. This was explained by a picture of a bird eating the largest of two piles of things. During the entire one-hour lesson, the concepts were not used in combination with the symbols. The authors of the method expected the students to discover the way these concepts worked for themselves. As in other lessons, this did not seem to happen during this period. After a one-hour struggle, no student seemed to have achieved mastery in using these symbols in comparisons.

Although the formal curriculum was the same as the curriculum in the other schools, one could question the delivery of the curriculum. The pressure on students to work was low, possibly caused by the lack of adverse consequences experienced for not working. So, there were days when students did not do much work. They sat at their tables and spent most of their time talking or quarrelling with their classmates. When history lessons were boring, no one did them.

Parental involvement

The reported contact with the parents of the students was the same in this school as in the more effective school. Teachers reported good contact with most parents and a lack of interest by other parents. This showed during testing days for the cohort. During these days, substantially more parents brought their children to school and walked them to their class, than on other days.

Most other contacts were teacher-initiated. These were the meetings during which the teacher and the parents discussed the report cards of the students. Most parents showed up for these individual meetings. Some parents showed interest in the school work of their child, others simply did not care.

In contrast to other schools described in this chapter, this school used parents in part of the teaching process. Like many other Dutch schools, this school had 'reading mothers' (in recent years, fathers had also begun to participate in this activity). During some reading lessons, the classes were split into groups of four students and each group read with one parent. The small size of the various reading groups allowed each student to have many turns at reading aloud during such a lesson. The problem experienced by this school was that there were insufficient parents volunteering for this task, and so students from higher grades functioned as assistants for the lower grades.

The headteacher/principal

The principal of this school was Mrs Boersma, who had twenty hours a week to run this school. During a large part of the first ISERP year the school was run by Mrs Koning, a deputy, because the principal was absent. As in the other schools, the main decisions in this school were made by the entire team during team meetings. Mrs Boersma was less visible than the principal of the more effective school. She interacted with her staff before the school day started and during the lunch and coffee breaks. Her leadership could be characterised as displaying interest on a personal basis. When someone had a problem, she talked with him or her during the lunch breaks. During a hard day for Mrs Wierden, she checked that the teacher was taking some time off to get some rest and was not overworking.

Mrs Terlet also seemed to have a large share in the actual running of the school: before the school day started she was always busy arranging practical matters and she seemed to have much knowledge about things that went on in the school. She checked agreements made between teachers and appointments made by visitors. Due to her involvement, the school seemed an organised place where teachers could devote their time to teaching.

The middle-socio-economic-status schools

Summer: the less effective school

General characteristics

This school was located in one of the older neighbourhoods, surrounded by small houses. The layout of the streets indicated that few cars were in existence when the neighbourhood was built. Turning the corner, one saw the monumental school building. Built in the 1920s, with two storeys, it stood like a central mark in the neighbourhood. In front of the school, there was a small space for climbing equipment; the large, square, paved playground was at the back.

Entering the school one saw the broad stone staircase in the central hall. The classrooms of the higher grades were on the top floor, the classrooms of the lower grades were on the ground floor. There were two classrooms at each side of the staircase on each floor. The school had a staffroom on one side of the building, which was also used as the principal's office, and a small gymnasium on the other side. The school also had a small kitchen.

The neighbourhood had gone through changes that were visible in the school. In the higher grades there were only students from Dutch working-class parents, while the lower grades included more ethnic minorities. In total the school served 135 students. There was a formal teaching staff of 5.5 and an actual teaching staff of 7. Most teachers worked part-time.

A day in the life of a child

The day in the school started in the small kitchen. Before school began the teachers walked in and out to greet one another and chat. In the corridors, last-minute improvisations were made for absent teachers. The first students entered the school building and walked around the corridors. At 8.30 the school bell rang and teachers walked to their classrooms. By that time most students had gathered in their classrooms. In the lower grades, the day started with students telling the class what they did yesterday after school time. There was discussion about toys and games that they played. In the higher grades these conversations were replaced by reading and discussion of a story from the Bible.

After these talks, Mrs Wubbels, the fourth grade teacher, arranged some practical matters. Today, she made an inventory of clothes which students had brought from home. There were sports clothes and someone had brought a pair of pyjamas. Mrs Wubbels showed the clothes and students explained the function of each item. The clothes hung all over the classroom, as a preparation for the fashion show. The discussion in class was about clothes which people in other cultures wear. A girl knew that people in Amsterdam wore torn-apart clothes. Next the teacher talked about tailors and showed one of their tools, a measuring tape. Mrs Wubbels measured one of the students and asked him how many centimetres he wanted to grow. This demonstration smoothly changed into the mathematics lesson. After the break, Mrs Wubbels wrote 'Theclothesarewashed' on the blackboard. Students had to divide this sentence into separate words. In the workbook for the language lesson there was an exercise which had the same assignment. After the introduction, Mrs Wubbels urged Johnny to get up from below his table and start work.

During the first part of the morning break, students consumed food and drinks which they had brought from home and walked around the classroom to chat and play games. The atmosphere in the class was relaxed. In a corner, some students wrote cards with descriptions to attach to the clothes. The second part of the morning break was spent outside in the playground. During this time, the teachers gathered in the kitchen for coffee and a chat. Given the number of part-timers, one met different faces, with new stories every day. Now and then a pupil from the kindergarten grades peeped in to watch their teachers or the visitors. These pupils were allowed to spend their break time in the corridors of the school. These corridors were thus inhabited by small humans strolling around with toys or just looking for their teachers. The break was scheduled for half an hour or until the time the teacher who had outside guard duty rang the school bell.

The grade 5 class of Mrs Jansen had a mathematics lesson. The teacher had led them through some questions and then the individual work period had started. In a corner of the classroom sat Peter, busy making a drawing. He had already completed the assignments and thus waited for the next lesson. Peter had started this drawing about half way through the language lesson earlier in the morning. His assignments for language were completed early too. In fact, during most lessons, the fact that Peter was drawing would not necessarily suggest that it was the drawing lesson.

In another corner of the classroom, Mariel, Wendy and Priscilla were busy correcting their work. The teacher gave them the book with the answering key for today's assignment. The students corrected their work themselves. According to the principal, this was done in order to teach students that they can learn from their mistakes. The girls took a pragmatic approach: they replaced their mistakes with the answer from the book and then assigned themselves high grades.

Teachers' teaching style

All teachers had a friendly way of interacting with the students. Most students seemed to like their teachers. There was no shouting at students and discipline remarks were made without raising voices. The style of teaching was traditional: working on exercises by asking individual students questions and assigning individual seatwork. The style of interaction created a warm atmosphere which gave the feeling more of being in a family than in a place of work. Although teachers reported to place firm demands on students, the amount of work actually demanded during school days could be easily achieved. A count during one morning revealed a total workload of six long addition sums and writing ten sentences.

There were notable differences in the teachers' capacity to maintain order. The same class worked well with one teacher, but showed many discipline problems with another. While students whispered during the individual work periods in Mrs Wubbels's class, they talked through most of the school day when a replacement teacher took over.

Mrs Jennings taught some of the classes, for part of the week. On one day, she began by changing the seating arrangements of the class. The seating arrangements had to be decided democratically, and had thus not been completed the previous day. During this lesson they started again. When the goal of the period was clear, the students started moving their desks around without waiting for further instruction. This resulted in several minutes of movement without clear purpose. During later periods, more discipline problems arose. Mrs Jennings started to write names on the blackboard of students who misbehaved. As the lesson continued, the list of names grew longer and longer. After the lesson, only a few of the named students stayed for a one-minute speech; most went home without waiting. This misbehaviour did not seem to have any further consequences for any of the students.

The headteacher/principal

The school had a full-time principal, Mr Johnson, during the first year of the research project, who took a job in special education after that year. As the school had by then become involved in a merger with another school, it was decided not to fill the principal position in this school again. Until the merger was completed, the school shared the principal of the school it would merge with, and Mr Smith, the grade 8 teacher, functioned as deputy principal.

When one entered the school building during the first year, Mr Johnson was always busy arranging some practical matter. One day he repaired the photocopier, another day he showed an unwanted salesman the way out. His handling of these activities allowed the teachers to concentrate on teaching. He was well liked by his entire team and the school's community. A year after he left, he was referred to as a good example for the new leaders.

During the interview Mr Johnson described having changed the school from an organisation with teachers who depended on the principal for everything, into a school with a more assertive team. Since then, the team had shared the decision-making in all important respects. He explained that his main focus was on creating a good pedagogical climate in the school. The main idea was that this climate was necessary to create the atmosphere required for learning. In addition, it was hoped that this climate, with its associated ways of behaving, would filter into the neighbourhood of the school. An important aspect of this climate was adapting the education to the needs of the individual student. Mr Johnson stated firmly that the regular educational system could learn much from special education in this regard.

The year after Mr Johnson left, the school met problems. The organisation of the school seemed to become less structured. During many school days last-minute problems had to be solved by improvisation, for example in the case of absence of teachers. Although the main focus, pedagogical climate, remained very well established, the school had lost a central person. In addition, the forthcoming merger created uncertainty.

School image

The school was well centred in the neighbourhood. Mr Johnson noted that before his arrival, parents had gossiped about the school and that this gossip had remained outside the school building. He reported to have changed this: instead, when parents started to talk about the school, he invited them in to see what was actually happening. This way, he tried to fight prejudice from parents, for example regarding the growing number of students from ethnic minorities.

After the departure of Mr Johnson, one teacher indicated that this pattern of outside gossip was emerging again. Parents started to talk about the school again on the street in front of the school. This time, the stories stayed outside. The stories were about the quality of the school, as the parents believed that it was declining, the rise of the number of ethnic minorities and the fact that parents felt that there would be negative results from their child being in a combination grade. These stories also started to have consequences. At the end of the second project year, teachers were frustrated, complaining about the fact that more and more parents were withdrawing their children from the school.

Autumn: the more effective school

General characteristics

This school was located in a village in the countryside. Although the church was still in its traditional place in the centre of the village, the village looked more like a neighbourhood in a city. A substantial proportion of the inhabitants did not make a living on the land, but instead travelled daily to nearby places for work. The characteristics of this community could be found in the school: despite being a village school, the school did not attract a typical rural population. Most students came from middle-class families. This resulted in classes with well-dressed, well-behaved students, who showed a knowledge of the Bible which pleasantly surprised their teacher.

The school was housed in a modern, recently renovated building. The design showed architectural skill in optimising the available space, creating much free space in a functionally designed building. In the centre of the school was the photocopier room, which was used a lot for creating worksheets. The classrooms provided ample space and new furniture. The staffroom was the largest of all of the schools visited and the principal's office could compete with managers' offices in any commercial organisation. At the back of the building was a large playground.

The school had a teaching staff of 10 teachers and 247 students. In past years, these students came from a wide area around the village, because it was the only Catholic school around. Over time a change has taken place and now most students came from the village itself. All students came from lower-middle-class to middle-class families. Because more and more students were in the 1.00 category instead of 1.25 category the school received funding for fewer and fewer teaching hours. This was the staff's greatest concern, because they saw colleagues disappear, which greatly weakened their own sense of job security. The school had the traditional division of labour, with females teaching in the lower grades and males teaching in the higher grades.

A day in the life of a child

Before school started the students played outside in the playground at the back of the school. The teachers came in one by one. Conversation between staff members in this school were mostly about politics and news. New educational policies were discussed and commented upon. There was also an interest in the society at large.

As the school bell rang, the students lined up in pairs. An area was marked on the playground, for each class, indicating where to gather. Teachers signalled the order in which groups were allowed to enter. Inside the building, other teachers supervised to see that there was no running. All students walked to their classroom in an orderly way and went to their tables. In most classes, tables were set in rows facing the blackboard in front. In some classes these tables were set completely aside with an open space around each table. The day began with a short prayer, recited in unison.

Mr Remmers, the grade 4 teacher, started the day with a short dictation. He read a sentence, after which the class repeated the sentence together. Signalled by Mr Remmers, the students wrote the sentence. After the dictation, a new series of words was copied from the blackboard to be learned for the following week.

Next, the mathematics lesson started. Mr Remmers walked through the classroom row by row, giving every student a turn to answer a sum from the 2× multiplication table. A boy who could not answer his question had to recite the entire table. Next, the class recited the 5× multiplication table. Mr Remmers then walked around asking individual students to do sums, ensuring that everyone had a turn. Students who were not called also stayed engaged during these tasks, watching their classmates. The second part of the lesson was spent doing addition problems from workbooks. During these tasks the students worked silently. The last part of the lesson was spent practising clock reading. Mr Remmers placed a clock in front of the class and gave students turns to read the time. Almost all students had their answers correct. After the morning break, the mathematics lesson continued with individual assignments. During this part of the lesson the students worked silently again. The occasional whispers were almost unnoticeable.

The next lesson of the morning was biology. This was taught by watching an episode from a schools television series. The students were attentive and responded actively when Mr Remmers asked questions afterwards. The last lesson of the morning was singing. Again, all students were involved and enjoyed the lesson.

In all, the class, consisting mostly of girls, was a sociable class. Students got along well together and there were no signs of conflict. The students cheered classmates who achieved good results and helped each other out when someone occasionally did not know how to solve a problem. There was some soft whispering during some lessons. Mr Remmers remarked that it was a noisy class. The noise level considered disturbing here was below the noise level considered acceptable in many other schools.

Teachers' teaching style

The teaching in this school was highly traditional. Because most teachers had been working in the school for one or two decades, the patterns were thoroughly set. All teaching took the form of whole-class teaching followed by individual assignments. All teachers had a firm routine in working according to this format and students were used to it.

Mr Bakker taught a grade 5/6 combination. He had split up the room with grade 6 sitting near the windows and grade 5 sitting near the door, with a separate teacher's desk in front of each grade group. Mr Bakker assigned some work to grade 6 and started teaching grade 5. He stood behind the grade 5 teacher's desk and conducted the group through the lesson with a thorough question and answer sequence. To achieve this, he occasionally glanced at the teacher manual which was open on the desk. Next, he assigned some seatwork to grade 5. He then walked to the grade 6 teacher's desk, from behind which he taught the grade 6 group interactively. Later on, he walked again to the other teacher desk to teach grade 5. One had the impression of having two rooms in one class.

Mr Zandstra taught his grade 4/5 class from behind his desk which was centred in the middle of the room in front of the blackboard. In contrast with the classes of his colleagues, the students were seated in groups of four or five. The day began with assigning an amount of work to the class. This work consisted of language lessons and mathematics, which took a few hours to complete. While the students worked, Mr Zandstra watched them from behind his desk and corrected them. Sometimes he interrupted the students to teach interactively with one group. Students with problems walked to the teacher's desk and got adequate and quick assistance. The atmosphere was one of an office where the silent workers were supervised by their direct chief. The pattern worked: while the code in most primary schools was to finish one book in each grade, the grade 5 group succeeded in finishing 1.5 books in the year. During the last phase of the morning, there was a lesson for the whole class during which a girl described a book that she had read. Mr Zandstra contributed to this period by telling an anecdote, which was enjoyed by the students.

During one lesson, Mr Bakker taught the students about the function of the rainbow in the story of Noah in the Bible. This was done in an interactive style, in which the students contributed their own knowledge. When one student began talking about the gold to be found at the foot of the rainbow (which was clearly not part of the teacher manual) Mr Bakker showed some confusion and changed the subject.

The headteacher/principal

The principal, Mr Konings, had served for a long time in the school. During the interview he focused on the changes that he had seen over the years in the village, and the way that these changes had affected the school. These changes seemed to concentrate on the larger influence of the city on village life. This could be noted in different social patterns (his status in the village had declined, for example) and the fact that the school had been confronted with different behaviour problems over the last few years.

Mr Konings was well informed about the school and its catchment area. He also knew which problems he wanted to tackle during the coming years. However, he predicted that changes would be complicated by the fact that his team was 'getting older'. Despite this fact, he was open to new ideas in the educational community and tried to persuade his team to adopt some of these ideas. The new projects he talked about focused on student social problems, which traditionally had not been considered part of the school's task, such as teasing or fear of going to school. He said that he wanted to tackle these problems in the coming years, but that it would be necessary to get the team on one line. He had high hopes that this would succeed.

Because of the experience of the staff, it was hard to assess the degree of explicit leadership involved here. The school ran smoothly, and gave the impression that little leadership was necessary. The team met once a month to discuss practical matters and every week to discuss problems with individual students. A remarkable event was that

Mr Konings walked into the staffroom one day during the morning break and said 'Boys, we have to go to work'. Everyone directly rose to their feet and went to their classroom.

School goals

The goals described by Mr Konings were to give everyone a basis for continuation at his/her own level of secondary education, to postpone referrals of special needs students for as long as possible and to watch and protect their social-emotional development.

The first goal was a goal described by most principals of Dutch primary schools. The educational process is aimed at this goal. Mr Konings explained that in the higher grades the school began the division in levels of achievement. This division set the different educational routes that would be followed by students in their secondary education, when they left the school.

The second goal was a consequence of the fact that the school was located in a village. When referral to special education was necessary the student had to go to another village. This brought extra problems: the student had a long journey to school every day and the student became separated from the rest of the community. Because of these problems, the school tried to keep the students for as long as possible.

The third goal was a consequence of the changing living patterns in the village. The village was now more orientated towards city culture. Because of these changes, the school was now more often confronted by pedagogical problems. The principal stated that he was busy organising an approach that would teach the teachers how to handle problems with individual students. He hoped that this would succeed in the coming years.

An interesting point to note is that Mr Konings was the only principal who, when asked, said that he did not have an image of an ideal school. He remarked that working towards such an ideal would mean frustration and a constant change of ideas.

Conclusions for Netherlands schools

Reading across the columns Table 9.1 presents an overall picture of the four schools described. The more effective low-SES school presents a picture of a school serving a disadvantaged population with an emphasis on success in academic achievement. Therefore, the teaching staff created structure and set routines. The less effective low-SES school showed more variance in daily patterns. Students controlled the speed during some parts of the day and teachers tried to maintain discipline, in which they did not always succeed. The less effective middle-SES school could be characterised by aspects related to the culture of the school. The school created a friendly atmosphere in which it tried to stimulate its pupils to learn. The more effective middle-SES school had created a solid and well-established routine devoted to work.

In the dimensions which were directly determined by government, few differences could be expected. Given the laws regarding funding and facilities, all schools were comparable in these aspects. The only notable exception was the less effective middle-SES school, which used parent contributions to fund some of its teaching hours. However, the amount actually charged to the parents was not enough to fund a

Table 9.1 Summary of differences between lower-SES and middle-SES schools across the twelve dimensions

Dimension of contrast	More effective low-SES (Winter)	Less effective low-SES (Spring)	More effective middle-SES (Autumn)	Less effective middle-SES (Summer)
General characteristics of the school	Adequate facilities Low-SES/ethnic minority population 165 students, 8 teachers	Adequate facilities Low-SES/ethnic minority population 240 students, 11 teachers	Adequate facilities Middle-class population 247 students, 10 teachers	Adequate facilities Mostly working-class population 135 students, 5.5 teachers
A day in the life of a child	Highly structured school day Consistency of daily patterns between/within classes Students work silently most of the day Strictly followed outlines Outside problems stay out of classes	Variance in daily patterns between/within classes Openly enthusiastic student population Occasional discipline problems Outside problems occasionally show	Perfectly established routines Day devoted to academic work Hardly any interaction between students during lessons	School day is more easy-going Occasional free time left over Social processes during academic work Teachers very friendly towards students
Teachers' teaching style	Whole-class/individual work teaching pattern Acceptable teaching skills exhibited by all teachers Order in all classes Some attempt at new ways of teaching	Whole-class/individual work teaching pattern Acceptable teaching skills exhibited by all teachers Between teacher differences in capacity to maintain order	Whole-class/individual work teaching pattern Acceptable teaching skills exhibited by all teachers Order throughout school Teaching closely follows methods	Whole-class/individual work teaching pattern Acceptable teaching skills exhibited by all teachers Between-teacher differences in capacity to maintain order Some flexibility in teaching
The curriculum	Traditional curriculum covered Speed of school day controlled by teachers	Traditional curriculum covered Speed of school day controlled by students Mathematics method does not fit with student population Native languages taught during hours for Dutch language	Traditional curriculum covered Relatively long maths and language lessons	Traditional curriculum covered Time left devoted to drawing

Table 9.1 (cont'd)

Dimension of contrast	More effective low-SES (Winter)	Less effective low-SES (Spring)	More effective middle-SES (Autumn)	Less effective middle-SES (Summer)
The influence of parents	Occasional contact with parents	Parents assist with reading lessons	Occasional contact with parents	Frequent contact with parents
The principal	Team-based decision-making Principal function primarily administrative Very outspoken principal	Team-based decision-making Principal function primarily administrative	Team-based decision-making Principal function primarily administrative Well-established school structure	Team-based decision-making Principal function primarily administrative School structured around principal who left
School expectations of pupils	High academic pressure School-wide evaluation system	Low academic pressure Consequences of behaviour/ work not always clear	Substantial amount of work demanded every day	Low demands during school days Extra time drawing Discipline system not always clear
School goals	Focus on achievement	Focus on continuation in high school	Focus on continuation in high school	Focus on pedagogical climate
Inter-staff relations	Good relations between staff members	Good relations between staff members More part-time teachers	Good relations between staff members	Good relations between staff members More part-time teachers
School resources	Government-funded	Government-funded	Government-funded	Government-funded Small parent contribution for extra teachers
Relationship with local authorities	Purely administrative	Purely administrative	Purely administrative	Purely administrative
School image	Positive image in town	Students withdrawn from school		Direct impact of neighbourhood Students withdrawn from school

substantial number of extra teaching hours, and probably funded little more than .25 of a full-time teaching job. No school had more than administrative relations with the authorities. This was because no special advantages would be expected from investing more energy into maintaining additional relations with the authorities. The main conclusion was therefore that the schools were comparable as regards funds and facilities.

Examination of other dimensions revealed further similarities between the schools which were less related to government policy. The first striking feature was that all schools adopted a teaching pattern of whole-class instruction combined with indi-vidual assignments. This pattern was observed in almost all lessons. All teachers knew how to ask questions of students so that the students stayed involved during whole-class teaching periods. Although one would expect to find new or inventive formats in more effective schools, these were never observed. One could hypothesise that this comparable teaching pattern resulted from similar training in the teacher training colleges.

Furthermore, all teams worked well together. The atmosphere in all schools was good and teachers helped one another out when there were problems. Also, all teachers shared the notion that they were working in a team and not as individuals whose only responsibility was their own class. Combined with the comparable ways of teaching, this gave the impression that Dutch teacher training had succeeded in producing certain standards of professional behaviour that would be typical for the Dutch primary school teacher.

The leadership structure of the schools was also similar. In all schools, the import-ant decisions were made by the entire team. This may be caused by the fact that the staff of the school was small, consisting of only six to eleven teachers. This created an atmosphere of a work group of professionals, instead of a hierarchical organisation. A second fact was that principals did not differ in training from the teachers whom they were leading, and usually only differed in the number of years of experience. Principals thus functioned more as coordinators of their teams than as leaders of their school. There were some differences in the personal style of the principals, for ex-ample in the degree to which they were visible during the school day. The principal in the more effective low-SES school was more visible than her counterpart in the less effective school. The principals in the mid-SES schools also differed in style, with the less effective school's principal being more of a hard worker and his counterpart seeming more reflective. Despite these differences, the main leadership style was shared team decision-making by all four principals. The principals differed from their teachers mostly by carrying the administrative load of the school.

The first contrast to draw is that between the more effective low-SES and the less effective low-SES school. Since the similarities were already listed in the previous paragraphs, the focus will now be on the differences. These differences are presented in Table 9.2. The schools serve a comparable population, so there should not be influences of the background of the students upon the processes described here. In general the patterns described in the less effective school seem to show more variance over time than the patterns described in the more effective school. This showed during the visits: after the first few visits to the more effective school, one could quickly learn what to expect. Visits to the less effective school were more unpredictable. Some days passed without interruptions, other days showed students refusing to work or a fight in the classroom.

Table 9.2 Summary of differences between low-SES schools on dimensions where schools are different

More effective low-SES (Winter)	Less effective low-SES (Spring)
Highly structured school day	School day is more easy-going
Consistency of daily patterns between/within classes	Variance in daily patterns between/within classes
Students work silently for most of the school day	Openly enthusiastic student population
Strictly followed routines	Occasional discipline problems
Speed of school day controlled by teachers	Speed of school day controlled by students
	Mathematics method does not seem to fit with student population
Native-language lessons for ethnic minorities during afternoons	Native-language lessons for ethnic minorities during Dutch-language lessons
High academic pressure	Low academic pressure
No parental assistance in class	Parental assistance with reading lessons
Outside problems stay out of classes	Outside problems occasionally show
Very outspoken principal	Less visible principal
Schoolwide evaluation system	Less formal evaluation of student work
Strictly followed rules	Consequences of behaviour/work not always clear
One teacher per teaching job	More teachers per teaching job
School has positive image	Students withdrawn from school

Next, a comparison can be made between the middle-SES schools. The differences between these two schools are listed in Table 9.3. In general terms for both the middle-SES and low-SES schools, the less effective school had a greater focus on the climate in the school, while the more effective school focused more on academic work. The less effective school thus spent more time trying to make students feel comfortable, for example by doing more socially orientated activities for relatively long periods between the lessons. The more effective school focused on teaching core subjects. More creative activities, like drawing or handicrafts, took place only at the end of the day. This difference in focus led to differences in school culture, which could be characterised as either more achievement-orientated or more climate-orientated.

From these descriptions of the four schools, two main differences arise which distinguish the more effective from the less effective schools. The first is the establishment of well-functioning routines. In both the more effective schools, the day was more structured and lessons continued in a standard and generally accepted way. Learning was the main daily routine and very few threats to this daily routine appeared – or, if they did, they were quickly dealt with. The second difference was the amount of material assigned. The more effective schools covered more of the curriculum than the less effective schools. It seemed to be the quantity of instruction and practice, rather than the quality that made the difference. Given the fact that all schools taught for an equal number of hours, the more effective schools succeeded in using the time more efficiently. When one looks at these two differences in the context of the twelve dimensions, both seem to be predominantly related to the child's experience of school and curriculum themes. From a wider perspective, differences can be found in the expectations and the goals the schools tried to achieve. The more

Table 9.3 Summary of differences between middle-SES schools on dimensions where schools are different

More effective middle-SES (Autumn)	Less effective middle-SES (Summer)
Middle-class population	Mostly working-class population
Extra work mostly academic	Extra work mostly drawing
Day devoted to academic activities	Occasional free time left over
Hardly any social interaction between students during lessons	Social processes during academic work
Relatively long mathematics and language lessons	
Perfectly established routines	Day is easy-going
	Very friendly teaching staff
Order throughout school	Between-teacher differences in maintaining order
No discipline system necessary	Discipline system of some teachers not clear
Highly traditional teaching	Some flexibility in teaching
Substantial amount of work set every day	Low demands on students
	Direct impact of the neighbourhood
Occasional contact with parents	Frequent contact with parents
Well-structured school	Structure centred around principal who left after a year
Focus on continuation in high school	Focus on pedagogical climate
	Students withdrawn from school

school-level-orientated dimensions (principal, staff, resources and school) seemed to contribute less to the differences between these schools. This does not necessarily imply that these were not important for creating an effective school, but rather that these dimensions are not as important as the instructional features of schools. We return to this theme in Chapter 13.

10 Europe – Norway

Trond Eiliv Hauge, Astrid B. Eggen, Marit Gröterud and Björn Nilsen

Introduction/context

There is a strong expectation from the Ministry of Education that all schools will follow stated guidelines in the national curriculum, and evaluate their work according to these criteria. These criteria include qualities of students' learning outcomes, both academically and socially; teaching; teacher collaboration and organisation of the work in schools. This view of the Norwegian school system is confirmed by external international reviews, which also point out the strong link between curriculum policy at national level and views about what constitutes school effectiveness in the system (Chapman and Aspin, 1995).

The Oslo middle-socio-economic-status schools

General characteristics

School 1 covered grade 1 through grade 9 and school 2 covered grade 1 through grade 6. School 1 will be called Fjord School and school 2 will be called Troll School. School 2 was the more effective of the two in terms of value added to pupil progress over time.

Both schools were situated within the metropolitan area of Oslo and were characterised as typical middle-SES schools. They were both located in the outskirts of the built-up area, bordering on to woods, but in two different parts of the city. Both principals characterised the schools' catchment areas as communities where people had a high level of activity, and where there were many organisations whose activities had a major impact on most people living there, as well as the general community's relationship with the school.

The schools were about the same size, taking elementary level into consideration; they had about the same number of students at grades 1–6 (439 at Troll School and 465 at Fjord School). But in total, Fjord School was the biggest, if all students and teachers serving grades 1–9 were taken into consideration. The total number of students and teachers at Fjord School were respectively 710 and 41. Troll School had 22 teachers.

The number of classes at elementary level were twenty and eighteen at Fjord School and Troll School respectively. The average number of students per class was twenty-six at Fjord School and twenty-two at Troll School. At Fjord School only two classes participated in the ISERP-study, but at Troll School the teachers preferred all three classes to participate.

Troll School was the newest of the two schools. It had recently celebrated its fortieth anniversary. The school started as a single building institution situated in the some-what rural area of Oslo consisting mainly of farmland. About the time Troll School was established, in 1959, Fjord School had already existed in its present location for more than forty years. The longer history of Fjord School was mainly due to its location closer to the centre of Oslo.

The most significant difference between the schools was that Fjord School was situated in a stable area where you could find lots of second- and third-generation inhabitants. Most students lived in detached houses and there were a few town houses.

Troll School, on the other hand, was placed in an area that had recently been de-veloped. Forty nationalities were represented in this area. Thirty-five per cent of the students at Troll School belonged to immigrant families, and many of the students with a Norwegian background belonged to families that had recently moved into the area. They lived in more densely built-up areas, in flats and town houses.

The stable, complete and partly conservative environment of Fjord School con-trasted with the new, vulnerable and dispersed environment of Troll School. The new inhabitants of Troll School's catchment area faced the challenge of creating a local environment, while new inhabitants of Fjord School's local environment found a well-established school, local leisure-time activities and a well-established parent group.

School goals

Both schools had school plans expressing the areas of priority in the school com-munity. The responsibility for developing these plans lay with the schools' principals. According to the national curriculum policy, both schools, in addition to developing school plans, implemented and adapted national curricular guidelines to local circum-stances, in teams of teachers working at the same grade level. This annual, monthly and weekly instructional planning was primarily the individual teacher's responsibil-ity and comprised mostly subject-related educational planning regarding objectives, activities and evaluation procedures.

In the frame of the school plans, the schools presented themselves with their mottoes; Fjord School's was 'The Progressing School' and Troll School's was 'The We-School'. For both schools, the school plans contained, in addition to the motto, a vision and goals for the different activities in the school, and the different educational areas to be given priority.

Fjord School gave focus to this vision for its education: 'A vital and creative school with learning and development in a confident environment'. This vision was further concretised into several goals for the overall school activities which were divided into four categories: 'Working conditions, Learning processes, Cooperation between home and school and Results'.

Further development of the teamwork in each section and a positive development of the communication concerning circumstances in each class were among the areas given priority. Evaluation of the teaching and learning processes was emphasised. Development of methods for improvement of the learning process, as well as methods for evaluation of the students' achievements and the school's activities, were stated as part of this overall evaluation process. The following statement represented the over-all goal for the teaching of students: 'Fjord School wishes that all students should be admitted to the upper secondary school they prefer.' The main theme for the school year was 'responsibility learning'. There was a clear lack of teacher participation and commitment in the development process of the school plan. Despite this, teachers were communicating an understanding of the importance of the goals in the plan.

The main vision for Troll School was 'learning through a confident, vigorous and joint environment'. According to the school plan, the following three areas had been given priority: Responsibility for learning, Adaptive education and Teacher co-operation. The three areas were further divided into subgoals. Adaptive education was further specified by division into: routines for diagnosis of students and the devel-opment of individual curriculum. In the area of teacher cooperation, the development of a team structure had been the focus. The plan contained a schedule for regular meetings between teachers, as well as a rationale for a special education team, a multicultural team and tasks for the different teams. Responsibility for learning had two dimensions: responsibility for the group and responsibility for one's own learning processes. This area had been classified into subgoals at different levels, representing the four categories: respect for other people, politeness, responsibility for yourself and for others.

The school plan of Troll School was the most substantial plan, and the process that led to it involved the teachers to a greater extent. The teachers at Fjord School were observers of the birth of their plan and hence their role became criticism of its content and the possibilities of implementing it in the classrooms. The singular plan of Fjord School contrasted with the corporate plan of Troll School. The content of the plans and the processes of developing and implementing the plans added to our understand-ing of Troll School as the cooperative school, focusing on educational and social issues in fields viewed as important by the teachers.

The principal

Both schools had had changes in principals over the past years. The principal at Fjord School was assigned to the school in 1988, but was absent on long sick leave and the first vice-principal acted in his place. Close after the ending of the ISERP studies at the school, another principal and vice-principal were assigned to the school. Due to these circumstances the reliable data about the management of this school is very limited. The teachers were also reluctant to comment on issues related to the leader-ship and management of the school. The teachers underlined a lack of contact and support from the principal, as well as vice-principal, but chose not to comment fur-ther on the problems this caused. None of the teachers we followed had had visits from either the principal or vice-principal during classroom instruction.

The leadership situation at Fjord School had probably, according to newspapers and teachers' statements, been the most important factor in the creation of conflicts over the past years. The combination of teachers representing different generations, and therefore different educational cultures, resulted in cooperation problems, together with a rhetorical attitude to solving this problem from the principal, which added new dimensions to the school conflicts and left old problems unresolved. According to teachers at the school the present principal lacked an understanding of the school's history. This lack of understanding was combined with a lack of tools to evaluate and diagnose the situation in order to improve the organisation. The result was a school organisation even more immature when he left than when he started. The lack of leadership in this process had resulted in a higher level of parent involvement, both through the parent council at the school, and in direct contact with teachers.

The principal at Troll School was quite new to the school, and her previous experience as vice-principal at two other schools coloured her statements about the local environment and school management in general, as well as her messages to the teachers. Two of the participating teachers found this annoying and disliked the comparison between schools. The principal underlined, however, that her experience had shown her the importance of searching in the local community for ways to improve the school, and discovering which aspects needed to be improved. She emphasised the participation of all teachers, both in specific development processes and, on a more general basis, during discussions about different educational and pedagogical issues.

Another important matter, she stressed, was her ability to 'be visible in the school'. She found that time pressure did not allow her to visit classrooms to the extent she had hoped for when becoming a principal of this school. She did not have any routines for visiting classrooms on a regular basis, but expressed a concern about getting to know the dynamics in individual classes. She would have preferred to spend time getting to know individual students, but found herself in a position where she had to give priority to a selected group of children, most often to those having some kind of learning or behavioural difficulties.

Her plan for developing the structure of the school organisation included delegating responsibilities. At the same time she communicated the urge to know, have first-hand experience of and understand every aspect of running the school herself. The management plan of the school, or rather the map of the school organisation, had several levels including grouping all personnel into teams. Different groups of personnel and leaders in the school had clearly defined tasks and areas in which they were primarily responsible for collecting information, developing procedures and raising issues with the whole staff. The organisation was hierarchical in the sense that the principal had the final responsibility and that the responsibility of other levels of the system was limited to part of the overall process. Along with this they had developed a system for information dispersal within the school. The principal expressed trust in the system they were building, but underlined the fact that the management system had only recently been developed and that this was still a very immature organisation.

The principal at Troll School felt a strong lack of competence in running the school in terms of budgeting, and found that she spent too much time on aspects in which she lacked interest and skills. Her field was educational leadership, and she took pride in the building of an organisation, managing the challenges the school presented regarding multicultural education, in teaching children with learning difficulties and in the integration of all children irrespective of ability and knowledge into one learning environment.

The influence of parents

All teachers and both principals in Fjord and Troll Schools reported that the parents were, in general, good supporters of the running of the school. Teachers also underlined that most parents at both schools were supporting the students in their individual school work as well as in building a stable school environment. Most parents met for their biannual conversations with the teachers, in which they received the teacher's comments on their child's advancement in subject-related work and the social life of the school. Most parents also met for the biannual parents meeting held for each class, where the teachers gave general information concerning the activities in the class in each subject, in addition to discussions about outside school arrangements. All classes elected two parents annually to serve as parent representatives concerning the whole group of students.

The parents' association at Fjord School had played an active role in changing the climate and it arranged meetings for all parents. One of these meetings resulted in a request that the principal should leave the school. As a group, concerned parents at Fjord School seemed stronger than at Troll School, which might have been caused by the somewhat tense communication situation at the school and the fact that they were of a slightly higher SES in this area.

Both participating teachers at Fjord School welcomed parents to be present during classroom instruction and to help out during excursions. Occasionally they had parents visiting in the classroom and when needed there were always parents available to assist the teacher on class trips and visits.

At Troll School, the three teachers, who belonged to the sampled classes, were aware of the diversity in background of the students and the fact that in the catchment area of this school several families were immigrants to the country or this part of Oslo. The participating classes at this school had therefore developed a 'family-group' programme that helped students to establish friendships and communications across different backgrounds. Most students were participating in these groups.

School resources

There were several buildings in Fjord School, which were three or four storeys high. The buildings reflected the different periods in which they were built. The school had sufficient classroom capacity, but according to the assistant principal, the school was lacking a larger auditorium for activities at elementary level.

The teachers at Fjord School described the textbook situation as good, but they would have preferred another textbook for Norwegian. The classrooms contained some additional hands-on materials. The teachers had a creative attitude to the use of supporting materials, and also made materials themselves. The classes did not have any encyclopaedias or reference books.

In most of the lessons the teachers were alone with the students in the classroom, but on some occasions teachers received practical help from parents. The classes were not entitled to extra teacher resources as there were few students with learning difficulties.

The Fjord School had two people working more or less regularly as substitute teachers.

Some buildings at Troll School dated back to the 1960s, but three pavilions had been added recently, due to the increasing number of children in the catchment area of the school. The principal and teachers were, however, complaining about a lack of adequate forward planning from the municipality, and had a constant struggle communicating to local educational authorities the need for sufficient classroom capacity and teaching materials. The school had reached a point where it had turned all possible rooms into classrooms. The consequence of this was that they had no library, group rooms or special rooms at their disposal. However, a new building had been planned to be finished within the year.

All teachers working at Troll School complained about the lack of hands-on materials for mathematics instruction. They thought the textbook was too difficult for the students, and looked forward to a change of textbooks in mathematics in grade 3. Our understanding of the situation was rather that the teachers did not take full advantage of the textbook's possibilities in creating a differentiated learning situation. These classes did not have any reference books available in the classrooms.

Troll School had received extra funding, earmarked to increase the number of teachers, as there were several students with learning difficulties, social problems and disabilities. The extra allocations were given over a three-year period integrated in a local development programme. The teachers said they appreciated the opportunity to discuss class matters with other qualified teachers. This situation had provided the students with an open attitude towards receiving help from adults.

The teachers' meeting room facilities in both schools, their working space and the adjacent rooms carried necessary Xerox machines, and were very pleasant, open and welcoming.

School image

Fjord School carried a feeling of anonymity. Teachers were centred round their tasks, they sat around tables most often speaking to the same colleagues. There was an invisible barrier to be crossed in order to be included in the conversation. They looked at you as an outsider, curious about why you were there, but reluctant to involve you in further conversation.

The school was in a difficult situation suffering from a lack of leadership and management. The teachers were reluctant to talk; they were concerned about the schools' ability to maintain the best parts of the environment, as well as to develop a good welcoming and cooperative school. For this reason they preferred the school's problems to remain within the group of personnel; 'We have had enough of being focused on in newspapers'. Their attitude was that outsiders' negative comments did not help to solve what they considered to be internal problems.

The school had, for several decades, been a 'community centre'. A lot of the local activities had been initiated from personnel at the school, in cooperation with parents living in the neighbourhood. During the past ten years the school had increased in size, both in numbers of students and of teachers. One explanation for the anonymity one felt when entering the school could have been the staff's lack of experience in managing a larger school and the making of bridges between old and new cultures.

At Troll School, all teachers said hello to everybody they met in hallways, the school yard or indoors, in teaching facilities or the teachers' lunch area. When entering the school a welcoming and including atmosphere struck the visitor. Walking around the corridors, most personnel turned to you to ask whether you knew your way around, if they could be of any help, etc. There seemed to be, despite the size of the school, an including atmosphere.

This school did not have a similar position as a 'community centre', nor an established position in the minds of the inhabitants of the catchment area, as Fjord School had. According to the principal, this fact was the main reason for involving the school in a local board of leisure-time activities, where several local organisations were represented.

Inter-staff relations

In both schools the teachers were organised in teams cooperating at the same grade level. The cooperation between teachers was, however, different at the schools, both generally and also between the teachers participating in the ISERP study.

At Fjord School, two of teachers that we met in the first year of the study, a man and a woman who had respectively nine and two years of experience, both chose to change school after our first year of data collection. During this year there was apparently a lack of collaboration among the teachers at the same grade level. During this academic year there was also a peak in the difficulties related to the management and leadership of the school. A total of fourteen teachers left at the end of the spring term in the first year. The teachers that replaced the two first-grade teachers were both new at this school. They were both women and had respectively three and two years of previous experience.

These new teachers both emphasised cooperation during teaching, planning and reflection even if the instruction in the classrooms was characterised primarily by the individual teachers' preferences.

The teachers at Fjord School were organised in teams consisting of teachers teaching at the same grade level. In addition to this team structure, there were cooperative units covering three grade levels. During the first year of belonging to the same team, these teachers' cooperative attitudes improved. Both teachers were of the general opinion that their school was not a typical communicative and cooperative school. They based these reflections on what and how issues were discussed, both at team meetings and at departmental meetings.

The classes observed at Troll School had had a more stable situation during the two years of study than classes at Fjord School. Only one of the classes had a change of teacher after year 1.

At Troll School, the tension between the vision stated in the school plan of developing a school characterised by fellowship and 'we-thinking', and the possibilities of developing an educational environment for all students regardless of learning abilities, was very apparent in the teachers team planning. In general, the three teachers who were followed in the second-year ISERP study reported that the school was a typical cooperative school, and underlined that they thought their team was cooperating in a good way.

Troll School had developed an information-dissemination system, where teachers were required to write minutes from all meetings which they then had to give to the administration. The administration and the principal would also give the teams forms to fill in and reports were to be written. The teachers in our sample had a reluctant attitude, due to the time that these tasks consumed.

Teachers' teaching style

The instructional style of the teachers were different in the classes at the two schools, but there were also some similarities in attitudes and behaviour concerning instruction. Observation data from ten lessons in each participating class indicated that students' attentiveness was somewhat greater at Fjord School than at Troll School. The mean effective teaching time was also somewhat higher at Fjord School, as was the case for teacher-led activity, student/group activity and management/organisation of the classroom. Troll School spent more time than Fjord School on teacher presentation of content, transitions, non-academic activity, group work, tests and procedural behavioural presentation. The major difference seemed to be represented in time used for teacher-led activities and for discussion and directions for assignments.

Teachers at Fjord School

The two teachers followed up in this school may be characterised and labelled as 'the conventional teacher' and 'the-teacher-as-an-actress'.

'The conventional teacher' did not avoid challenges, but she preferred teaching activities and educational programmes which made it possible for her to stick to her routines. She enjoyed teaching in primary school and was proud of being a teacher and proud of her work in the classroom. Her attitude to the effort put into preparing activities for the class was relaxed.

Our main impression of 'the-teacher-as-an-actress' was that she was gifted, in most situations, at encouraging the students to be involved in the activities related to a subject. The teacher made use of voice, body and facial expressions, both when communicating with the whole class, and in contact with the individual student. The teacher emphasised variations in teaching methods and learning activities, and had a special creativity in the facilitating of these activities. She spent time figuring out ways of using the resources available and refurbished the classroom depending on her analysis of practical and other educational reasons.

Both teachers emphasised the development of socially aware children; students that during a socialising learning process, became good citizens. On several occasions they told the students to pay attention to one another, to wait patiently for their turn and to help and include all students, regardless of their abilities in the subjects. They were also aware of the different needs that their twenty-four students had. For this reason they appreciated textbooks that facilitated differentiated educational programmes.

The mathematics lessons in both classes followed a very similar structure. A large proportion of the effective teaching time was spent on individual work, during which the students were sometimes encouraged to cooperate. Most of the time the students would pay attention mainly to their own work and only turn to other students to seek advice in solving problems. The periods of uninterrupted individual work were somewhat longer in the classroom of the second teacher. In the other classroom there were more frequent interruptions, giving messages or explaining mathematical concepts. This class also tended to spend more time introducing new concepts and corresponding tasks.

Teachers at Troll School

In characterising the three teachers in this school we had chosen three labels: the 'maternal teacher', the 'discipline-orientated teacher' and the 'friendship-building teacher'.

'The maternal teacher' talked about her students using the expression 'my children', and she was, in many ways, acting as a second or third parent. The observation data also indicated a higher proportion of non-subject-related work in this class compared to the others. Interview data supported this, when the teacher underlined her intention to give all the students time to tell stories, show items, etc. This class used tests to a greater extent than all the other teachers in the project, and during the lessons at which we were present, two tests were administered lasting fourteen and twenty-five minutes.

'The discipline-orientated teacher': this class was probably the most challenging class to manage, according to our observations, which showed more time in this class spent on disruptive children, whereas there was almost no time spent on discipline matters in the two other classes during two years of study. The strict atmosphere in the class was striking. On the other hand, of all the classrooms visited at this school, this classroom was the most appealing when it came to the display of students' work.

'The friendship-building teacher' gave the students time to bring out a personal 'message' to the class, and she sometimes spent a major proportion of the lesson in establishing possibilities for building relationships among the students and between students and teachers.

The observation data from the three classes indicated some interesting similarities and differences between the classes. The classes of the second and the third teacher had about the same ratio between time spent on individual work activities and time spent on teacher-led instruction. The first teacher, on the other hand, put more emphasis on teacher presentations and whole-class discussions about mathematical concepts.

The dialogue in the classrooms were different in the way the teachers initiated question–answer sequences. The first and third teachers both encouraged the students to offer their own reflections, though on most occasions in accordance with the teacher's main focus. These teachers would generally give the floor to those students who raised their hands, signalling their desire to answer. The second teacher also did this but she would in addition ask the students who were not raising their hands, and who thus seemed uncertain, to answer and hence encouraged these students to participate orally in the question–answer sequences of the lesson. There was in all three classrooms little subject-related communication initiated by the students.

Students achievements and attitudes

At Troll School the three classes followed up in the study showed quite different achievement outcomes in mathematics (CTBS-test) and Norwegian (dictation). The total gain in CTBS scores over two years of instruction was largest in the class of the 'friendship-building teacher'. The class of the 'discipline-orientated teacher' had the smallest gain in CTBS testing. The 'maternal teacher's' class, scoring medium in CTBS testing, was in the lead in the two Norwegian-language dictation tests conducted during grade 2. In this test the class of the 'friendship-building teacher' had the lowest score.

At Fjord School the results on the CTBS test showed that the classes were closer in total gain during two years of instruction than the classes at Troll School. The class of the 'actress teacher' was, however, a little ahead of the class of 'the conventional teacher'. In the Norwegian dictation test the two classes had almost identical results.

The overall results of the Norwegian dictation test gave the best average results on the single test to Fjord School, but the measure for gain over the school year put Troll School in the leading position. This pattern was the same for CTBS testing; Troll School held the best results for learning gain, while Fjord School was in the lead regarding mean results on the single test. Troll School was therefore the more effective.

Conclusions on the Oslo middle-socio-economic-status schools

Fjord and Troll School were chosen for this contrasting case study because of similar SES characteristics, but differences in effectiveness, as assessed by the Norwegian ISERP research team during the study. The study showed two schools functioning quite differently. Differences were found both at the organisational level and the class level in the schools.

Fjord School expressed itself by a more tense and closed communication pattern between the principal and the teachers than Troll School, a situation that was also evident when analysing school–parent relationships. Parents at Fjord School had clearly expressed that they wanted a new principal. The principal at Troll School seemed to be more open-minded to the teachers and concerned to develop a corporate working culture.

School planning and evaluation procedures were also different in the two schools and involved the teachers quite differently. At Fjord School, teachers had a reluctant attitude to such work and did not see the obvious benefit of it.

The case-study classes at Fjord School changed their teachers after the first grade. For one of the classes, this change gave the class a much better working and communication situation. Only one class changed their teacher at Troll School. When looking at the situation in the second year of study, there were striking differences in the teachers' teaching experiences in the schools. Teachers in Troll School were older and more experienced. As a group, their attitudes to teaching and towards students also seemed different: they were more concerned about the individual students and their needs.

Parents at Troll School seemed to be much more relaxed about students' academic achievements than parents at Fjord School. This may be one of the reasons behind the different visions and overall goals in the school plans. The 'We-School' profile and the priority given to taking responsibility for learning, suitably adapted education and teacher collaboration at Troll School fitted into a pattern of a school very concerned about their students and the learning environment. This seemed to be an accepted message among the diversified group of parents at this school. Fjord School seemed to be more concerned with expectations coming from secondary education.

Looking at the criteria for school effectiveness that we have used in this study, we may conclude that Troll School was more effective than Fjord School. This is the case when using quality standards for leadership and communication in the school organisation, cooperation between teachers and teaching, and also when looking at the traditional measure for school effectiveness and student outcomes.

The Trondheim middle-socio-economic-status schools

General characteristics

The two schools, Asp School and Bang School, were in typical residential areas on the outskirts of Trondheim (*c.* 180,000 inhabitants), but in different school districts. Apart from their size and number of classes, the two schools were similar in several ways. Both schools were situated in residential areas, with little industry or workshops. The housing was mainly dense, low-rise housing. There were a few high blocks close to Asp School. Asp School was situated in a well-established area, while Bang School was located in a newly developed area without strong traditions and with relatively few cultural and free-time activities established for children and young people.

Asp School, the more effective school, had 261 students, while Bang School, the less effective school, had 420 students. The average class size in both schools was twenty-four students. The staff in Asp School consisted of one principal, one vice-principal and eighteen teachers. The staff in Bang School consisted of one principal, two vice-principals and forty teachers.

The schools both had large, open playgrounds, with open country, lawns, areas for ball games and playing, and asphalt surfaces close to the school buildings. They were also sheltered from traffic, except for that to and from the schools.

Both schools had open-plan classrooms, each year being located in a shared area, but with an individual 'home' area for each class. The teachers at each level were organised in teams which cooperated in planning and teaching. Asp School was older but the schools did not have significantly different designs architecturally.

There were no private schools competing for students in the area and more or less all the children in the schools' catchment areas attended these schools. Special education was planned and carried out by each class-level team. Application was made for extra resources for individual students in need of additional support. These resources would normally be linked to the team. A number of foreign-language-speaking families lived in Bang School's catchment area and children from these families who attended the school were integrated into the individual classes.

Both schools had organised School-Free-Time groups, in which the youngest students could have places both before and after the obligatory hours of normal school.

A day in the life of a child

There were many similarities in the school days experienced by Per, Mons and Arne in the two schools. Observations, nevertheless, showed qualitative differences which may be related to how the students' motivation and learning strategies were stimulated by the teaching arrangements.

The classroom observations were made in mathematics periods in the second class. The observers of the students followed them through a whole day at school.

Asp School

The teachers were asked to select a student who represented average ability in the mathematics class. The selection was made before we had access to the results of the CTBS-tests. It transpired later that Per's results in these tests were in the upper level.

Per takes many initiatives in the class, both academically and socially. These initiatives made him the centre of attention and he was thus given much feedback, both as regards academic work and social behaviour. He made himself particularly prominent when the class-level group was split: he was one of the first to be allowed to go to the blackboard during the class teaching, was allowed to answer frequently in the class and to tell his story in the listening corner. He collected in books even when it was not his turn and on several occasions was given recognition for his ability to accomplish the tasks. He had many conversations with other students and with the teachers.

In an academic context, he put emphasis on and energy into work which was easy to check, and at which he was competent. It was obvious that he was able to carry out the mathematical work in the lessons in most of the mathematics periods. For this student it was a matter of solving 'routine tasks'. He nevertheless involved himself actively in the ongoing work and sought regular confirmation that he was answering correctly. It appeared to be important for him that his 'good results' were recognised both by the teacher and by his fellow students.

The student said that he enjoyed the mathematics periods, 'especially when he was allowed to do sums that he understood'. The teacher regarded the student as awake and active, and felt that he followed the teaching well when he was interested.

It appeared that the student had a considerable need for positive feedback from his teachers and fellow students and exerted himself to achieve this in areas in which he was competent and interested. Perhaps this was linked to a need to maintain a positive image of himself.

But what happened when the student met academic challenges which he was not able to understand and handle immediately? In situations which we observed, he distanced himself, or put less weight on work which required more continual, long-term effort and which he did not understand at once. The teachers thought this was because he found some tasks boring and wanted them to 'help him get started'. He was able 'to get started' either when he was given such clear explanations that he was certain that he was 'competent' for the task, or when he was able to avoid the difficulty by beginning with other routine tasks.

Bang School

Mons scored in the middle of his class (class 2) in all the CTBS-tests. He gained a high mark in the maturity test, however. It appeared that Mons adapted his academic effort and involvement so that it could be accepted by the teachers. He had thus 'covered himself' so he could get by without making much effort. He did not avoid required work, but some of his effort was of more symbolic value and did not appear to be inspired by any great academic interest. Mons had to follow the teaching so that he was informed about what was happening and could show he was participating. He could also take the initiative to stand out, but when the teacher had registered his effort he 'fell back' to making less effort.

The teachers often tried to establish an academic dialogue aimed at solution of a problem when they felt that Mons was not working up to standard and needed guidance. Mons was, however, very concerned as to whether he had given the right or wrong answers, and the teachers gave him feedback on this. He was willing to carry on working with similar questions if he was given positive confirmation that he was answering the questions correctly – until he ran into the next problem. When he had answered incorrectly he wanted to be given a standard answer for the correct way to answer the question and was not very interested in the teachers' efforts to increase his understanding of mathematics.

Our observations suggested that the implementation of the teaching varied in the two classes, even if the system was based on common planning. The observations also showed that the students reacted to guidance differently, for example, in the case of Arne in class 1. Arne had the highest marks in all the CTBS-tests in this class. He was active in the class, commenting on the questions, participating actively in discussion of solutions and answers, and trying to find alternatives and possibilities. His interest did not stop if he was not completely satisfied with an answer which he himself, or the group to which he belonged, had reached, but instead carried on with his reasoning. Arne seemed to build his knowledge creation on understanding, and he therefore allowed himself to become involved in the learning process itself. The consequence was that he did not have to load his memory with details. This did not mean that he placed less emphasis on detailed knowledge in the learning situation itself; in fact, the reverse was true, in that he was very concerned with details: those that dictated whether the solution he found was good or bad, right or wrong. The details were, however, only the building-blocks in the process; it was the general knowledge which was stored. The teacher did not have to direct Arne's work effort, because he involved himself in the learning process itself. It was often Arne who asked the teacher for permission to start on new tasks. When he was stuck, it was natural for the teacher to guide his learning by entering into a discussion on the subject with him.

Teachers' teaching style

The teaching arrangements in the two schools were very similar. The guidance service in the municipality had, for a number of years, run courses in pedagogy for elementary schools, for teachers starting with class 1. It would appear that these courses may have had a strong influence on the teachers' thinking.

The teaching area contained the 'listening corner', suitable for conversation between the teacher and the class, and an area for work. The students sat on low benches, without work tables, in a semi-circle in the listening corner. The corner was equipped with a blackboard, flip-over board and felt-pen board. The students sat close together, as well as close to the teacher, so that the possibilities for contact were good. The students' work tables were arranged in varying groups in the work area, most frequently as four tables pushed together, with the students sitting around them.

This form of organisation was closely linked to the pattern of teaching for each period. The period started in the listening corner, where the teacher presented the material to be covered and the related tasks in an interactive teaching process. The teachers wanted to establish a close communications relationship with the whole class, by involving the students in conversation on the subject, both with the teacher and with one another. More social questions, working arrangements, events in the news and information were raised in the listening corner. Almost all activity was teacher-initiated and teacher-run, even though the students were involved in the interactive teaching. The teacher also tried, however, to clarify both the students' interests and knowledge through conversation, rather than just checking their level of achievement. About a third of the period was spent in the listening corner.

The students went to their work tables after the tasks had been presented. Solution of the tasks was normally carried out on an individual basis, occasionally in small groups. The students could talk to one another, both socially and on the work in hand. In the meantime the teacher walked round, guiding the students. They checked their understanding and related it to earlier experience. The intention was to take the individual student's academic level as a basis for supporting the students as effectively as possible in their work on each subject.

The teachers at both schools had good contact with the parents, giving them abundant information on teaching and life in the class. The classes has a weekly working programme, showing the topics for the week's work and the problems to be solved, which were sent home to the parents. There was also continuing contact via communications arrangements, such as 'post folder', 'letter book' and 'end-of-the-week messages'. The parents could be given various follow-up tasks via these channels, such as checking homework and helping the students with their problems.

The class-level teams planned the teaching together, and the teachers in both schools said that they had a shared view and attitude to the teaching and the school.

The students were organised in somewhat different ways at the two schools. Two teachers each had responsibility for a class at Asp School. The teaching, however, was mainly organised as one large class, with the teachers taking turns to lead the class. Both teachers participated in guiding the students, regardless of which students belonged to their own class. The teachers therefore cooperated quite closely, not just at the planning stage, but also in the teaching work. The teachers could build on a shared experience from the teaching when they were assessing the work and planning the way forward.

Each class was taught by its own teacher at Bang School, even though the teachers occupied the same shared area and had also shared the planning process. The teachers therefore had less opportunity to give each other direct feedback and influence each other's practice, than was possible at Asp School.

A closer analysis showed that the teachers at Bang School had a somewhat different approach to mathematics teaching. As noted, they planned together. This led to establishment of the same basic structure, both as regards rules and arrangements in the class and also regarding teaching schemes. They believed that it was important to build a strong academic base as regards understanding of mathematics. This was guided by following the progression in the teacher's manual closely, and by giving the students the same tasks. Students who showed quickly that they understood and who were quick, got extra tasks and could go further in their books, but the class was kept together when new material was presented.

The differences between the classes emerged, first and foremost, in the conversations on the subject in the listening corner and in the guidance work. The teacher in class 1 normally formulated mathematical problems as 'open' questions. This allowed an opportunity for reflection and problem-solving, so that the students could work out alternative answers. The teachers did not tolerate laughter from the students if one of them gave a strange or wrong answer. The teaching environment was intended as a support for the students' imaginations. The teacher was mainly focused on a subject dialogue in guidance situations, in which she tried to find out what each student could manage and how they reasoned, by 'driving' the students forward. This was the basis for expectations as to the student's later efforts. The teacher was not at all satisfied if, when students managed tasks which 'others' managed, they did not utilise their capacity in so doing.

The teacher in class 2 gave guidance based on the students' right or wrong answers to a much greater degree, without checking their understanding. She assumed that a right answer indicated understanding and was satisfied when students showed that they could get the right answers. It could then be that some students did not utilise their capacity and that they were also satisfied when they got the correct answers, even when they could have gone on to more complicated tasks.

The third teacher in the team taught in both classes. Her experience was that the classes functioned differently: the students in class 2 were more competitive, more interested in confirmation that they had counted correctly and less so in the logic of their reasoning. They were also less enthusiastic about mathematics as a subject and expressed a lesser degree of confidence in their own skills.

The curriculum

The plans which formed the basis for teaching could have existed at three levels: the national curriculum, local curricula for the municipalities, districts and schools and teaching curricula for the team or class. The schools were free to establish a sequence for learning with interpretation, priority and definition of goals, weighting of topics, choice of work forms and systems for evaluation, sequence and progression in the work.

Neither Asp nor Bang School had developed a local curriculum for mathematics teaching, but each team made an annual plan. The annual plan included a list of topics, with the period during which they were to be covered. The teacher's manual, which was assumed to reflect the national curriculum, formed the starting point for the annual plan.

The teaching plan in both schools was built up in the form of weekly plans indicating the topics and tasks for each subject in the course of the week. The weekly plans were delivered to the students and sent as information to their homes.

Progression in mathematics as a subject could be characterised as gentle. The idea was that it was important to build up a solid foundation for mathematical insight in all the students. The teachers' manuals therefore had many practice questions for each topic. There were extra problem books in addition to the normal textbook. At the end of the first class it was expected, for example, that the students would understand numbers from 0 to 100 and the positioning system for single digits and tens; by the end of the second class the students would not yet have worked with numbers in the range over 1,000, nor with decimal numbers and fractions, nor with division.

Much emphasis was placed on individuality, and the students could, to a certain extent, choose the scope and level of their work problems themselves. The teacher directed this, however, by guiding it. The students were, in general, held together within the same chapter in the textbook, but those who were fastest and who had documented their understanding were, to a certain extent, allowed to work further on, or to have problems from other textbooks. Most problems could be solved on an individual basis, but a few were handled as group work.

The textbook had a number of tests after each main chapter, so that the students could check their understanding of the mathematical topics in the chapter. The students put their results into a histogram to visualise their own progress.

The principal

The formal organisation and leadership structures in both schools were quite similar. The differences emerged first and foremost in how the leadership and organisation functioned in reality, i.e. when it came to cooperation between the teachers, and innovative activities.

The principal and the vice-principals formed the schools' formal leadership group. Resources for administration were calculated on the basis of the school's size; two people at Asp School and three at Bang School. All the members of the leadership groups at both schools had some teaching duties so that they maintained practical contact with the schools' primary tasks. The principal had overall responsibility for educational leadership, personnel responsibility, budgetary responsibility and responsibility for external contact, while the vice-principals had responsibility for more specific management and administrative tasks. The group had regular meetings at which they had continuing discussions and distributed tasks to one another. The leaders at Asp School had closer cooperation than those at Bang School.

Both schools organised the teachers in class-level teams, who had responsibility for most of the teaching at that level. A team followed a class for several years. The team teachers should, for class 4 and upwards, be qualified to teach Norwegian, mathematics and English. Subject teachers were involved for specific subjects at higher levels, but not to the extent that the team concept was destroyed. The team was expected to work with planning the teaching and evaluation, subject matter and questions relating to the students. Neither of the schools had established subject departments.

Two to three class-level teams were placed together to form a 'mega-team', to work with matters at the school level, for example to work with the school plan, school evaluation, activity days and practical questions covering several class levels.

Asp School

At this school, the mega-teams comprised first and sixth levels, second and third levels and fourth and fifth levels. Each mega-team chose a leader who, together with the principal, vice-principal and a representative of the teachers' trade unions, formed an educational leadership group at the school. This group was given its mandate by the teaching staff as a whole, with the approval of the principal. The group discussed pedagogical questions, formed plans and made arrangements necessary for the pedagogic work at the school level. They took initiative in development of the school plan, development projects and work with school-based evaluation. The principal's position in the group was not greatly different from that of its other members. The principal had, in matters that were taken up, only the power of reason, as did the other members.

Bang School

At this school, mega-teams were based on which class-level teams shared the main areas of the school: first, second, third and fourth classes, fifth and sixth classes and seventh, eighth and ninth classes. The three leaders were linked to each of the mega-teams, but participation in their meetings was not systematic. These teams did not meet frequently and had not yet found their role. Several of the teachers had low expectations of the potential function of the mega-teams, unless they took up matters which affected the teachers to a greater extent than at present.

A planning group had been elected in the school to lead the educational work along with the principal. Its tasks had mainly been to arrange educational discussions on the basis of topics suggested by the teachers.

Both schools had school plans. These should have clarified local goals, described central areas of activity and clarified areas of priority for educational development. The plan should have shown how the school would work to improve the quality of its teaching and activity in general.

Asp School

The teachers and the leadership had, together, defined the school's main goals, with emphasis on responsibility, caring and cooperation. There were good links between these goals, the goals at other planning levels and areas of priority for educational development.

The work with school-based evaluation was systematised. The school's developmental areas would, from year to year, be taken up for evaluation, and the school aims for systematic improvement, both of its practice and plans, in the relevant areas. The school carried out a major evaluation of both form and content in its team work, just before the initiation of the ISERP project. Both this work and systematic sharing of experience, formed the basis of the school's common plan for school and home work and for arrangements which were repeated from year to year – i.e. development of a plan for practical, social and cultural work which systematises teaching in that area. The various tasks aimed to help the students to develop respect and responsibility for the environment, culture and working life around them.

The teachers sought the development of local curricula for each subject. Sharing of experience ensured, however, a degree of stability in the work; positive experience and ideas were passed on. Herein lay part of the explanation for the teachers from the first and sixth classes forming a mega-team. The sixth-classteachers would, in principle, go 'down' to the first class in the following year, and thus shared experience from this level. The school also had a project in which the first and sixth classes cooperated, in which students from the sixth class supported those in the first class both socially and academically.

It was obvious that the evaluation culture developed in the school also influenced the teachers' evaluation work in the teams. The teaching team analysed and assessed methodological questions in relation to the teaching arrangements. The teachers had an insight into each other's teaching, in that they all taught in class-level areas, and therefore approached one another in their discussion of practical theory.

Bang School

The teachers and the leadership had developed a 'shared platform' encompassing both academic and social goals. The teachers in the ISERP-team referred to this as the starting point for their planning. The school plan was otherwise built up according to a standard set by the local school authorities. Both the teachers and the leaders regarded the planning as going through the motions, an obligation, and expressed the view that it was not 'theirs'. It had largely symbolic, rather than practical, value. It was difficult, for example, to see connections between the goals for the individual sub-areas and the areas of priority for educational development defined for the school. However, the school had involved itself in one sub-area, 'positive school environment', had developed plans and followed up the work in practice. There was a good correspondence between goals and project planning in this area.

The school had not carried out any form of systematic internal or external school evaluation. The school culture therefore gave very weak support for the evaluation work. Sharing of experience had been tried out in some mega-teams, but this had often led to situations that were not constructive, characterised by attack and defence.

Both ISERP-teams in the two schools practised innovative teaching, though this did not emerge particularly clearly in the mathematics periods. The teachers' innovative approach had broader support in the school culture at Asp School than at Bang School.

Asp School

The principal at this school advocated a cooperation-orientated leadership of the school:

> I lay the groundwork *so* that the teachers are able to practise leadership them-selves, that is to say, I arrange the situation *so* that I can delegate leadership tasks to the teachers. For the teachers are *also* supervisors in their classes and in their teacher teams.

The teachers had a clear conception of the principal as the force behind the major lines and links in the school's activity. They were more doubtful as to what extent he was informed of, and knew about, the daily teaching activity. The situation led to the experience that the principal handled leadership at the school level while the teachers had responsibility for and led the educational work at the class level.

It was, however, obvious that the school-based planning, the links between the local curricula, the follow-up school evaluation, the contact between the leadership and the mega-teams, and the frequency of meeting, all contributed to the creation of an educa-tional cohesiveness in the organisation. It was related that, for example, all the level teams functioned approximately according to the same model as regards planning, shared teaching arrangements and follow-up evaluation. 'Frustration meetings' aimed at processing conflicts were arranged when problems or disagreements arose.

Competence was developed via sharing of experience, continued planning, evalua-tion and innovative work. The leadership also tried, with limited resources, to develop competence through a further education programme.

Bang School

The leader of the school described it as 'a happy anarchy', in which there were oppor-tunities for taking the initiative for those who wished to do so. The group of teachers involved in 'positive school environment' were an example of this and had the leaders' support. The school was team-organised but it was entirely up to the team to decide its working form and follow-up of the school plan. The educational community in the school was weak, even though the teachers had a good social fellowship. The school plan and evaluation work did not function as a framework for the educational leader-ship. The work was adjusted to some extent, in that each team had to submit year plans at the start of the year, and because work in the open areas was visible for all. The school also lacked a well-thought-out programme for competence development.

In this situation it was not surprising that the planning group's function was limited to organisation of educational discussions, without any special commitment from the individual teachers.

Inter-staff relations

The ISERP-teams in the schools cooperated on a wide range of tasks, including planning of teaching and evaluation; they took up matters relating to the students, difficulties relating to both teaching and colleagues, and consideration of how the teaching and the school functioned. The teachers spent more time at the schools than the time stipulated for cooperation. They had developed open relationships to one another, both professionally and personally. The ISERP-teams resembled each other more than their schools did. An integrated cooperative situation was less normal at Bang School than at Asp School.

Asp School

The teachers regarded themselves as part of an educational unit with a generally shared view of the school and teaching. The team was a part of this basis and there was a clear working fellowship in each team. The teachers spent a lot of time at the school on planning of teaching, and time was also allocated to general staff meetings for discussion of matters related to the work in the classes, or to the activity of the school as a whole.

Bang School

The size of this school, with forty teachers altogether, made it more difficult to create a professional and educational fellowship. There was nevertheless a good social atmosphere amongst the teachers and between them and the leadership. The teams functioned, however, in isolation, and were therefore very different from each other. There was also little interplay between the teams concerning educational matters, even though they were organised as mega-teams.

Conclusions on the Trondheim middle-socio-economic-status schools

The schools had quite similar conditions apart from their size and the fact that Bang School had both elementary and lower-secondary levels. Both schools had open teaching areas, each level consisting of two classes taught in the same area. The teachers were organised in class-level teams, with responsibility for planning and implementation of the teaching. The socio-economic status (SES) was comparable for the two catchment areas, although Asp School was situated in a more established residential area.

Differences appeared, first and foremost, in leadership and organisation. Asp School emerged as a significantly more integrated organisation, in which the principal put a greater degree of emphasis on educational leadership. The educational programme was more unified than at Bang School, even though the teachers felt that they handled the educational work themselves, and that the leadership did not really know very much about what went on in the classrooms. Neither of the schools had local curricula for individual subjects; the planning followed from the textbooks. One of the teachers at Asp said, nevertheless:

> We have a local curriculum for the school which gives directives for teaching and learning activities. The plan shows how to establish a progression for the classes weekly plans from first to sixth class, so that the students have gradually increasing responsibility for their own learning.

Change and development of plans and improvement in practice had systematic school-based evaluation as their starting point. The schools went their separate ways here. Bang School did not have any form of systematic evaluation but the reverse was the case with Asp School. This did not just mean that topic after topic was taken up in relation to the school plan from year to year. It was also that the evaluation work was of a quality which contributed to professional dialogue. This could be exemplified by the following statement from a teacher:

> Some aspects of our practice have not been so very good; these have been taken up in the course of our school-based evaluation work and this has led to improvements. These concern matters which we did not talk so much about earlier. The school-based evaluation has therefore been a catalyst which has given us an opening for talking about these matters.

The following was said at Bang School:

> Many teachers are afraid of school evaluation. We are probably afraid of being found out doing something wrong, instead of thinking of it as guidance so that we can do something better. When it goes so far that individuals feel a sense of accusation, they go into the trenches very quickly. I have experienced conversations about educational work in which the two sides differ, ending up with two angry teachers in opposition to one another. Nothing happens, and what could have been constructive becomes the opposite. This sort of approach does not create a good environment.

The school plan at Asp, unlike Bang's, was remarkable in its emphasis on the links between goals in the various sub-plans, and between goals and areas of priority for educational development.

Asp School was among the Norwegian schools which ranked the highest as regards achievement level in mathematics, as shown in the CTBS-tests. Bang School had an average position. The same achievement pattern was found on the Norwegian dictation test. If we look closer, at the individual classes, we see that one class (1) lies right in the uppermost group as regards both level and gains while the other class (2), lies solidly in the middle group. But this is not the case in the Norwegian dictation test.

The results from attitude tests, indicated that positive attitudes to school and school-work characterised the students' responses at Asp School to a larger extent than at Bang School. More positive responses were given on nearly all items in the test at Asp School.

The ISERP-team at Bang School had perhaps just as good cooperation on planning of teaching as did the team at Asp School, and shared their experience with each other. The leadership appreciated their work. A closer analysis showed, nevertheless, that implementation of the teaching plans was different in the two classes. The differences emerged first and foremost in the professional dialogue in teaching, and guidance situations. One could see, in class 1, that the teacher was aiming for a communicative form of teaching, in which she, to a large degree, asked open questions which promoted reflection and alternative thinking in the students, and which she linked to the students' everyday experiences with comments and examples. In her guidance she entered the students' world, to get a picture of how they thought, and she says:

> The students and I cooperate, in a way, in explaining. I check what the problem is, and the students get help to explain the problem to themselves.

Expectations of what the student could work on were adjusted based on a view of the student's level.

It would seem that the teacher in class 2 was more 'achievement-orientated', i.e. orientated towards what were the right or wrong answers to the problems. She presented the 'right' way to answer the problem and posed control questions. She intended to support the students' way of thinking in guidance situations but often fell into a response of right or wrong. This could lead to the students thinking that mathematics was about doing things the 'right' way. Both they and the teacher were then satisfied when the problems were done in the specified way. This could mean that many students were not challenged very much, especially as the textbook had a fairly gentle progression. Solution of the mathematical problems could become routine work.

The teachers in the team, especially the third teacher who taught in both classes, felt that class 1 was more involved and positively interested in the mathematics teaching than class 2. Our view was that the students 'got more from' the teaching in class 1; the students in class 2 could live up to the expectation 'they'd get the right answer' without having to make very much effort.

Planning continued on the assumption that the teachers thought and acted alike in the mathematics periods, due to the fact that they did not have much fellowship in the teaching situation and no opportunity to observe each other's work. They could not attain insight into each other's practical theory.

It may be that the team teachers at Asp School were just as different to start with, but they had a form of organisation and belonged to an evaluation culture which led them to confront each other with their shared experience to a much greater degree, and in which they, in the planning process, discussed each other's practical theory to a much greater extent.

Conclusions for Norwegian schools

What are the lessons that can be drawn from these contrasting school analyses which are summarised in Tables 10.1 and 10.2? Two major factors or domains are revealed in the study. One is connected to the teachers' way of teaching, their instructional style and pattern of communicating in the classroom and how they manage their work together with the students. Another one is part of the overall management and collaborative structure in the schools, where the principal is the key figure in setting the agenda for common planning, vision-making and experiential learning. The most effective school shows high quality on both factors and on the interplay between them as well.

In studying the practice of teaching, we have become aware of two kinds of stimulating classroom environments for students' learning. Teachers who care for their students in a friendly, maternal way, and who are socially and academically orientated, produce the most effective teaching. The same holds true for teachers who are able to share and discuss classroom work with each other in a confident manner, not only at the planning stage, but also during teaching and afterwards.

In analysing school climate, inter-staff relations, cooperation and leadership in the schools, we are inclined to conclude that a collegiate, collaborative culture, nurtured by a principal who believes in joint planning and vision-making, who is culture-building and supportive of her teachers, is fostering the most effective school. Two of the schools in the study show characteristics of this kind.

The study reveals a consistent interplay between the two major factors or domains described above, in such a way that a collegiate, collaborative structure and a culture-building principal creates a supporting infrastructure for effective teaching, when the teachers are responding to it in an appropriate manner. The condition for this conclusion is, however, that the infrastructure must be supportive, have personal meaning for the teachers and be experienced as worthwhile for their teaching.

Some of our findings seem to fit quite well into the international picture of the effective school. The leadership style found to be most effective in our schools seems to reflect functions belonging to an organic school organisation, but upheld by the democratic traditions dominant in Norwegian society.

Hargreaves (1994) differentiates between collegiate and contrived teacher collaboration, the latter found to be more inefficient than the former in supporting teachers' professional work in the classroom. Our study seems to support this conclusion. We may add to this that the positive interplay between the organic leadership style and the collegiate collaborative structure in the effective schools, seems to nurture the ownership in school among teachers, which also seems to affect their commitment to joint planning, vision-making and evaluation in school, in addition to practice of teaching. Signs of this are found in our more effective schools, which are also confirmed in other Norwegian studies (Hauge, 1982, 1995).

The teaching style and classroom management profile found in the most effective schools, are consistent with some of the basic aims and principles laid down in the national curriculum guidelines. We may conclude that the balanced practice of teaching concerning social and academic learning, and the consistency and coherence in what teachers are doing, seem to be quite important effectiveness factors in our schools.

School effectiveness dimensions like parental involvement, school curriculum and school resources seem to be of minor importance in discriminating between the Norwegian case-study schools. The reason for this is the fact that these relations are to a large extent regulated through common national/local frameworks and norms. Every school, for example, has to follow the national curriculum guidelines for teaching; parental involvement is regulated through formal democratic bodies at school level, and by the practice of parental class meetings as well; in addition, the economic situation for each of the schools in this study was very similar, despite minor differences in resources provided for special education. This may be seen as a result of a national policy for equitable education for all and the idea of comprehensive schooling.

Table 10.1 Summary of characteristics of two Oslo middle-socio-economic-status schools

Dimension of contrast	More effective school (Troll)	Less effective school (Fjord)
General characteristics of the school	439 students in grades 1–6 Conventional school building Typical middle-SES school Recently developed living area, mixed with old houses 1/3 immigrant families	710 students in grades 1–9 Conventional school building High-middle-SES school Well-maintained and stable living area Second- and third-generation families
A day in the life of a child	Middle test scores in the three case-study classes Students are in general positive about their teachers and school One case-study class got a new teacher the second year	High test scores in the two case-study classes One of the classes had a negative attitude to their class-teacher and school in general Both case-study classes got new teachers the second year
Teachers' teaching style	The class-teachers are inclusive in their way of teaching. They are concerned about the individual students and their needs Teachers in this school use more time on class organisation and social regulation than teachers in the other school	Teaching seems first of all to be academically orientated Effective teaching time is somewhat higher in this school than in the other Student attentiveness during lessons is somewhat higher in this school than in the other
The influence of parents	Case-study classes run a special 'family-group' programme Parents are generally supportive of the school, but need encouragement to be so	Parents are quite concerned about the leadership and management functions at the school Parents are interested in what is happening in school and the development of their children

The principal	The principal is quite new to the school, she works on rebuilding team structures and responsibilities. She is focusing on educational leadership	The principal has difficulties in communicating with the teachers. His authority is questioned He was removed from the school after the study
School goals	Well-articulated visions and goals, focusing on the 'We'-school. A balanced view on educational and social issues The teachers are cooperating in making the development plan	Well-articulated visions and goals, focusing on the 'progressive' school and academic outcomes The development plan is a product of the principal's initiatives and writings
Inter-staff relations	Teachers are inclined to say that the school is a typical cooperative school Staff relations are open-minded and supportive	Teachers are inclined to say that the school is not a typical communicative and cooperative school An abnormally high proportion of teachers quit the school after the first year of study
School resources	The classroom capacity is too low for the intake of pupils Extra funding is given due to several students with learning difficulties in accordance with a local development programme	The classroom capacity is sufficient The teachers complained about textbook situation
School image	The school carries an open and inclusive atmosphere The school is working on various network-building projects in the local community	The school carries a feeling of anonymity The staff climate reflects ongoing conflicts between the principal and the parents

Table 10.2 Summary of characteristics of two Trondheim middle-socio-economic-status schools

Dimension of contrast	More effective school (Asp)	Less effective school (Bang)
General characteristics of the school	261 students in grades 1–6 Typical middle-SES school Open-plan school building Situated in a well-established residential area	420 students in grades 1–9 Typical middle-SES school Open-plan school building Situated in a newly developed residential area without strong traditions and relationships. A number of foreign-language children attend to school
A day in the life of a child	High test scores in the case-study classes Positive attitudes to school and school work	Average test scores in the case-study classes Less positive attitudes to school and school work than at the other school
Teachers' teaching style	Teaching is organised in large classes and two teachers share the responsibility for one class working in their home area The teachers cooperate quite closely also when teaching and share responsibility for the follow-up of individual students	Each class is mainly taught by one classteacher in their home area The two case-study teachers are inclined to follow the teacher's test book manual quite closely. They differ in their way of using open-ended questions to the students
The influence of parents	Good relationships with parents by the use of weekly working programmes for the students, 'letter book' or 'end of week messages'. Parents can be given various follow-up tasks Parents are in general positive about school	Good relationships with parents by the use of weekly working programmes for the students, 'letter book' or 'end of week messages'. Parents can be given various follow-up tasks Parents are in general positive about school

The principal	The principal is focusing on educational leadership and advocates a cooperative leadership style. All teams of teachers are functioning according to the same model of planning and evaluation	The leaders describe their school as 'a happy anarchy', in which everyone is free to take initiatives. All teams of teachers are given much freedom in modelling their work
School goals	Goals are focusing on responsibility, caring and cooperation. The educational programme is well integrated and unified in the organisation as a whole. The staff has a shared ownership in the development plan. School-based evaluation is systematic and continuous	Goals include social and academic areas grounded on standards set by the local education authority. The ownership of the development plan is loose both among teachers and leaders in school. School-based evaluation is only a starting point for school development planning. The staff are reluctant to use systematic school-based evaluation
Inter-staff relations	Teams of teachers have a clear and supportive working fellowship. Teachers spend a lot of time at school on planning of teaching and in meetings	There is little interplay between teams concerning educational matters. In general there is a good social atmosphere among the staff, including the leadership
School resources	Normal conditions according to local standards	Normal conditions according to local standards

11 Europe – the Republic of Ireland

Desmond Swan and Dympna Devine

Introduction/context

The Irish Republic is a sovereign state comprising about three-quarters of the island of Ireland, with a population of about 3,500,000. The state was established in 1922 and has a written constitution which views education primarily as a parental responsibility. A traditionally Christian country, and a member of the European Union, Ireland has close cultural links with mainland Europe, while historically and as a largely English-speaking country it enjoys close links also with Great Britain, the United States and other English-speaking countries. The country's low population density presents a particular challenge to education in rural areas. It is government policy that the Irish language must be studied by every pupil in primary and secondary school. Although it is not legally required to attend school until the age of six years, a large majority of children are already in school at four, while almost everyone will have completed at least one year of school by the age of six.

The low socio-economic-status schools: general characteristics

Secret Garden: the more effective school

Secret Garden, which is run by an order of teaching nuns, is located in the inner city in an area characterised by high levels of unemployment. Housing comprises a disjointed mixture of tower apartment blocks built in the 1960s and terraced red-brick houses dating back to the 1920s, with no front gardens and small yards to the rear. There is some division in the community between what are locally described as the 'flatsies' and the 'poshies', depending on the individual's home accommodation. This division is evidenced not only in differences in living standards between families who live in the houses and those who live in the tower blocks, but also in the setting up of separate facilities such as community centres and nurseries. The problems of the general community, but particularly those in the tower blocks, are similar to many in deprived areas, with high unemployment and crime levels coupled with extensive drug abuse. A new problem for the area has been the spread of Aids and in one of the classrooms under observation in this study one child was being reared by her grandmother following the death of both parents from the disease.

On approaching the school grounds one notices the snarling dogs roaming freely on the scorched grass areas surrounding the tower blocks, and the stare of the occasional local who studies strangers to the vicinity with suspicion. Walking through the gates of the school grounds, however, one immediately experiences a sense of release and escape from the desolate and threatening environment outside the high grey convent walls. It is like entering a secret garden with blossoming trees, the sound of birds singing, flower beds and open grassy lawns. The primary school is a two-storey building of grey brick, and is modern and free of graffiti. There is a playground to the side, a small school garden to the rear and further up the drive is the main convent building, with a church alongside. Classrooms are bright and spacious with views on to the convent grounds.

There are two front entrances to the school building which lock automatically from the outside, ensuring that unauthorised individuals are not allowed access to the school. School corridors are very neat and tidy, with walls decorated with pictures, children's work and posters about health and safety. Coats are neatly hung in rows with each child assigned a particular coat hook with her name on it. The school hall is a very cheerful place with full length windows and murals painted by the children on every available piece of wall space.

There are sixteen full-time teaching staff, the principal, a secretary and a teacher's aide who is employed on a government employment scheme. It is a co-educational school up to first grade, and a single-sex girls' school thereafter, with boys leaving to attend the local boys' school for the remainder of their primary education. Average class size is twenty-eight. The children wear a school uniform and there are very specific rules about tying back hair, wearing jewellery and general cleanliness.

Tower View: the less effective school

The school is located in the same catchment area as the more effective school already described. The area is bleak and depressed and the road leading up to the school is frequently littered with burnt-out cars. Bollards have been erected in 'through roadways' to reduce the incidence of 'joy-riding' (youngsters racing stolen cars at high speed). A former military barracks converted for use as a primary school over fifty years ago, it has retained its prison-like character, with a high grey boundary wall, large steel gates and windows hidden by steel bars. Guard dogs peer through a gate in an enclosed yard and are used for security at night. The building is old and poorly maintained, splintered in structure and with the decor inside dull and dated. It does not have the appearance of a school and, in contrast to the more effective school already described, provides little respite from the immediate environment, mirroring its run-down, oppressive character.

This school is run by a male religious order with five lay teachers and the principal who is a member of the religious community. It is an all-boys' school serving grades 2 to 6, with boys below grade 2 attending the local convent school. Average class size is twenty-three. There is a school uniform which all children were wearing. Two of the teachers teach in one building which also houses the principal's office and the reading room. This latter room is used by the principal (who is also a qualified remedial teacher) for working with children with reading difficulties but it is very poorly resourced and seems to be treated as a room for storing surplus furniture. The second building – across the school yard – has three classrooms, a staffroom and staff toilet. The third building houses the school hall which teachers are reluctant to use as it is too big to heat. The corridors in each building are long and narrow with the occasional statue and religious portrait along the walls. Classrooms are small and furnished with traditional two-seater benches. All windows are fitted with steel grids and there are no sink areas in the classrooms themselves.

A day in the life of a child

Secret Garden: the more effective school

The pupil chosen for the child study is an eight-year-old girl named Ann. She has blonde hair tied neatly in a pony-tail with a hairband and rosette. She is tall for her age and sits towards the back of the class, sharing a group with four other children. Each group in the class is named after a flower and Ann's group is called the 'bluebells'.

The day begins with the children entering the classroom in a line, the teacher keeping a watchful eye for possible misdemeanours. Following a prayer, school work begins with a mathematics lesson and from this period to the end of the day Ann is kept busy. The mathematics lesson entails class discussion of two-digit addition and subtraction problems followed by completion of work from the blackboard. An Irish-language reading lesson follows with a lively mixture of questions and answers, reading aloud and drama to illustrate the story. Questions in Irish are repeated and rephrased so that children get a good grasp of what is being taught.

Break-time follows with eating of snacks and fifteen minutes' playtime in the school yard. An English lesson on 'Capital Letters' is then completed using whole-class instruction and Ann enjoys the 'mistakes' the teacher deliberately makes in writing sentences on the blackboard. The lesson concludes with children completing written work from the blackboard and Ann works away quietly while the teacher completes Irish reading and begins English reading with groups of children at her desk. Lunch break is signalled by the ringing of the bell and after saying a prayer and eating their lunch (supplied by the local authority) the children are again sent to the yard to play. The afternoon period is spent completing a religion lesson, and on correction and assignment of homework, and as a special treat (which happens once a month) a video of the 'Lion King' is shown to the two second grades.

The teacher describes Ann as a hardworking, mannerly girl. She says that Ann's mother is a single parent who finds it difficult bringing Ann up on her own. She is very ambitious for Ann and is very supportive of her in her school work. Ann describes the school as a happy place and says she has lots of friends here. Her favourite part of the week is when they do the 'fit kids' programme. She likes her teacher, whom she describes as sometimes cross but always fair.

Tower View: the less effective school

The child study involved an eight-year-old boy named Andrew. He is of small stature with fair hair and blue eyes and has a lively appearance. He is seated at the top of the classroom near the teacher's desk, sharing a group with six other boys.

Andrew's school day comprises a mixture of oral and written work. The day begins with a lesson in the Irish language which both the teacher and children seem to find tedious, encapsulated in such comments of the teacher as, 'I think you've all gone to sleep, wake up down there'. The lesson is frequently interrupted by inattentive children and, while Andrew is not one of these, he is constantly checking his watch as if wishing the lesson was over. The mathematics lesson follows a similar pattern with discussion of the text (the topic being covered is 'Time'), and completion of work, drawing clocks and filling in the time, in a mathematics workbook.

An English reading lesson follows the break and the morning session is completed with a story about the Fianna (an ancient warrior tribe in Irish mythology) which is recounted expressively by the teacher much to the delight of the children. However throughout this lesson the teacher has an uphill struggle maintaining order and is frequently heard to say 'You're taking the fun out of it . . . stop carrying on'. All are delighted when the lunch bell sounds and sandwiches and milk, supplied by the local authority, are distributed, with the children racing out to the yard when they have finished eating. Afternoon teaching begins with a lesson on the 'Safe Cross Code'. This involves talking about safety on the road and colouring in a workbook on road safety.

The atmosphere in the classroom is pleasant and easy-going, and the children have a warm, open relationship with their teacher. Andrew spends a good deal of time 'off-task' however, chatting to his group mates. He is never involved in any serious misdemeanours and always makes an effort to complete his written work and participate orally. The teacher describes Andrew as a good worker and an independent child who occasionally needs to be pressurised into working to his ability. She describes his home background as being relatively stable and that his parents take an active interest in his school work, ensuring that homework is always completed. Andrew says this was a typical school day and that he enjoys coming to this school, although he complains about the school building which he describes as 'old-fashioned'. He likes his teacher and describes her as good fun and not as strict as other teachers in the school.

Teachers' teaching style

Secret Garden: the more effective school

There are two second grades in this school and observation was carried out in each one. In both classes, however, common patterns of instruction and classroom management emerged. Both teachers emphasised maintaining discipline, while class rules and procedures were clearly understood by the children. Rules were implemented consistently and discipline enforced fairly. Both teachers also placed a high premium on positive reinforcement and there was continuous evidence of praise for positive behaviour and good work efforts. Discipline, praise and consistency in dealing with children were seen by both to be crucial aspects of providing a safe and secure environment for these children. A low level of noise was tolerated and teachers were quick to identify and respond to children who were distracted. Instruction generally involved whole-class teaching followed by individual instruction of children with learning difficulties. Questioning of children was a frequent feature of all lessons but this tended to be of a factual nature rather than focusing on the development of higher-order thinking skills. There was very little wasting of time evident in either class and the transfer of children from one topic to another was carried out without major disruption. One of the teachers was particularly well organised and wasted no time at all. She was constantly working with children at her desk or checking through reading while the remaining children worked at their desks, finding the time also to listen to stories and news items from individual children. She was highly efficient and business-like in terms of classroom management, but warm and caring in her interactions with individual children. The other teacher exhibited a more relaxed teaching style, and, while equally efficient in classroom management, more of her individual personality was brought into her teaching style.

Tower View: the less effective school

The teacher is a middle-aged woman who describes herself as having become 'stale' in her teaching, lacking the enthusiasm she initially had at the start of her career. Un-doubtedly the lack of mobility in the teaching profession has contributed to this sense of disillusionment, as she has little opportunity of transferring to another school. She clearly finds her work an uphill struggle and stated that she has taken time off in the past due to pressures in the job. She grew up in the locality, but feels that the area has changed considerably since she was a child. Nonetheless, she states that being from the area has helped her in her dealings with the parents, who talk to her more readily than to other teachers. She cares deeply for the children, but seems unable to cope with the demands they place on her. Most teaching is whole-class orientated, although children are divided into groups for both mathematics and reading. She makes a point of checking through each child's work every day, but finds this difficult given the time spent maintaining discipline. A great deal of time is devoted to classroom manage-ment and a lesson is never completed without some time being given to correction of disruptive pupils.

The curriculum

Secret Garden: the more effective school

The curriculum followed in this school adheres to guidelines set by the Department of Education. While the principal does not become directly involved in curricular issues, she was instrumental in drawing up a 'School Plan' by organising attendance of all the staff at a course related to school plans in a local Teachers' Centre. She states that both she and her staff have benefited greatly from the process of discussion and collaboration emanating from putting the school plan together and that definite im-provements in curricular practice are evident since putting the plan in place. Speci-fically, she feels it has given teachers greater confidence in affirming their own teach-ing style and methods and has ensured greater continuity and consistency in the edu-cation of children throughout the school. She stresses that drawing up the school plan is an ongoing process and describes it as a 'living document' – constantly open to regeneration and change, responding to the needs of children in the area at any given time. A high premium is placed on ensuring the availability of resources for imple-menting the curriculum and these are constantly renewed and updated. Particular emphasis appears to be placed on encouraging activity in the children ('to counteract the TV syndrome') and subjects such as physical education, music, drama and reading are emphasised. As an example of this all children are participating this year in a 'Fit Kids – Fit for Life' programme, and a performance of their skills will be given at the Christmas concert. Each year a fund-raising 'Readathon' is completed (with funds raised going to the school and a national charity) and illustrations and synopses of books read by children are displayed on the walls of the school hall. Yet another example is the existence of a school garden which all children in the school have a role in maintaining. This gives them the opportunity to see things grow and become more aware of the changing seasons. The theme of watching things grow is carried through to the classrooms where, in both second grades, each child had planted sunflower seeds which they tended and cared for throughout the school year.

Tower View: the less effective school

The curriculum followed in this school is similar to all primary schools in Ireland. The teacher stated that the programme for second grade is completed each year by most students, which she attributes to the small class size (twenty-three pupils) and therefore the opportunity to give appropriate attention to each individual student in whatever area they are experiencing difficulty. Of particular note, however, is the absence of organised extra-curricular activities, with only football and hurling (a traditional Irish game) played after school hours on occasion. There is a particular emphasis on developing reading and writing skills and the teacher feels that very few children 'slip through the net' in these areas. There is no collaboration between teachers in relation to curricular issues, although they have expressed an interest in completing a school plan. They are currently waiting for the principal to organise attendance at a course to give them guidelines on implementing this plan. The teacher is particularly frustrated by the lack of teaching resources in the school and says that it is difficult to implement the curriculum in an interesting and enjoyable way without an adequate supply of learning aids. She enjoys teaching art but rarely does painting with the children as the nearest source of water is from a tap in the school yard, thus making it impossible to organise an art lesson without major disruption.

The influence of parents

Secret Garden: the more effective school

Both the principal and teachers state that the relationship between the school and parents is very positive. There is an acute awareness that parents may feel threatened by the school environment and efforts are made to overcome this by making the school open, welcoming and supportive and above all by treating parents as equals – 'let them feel that what they have to say is important'. There is a history of parental involvement in the school which centres not only around fund-raising but also on helping teachers in the classrooms with activities such as art and crafts. A parents' association was established in the last year and suggestions made by the association towards improvements in the school are followed up by the principal. An example of this was a suggestion that boys leaving the school at first grade should have a formal leaving ceremony. The principal and staff agreed and for the first time a mass and presentation of scrolls to the young boys was held at the end of the last academic year. Efforts are currently being made by the association to employ a drama teacher after school hours for the children and this is being actively supported by the principal.

While the school has not yet been allocated a home/school liaison officer, a system of promoting home/school links has been in place for the past number of years, by making a member of the religious community available to do homework with children in the 'flats' (apartments for low-income families). For this purpose a flat has been assigned to the nuns, which they have renovated and which provides space and a pleasant environment in which the children can complete homework. The principal says that this system has worked very well as the sister can relay messages from parents to teachers and acts as an important link between the most disadvantaged children and the school. Understanding and empathy appear to be explicit features of this school in dealing with parents and this is reflected in the reluctance of the principal to suspend children for misbehaviour, knowing that such behaviour is rooted in difficulties the children and parents are experiencing at home.

Tower View: the less effective school

Relations with parents appear to be good, although they are not directly involved in any of the day-to-day activities of the school. Both the teacher and principal mention the difficulties parents experience in coping within a disadvantaged environment, along with problems of illiteracy which impact directly on their ability to help their children with school work. While there is therefore an appreciation of the difficulties of parents in the school, there is no attempt made to establish a sense of community involving parents, children and teachers. There is a strong sense of despair among the teachers, with little belief in an ability to overcome these problems – they seem imprisoned by the deprivation of the general area. Some parents have been physically and verbally abusive to teachers, although this was seen to be the exception rather than the norm. There seems to be little interest in increasing involvement of parents in the school and the teacher stated she would find it intimidating to have parents come into the classroom to help with school work (as recommended in a recent 'home/school liaison' course which she had attended). Parent/teacher meetings take place twice yearly, at the beginning of the school year to set parameters for pupil performance, and towards the end of the year to assess progress. The teacher complained of the lack of contact with the fathers of children and feels it is very difficult for mothers to cope with their childrens' problems on their own.

The headteacher/principal

Secret Garden: the more effective school

The principal is a woman in her early forties and is a member of a religious community of teaching nuns. She has considerable experience as both a teacher and principal and has been principal of this school for the past six years. She is quietly spoken, highly organised and totally committed to the children and staff of this school. She sees her main role as facilitator – to provide a happy working environment for both teachers and children and to give people 'freedom to use their gifts and to work responsibly within a free and easy atmosphere'. Consultation with others is a key feature of this facilitation process. In this regard she has an open-door policy and feels it is important to give time to listen to the problems, difficulties and worries of those she comes into contact with in the course of her work. She has an intimate knowledge of the children and their families and takes an active interest in what is happening in their lives. This was evidenced on one particular visit to the school when the principal talked to a young student in her office about her father's serious illness, discussing a picture with the child that she had drawn about her father. On visits to classrooms the principal always talks to the children, inquiring about family events or simply asking how they are. Her office is decorated with photographs of childrens' activities and the occasional picture or card which some children have made for her.

She has an excellent relationship with her staff and says she is guided by their experience and expertise in making decisions relevant to the school. Monitoring of staff is carried out formally through submission of monthly schemes and end-of-year progress reports and informally by the principal walking freely in and out of classrooms with messages for teachers and pupils. Specific roles of responsibility are assigned to staff members (such as library administration, religious celebrations/events, resource maintenance etc.) and every eventuality in the school year seems to be taken into account. There is a high level of consultation with staff and an emphasis on collaboration and cooperation. This has been particularly worked upon and improved upon since the introduction of the school plan. She is very professional in her role as principal although she is reluctant to apply this term to herself – believing it conjures up notions of distance and rigidity. Her personality is very much in evidence in her management style – an openness and enthusiasm for her work and an acceptance that she cannot be an expert in all things, leaving areas she is not confident in to others. She is very comfortable in her role as principal and is not afraid to confront difficult issues, expecting staff to be honest and 'up front' with her in relation to her performance as principal.

Tower View: the less effective school

The principal is a quiet, shy and introverted man in his early fifties. He has been principal of this school for three years. As an individual he is self-deprecating and seems to lack any vision for the school. He is clearly uncomfortable in his role as principal, having taken up the appointment at the request of his religious superior. He expresses confidence in his staff and is willing to let them carry on with their role without any interference or intrusion from him. Teaching plans and monthly progress reports are not checked. His tendency not to become involved in classroom issues was identified as a problem by the teacher under observation, who stated that clear leadership is lacking in the school, with very little communication about school policy or backup support, particularly in relation to disciplining the pupils. He is kind and gentle in his dealings with the children (for example, he organises a trip to the mountains for children in the school most Saturdays) but neither the teachers nor the children perceive him as an authority figure in the school. He admits to being very disorganised in his work and mentions specific plans which have not yet been realised because he has not got around to doing them. Specific mention was made of attending a course on establishing a school plan, but the commitment to doing this, or the concept of such a plan as a vibrant 'living document', was absent. His style of management is reactive (for example, the school yard was recently tarred only when it deteriorated to dangerous levels) and he is satisfied to let the school run on the initiative of the staff. The teacher under observation says this is very frustrating for the staff, who already feel overburdened with the work they do in their classrooms.

The teacher, while loyal to him and therefore unwilling to criticise him openly, stated that he is not suited to the position of principal and that there has been a history of ineffective principals in the school for the past ten to fifteen years. This she attributes to the shortage of effective personnel within the religious community from which to select principals. The problems in the school cannot therefore be attributed to one individual, but arise from policy decisions taken over time by the religious order governing the school. She expressed the view that the problem would only be solved by bringing in 'new blood' and was quite emphatic that none of the existing staff members would be suitable as a possible replacement, given the history of animosity that has developed among some staff members over the years.

School expectations of pupils

Secret Garden: the more effective school

The principal specifies that the most important goal of the school is the development of high self-esteem in the children, stating that the school should 'foster a happy atmosphere in which children can learn, use their gifts, bring out their potential and sense of self-worth and so face life with courage, confidence and independence'. She is very aware of the difficulties facing these children when they leave school and, while high academic standards are emphasised ('Teach each programme well and prepare children for second-level, i.e. secondary, schooling'), it is on the area of personal and social development that particular stress is placed. This is reflected in the emphasis on physical and creative activity throughout the school (music, art, drama and sport) and on extending academic activities (such as reading) beyond the classroom, but making children aware that what they learn is a skill for living and leisure. Thus the 'Readathon' encourages children to read for pleasure and the running of the 'Book Fair' provides parents with the opportunity and encouragement to purchase books for their children. There is also a distinct emphasis on promoting a religious ethos in the school, reflected in 'teaching children to respect themselves, each other and God and the mystery of life', and religious occasions are taken very seriously with one teacher assigned specific responsibility for organising church-related events.

Tower View: the less effective school

The development of social skills is identified by both principal and teacher as being an important curricular goal for the school. This specifically entailed teaching the pupil to be able to work on his or her own as well as being polite and mannerly in conversation. There is, however, no consistent policy within the school on discipline and the teacher states that complaints about disruptive pupils are rarely followed up satisfactorily. The school places an important emphasis on ensuring that all children leave the school with basic reading and writing skills. Assessment is by each individual teacher and the principal does not become involved.

School goals

Secret Garden: the more effective school

Specific school goals relate to the maintenance of high standards and efficient running of the school. Securing the school building has been a major priority, and in the past few years all windows have been replaced and an alarm system put in place. The principal is determined that school activities will not be curtailed or limited due to vandalism, as evidenced in her continual replacement of shrubs to the front of the school despite the likelihood of repeated theft of these. Securing the appointment of a full-time home/school liaison officer is an immediate concern; the continued development and extension of the school plan was also specified as an important priority for the future.

Tower View: the less effective school

The principal was very vague in his description of school goals but when pressed did specify that he would like to establish a parents' committee, draw up a school plan, and refurbish the school building. However no plan of action or timetable has been drawn up for the achievement of these goals, and there appears to be no urgency in implementing them. The teacher was very frustrated by the constant vandalism to the school building and the consequent lack of resources, but improving security in the school was not mentioned by the principal as a source of concern.

Inter-staff relations

Secret Garden: the more effective school

Relations between staff members in this school are very positive, reflected in the fact that there is little staff turnover, with some of the teachers having been in the school for over twenty years. While there is little scope for movement from one school to another in Ireland, teachers in this school seem very content to remain here. The relationships between staff members extend beyond their professional roles and strong friendships have evolved over the years. A specific emphasis is placed by the principal on collaboration and, since her appointment, teachers of similar grade levels are encouraged to work together on class schemes. This has been facilitated by working together on the school plan which encouraged teachers to share their ideas and teaching methods with one another and, as a result, gave all teachers greater confidence in their own ability and worth. Responsibility for discipline is also shared among staff with an agreed policy of ensuring high standards of behaviour in all children, not just those in the teacher's own class. The staffroom is very warm and welcoming with a homely atmosphere. It is an easy place to relax in and coffee breaks are full of chat and lively discussion. Teachers are obviously at ease with one another and seem happy and enthusiastic about working in this school.

Tower View: the less effective school

This school exhibits an extremely isolationist approach to teaching. Due to the physical layout of the school the staff work in two buildings and there appears to be no collaboration or interaction between them in carrying out teaching duties. The staffroom is a cold impersonal place and there is very little communication among the teachers. There appears to be some hostility between male and female members of staff, to such an extent that teachers do not always go to the staffroom for their lunch. Much of the conversation that does take place is negatively orientated, and one member of staff during one observation period spent his time staring through the windows at children playing in the playground, making derogatory comments about their appearance and behaviour. The teacher under observation stated that, in her view, it is the staff more than the pupils who have suffered as a result of the ineffective leadership in the school and that the teachers do their best within a poor working environment.

School resources

Secret Garden: the more effective school

This school has a very good stock of resources and teachers are supplied with the equipment and activities they need in fulfilling their teaching duties. Funding for resources comes from government grants and a small amount from local fund-raising. A particular emphasis is placed on maintaining equipment in good condition, thus ensuring that it can be passed from class to class from one year to the next. The resourcing of the library (which is currently being redecorated) is a top priority and new books are purchased every year.

Tower View: the less effective school

There is little evidence of adequate resourcing in the school. Money has been spent on television sets, video-recorders, games, etc. over the years, but they have all been stolen or vandalised. Only some weeks prior to the observation, attempts had been made to burn down the school. The teacher described the situation as hopeless and the constant vandalism as wearing down the spirit of the staff. Government funding is inadequate to deal with the problem and is mainly used for heating and cleaning expenses, with local fund-raising kept to a minimum due to the high levels of un-employment in the area.

Relationship with local authorities

Secret Garden: the more effective school

The principal describes her relationship with the school board as 'friendly, supportive and easy'. She describes her relationship with the School Inspectorate as excellent, making them feel welcome on their visits, but stressing their role as encouraging and affirming the staff in their work. Her dealings with the Department of Education revolve around securing extra funding and facilities for the children. The principal has an active involvement with local community workers (social workers, nurses, youth workers, police) and meets with them once a month to share information on what is happening locally that will be of relevance in her work with the children.

Tower View: the less effective school

The principal described his relationship with local authorities (Board of Management, School Inspectorate and Department of Education) as being good, but was not forth-coming on details of those relations.

School image

Secret Garden: the more effective school

The principal feels the school has a good reputation in the local community and that it is perceived to be 'a good school where children are happy, well cared for and are taught well'. A recent problem in the community, with implications for the school, is the incidence of Aids in certain families. Some parents have withdrawn their children from the school, sending them to schools outside the local area. While no child in the school has Aids, the principal and staff have discussed the issue and have agreed that precautionary measures in dealing with all children injured in the school should be introduced.

Tower View: the less effective school

The principal believes the local community perceive the school in a 'reasonable' light. He states that upwardly mobile parents often send their children to schools outside the area, but feels they do not necessarily get a better education as a result. No attempt is made to publicise the school in the local community and there are no school concerts, open days, etc. to display school work to the parents.

Conclusions for low-socio-economic-status schools

The schools described here are similar in a number of respects. Firstly, the catchment area for both is the same, resulting in a similar student body in terms of home background and general social context. Given the single-sex nature of both schools, it frequently happens that pupils in each belong to the same family. Secondly, the national curriculum is implemented in the two schools, with similar mathematics and reading programmes being followed. Thirdly, both schools are run by religious orders and have a long tradition of serving the local community in the field of education. Teaching styles were also comparable because of a strong tendency to use whole-class teaching followed by completion of written assignments. There was no evidence of group work or cooperative learning in either school.

Despite these similarities, substantial observable differences were evident in the two schools as summarised in Table 11.1. These differences reflect the substantially different working environments for both teachers and children. Overall, the impression in the more effective school is of a proactive style of management and teaching, with the school perceived as being a vital part of the children's lives. Difficulties encountered by the children are worked on diligently in an effort to overcome them. While it must be stated that the teachers in general in the less effective school are also concerned to help students, an overriding sense of despair exists in the school. Teachers are coping, but only just.

An element in explaining these differences is the personality of the principals in both schools. The open, confident and disciplined personality of the principal in the more effective school is reflected in the pursuance of specific school goals, with an overall vision in mind. The principal of the less effective school is introverted and shy and seems incapable of leading in a clear, organised way. Unsuccessful attempts to maintain discipline, and repeated vandalism in this school also affect, in a very real

Table 11.1 Summary of differences between the two lower-SES schools across the twelve dimensions

Dimension of contrast	More effective low-SES (Secret Garden)	Less effective low-SES (Tower View)
General characteristics of the school	Modern, well maintained in pleasant surroundings; 'haven'	Very old, bleak, poorly maintained; 'prison-like'
A day in the life of a child	Highly structured, clear focus, intensity of learning, silent	Unstructured, laissez-faire, slow pace, student inactivity, noisy
Teachers' teaching style	Consistent and efficient, minimal misbehaviour – does not detract from learning	Haphazard approach, discipline problems have a wearing effect on teacher and students, detracts from learning
The curriculum	Ongoing curriculum development and implementation of school plan	No school plan has been developed
The influence of parents	Policy of inclusiveness with accommodation to parent needs	Minimal contact with parents
The principal	Highly organised, visible, proactive in managerial style, democratic leadership in evidence	Disorganised, reactive managerial style, little leadership in evidence
School expectations of parents	Develop high self-esteem and high standards in academic and social sphere	Reinforcing basic social skills and 3R's (Reading, Arithmetic and Writing)
School goals	Clearly defined, highly specific	Vague, imprecise
Inter-staff relations	Warm, friendly, lively and enthusiastic	Little personal interaction, depressed, feelings of being trapped
School resources	Well equipped, emphasis on maintenance and strict stock control	Poorly resourced due to repeated vandalism. Poor stock control
Relationship with local authorities	Friendly with emphasis on active support for work in the school	Considered good but little direct contact encouraged
School image	Considered good	Considered reasonable

way, the ability of students and teachers to work together effectively. These problems are compounded by the historical context of the school, with a pattern of ineffective principals having been appointed from a declining religious-order population in the past twenty years. The all-boys setting of the school must also be borne in mind in terms of discipline issues.

The middle-socio-economic-status schools: general characteristics

Country Lane: the more effective school

This school, which is located in a densely populated, middle-class area in Dublin city, is tucked away at the end of a narrow winding lane, totally secluded from the hustle and bustle of city living. The back gardens of expensive detached houses open on to this lane. The land on which this Church of Ireland co-educational school was built was donated by a local parishioner thirty years ago. His house, which is reminiscent of an old country farmhouse is adjacent to the school.

The school building is modern and has the appearance of being well maintained. The playground is small and visitors must park their cars in the lane leading to the school gates. Inside, the school is spotless and a sense of calmness and order is palpable as one walks along the corridors. A buzz of activity emanates from the classrooms, which are bright and airy. Children's work is displayed on every available space, both inside and outside the classroom walls. Three years ago a substantial extension was added to the school, comprising a hall, reading room, staffroom and office.

The school serves a middle- and upper-middle-class population. Many of the children do not live in the local area, and some travel up to twenty miles to attend the school. The principal states that many children choose this school not only because of its excellent reputation, but also because religious doctrine is not taught during school hours. There are eleven members of staff, comprising ten teaching staff and the principal. There is a high level of staff stability, with a majority of staff having worked there for over five years. The principal has been in the school for twenty-six years and the vice-principal for a similar length of time. Classes are organised along grade levels, with one class for each grade. Average class size is approximately thirty-two children. There is a full-time remedial teacher who works with groups of children from each class, and a resource teacher whose responsibilities change from week to week as needs arise.

Cherry Orchard: the less effective school

This school is located in a middle- to upper-middle-class suburb in Dublin. It is a co-educational convent school up to grade 1, becoming single-sex from grade 2, when boys leave to attend the local boys' primary school. The school entrance has changed considerably in the past year, following the sale of a substantial proportion of land to private housing developers. The former avenue leading up to the school is now lined with highly priced detached suburban homes. Building work is ongoing and the sound of bulldozers can be heard in the distance from the classrooms.

The convent grounds are dominated by two large buildings to the front, comprising the convent itself and a newly built secondary school. To the rear of the convent is the primary school. This is a large, two-storey building, which has been extended and added to over the years. Entry to the school involves crossing an enclosed yard and walking along a perspex-roofed corridor. Inside, the school has a sixties-style decor, with green tiles up to waist level along the walls and religious statues and portraits dispersed throughout. High ceilings and wooden floors abound, creating an echoing atmosphere. While children's work is displayed along corridor walls, it has little impact on the institutional character of the building. Arrowed signs pointing to the direction of the principal's office are displayed intermittently throughout the school, as this office is tucked away on the first floor. New windows have been installed and overall the school building is very well maintained. To the rear of the school two classrooms have been located in prefabricated buildings, installed last year. The second grade class is one of these. It is a large, bright and warm room with two toilets at the rear. There is a sink area and the classroom walls are covered with a combination of the children's and teachers' work.

There are fourteen full-time teaching staff, the principal and a part-time secretary. There is a school uniform which all of the children were wearing. While the school is run by a religious order, only two nuns teach on the staff.

A day in the life of a child

Country Lane: the more effective school

The school day begins at 8.40 a.m. and Peter, a bright-eyed, brown-haired boy settles into his group at the back of the class. There is no school uniform and he is dressed in a jumper and jeans. The teacher allows five minutes for 'settling down' before starting work for the day, which begins with correction of homework. Peter participates eagerly in the checking of spellings and tables and is delighted when he gives a correct answer. An oral Irish-language lesson follows with emphasis on activity to illustrate the meaning behind Irish phrases. Peter's attention during this lesson is intermittent, particularly when the teacher focuses on one child or group in the classroom. Reading of an Irish-language text follows, with the children then assigned a written exercise on the text.

The mathematics lesson following the break focuses on identifying three-digit numbers and Peter seems to have little difficulty in understanding the lesson. Whole-class teaching is used by the teacher, writing three-digit numbers on the white board and asking children to pick out the hundreds, tens and units. Peter enjoys the written mathematics exercise (drawing three-digit abacuses) and is very methodical and careful about drawing neat, straight lines. There is a lot of discussion in his group about the mathematics problems, and noise levels in the classroom at this time are quite high. Rehearsal of the school play 'The Gingerbread Man' follows. Today the emphasis is on practising songs and Peter participates enthusiastically, doing actions to the words and putting every effort into his singing. The teacher then reads the children a story about dreams, holding their attention through questioning and discussion at different points of the story. A worksheet is distributed on which the children must write a creative account of a dream they had.

The afternoon session is devoted to assignment of homework and an art lesson, making picture-frames for the children's favourite photograph. There is a buzz of activity throughout the lesson, with the teacher moving from child to child giving assistance where needed.

The teacher describes Peter as a lively, intelligent child, who is enthusiastic and cooperative in his work. She says his parents are extremely interested in his school work and very supportive in encouraging him to work to his potential. Peter says he likes this school and that he particularly loves doing the school play.

Cherry Orchard: the less effective school

The child chosen for observation is a fair-haired girl named Martina. She is neatly dressed in full uniform with her hair tied back in plaits. The class is organised into groups identified by colour, each group comprising six or seven children. Martina is in the 'red' group and is seated at the back of the classroom.

Martina's school day begins at 9.10 a.m. with recital of a morning prayer followed by discussion of any news the children may wish to share with the rest of the class. The teacher then assigns work from the religion textbook which entails colouring in a picture of a biblical character. An oral Irish-language lesson follows which involves repetition in unison of phrases related to a story shown on a film slide. There is a great deal of shuffling of chairs during this lesson. The children seem restless and Martina occasionally colours in her religion work. This lesson concludes with reading instruction in the Irish language, with children asked to read in rotation two sentences from the textbook. The lesson is completed with the recital of poetry and a game requiring the following of instructions in Irish.

On return from the school yard following a break, a mathematics lesson is completed, involving subtraction and addition of three-digit numbers. A traditional approach towards the teaching of these sums is used with no regrouping of numbers, and concepts explained using the blackboard rather than concrete materials. After completion of a page in the mathematics textbook it is lunch-time.

The afternoon session entails correction of sums completed prior to the break and creative writing based on a biblical character. An English-language reading lesson is also completed with reading of the text by individual children followed by a question-and-answer session on the text. The final hour is the class 'video-time'. The video room is located in the main school building and the children walk to this in a neat and orderly line. On return to the class a prayer to end the day is recited and the children leave for home.

There is a pleasant easy-going atmosphere in Martina's classroom with very little misbehaviour, despite the children being visibly bored during many of the lessons. The teacher describes Martina as a very earnest child who tries hard in school. She says her parents are keenly interested in her progress and very supportive, ensuring that homework is always completed to a high standard. Martina says she likes this school because there is no 'bullying', but thinks the building is very old. She is pleased to be in the new classroom.

Teachers' teaching style

Country Lane: the more effective school

Peter's teacher has a gentle approach in working with the children. Teaching usually consists of whole-class instruction, followed by completion of worksheets or of a page in a workbook. Individual children are then free to ask for assistance when required, and the teacher moves about the classroom correcting mistakes and monitoring written work. There is a strong emphasis on developing higher-order thinking skills through questioning and discussion. Children are praised frequently and the teacher has a very good relationship with them. While major interruptions due to misbehaviour are rare, there is generally a high level of noise during children's written work. The teacher is frequently heard saying 'ssh' or 'It would be lovely if you stopped talking', but is most often ignored. Many of the children, including Peter, spend a good deal of time 'off-task', particularly when written work is finished. Instructions for follow-up activities are rarely given and children amuse themselves chatting, walking around the classroom or going to the toilet. The teacher states that she allows freedom of movement 'within reason', but children are not allowed to leave the classroom without permission.

Cherry Orchard: the less effective school

The teacher is a woman in her thirties. She was formerly employed as a full-time member of staff but is now working on a temporary basis in the school, having relinquished her permanent status following a career break of five years. She will be teaching this class for the remainder of the school year. Her style of teaching is very traditional, characterised in the main by whole-class instruction and a good deal of oral instruction. While her relationship with the children is friendly, there appears to be very little personal interaction with individual children. There are no discipline problems and any minor misdemeanours are efficiently dealt with. She says that this is a lovely school to work in and one where it is 'very easy to fit in'. She states that she has become uninterested in teaching as a career and would like to see herself move into some other area of work. Teaching, for the moment therefore, is a means of earning a living.

The curriculum

Country Lane: the more effective school

A standardised curriculum is implemented by all schools and this school differs from others only in that religious doctrine is taught outside school hours. Whole-class teaching is used predominantly, with individual and group instruction for reading and mathematics when required. The principal does not become directly involved in curricular issues, but sees her role as ensuring that there are sufficient resources for teachers to help them implement the curriculum. She actively encourages children's participation in extra-curricular activities such as art, French, dance and music, which take place after school hours. In the previous year a substantial proportion of time was devoted to drawing up an official 'School Plan', for which a sub-committee for each subject area was organised. Teachers shared information and ideas which have now become part of school policy in implementing the curriculum.

Cherry Orchard: the less effective school

The curriculum followed in this school is in line with guidelines issued by the Department of Education. Whole-class teaching is mainly used, with individual and group instruction for mathematics and reading instruction when required. The emphasis appears to be on implementing the curriculum on the 'tried and tested' basis, with adherence to traditional modes of instruction because 'they work best'. There is a remedial teacher in the school and children are withdrawn from class to attend the 'reading room' several times each week. The principal becomes involved in curricular issues only to the extent of initiating discussion on improving classroom practice. She has found the implementation of the school plan to be very useful in encouraging discussion on school policy in general and in particular sharing ideas in relation to art and music teaching. A private physical education instructor is employed in the school for two days per week. There is also a strong emphasis on extra-curricular instruction towards which the children pay a small fee. Subjects offered in this regard include art, ballet, Irish dancing, French, swimming, tennis, and music.

The influence of parents

Country Lane: the more effective school

There is a very positive relationship between parents and teachers in this school. Most contacts are teacher-initiated, but there is an 'open-door' policy, with parents welcome at any time once prior notice has been given. The principal is concerned that parents are kept informed of all events in the school and are also consulted on any major issues which may arise, for example in relation to discipline policy or sex education. Parents are not involved in any of the day-to-day activities of the school and formally meet the teachers once a year for a progress report on their child's performance. However, the teacher states that she meets all parents, on average, eight times over the school year through appointments.

Cherry Orchard: the less effective school

The principal states that the school has a friendly, open relationship with the parents. There is an active parents' association, and relations between school personnel and the association are described as being excellent. She is anxious that the school is perceived in a warm light by parents and ensures that she is available to meet and discuss areas of concern at all times. Her motto is one of 'prevention is better than cure' and this is ensured by enabling parents to 'communicate regularly with the school about factors that are likely to affect the behaviour of their children in school'. This emphasis on an open, friendly policy is demonstrated by the organisation of fund-raising events, which are considered by the principal to be important as 'social events' in themselves – building a sense of community, rather than simply for raising money for the school. Parents have been involved in decisions relating to changes in the approach road to the school and participating in the upkeep and maintenance of the school building itself. A number of parents are also involved in administering the school library.

The headteacher/principal

Country Lane: the more effective school

The principal is a smartly dressed woman in her mid-fifties. She is lively, enthusiastic and clearly enjoys her work. She is very proud of the school and has spent the past twenty-six years moulding it into a place that is 'maintained well, bright, clean, heated, with modern well-kept equipment that serves the needs of children and teachers'. She is highly efficient and while she does not interfere in any direct way with teachers' professional role, she likes to be kept informed about what is happening in every classroom. Monitoring of teachers' work involves checking through fortnightly schemes and monthly reports, of which copies are kept in her office. She particularly stresses the need to be kept informed of all contacts with parents and insists that all such contacts are made known to her in advance. This is to ensure that she will not waste another teacher's or parents' time in the future by being caught 'off-guard' on any issue and not being able to deal with it competently at the time.

She places great emphasis on communication and sees the absence of communication as being the major contributor to problems in both the home and the school. Her philosophy on the importance of communication comes through in her management style, which she describes as being proactive and democratic, ensuring wide consultation with staff members and a commitment to discussing detailed ideas and plans she has for the school. She is thorough and precise in her work and when implementing policy changes, informs herself of the latest research on the area. A recent example of this was the drawing up of a discipline policy. This was only finalised after informing staff and parents of the latest research on the area and discussing with them their views and priorities. She sees the lack of time given to communication as the biggest change in modern society, and feels that it directly impacts on the lives of children whose needs are often forgotten in the hustle and bustle of modern living. She invests a great deal of her own personal time in running the school, as evidenced by a recent weekend in which she and her husband spent their time preparing books donated to the school, for a book sale. She places great emphasis on private fund-raising, not being willing to wait for the Department of Education to supply funds before getting things done.

Cherry Orchard: the less effective school

The principal is a woman in her mid-fifties; she has been principal of this school for ten years. She is a matter of fact, direct person, initially appearing quite abrupt in manner. She is highly organised and efficient and seems very comfortable in her role as principal. She states that she attaches extreme importance to communication and expects openness and honesty in her dealings with others in the school. An example of this openness is to be found in her attitude towards her office – the door is always left open and 'nothing is kept hidden because the office belongs to the school'. This encourages, she feels, a degree of self-sufficiency in the teachers and ensures that they can take over administering the school should she be absent. She describes herself as 'a teacher with a post of responsibility for administration', rather than as a principal or 'executive' of a school organisation. The latter term she particularly rejects given its business-linked connotations. She makes little distinction between herself and the staff and does not exclude herself from duties such as yard supervision simply because she is principal. She places an important emphasis on establishing a sense of community in the school by highlighting special occasions/achievements of individual children over the school intercom system and ensuring that parents, staff and children are happy coming to school. Maintaining high standards of discipline is considered very important and school policy on discipline, i.e. 'good behaviour', has been drawn up in consultation with parents, teachers and children in the school.

The principal describes her relationship with the teaching staff as 'very friendly' and feels this is due to the emphasis she places on 'personal aspects of their lives as much as professional'. There is no official monitoring of teachers' work – she trusts each one implicitly to carry out their role efficiently and professionally, and copies of monthly reports are kept in her office for Department of Education purposes only.

School expectations of pupils

Country Lane: the more effective school

There are high expectations both academically and socially for children in this school. The principal is very proud of the fact that scholarships for entry to highly regarded private secondary schools are frequently won by students of sixth grade. She attributes this to the overall standards of excellence running through the school and the commitment of the staff in helping any child who wishes to enter for the scholarships. She stresses, however, that children who decide to enter for scholarship exams are not singled out for special treatment and that all children are given equal treatment in the school. As an example of her commitment to high academic achievement, the principal introduced standardised 'exam papers' (compiled by the teachers themselves) from third grade to sixth grade, to be completed in the school hall at the end of the school year. Her objective in formalising summer assessments was to familiarise children with exam procedures in a gradual and informal way. There was some resistance from staff members to this idea and a compromise was reached by ensuring that end-of-year reports were based on teacher assessments of the child's yearly progress, rather than on the results of the end-of-year exam. The development of self-esteem is also a top priority, reinforced through positive appraisal of children's work and ensuring that children feel happy and secure in the school environment.

Cherry Orchard: the less effective school

A school pamphlet is distributed each year to parents of incoming children. School aims are stated as being to 'develop the intellectual, physical and aesthetic talents of the children in its care within a framework of a growing social awareness and religious values'. The principal states that these aims are achieved through creating a warm and friendly atmosphere and by the dedication of the teaching staff, the guidance of the religious personnel and the commitment of the parents in giving time and energy to the school. Developing high levels of confidence in the children is also considered important and is ensured through praise for childrens' achievements and efforts, and encouraging them to 'speak openly and know they will be listened to with respect'. Through ensuring high standards of discipline, care is taken to focus on the behaviour rather than the child, with the ultimate aim of 'control of self and the ability to behave in an accepted fashion without being commanded, and the ability to make decisions in the light of Christian values'.

School goals

Country Lane: the more effective school

Specific school goals achieved in the recent past by the principal include extending the school building, a major task which she has worked towards over the past five years.

She is very proud of this achievement, particularly of having raised £92,000 over a period of three years toward the cost of the extension. Her diligence and perseverance in achieving goals is evident from her repeated visits to the Department of Education where she managed to speak directly to the Minister for Education to plead her case for extra funding for the school. The second major goal achieved in recent years has been the completion of the school plan, which entailed detailed assessment of work carried out in each classroom, with ideas shared and discussed on changes and additions to the school curriculum. Current goals being followed include the drawing up of an introductory handbook on the school for the parents of incoming students. This booklet will detail school policy on issues ranging from discipline to assessment and will provide an overview of the ethos of the school.

Cherry Orchard: the less effective school

Specific goals mentioned by the principal in the coming year include updating and expanding upon the school plan and maintaining the school building in good order through painting and redecorating.

Inter-staff relations

Country Lane: the more effective school

Staff members are very friendly with one another and appear very close. This is facilitated by the insistence of the principal that all problems, both personal and professional, are dealt with sensitively and with concern. She stresses that if any particular member of staff is under stress, other members rally round in support, providing any assistance they can. As principal, she sees her role as keeping staff as stress-free as possible and states that even if problems are of a personal nature she will try to help. At the end of each year, one member of staff is usually singled out for special praise on the basis of work done during the school year. Parents are informed and a gift is presented to that teacher. The principal describes the staff as 'gorgeous' and the atmosphere is very relaxed and informal in the staffroom. There is a lot of collaboration among staff, particularly in the areas of music, art and drama and each Christmas a school concert is organised jointly by all the teachers.

Cherry Orchard: the less effective school

There is a high degree of staff stability in this school and many of the staff have been teaching here for over twenty years. Firm friendships have evolved as a result and this is evident in the warm, open discussions which exist at break-times. There is high praise for the principal who is described as being 'open and fair-minded in her role, concerned for the welfare of the teachers and pupils'. There appears to be a great awareness of the diverse talents and interests of staff members and an openness therefore to sharing ideas.

The staffroom is very large and slightly impersonal with a 'hollow' feel – due to the wooden flooring and high ceiling. It is functional rather than comfortable and more like a kitchen than a resting room. An elderly member of the religious order makes tea/coffee for teachers during their break. Official staff meetings are held monthly, but frequently impromptu meetings are called during breaks to make decisions on matters needing immediate attention.

School resources

Country Lane: the more effective school

Funding is not a problem in this school and as a result teachers are free to furnish their classes with resources as they need. There seems to be a strong emphasis on reading resources in the school and classes were very well stocked with reading materials. Teachers are encouraged to develop their talents and funding is provided if they wish to pursue qualifications in particular areas.

Cherry Orchard: the less effective school

Funding is not a problem for this school and resources are made available to teachers as they require. Great care is taken of the maintenance of the school building and school equipment, with an emphasis on children showing respect for school property.

Relationship with local authorities

Country Lane: the more effective school

The school enjoys an excellent relationship with the Board of Management, particularly with the chairman who is also the parish vicar. The principal stresses that she has a healthy respect for 'the collar' and would find it difficult to work with somebody she did not respect. She describes as 'excellent' her relations with the School Inspectorate and, as highlighted by her persistence in visiting the Minister for Education, she has no hesitation in using contacts within the Department of Education to promote the interests of the school.

Cherry Orchard: the less effective school

Relationships with local authorities are described as being 'very good' with visits from the School Inspectorate (who the principal says, are very approachable) approximately every four years. The school Board of Management is described as being very supportive, which the principal attributes to the positive sense of community encouraged between all those involved in the school.

School image

Country Lane: the more effective school

The principal states that people in the community describe her school as the 'little school down the lane' – a description which she feels does not do justice to the development and expansion of the school over the past number of years. She does not believe in actively promoting the school and says that her standards of excellence are made evident by the performance of the children and by word of mouth in the school community. She does not like drawing attention to herself and prefers to be judged by her successes.

Cherry Orchard: the less effective school

The principal states that the school is perceived as being a caring and happy place for children. She also states that the age of the school building, and its outward disjointed appearance, may be 'off-putting' for some parents, as is the fact that parents must drive down an avenue to take their children to school. However, the fact that it is a school with an established religious tradition, ensures that overall, it is held in a very positive light within the local community.

Conclusions for middle-socio-economic-status schools

The schools comprising the middle-SES sample have a number of features in common. Firstly the children come from a middle-class social background, with the schools themselves located in prestigious suburbs of Dublin. Due to the relatively stable financial background of the parent body, funding for both schools is not a problem, with fundraising activities a priority for both throughout the school year. Secondly, as with the schools in the low-SES sample, the national curriculum is implemented in both schools with similar mathematics and reading programmes being followed. Thirdly, the staff in both schools enjoy warm, friendly relations and appear highly cooperative on teaching matters.

Notwithstanding these similarities, differences were identified between the two schools. These are summarised in Table 11.2. Overall, differences seem to revolve around the pattern maintenance and the smooth running of the school classified as 'less effective' and a sense of enthusiasm and innovation in the 'more effective' school. This was particularly evident in the classroom atmospheres in the two schools – a buzz of activity in the 'more effective' school (with children not always working on what they should) compared with quietness and a sense of restraint in the 'less effective' school. The difference between each principal's style of management is also worth noting. The principal in the 'more effective' school constantly pushes the parameters for learning, in all respects, while the principal in the 'less effective' school seemed most concerned with adhering to tradition and minimising change in school matters.

Conclusions for Ireland schools

The study outlined in this chapter has highlighted similarities and differences in effectiveness both within and between a small sample of Irish primary schools in low-SES and mid-SES environments. In this regard what is perhaps most striking about the quantitative data gathered (focusing on children's achievement in mathematics and children's attitude towards and experience of school) are the large differences that exist between low-SES schools and the relative similarity between the mid-SES schools.

In relation to the low-SES schools (Secret Garden and Tower View) differences were identified in mathematics achievement (particularly computation skills) and in attitudes toward school, with children in Secret Garden, the more effective school, expressing overall a more positive experience of school than their counterparts in

Table 11.2 Summary of differences between the two mid-SES schools across the twelve dimensions

Dimension of contrast	More effective mid-SES (Country Lane)	Less effective mid-SES (Cherry Orchard)
General characteristics of the school	Modern, welcoming	Old, dull
A day in the life of a child	Flexible, creative, pupils had freedom of movement	Routine, boring, movement restricted
Instructional style of the teachers	Whole-class teaching, time for individual children	Whole-class teaching, little personal interaction with children
The curriculum	Willingness to try new initiatives, school plan developed	Adherence to tradition
		School plan developed
The influence of the parents	No direct involvement in school activities	Involved in school library
The principal	Energetic, organised, enthusiastic	Efficient, emphasis on smooth running of school by maintaining status quo, little monitoring of staff
	Monitoring of staff	
	Democratic leadership with proactive input from principal	Highly democratic leadership
School expectations of pupils	High emphasis on academic performance and self-esteem	Confidence-building and self-discipline
School goals	Constantly being worked upon and updated	Immediate focus rather than long-term planning
Inter-staff relations	Excellent, very friendly	Long standing friendships, cooperative
School resources	Plentiful supply, constantly being updated, emphasis on reading	Adequate supply
Relationship with local authorities	Excellent	Very good
School image	Very positive	Reasonably good

Tower View. Table 11.1 highlighted distinct differences between the two schools on all of the twelve dimensions specified within the ISERP project. Cultivation of a positive school climate is frequently cited as a major distinguishing feature of effective schools (Mortimore *et al.*, 1988; Teddlie and Stringfield, 1993) and in this study the positive school climate in Secret Garden is evident, ranging from the 'haven-like' quality of the school grounds to the experience of both the teachers' and children's school day as consistent, organised, task-orientated and supportive. Looking at the mid-SES sample in Table 11.2 (Country Lane and Cherry Orchard), the situation is more complex. Greater rates of pupil improvement in mathematics were evident in Country Lane although the overall achievement levels of the two schools were quite similar. The emphasis on higher-order questioning and concrete learning observed in Country Lane, but not in Cherry Orchard, provides some explanation for this. Interestingly, however, children's views of their experiences in both schools were quite mixed and in general more varied than those expressed by the children in the two Low-SES schools.

Such findings confirm the particular importance of schooling for children in low-SES environments and the manner in which a negative experience of schooling not only affects levels of achievement but also self-concept and attitudes toward school and learning. Within the Mid-SES sample the lower differences in children's attitudes, experience and achievement suggest that school effects are mediated to a great extent by home background influences. In other words, middle-class parents with their greater economic and cultural resources ensure the success of their children's education. Within the low-SES environment, parents' levels of contact with the school will in contrast be influenced by the school's willingness to encourage and facilitate such contacts. This was clearly highlighted in this study by the different policies evident in low-SES schools in relation to parents, with a highly proactive policy of inclusiveness in more effective Secret Garden and a laissez-faire, minimalist approach in less effective Tower View, despite the similarity in parental background for both schools.

At a more general level, the study identifies the important role of the principal in encouraging a cooperative approach to teaching – where teachers feel a sense of ownership of the school curriculum and their role in implementing it. The development of the school plan was a factor which seemed to facilitate a 'collaborative culture' (Hargreaves, 1994) in the more effective schools in each SES category, where a distinct sense of enthusiasm and commitment to development was clearly in evidence.

From observing the work of teachers and principals in each of the schools, however, it became clear that the terms 'more effective' and 'less effective' were not always adequate to describe their behaviour. Schools are complex organisations and do not fall readily into either category. All teachers and principals in the study appeared to be committed to the children in their schools but the distinguishing features in terms of whether the schools were more or less effective hinged on the desire to explore and search for further ways of improving practice, and an openness and commitment to change when required. In relation to the low-SES schools, their historical context in terms of the differing priorities of school management over the years must also have been an influential factor. The 'climate of disconnectedness' (Teddlie and Stringfield, 1993) in Tower View cannot simply be reduced to the inadequacies of the principal alone, but must be seen in the context of a laissez-faire approach by school management over a long period of time.

12 Europe – the United Kingdom

*David Reynolds, Shaun Farrell
and Wynford Bellin*

Introduction/context

Education for children in the UK starts at the age of five when pupils attend infant school. Prior to this, approximately 45 per cent at age four and 35 per cent at age three will have attended formal state-provided or company-provided nursery schools with maybe a further 30–40 per cent attending childminding schemes of some kind. Only at age six, in the second year of infant school, would all children have begun their academic studies, in this case in the areas of mathematics, reading and writing. Children attend school for about 195 days per year, for an average of six hours per day, although the time spent in the classroom varies according to how individual schools structure the timetables. The school calendar begins early in September and concludes in mid-July with three to four week vacations at Easter and Christmas.

The low-socio-economic-status schools: general characteristics

Trelent: the more effective school

Trelent School has a roll of about 350 pupils between the ages of five and eleven, and an additional reception class for the under fives. The school shares a site with a community centre, which many of the school's parents attend for both social and educational purposes, particularly the ethnic Asian parents. The school staff comprises thirteen teachers and eight further support staff concerned with second-language support, special educational needs and the like. In addition to the employed staff, it is not uncommon to observe parents in classrooms and open-plan areas outside the classrooms, listening to pupils read or supervising small groups undertaking academic activities. The levels of staff turnover have been zero throughout the ISERP study and have reportedly been minimal in previous years; the two classteachers involved with the ISERP pupils during the period under discussion had been employed at Trelent for seven and fifteen years respectively and each had at least fifteen years' teaching experience.

It is worth noting that at Trelent the school secretary, the lunch staff, the part-time library assistant and other ancillary staff are treated in the same manner as the teaching staff and that they universally pursue the school's goals with as much enthusiasm and commitment as the teachers. Indeed, they have reported that their role is often extended to that of pastoral or welfare person at the behest of individual pupils, where they act as an intermediary between pupil and headteacher, even though the headteacher is always available to the pupils. In general terms, the school staff at Trelent can best be described as 'proactive', with the staff acting as one in pursuit of common educational goals.

The pupils at Trelent come from a mainly ethnic Asian background or are from low-SES white families. The annual free-school-meal entitlement for the school is consistently at or above the 30 per cent level and their test scores on Midshire tests reflect the presence of English as a second language for many pupils during the infant years, but is overcome by the junior years to give scores significantly in excess of prediction by age seven. In fact the gain above prediction for Trelent at age seven, was equal to the loss below prediction for Ford Junction (the less effective low-SES school). Furthermore, at the end of the first ISERP academic year the mean scores for Trelent in comprehension, mathematics, computation and applied mathematics exceeded those of Hillcrest, the less effective mid-SES school described below, with Hillcrest having a free-school-meal entitlement consistently below 5 per cent.

Trelent is located near to the Ipminster city centre behind several backstreets and neighbouring large retail outlet. The school has been rebuilt during the last fifteen years and has several prefabricated teaching huts on the site, which also contains a sizeable field area and concrete playground. The main building houses the majority of classrooms, a large school assembly hall/gym and the staff common room and administrative offices. The catchment area is in a socially and economically deprived part of Ipminster, situated in the inner-city 'zone of transition' area. The housing is predominantly small and terraced, and small shops and workshops, together with several small factories, provide a limited source of employment in the area, which has a mostly unskilled or semi-skilled adult population and an unemployment rate of approximately 20 per cent – double the British average.

The school sets itself the mission of serving the local community and views the diversity of its pupil backgrounds as a resource to be called upon in pursuit of its educational goals. It retains an equal commitment to both the Asian and white communities and has virtually no attrition in favour of neighbouring mid-SES schools, due in part to its status in the locality and in part to its academic achievements and reputation among the Asian population.

Ford Junction: the less effective school

Ford Junction is a low-SES school occupying a split infant/junior school site with a roll of about 200 pupils attending the junior school between the ages of seven and eleven. The school staff consists of ten teachers and no further support staff other than the normal school secretary and lunch staff. There is a moderate staff turnover, together with a core of teachers who have been employed at Ford Junction for some fifteen years and more. Staff turnover is typically caused by either the breakdown or retirement of older teachers, and there is also a pattern of young ambitious teachers coming to the school for a short time period and moving on.

The school is attempting to be proactive in its approach to staffing and has recently made shrewd appointments of two committed mid-career teachers. Unfortunately, the staff problems have historically been related to the long-term illness of two long-serving staff members. This situation has ensured a steady flow of supply teachers and engendered a sense of instability and lack of cohesion for the generally small staff group, as well as for pupils. The teachers involved during the first two years of ISERP are not atypical for the school, having been employed at Ford Junction for one year, nineteen years, and twenty-three years respectively, one of the latter being periodically absent. In contrast with Trelent, the ISERP UK team never observed a parent in the school during the two school years reported on here.

The pupils at Ford Junction come from an almost universally white low-SES background, mainly from the surrounding state-built housing estates. The annual free-school-meal entitlement for the school is consistently above the 50 per cent level and its county test scores are consistently below prediction. In terms of the ISERP first-year test scores, Ford Junction scored bottom in both mathematics tests and second bottom in comprehension.

Ford Junction is located in a socially and economically very deprived outlying area of Ipminster. It is surrounded by decaying public housing estates built originally in the 1930s which were added to during the 1950s and 1960s. The estates are used by the local authority for 'dumping' 'problem families', who have previously smashed up their former accommodation or failed to meet rent agreements. The estates are severely deprived, environmentally low grade, have few if any public facilities or amenities, and are reputed to have one-, two-, three- and four-generation 'problem families'; one of the ISERP teachers has taught the grandchildren of pupils she taught earlier in her career!

The school sets itself a 'childminding' mission with little emphasis being given to its educational role. Typical comments from staff during the first two years of observation have been along the lines, 'you have to understand what we're up against', and, 'it's all we can do to keep them on site, poor devils'. This ethos of apology pervades the teaching staff and is reinforced by the sterile corridors which run throughout the school, broken only by the occasional door with cracked glass, or the 'Man United Rule OK' graffiti etched carefully in the cold plaster walls.

A day in the life of a child

Trelent: the more effective school

The child chosen for the child study is named 'Ericsanna Mohammed' who was the median-scoring pupil across the ISERP tests at Trelent during the first ISERP year. At the time of observation Ericsanna was a nine-year-old girl in her second year of junior schooling. She is of Bengali decent and is a second-generation British citizen. Both her parents work in a local factory and English is the third family language after Bengali and Arabic. Mr and Mrs Mohammed have a very strong work ethic and a strong commitment to their children's education, and Ericsanna is encouraged by them to believe that school is very important to her future. Every evening the work of the school is reinforced by the moral lessons that she receives in her religious teaching. Ericsanna's attendance record was typical for the Trelent cohort under study – she had missed eight days of schooling during the first two ISERP years and she is always well presented and tidy in her appearance.

Ericsanna is popular with her peers and her teachers, and is a conscientious well-behaved pupil. Her classteacher, Mrs Meadows, stated that Ericsanna was a 'typical pupil in her class, polite and hard working'. Ericsanna lives with her parents and her brother, who is a year younger and also attending Trelent. Her family live in a rented terrace house about 800 metres from the school and walk to school daily with several friends and an accompanying parent, occasionally her mother on a rotation basis with other parents.

Ericsanna's attitude towards school is generally positive, although she feels that she struggles with some of the mathematics. She likes her classteacher and has many friends in her class whom she likes to work and play with. The school day begins at 9 a.m. with registration, which is undertaken in silence with the pupils raising their hands in response to their name being called out. This is often followed by a 'look and show' session where pupils are encouraged to bring items of interest from home to share with the class. During such sessions the teacher typically interacts with the pupils in a friendly and informal manner whilst undertaking administrative tasks such as checking meal arrangements and collecting school-photograph or outing money.

The school assembly runs from 9.15 to 9.45, with the school filing into the assembly hall/gym. All teachers attend with their classes, and stand, ensuring that order is maintained. Absolute silence is expected and insisted upon. The assemblies are appropriately multicultural and involve pupils reading in groups or presenting to the whole school. The headteacher also makes announcements, and compliments individual pupils on good work that he had observed during the previous day. He also praises examples of good behaviour which he will have observed first hand or had reported to him. He knows and uses all the pupils' first names and often adds an informal comment about the individual pupil.

Lessons begin immediately following assembly, with a half-hour break between 10.30 and 11 a.m. and lunch at noon. There is no afternoon break for the junior pupils and school finishes at 3 p.m. with the majority of parents collecting their children and taking the opportunity to check progress with classteachers.

Mrs Meadows is an experienced teacher who has been at Trelent for seven years. She is well liked by the class and adopted a firm and formal style of teaching which combined a considerable amount of whole-class teaching with periods of individual and small-group academic activities. The emphasis throughout the day was on the academic and classroom routines, and teacher expectations were sufficiently well inculcated virtually to render poor behaviour a non-issue. Mrs Meadows offered public praise to individuals and also to the whole class throughout the day, and consistently demanded the best of each individual child. The day was tightly structured and all lessons and materials appeared to be well prepared, with links being made with previous learning and a careful monitoring of each individual's progress.

Ericsanna was on-task for more than 90 per cent of the time throughout the day, she appeared engaged in her learning and was well motivated by the tasks and curriculum. During periods of group work she would interact with her peers, discussing task-related issues on most occasions. During individual work she would work silently and conscientiously with the occasional inquiry to a peer when she got stuck. During the day Ericsanna had two mathematics lessons, one silent reading session after lunch (a parent attends these sessions and listens to individuals read aloud in the craft area outside the classroom) and worked on two tasks related to the topic which was being covered, Egypt. One of the tasks involved integrating mathematics and writing and the final task at the end of the day was reserved for creative pursuits such as painting or drama. It is notable that at this time most other schools were also covering topics related to ancient civilisations as required by the national curriculum, the point being that while most others were doing the Romans or Vikings, Trelent was adopting a topic of greater relevance to its ethnic composition.

Mrs Meadows continually monitored the class throughout the day and during individual and small-group activities she would walk quickly around the class monitoring progress, checking for understanding and prompting improvements. At no time were pupils allowed to form a queue at her feet; they were to first seek answers by thinking carefully, if unsuccessful they could seek peer assistance, and in the final analysis they could raise their hands and she would attend to their inquiry by asking questions in order to facilitate self-solution.

Throughout the day Ericsanna appeared to be engrossed in her learning. At no time did she stray from the task set and she reported that she finished most tasks to her satisfaction within the time allocated.

During morning break, Ericsanna joined her friends on the playground and ate a snack and talked about the events of the morning and about pop music. At lunchtime she played for a while and joined her year group in the dining hall where she ate her sandwiches and interacted with her peers.

Mrs Meadows stated that she would miss teaching this class next year since they had been a pleasure, but they would move up into the school's 'top bay' which combines the pupils from ages nine to eleven for their final two years. This arrangement is a new initiative in the school and allows two classes to share three teachers giving potential for teachers to teach their specialist curriculum areas in a more formally differentiated structure, more akin to the system of secondary schooling.

Ford Junction: the less effective school

In contrast to the tightly structured day experienced by Ericsanna at Trelent, Steven Jones's day at Ford Junction was characterised by noise and inactivity, with short spells of on-task learning. Steven was the median-scoring pupil across the ISERP tests during the first ISERP year. At the time of observation Steven was about to turn nine, and in his second year of junior schooling, having previously attended the Ford Junction infant school. Steven comes from a single-parent 'uncle' household and has two younger sisters and an older brother. His mother is unemployed. The family live in a semi-detached rented house on one of the estates which borders the school playing field. Steven reports that he stays up late at night watching TV and has a paper round before school begins. His classteacher, Miss Beedy, reports that he is often late for school due to oversleeping and our data suggests that his attendance is typical for his class, with twenty-two days absence during the first two ISERP years.

Steven describes school as 'all right but boring' and expresses great affection for Miss Beedy. His behavioural record is not good and his previous teachers remember him as happy and lively, but 'quite a handful'. Steven is part of a 'gang' of Manchester United supporters who spend most of the day talking about soccer and chanting 'oh ah Cantona' about the classroom, using carefully rehearsed strategies to avoid work and also the gaze of Miss Beedy.

Steven has little to say regarding the school curriculum and the activities undertaken at school, his attitude towards school is one of resignation to the inevitable and his long-term aspirations are realistically limited, although dreams of glory at Manchester are jovially forthcoming.

Steven walks to school across the school playing field, usually accompanied by his mother and younger sisters who are dropped off at the Infant school. On the day of the observation Steven arrived at school on time, entered the sterile corridor where he hung his kit-bag and joined his friends in the playground. The headteacher arrives at school at 8.15 in the morning in order to supervise the playground, a task he insists he must undertake throughout the day. The school day begins with a bell at 9 o'clock and the pupils line up in the playground in their class groups and are escorted by their classteachers to the classroom. This process takes about five minutes due to several pupils, including Steven, loitering in the corridor. Miss Beedy monitors the pupils as they enter and shouts 'settle down'; she is prone to shouting and attempts unsuccessfully to employ overt behaviour-modification techniques.

During registration there is a lot of wandering around the classroom and also a lot of noise and shouting. Miss Beedy shouts out the pupil names and they shout in reply, 'Yehs Miss Beeeedy!'. Steven wanders about the classroom and talks with friends whilst feigning getting something from his drawer. Assembly is at 9.15 and involves the class lining up outside the classroom and being escorted noisily to the assembly hall/gym. The headteacher conducts assembly which includes a hymn and prayer and recognition of the school football team's victory against its neighbour, Finchtree. The pupils sit in class rows, some in uniform, and most yawning and fidgeting. At 9.45 the pupils are again escorted to the classroom and supervised by Miss Beedy as they enter. Miss Beedy shouts instructions and repeatedly shouts for the class to settle with their mathematics workbooks. This process takes about ten minutes and eventually Miss Beedy shouts out the task instructions while several pupils, including Steven, continue to procrastinate.

As Miss Beedy repeats the instructions she asks if all are clear about the task and receives no response. Most pupils are now at their seats talking and arranging their books and equipment. Steven sits at his desk which he shares with five of his friends and proceeds to blunt his pencil on the side of the desk. He holds his pencil up seeking permission to sharpen it. Miss Beedy is busy settling the final stragglers and moving about the room monitoring individuals' settling. The level of noise in the room is not conducive to academic work, although a group of girls on one table conscientiously settle and work. The on-task figures for this class fluctuate between zero and 40 per cent throughout the school day, with Steven spending only about 10 per cent of his classroom time on-task. At about 10.15 Steven decides to get up and sharpen his pencil. This takes about six minutes as he takes the long route to the sharpener, interrupting others, and interacting with his friends en route. The sharpening itself is worth about two minutes as the pencil shortens by about an inch.

It is worth noting the skill with which Steven has developed the strategies employed here, his ability to avoid detection or drawing attention to himself is well honed and goes unnoticed throughout the day. In fact the only time that Miss Beedy speaks to him is when she visits his table periodically to monitor progress or assist with an inquiry, that is if he is present during such visits. By break-time at 10.30 Steven had done two sums in his workbook and had got one of them wrong, but as soon as Miss Beedy announced that it was time to pack away for break Steven and his friends were the first table sitting in silence. Miss Beedy shouted for others to be ready and rewarded Steven's table by allowing them to leave first.

Miss Beedy was in her second year at Ford Junction and had one previous year's experience elsewhere. She had been inducted into the culture of the school by the older time-served staff members and had received no appraisal or support from the senior staff although the headteacher had been very supportive since her employment at Ford Junction. Her approach to her teaching is largely determined by the perceived needs to maintain order in the first instance, and to contemplate education as a secondary concern. This approach was typical for the school during the period described although recent staff appointments and initiatives from the headteacher are beginning to change the ethos.

Steven plays football on the playground during break and lines up with his class at 11 o'clock. The class is again escorted into the classroom and Miss Beedy shouts for the pupils to settle and shouts instructions regarding the forthcoming project lesson on the Vikings. This routine takes about ten minutes and Miss Beedy then begins to ask questions of the whole class. The questions are closed and pupils shout out the answers even though they are repeatedly shouted at to put their hands up. After about five minutes of questions, including a few deflecting comments shouted out by pupils, Miss Beedy shouts out the task instructions which involve building a longboat. The pupils meander toward the craft area and help themselves to the required materials. Miss Beedy waits at Steven's desk and demonstrates the task to them. Steven asks if he can be excused to go to the toilet, which he is allowed to do after being cautioned that break was only twenty minutes ago and that he should have gone then. He eventually reaches his desk, after observing the progress of several other groups, and actively participates in the construction of a cardboard longboat with cocktail-stick oars. By lunch-time all pupils have constructed a longboat. Steven's is rather misshapen and the edges are ragged. 'That's OK,' he responds, 'they wouldn't 'ave been able to get it straight back then.' When asked 'when was that?' Steven was unable to reply.

At lunch-time Steven played football and had playful fights with his friends. The headteacher supervised the playground and interacted informally with several of the pupils. Steven had his lunch with the rest of his year group and ate the free school meal he was entitled to. After eating, he once again played soccer in the playground, and was warned once to be careful of others.

The afternoon activities involved painting the longboats and adorning the sides with foil shields. Steven's on-task behaviour was consistent with that observed during the morning session, although he comfortably completed the task by break-time. Ford Junction retains a short afternoon break, as Miss Beedy explained, 'so that they can go to the toilet, because they are not mature enough to have control!' Following afternoon break the longboats were left to dry at the side of the room. The final activity for the day was to finish writing a letter begun the previous day and then to read a book. Steven had been absent the previous day and so spent the session, or at least a small part of it, writing his letter. Several other pupils finished with time to spare and spent long periods apparently choosing a reading book, but actually talking and wandering around. The level of noise in the classroom remained consistently high throughout the day, led, it has to be said, by the example of the shouting Miss Beedy. Steven left school at 3 p.m. and walked away with several friends.

Steven's day was reported as being typical for him and his class; his coping strategies and procrastination tactics were similar to those adopted by many of the class members, although it must be stressed that there was a very small core of hard-working, attentive pupils on one table. They appeared to be a class within a class, self-motivated and making the best of the context within which they spent their educational careers. This group were almost taken for granted by Miss Beedy throughout the day, presumably because they were not a problem and needed less attention.

Teachers' teaching style

Trelent: the more effective school

During the first two years of ISERP, three teachers were involved with the cohort under study. During the first year Mrs Mound had a class of thirty-two ISERP pupils aged seven years, and Mrs Meadows had twenty-four ISERP pupils and six aged-eight pupils, who were overspill from their year group class. During the second year of the study, Mrs Meadows taught Mrs Mound's original ISERP pupils and Mr Polity taught Mrs Meadows's original ISERP pupils, along with the eight pupils from the year above. Mrs Mound retained four of her original class who had been identified as having special educational needs, as she had a background in special education and the SEN assistant was based near her classroom.

Instructional style varies as pupils progress through the school. In early years there is an emphasis upon acquisition of basic skills, especially in English where the students are weak. This is done through didactic and academically focused teaching, using whole classes. Later in their school life, pupils experience greater emphasis on use of the basic skills, and the school situation will be more progressive and project-orientated.

Ford Junction: the less effective school

In general, the teachers use the customary primary school method of a combination of a whole-class instruction, followed by pupils working in groups, with some form of conclusion at the end. It is worthwhile saying that the instructional style of the teachers in this school is compromised by frequent disciplinary interventions, and by very frequent whole-class instructions about behaviour and attitudes, the work rate and noise. So, in fact, much of the lesson time is never used for curriculum transmission; instead it is used for routine procedure, sanctions and warnings.

The curriculum

Trelent: the more effective school

This consists of maths, science, English, history, geography and information technology, and is laid down in the form of a national curriculum.

The school's resource base enables it to develop its own 'project' material to integrate knowledge, and to use visits, trips, etc., to local cultural resources (such as museums).

Ford Junction: the less effective school

The school follows the national curriculum, and as such is much the same as any other British primary school.

The influence of parents

Trelent: the more effective school

Very well-developed relations with parents exist. There is a nursery school on the same site as the school which operates on a 'mother and child' principle, and most parents are therefore used to visiting the school grounds. There is also an active parent–teacher association and parent assistance is also used in the classroom. Formal year meetings and an annual governor's report involve 80 per cent of parents and a high level of informal contacts also exist.

Ford Junction: the less effective school

We at no time saw a parent in the school and were told that the school finds it very difficult to involve them. Attendance at the yearly meetings, at which parents are invited to look at the work of their children, is said to be somewhere around 30–40 per cent, which is an extremely low rate of participation for this kind of event. Participation in formal school activities is also very low. The only involvement from parents would appear to be when parents come to the school to complain, which they are said to do quite frequently. The school had tried to involve parents, but had not had success and tended to give up in this area.

The headteacher/principal

Trelent: the more effective school

The headteacher is a very acute man in his mid-forties. Trelent is his third headship, which he took specifically for the opportunity to be a headteacher in a multicultural school. He is a highly intelligent individual, with an interest in the field of school effectiveness and a sound understanding of research issues – we remember him telling the staff that they shouldn't worry that the pupils were performing badly at intake, because this meant that their gain would be greater!

He shows keen dedication to his job and his school, working from 8.00 a.m. until 5.00 p.m. at school, before taking work home.

He began by restructuring the school from the top down, by removing incompetent and racist staff. He then became bottom-up and now practises completely lateral distribution of authority, with excellent relations with both staff and pupils. He has a strong presence around the school and is clearly both respected and liked by his school. He has strong involvement in the community out of school, with the ability to network in order to bring to his school additional resources and contacts.

Ford Junction: the less effective school

The headteacher of Ford Junction is difficult to type, in that he appears moderately competent, but sometimes appears not quite fully involved in the day-to-day life of the school. He is committed and thinks and cares about the school a lot, yet he is very formal with his staff and tends neither to support nor pressure them. At break-time for example, the headteacher always goes out with the pupils, and doesn't spend the time in the staffroom required to foster good relations or understand staff perspectives. This lack of involvement suggests that, although competent, he is not developing an effective school. However, he has a good relationship with the children in the school, whom he obviously cares about a great deal.

School expectations of pupils

Trelent: the more effective school

Trelent employs strong use of reward-based control; academic, cultural and sporting effort and success are all identified and congratulated at the daily multicultural assembly.

Ford Junction: the less effective school

There is a sense that the school is strongly punishment-orientated rather than reward-orientated. The staff perception is that the children would abuse rewards, and so there are no merit awards or house systems. Basically the school runs on the principle of punishing of the bad, rather than on rewarding of the good. It is reactive, responding to problems, rather than proactive, seeking to prevent problems.

School goals

Trelent: the more effective school

Trelent is predominantly concerned with academic work and serving the local community. It also aims to raise the aspirations and expectations of the pupils and their families.

Ford Junction: the less effective school

In many ways the goal of the school is to childmind. The children are perceived as having little potential, which staff justify by the fact that they arrived at the school with appallingly low reading ages. The estimate is that about two-thirds of the children entering the school would have a reading age of more than two years below chronological – which is a seriously disadvantaged population. Therefore, for the majority of pupils, any serious attempt at achieving academic goals is deemed pointless. However, if there are children with obvious talents, the school will apply real effort trying to help them, and actually sees its job as the rescue of the small number of children from respectable families, who may have a chance to escape from the estate and from the socially deprived community that surrounds the school. But essentially, the main goal is of childminding, which, when in day-to-day classroom practice is about survival. It is about avoiding losing children out of the classroom, and about preventing children from beating up other children. The day-to-day battle of the school is simply to survive.

Inter-staff relations

Trelent: the more effective school

Staff relations within the school are very good, and are both warm and professional. There is a strong commitment to supporting and helping one another. It is one of the few schools in which the staff discuss individual pupils' problems at break- and lunchtimes. There is a high level of informal transfer of knowledge about pupils. (The school is now trying to develop formal procedures only because of the requirements of inspection.)

Ford Junction: the less effective school

Staff relations at Ford Junction are generally good, but there is a culture within the staffroom of considerable hostility towards the children. Staffroom breaks are typically filled with discussion of what the children had been doing in the class, with much laughter about some of the activities and some of the problem children.

School resources

Trelent: the more effective school

The pupils, families, community and teaching staff are the main resources at the school. There are also a number of teaching assistants for language support and SEN who are employed to their fullest potential.

In material terms the school is equipped much like most primary schools, with a globe in each classroom, computers, etc.

Much use is made of materials provided by parents and the local community, which reflects the multicultural modifications to the curriculum made by the school, and also the support which is evident from the community.

Ford Junction: the less effective school

The school has computers, globes, etc., and a library which is provided by the county. Each classroom also has its own stock of reference, text and literature material. The main resources which are used regularly and plentifully are the art materials bought predominantly out of school resource funds.

Relationship with local authorities

Trelent: the more effective school

Trelent has very close relations with the local authority, evoked largely by the school's vibrant and pleasant atmosphere, which prompt visits from advisors, etc. Iserpshire LEA also uses the school to exemplify its good performance as an LEA, and thus brings a wide variety of visitors.

Ford Junction: the less effective school

These relations are not particularly close. The local authority appears to wash its hands of what it sees as a problem school, with very few visits from inspectors or curriculum advisors, and very little help from the district.

School image

Trelent: the more effective school

The school has a positive image within the local community, fostered by the school's emphasis on image management, now necessary in the British market-orientated educational system. Use is made of press releases and the local radio station and its 'no touch' rugby team at important rugby matches.

Ford Junction: the less effective school

This school places little emphasis on image management and as a result is beginning to lose pupils to primary schools around the estate. The attempt at image management made recently is some redecoration, made possible by sums of money released to fund new buildings following amalgamation with a local infant school. Image management here is viewed simply as improvements, for example, to the school decor in areas such as around the doors, where parents and visitors enter the school, rather than a more widespread, proactive policy.

The middle-socio-economic-status schools: general characteristics

Sea View: the more effective school

This school is situated in a rural village on the outskirts of a large industrial town. The village is a mixture of old village population, and new high-income, mid-SES executives from the city, who live in this village six or seven miles away. The community is very advantaged. It would be impossible to find more than a few people unemployed. Those who are are casualties of a recent shake-out in middle-class jobs. Even the lower-SES population in the village tends to be a very respectable rural people – skilled working class or farm workers. The free-school-meal rate of the school is virtually non-existent, with perhaps one or two pupils in the school having free school meals, by comparison with a 20 per cent rate for the country as a whole. An example of the affluence which characterises the school's intake is that almost every child has his or her own personal computer in the bedroom by the age of nine.

The school has about 170–180 pupils, creeping up from 160 a few years back, because the school is allowing itself to recruit a small number of extra children from areas outside its own catchment. The school is heavily over-subscribed, due to its popularity, and is slowly taking extra pupils, but will not allow itself to become swamped. The average class size in the school is lower than for most other schools, with figures being in the mid-twenties rather than the low thirties found elsewhere.

The school consists of one main building which has spacious and attractive work and library areas. Additional prefabricated huts house three classes, and a large school hall doubles up as a gym. The school is located on the edge of the village and faces beautiful countryside on three fronts. During the infant years and, to a lesser extent, the junior years, the school exploits the learning potential of the available countryside to its fullest and typical lessons during the summer months include nature trails and projects. During the junior years the history of the village and its population provide additional resources which make the curriculum immediately relevant to the pupils.

The school mission is academically focused with a strong element of local commitment to the village. High expectations and standards are made explicit through the school for pupils and parents, in a way that places the school at the centre of a partnership with parents, pupils and wider community. The staff consists of six teachers, including the headteacher, and staff turnover is virtually non-existent. In essence a happy settled staff work together as a collective, based upon security and stability.

Hillcrest: the less effective school

In contrast to Sea View, Hillcrest is a much larger school with just over 400 pupils and is housed in brand-new buildings. The school is only four years old, being situated on a new owner-occupied estate on the outskirts of Ipminster. It is planned that the school will increase by another hundred with the number of pupils coming into the school in future years, leading to potential rises in class sizes. The catchment area is a new middle-class estate of mostly first-generation middle-class families. There are some small housing association blocks of flats within the estate, resulting in the first intakes of ethnic-minority pupils into the school, and the head is very pleased that its balance is improving in this way. The proportion of low-SES children has increased in the school, but free-school-meal rates are still consistently below 5 per cent. Since the school is growing rapidly, it is clear that the staff are not constant. New staff join as the school grows, and because of the ideology of the school it also loses quite a number of staff who find that they do not necessarily adopt the school party line. The turnover is comparatively very high; what is more, the staff are mostly young and inexperienced: there are very few teachers over the age of the low thirties. The school is therefore in a situation of rapid growth, with frequent staff turnover, a young staff, inexperienced and insecure in a climate, as you will see, of progressive ideology.

It is a pervasive progressive ideology which defines the school and its mission. The focus here is less upon academic development and more upon an ill-defined holism. Whole-class teaching and individual pupil seatwork are a rarity until the later junior years and then remain an exception to the norm.

There is a caring ethos within the school which is freely expressed by staff members, but there is little evidence of its educational or structural foundations. In many ways the staff are a fragmented group of individuals struggling to adopt an imposed approach which many find difficult to define. The pupils are always well presented in their school uniforms and arrive at school well equipped. It is noticeable that the level of maturity at Hillcrest is less than that observed elsewhere in the ISERP study. Pupil interaction is typically brief and unfocused, both within the classroom and beyond.

The school buildings are very new and constantly expanding. There has been a steady rise in finance which allows the school to boast having among the best and most up-to-date equipment in the county. The decor of the school is brightly coloured with McDonalds-style fixtures and fittings. Indeed, entry to the school buildings would suggest a great potential for learning; it is only upon closer inspection that the foundations for learning are found to be absent.

A day in the life of a child

Sea View: the more effective school

The child chosen for the study is called Edward Walsh who was the median-scoring pupil across the ISERP tests at Sea View during the first ISERP year. At the time of observation Edward was a nine-year-old boy in his second year of junior schooling. His father is the manager of a large retail store in Effecton and his mother spends most of her time caring for his younger brother and tending house. Both parents are regular attendees at parents' evenings and Mrs Walsh occasionally attends school to assist teachers by listening to pupils read etc.

Both parents are strongly committed to Edward's education and regularly supervise his homework. Edward has a high attendance record and reports liking school and his classteacher, Mrs Shaw. Edward missed four school days during the first year of the study, two due to his parents taking their annual holiday.

Edward is popular with his peers, as demonstrated by the ISERP sociometric instruments, and is described by his teacher as an able and likeable pupil who is mature and willing.

The family own a large detached house in Sea View and Edward is accompanied to school each day by his mother. Edward's attitude toward school is very positive and he reports being happy with his work, which is usually neatly presented and mostly correct and creative, according to Mrs Shaw.

The school day begins at 9 a.m. when Edward joins his classmates on the carpet near Mrs Shaw's seat. The register is quickly taken, with each pupil saying 'Good morning' to Mrs Shaw in turn. Mrs Shaw interacts with individuals during registration and allows them to share their experiences of the previous evening with the class. At about 9.05 a.m. all the pupils are seated at their desks which are organised into ability groupings of about six pupils per group. The day begins with ten minutes of rapid-fire sums, which most pupils raise their hands to. Mrs Shaw is careful to seek out non-hand-raisers and elicit responses.

Following this rapid-fire session, Mrs Shaw introduces the morning task to the whole class. She asks several questions and ensures that all understand before continuing. Careful presentation and correct punctuation are stressed, as Mrs Shaw writes the title and date on the marker board. The class are then encouraged to share their ideas and comment on the task. Mrs Shaw frequently adds statements which reinforce what is expected, both in terms of content and also conduct – 'It's good to be busy and get on with things straight away'. Mrs Shaw continues to ask questions and seek understandings from the class for several minutes. Edward raises his hand often and is given the opportunity to contribute at least once. During this process between 80 and 90 per cent of the class are attending constantly, with Mrs Shaw prompting the one or two pupils who are not. Positive feedback and discussion is a feature of Mrs Shaw's natural teaching style, although she is equally quick to prompt correction and careful thought when necessary. At about 9.20 a.m. Mrs Shaw asks the class what they have to remember. The entire class replies 'neat handwriting'.

The pupils now attend to the task set. All are on-task and Mrs Shaw proceeds to distribute 'gold stars' for work undertaken the previous day. At the same time she monitors the room and prompts individuals to concentrate. Edward works carefully and conscientiously, moving from his seat only to get a dictionary. Mrs Shaw checks on the progress of individuals as she moves about the class and asks pupils to hold up their books to see if everyone has done enough work. All pupils respond immediately. She prompts several to work harder and the class returns to the task.

At 9.40 Mrs Shaw asks all to finish off neatly and pack away and get ready to practise the class song for the school concert. After a few seconds all have finished their work and sit ready for instructions. Mrs Shaw arranges the pupils into their singing positions and the class rehearse the song. Edward sings enthusiastically and Mrs Shaw offers praise to the whole class, selecting individuals as examples to follow.

At 9.57 the pupils return to their seats and Mrs Shaw offers universal praise and encouragement. The class then line up and leave for the school assembly, which is from 10 a.m. until 10.20. Edward and his class file silently from the room and enter assembly in an orderly manner. The headteacher conducts the assembly and distributes prizes to individuals and also praises school sports teams on their results.

Morning break follows assembly and Edward joins his peers on the tarmac playground for a game of soccer. The game is lively and loud but played in a sensible manner. Break-time is supervised by another classteacher and there is little incident requiring her attention. At 10.45 the bell rings and Edward and his class line up outside their classroom. Mrs Shaw supervises their entry and instructs them to get out their maths workbooks. The classroom is bristling with movement and noise as they settle down. Mrs Shaw prompts individuals to settle and selects two to distribute worksheets. The task involves giving coordinates to landmarks on a map of the village. Mrs Shaw stands at the front of the class and outlines the task using examples on the board. She asks several questions and relates the task to work undertaken yesterday. Edward pays close attention, as do his classmates, raising their hands when questions are asked and offering comments when invited to do so.

Mrs Shaw explains the reasons for needing to know coordinates and asks the class to give examples of times when they might need to use them. Edward offers an appropriate response, and after elaborating Mrs Shaw gives him praise. This process continues for about ten minutes until 11.20 when Mrs Shaw feels that all understand the task and are capable of completing it. At 11.20 the pupils are instructed to begin, and are told that after they have finished, and she has seen their work, they may colour in the map. Edward immediately begins to work and takes part in quiet discussion with those at his table. Mrs Shaw works with a group of pupils who are in the lower ability range and continually monitors the class, offering praise and prompting as required.

At 11.45 the noise level begins to rise as most (including Edward) have now completed the task and are beginning to colour the map. Mrs Shaw prompts noise reduction – 'shhh' – and asks several individuals to bring her their work. Edward has completed his coordinate work satisfactorily and is encouraged to colour carefully. At noon Mrs Shaw asks all to finish off where they are and place their worksheets in the centre of the table. She then stands at the front of the class and fires questions at the class using a large map on the board. Pupils raise their hands enthusiastically and Mrs Shaw takes them on a 'walk around the village using the map': 'If I am at the shop what are my coordinates?'. 'If I go to the church what are they now?' 'Who can tell me what transformation took me from the shop to the church?' Mrs Shaw takes several answers and then explains the methods required to answer her question. She then proceeds to travel about the map via questions and answers with the class until she finally arrives back at the school.

Lunch is at 12.30 p.m. until 1.30 p.m. Edward has his sandwiches and plays soccer with his friends. He eats in the school hall and conversation varies between the events of the morning and the previous evening. When the school bell rings he joins his class and waits for Mrs Shaw to supervise their entrance. Two monitors are already in the classroom making sure the register is delivered and the board is clean. At 1.31 the pupils are all seated and Mrs Shaw instructs them to get their reading books out and do some silent reading. The class responds immediately and silence continues for the next half hour. Mrs Shaw takes the register and listens to several individuals read for her whilst preparing material for a later task.

At 2 p.m. Mrs Shaw instructs the class to put their books away and sit ready. She asks two pupils to distribute art material and stands at the front of the class. The pupils are instructed to complete the work begun during the morning, the writing and the mathematics; once they have finished they are to get into pairs and design a map of the village which must have buildings and landscapes on it. Mrs Shaw asks for ideas of what they might include and asks the pupils what material they would use for the suggestions. At 2.15 the classroom becomes a hive of activity. Edward finishes off his writing and takes it to Mrs Shaw who offers praise and prompts self-correction and care with punctuation. Edward returns to his seat, does his corrections and finds a partner to work with on the map. By 2.25 all pupils are constructing their maps, Mrs Shaw claps her hands and gets immediate silence. She asks one pair to show the class their map, then asks the class what else they might add and takes several responses. The class then return to their task with Mrs Shaw working with a pair of pupils in the lower ability range, asking them questions and prompting their ideas. Edward and his partner make steady progress as the classroom buzzes with a working noise level. At 2.50 Mrs Shaw demands 'Stop!' and the class freezes in silence. She gives clear and precise instructions for tidying up in such a way that will allow the pupils easily to complete their maps tomorrow. The class then becomes alive with movement as the pupils carefully tidy away and settle in their seats with their arms crossed. Mrs Shaw stands at the front of the class, waiting and prompting. Once the class are all seated in silence she reads a few pages of a story to them and then instructs them to collect their coats and wait quietly at the door. The school day ends at 3 p.m. and Edward is collected by his mother and younger brother.

Hillcrest: the less effective school

The child chosen for this study is called Emma Edwards who was the median-scoring pupil across the ISERP tests at Hillcrest during the first ISERP year. At the time of observation Emma was a nine-year-old girl in her second year at junior schooling. Her father is a self-employed electrician and her mother is a hairdresser. Emma is the middle of three girls in the family and her younger sister attends the infants at Hillcrest. The family own their own semi-detached house on one of the new estates adjoining Hillcrest.

Emma is a well presented young girl who always wears school uniform and is tidily turned out. She is generally polite, although her teacher says she can be 'a bit of a madam'. During observation Emma was seen to be open to interaction with her peers although, as with many of the Hillcrest pupils, she did not seem to be part of a close friendship network.

The school day begins with registration at 8.50 a.m. with the pupils sitting at their desks and Mr Jones at his. The pupils interact informally during roll call and several have to be prompted to reply. At 9.05 the class leaves for school assembly. There is no orderly exit from the room or passage through the school, however, and on arrival the pupils order themselves before entry to the school hall. At the front of the hall Mrs Gump (the headteacher) stands waiting and listening to the 'Mammas and Pappas' music, which greets their entrance. When the entire school is present the headteacher conducts an assembly which is a combination of announcements and prayer.

At 9.45 the pupils return to their class and Mr Jones enters. There is a buzzing of small voices as they settle, and Mr Jones interacts informally with several individuals. Mr Jones begins to discuss the nature video the class watched yesterday. Several pupils interact in whispers as he talks and puts questions to the class. Pupils raise their hands and several call out answers and comments. Mr Jones discusses the aspects of the video on bees and their life-cycle. Emma listens quietly but is distracted by her neighbour. Mr Jones prompts them to pay attention. At any given point about 40–60 per cent of the pupils are attending, with the others talking or being distracted by one another. Mr Jones asks several specific questions and offers answers, often without giving the pupils time to contribute. Several persist in raising their hands, including Emma occasionally, and Mr Jones intermittently responds to them. Although Mr Jones is addressing the whole class he often has to prompt individuals to attend, which breaks the flow of ideas. He outlines the task, which is to describe the life-cycle of bees and gives several key ideas to include. The pupils then get their pencils and paper, and the classroom can be characterised as noisy with a lot of movement. After about five minutes most pupils are at their seats. Mr Jones spends much of his time reclarifying the task for those who had not paid attention – 'Who has been day-dreaming?' By 10.25 all are working at their desks, but there is a good deal of talking (rarely task-related) and much fidgeting. By this time Emma has written two sentences and is talking with her neighbour. At 10.30 the school bell goes and the pupils begin to pack away. Mr Jones responds, 'it will be break when I say so'. The pupils sit up straight and wait to be allowed out to break and Mr Jones releases them one table at a time. Emma exits and gets a bag of crisps which she eats in the playground. Another teacher is supervising play, and Emma and several of her peers gather round the teacher, one sitting on her knee. Much of the interaction is dominated, or initiated, by the teacher as Emma and her peers vie for attention. At 10.50 the bell rings and the class re-enter their room. There is much noise and movement and by 10.56 about 60 per cent of the class are seated. Mr Jones continues to clarify the task and offer guidance to individuals. Several approach him for help, including Emma, and are told, 'It's up to you what you do – make sure it's really inventive.'

Mr Jones joins a table with three special-needs children and works with them. Emma in the meantime has added a couple of sentences to her work, but has gone to talk to a pupil at another table. At this stage about 50 per cent of pupils are on-task. Mr Jones remains at the SEN table for about fifteen minutes and rarely monitors the room, while Emma and most of her peers are moving and interacting freely with occasional additions to their work being made.

At 11 a.m. Mr Jones stands and moves about the classroom monitoring progress, and most of the pupils immediately settle to their seats and begin work. Emma has now written several sentences and Mr Jones discusses what she might add. Several pupils approach Mr Jones with their work and with questions. Emma immediately sees a way to lose his attention and begins to talk to her neighbour. A few pupils have finished the task as they define it and go to the list of tasks at the front of the class. The list covers all tasks for the day, and the pupils determine how they define the tasks and in what order they complete them. The intention is to encourage the pupils to be 'self-directed'. Emma settles briefly and works steadily for about five minutes. Then, having written about half a page, she draws a picture to fill the space. While drawing she takes great care of her work and refuses to be interrupted by her peers.

Mr Jones meanwhile continues to move about the class working with individuals and responding to questions, strongly encouraging self-help – 'Go away and think about it.' At 11.15 Emma places her finished work in a basket at the centre of her table and goes to the task list to choose what to do next. Mr Jones returns to the SEN group and gives them praise and two 'tokens' for their good work. Emma has taken out her mathematics book and begins to finish the sums which she did not complete yesterday. Mr Jones continues to work with the SEN group and occasionally monitors and prompts the class, about 60 per cent of whom are on-task. Most of the class then settle to their work. Emma talks with her desk-mates while working with her calculator. She has answered three sums, two of which are incorrect. Mr Jones moves to another table and has his back to most of the class. Several pupils, including Emma, move about and most are now off-task, anticipating lunch, even though there is still an hour to go.

By noon several pupils have gathered around Mr Jones to show him their work, Emma retrieves hers from the basket and joins the queue. Mr Jones offers praise and comment to each pupil 'Have you finished? That's lovely.' He checks that he is interpreting their work correctly and comments accordingly: the pupils are clearly dictating the criteria for the teacher's comments. After several minutes, Emma shows Mr Jones her work. He responds with praise for her lovely picture and asks her questions about it, before she returns to her sums.

After dealing with the queue, Mr Jones returns to the SEN table and works with the pupils as a group, asking them questions and offering answers. Emma talks with her table-mates as she continues with her sums. At 12.40 p.m. the class begins to pack away ready for lunch at 1 p.m. There is considerable noise and a lot of movement. Mr Jones monitors from the front and waits for the pupils to settle. By 12.53 the class are all seated upright waiting for lunch and Mr Jones gives them a short twenty questions quiz to see which table will go to lunch first.

During lunch Emma plays with several other girls until it is their turn to eat. She gets her sandwiches and enters the hall where she eats with her friends. After food they return to the playground and talk to the lunch staff. The bell for afternoon lessons rings and Emma and her class enter the classroom. Mr Jones calls the register and instructs the class to get changed for games, at which point the classroom explodes with noise and movement as they scramble for their kit. After about fifteen minutes the pupils are standing at the door ready to leave for the field. Mr Jones tells them to meet him on the field and he goes and gets the equipment.

Emma and her peers run about and do cartwheels while waiting for Mr Jones, who on arrival puts them into three rounders teams (one team is to watch on a rotational basis). Emma is in the first team to watch and she sits and talks with her friends as the others play. At 2.50 Mr Jones takes the pupils back to class where they get changed and sit waiting for the end-of-day bell. At 3 p.m. Emma is met by her mother and sister and they leave for home.

Teachers' teaching style

Sea View: the more effective school

There is a very strong emphasis on whole-class teaching at Sea View, as well as a strong didactic orientation in both of the first two years of schooling.

Hillcrest: the less effective school

Very little use is made of direct whole-class intervention at Hillcrest. Teachers are very much the facilitators working with individual children and sometimes working with children in groups.

The curriculum

Sea View: the more effective school

The National Curriculum is presented in both integrated and differentiated forms. The school adopts a two-year mathematics curriculum, which allows for in-depth focusing on curricular areas. There is evidence from the ISERP data that the pupils test scores were an underestimate in ISERP year 1, due to the universality of the test in curriculum terms. However, at the end of the second year the pupils were scoring highly on all test items, having been exposed to the entire mathematics curriculum over the two-year period.

Hillcrest: the less effective school

The National Curriculum is taught in a totally integrated manner. It is very difficult to identify specific curricular content, and teachers tend to assume that the self-directed mode of learning incorporates an array of curricular areas.

The influence of parents

Sea View: the more effective school

Sea View appears to have very well-developed parental links, including very high attendance at open evenings to look at their child's work.

Hillcrest: the less effective school

The school tries very hard to establish parental links, but this is mostly because it feels the need to explain its ideology to parents, who, perhaps because they are first-generation middle-class, tend to be hostile towards some of the more progressive ideology. So, while the school is trying to involve parents, it is essentially trying to explain to parents, rather than to involve them. It is worth saying, though, that there is a very high level of turnout at all school functions. Parents would also normally attend the meetings that are held to inform them of their child's progress.

The headteacher/principal

Sea View: the more effective school

The headteacher at Sea View is highly orientated towards the curriculum. When appointed four or five years ago, she simply took the old curriculum apart and rewrote it, aiming to start the children off very broadly on entry into the school, in junior year 1 of their education, and then slowly narrow the focus. The effort that went into staff development and into the reshaping of the school curriculum is really quite extraordinary. Day-to-day management of a school of this type, with this type of catchment area, is little other than management by walkabout. There are very few problems now with the curriculum set, and there are very few changes to make. The school has got as big as it is going to. The headteacher practises strong laterality. She is in with her staff every break- and lunch-time. Most decisions about matters are simply emerging. It is worth saying that when there is need for ruthlessness, as there was over the curriculum planning, the headteacher showed it and in fact pushed out a couple of the old teachers who could not ideologically or practically run with the new curriculum.

Hillcrest: the less effective school

To understand Hillcrest, one must understand the headteacher. She has a very strong progressive orientation and believes that the role of primary education is not just to develop economic talent, but also to develop social outcomes of the children, their capacity to work independently and their capacity to work collaboratively with others. The headteacher proactively staffs on the basis of the people that she believes will actually run with this ideology. The strange thing is, however, that the headteacher, although highly committed ideologically, is very aloof from the normal running of the school. She rarely ventures out from her office, and spends little time around the classrooms, where a rather young and fragile staff would probably greatly appreciate her support. She has a sense of ideological consistency and ideological commitment to primary progressive practice, but not administratively or organisationally. She works her staff extremely hard; they are expected to be there at half past seven in the morning. She is very hands-on and insistent in terms of curriculum documentation, looking at children's homework books and so on, and she herself works extremely hard, arriving at half past seven and rarely leaving until half past six in the evening. There is evidence of some difficult relations between the headteacher and the staff. This is because, if the staff sometimes do not live up to her strong progressive commitment, this causes difficulties, and her progressive ideology, and the small number of teachers available who actually share this nowadays, has led her to make poor appointments to her management position within the school. Basically, the number of people to choose from, if one has a strong progressive orientation, may not be very large, and can result, as in this case, in appointments not necessarily going to the most able candidates.

School expectations of pupils

Sea View: the more effective school

There is a strong use of reward-based control and strong use of reinforcements, both intrinsic and extrinsic, for academic, cultural and sporting effort and achievement.

Hillcrest: the less effective school

Hillcrest has a very strong commitment to rewarding children's positive behaviour, rather than punishing bad behaviour. This is done via the house system and merit systems.

School goals

Sea View: the more effective school

Sea View has a very strong commitment to academic outcomes. The majority of the parents in this catchment area expect high levels of academic outcomes from the school. In addition, the school also tries to encourage creativity and personal and social development by using interesting project work and the like in the curriculum.

Hillcrest: the less effective school

Hillcrest also has a strong commitment to developing children socially and academically, but the major commitment here is towards the children developing responsibility for their own learning. There is very little emphasis on active instruction of children. The key element is that children are regarded as being potentially able to educate themselves. There is, therefore, very little effort devoted to skilling them.

Inter-staff relations

Sea View: the more effective school

Staff relations at Sea View are very good. The staff appear to be friends with one another and appear to have strong social links, as well as forming very cohesive staff groups within the school.

Hillcrest: the less effective school

There is a considerable amount of tension and a limited amount of collaborative planning or curriculum design evident at Hillcrest. The staff are universally very young and seek comfort and assurance from each other. They are carefully selected and inculcated into the progressive regime, as well as into the ethos of insecurity and underlying covert hostility.

School resources

Sea View: the more effective school

Resources at Sea View are standard for primary schools in England. The locality and surrounding countryside and village culture is integrated and exploited as a learning resource to its full potential. The pupils, parents and staff are the air which the school breathes.

Hillcrest: the less effective school

The resources available at Hillcrest are luxurious by English primary school standards. This is largely due to the size of the school which ensures a large resource budget. There has also been additional resources due to the newness of the school's creation. There are no tatty books or dated reference material, for example. The art and craft resources are unique in the experience of the research team, and are a reflection of the means by which the school attempts to deliver the curriculum.

Relationship with local authorities

Sea View: the more effective school

Relations with outside agencies are non-existent; there is no contact at all. There would be no reason for the District to be involved, because it's a very good school and the District does not bother with the very good schools.

Hillcrest: the less effective school

Relations with outside agencies or the local authority are not close at all, because the school is seen as something away from and different from the philosophy of the advisory and inspection staff.

School image

Sea View: the more effective school

Image management has been strong and the school has put some effort into attracting increased intakes, which has clearly worked. However, it should be said that the school does not really need to manage its image.

Hillcrest: the less effective school

The school is aware of a need to present itself and its philosophy better to its catchment area and so is trying image management.

Conclusions for UK schools

Tables 12.1 and 12.2 show a summation of the characteristics of the schools for the two different socio-economic contexts. In general, the directions of the contrast between the two lower-SES schools are as expected in view of the school effectiveness literature, with such areas as the curriculum showing no differences because of the state national curriculum imposed on all schools. The more effective school shows higher expectations, a more assertive headteacher, a more directive and academically orientated teaching style, and more involved parents. In areas such as resources and inter-staff relationships, differences between the schools are only small.

For the middle-SES schools, the picture is complicated by a clearly different, and experimental, ideology present in the less effective school. Whilst the more effective school possesses many of the characteristics that one might expect (an assertive headteacher, positive expectations and a classic active teaching model for basic skills like mathematics), the less effective school is handicapped, not just by scoring 'low' on some of the conventional effectiveness correlates, but also by the effects of attempting to run with a relatively rare, if highly advanced, educational philosophy that has been only partially turned into a strong technology of schooling. In this respect, the middle-SES schools of the UK study are interestingly the same as, and yet different from, those of other countries reported earlier.

Table 12.1 Summary of differences between the two lower-SES schools across the twelve dimensions

Dimension of contrast	More effective low-SES (Trelent)	Less effective low-SES (Ford Junction)
General characteristics of the school	Size 350 pupils Minimal staff turnover Major ethnic minority, Asian; some socially deprived whites School staff sees role as generation of upward mobility for Asians	Size 200 pupils Average staff turnover White low social class; public minding School sees own role as child-minding
A day in the life of a child	High time on-task Teacher continuously monitors the class Setting is used to reduce the range of achievement, thus permitting more direct teaching	Low time on-task Teacher continuously attempting to keep order Time wasted through poor management of classes
Teachers' teaching style	Strong emphasis upon basic skill acquisition in science, maths and English High proportion of whole-class academically focused direct teaching Rapid lesson pace Maximisation of time for academic matters	Emphasis upon social as well as academic development, seen as important because of children's background Mixed whole-class and group Much time used in administrative routines etc.
The curriculum	Standard determined curriculum	Standard determined curriculum
The Influence of parents	Very well developed formal links and informal access	Parents rarely attend formal events and never informally
The principal	Committed to the development of a multi-cultural school Acute mixture of goal-setting and laterality	Competent, yet distant from his staff Mixes a lot with the pupils with whom he has an excellent relationship
School expectations of pupils	Excellence to be aimed at in all spheres	School is reactive upon events
School goals	Academic achievement, the transformation of children's occupational prospects	Childminding, survival
Inter-staff relationships	Very good relationships	Good relationships
School resources	Excellent material support in audio-visual material, books, etc. made possible by additional funding attached to the ethnic pupils	Good level of resources
Relationship with local authorities	Very good with the school used for LEA visitors	Not close
School image	Attempt to use new media etc. to attract and hold pupils; some success	Little attempt made

Table 12.2 Summary of differences between the two middle-SES schools across the twelve dimensions

Dimension of contrast	More effective mid-SES (Sea View)	Less effective mid-SES (Hillcrest)
General characteristics of the school	Very socially advantaged, rural community Size 180 Spacious and attractive buildings	Newly built middle-class housing Rapid increase in numbers over 6 years to 400+ creating instability and change
A day in the life of a child	Whole-class interactive teaching predominates Heavy use of reward systems Rapid curriculum pace, conceptually difficult material Very high time on-task	Moderate time on-task An emphasis on the importance of children learning for themselves
Teachers' teaching style	Whole-class active, interactive teaching is emphasised Strong didactic orientation Limited individual work	Teachers seen as facilitators Heavy use of individual work
The curriculum	School has a broad, thematic approach with an integrated curriculum	School has a broad, thematic approach with an integrated curriculum
The influence of parents	Very well developed; virtually 100 per cent attendance at open evenings	School is attempting to use parent evenings etc. to explain its progressive pedagogy
The principal	Curriculum orientated, pushy, driven Considerable attention given to staff development	Strong progressive orientation, hires zealots Isolated from staff who, being mostly young, need greater support Very hard worker, works long hours
School expectations of pupils	Strong reward-based control; use of reinforcement for academic cultural sporting effort and achievement	House system, merit system use
Schools goals	Very strong commitment to academic outcomes, with commitment to creativity and personal development through an innovative curriculum	Very strong commitment to children learning for themselves
Inter-staff relations	Excellent	Much friction, high turnover; young staff and remoteness of the principal
School resources	Excellent with the community used as a resource	Excellent
Relationship with local authorities	No relations – no need for district support	No relations
School image	Some attention to this, but the reputation of the school has its own effects	Considerable attention being given to sell the progressive technology

Part III

Conclusions

Creating world-class schools

13 Comparisons across country case studies

Charles Teddlie, David Reynolds,
Bert Creemers and Sam Stringfield

Introduction – the cross-national ratings

In the previous nine chapters, the case studies of all the countries involved in ISERP were presented. Information from these will be used in this chapter to generate comparisons across the countries. The following research questions, first stated in Chapter 1, are addressed in this chapter: –

1   *Which* school and teacher effectiveness factors were associated with schools/teachers being effective in different contexts?
2   How many of these factors were *universals* and how many *specific* to certain contexts?
3   What might explain *why* some were universal and some specific, and what were the implications of any findings for policy, for practice and for the school effectiveness research base?

This chapter contains information from several sources, including the following:

*   responses from each country's research team members to queries concerning the twelve predetermined case-study dimensions (see Table 2.3), as these dimensions relate to their own particular country;
*   assessments by the core research team of the power of the twelve dimensions to contrast between differentially effective pairs of lower-SES and differentially effective pairs of middle-SES schools based on evidence from the case studies;
*   other evidence from the case studies as contained in Chapters 4–12.

This chapter is divided into three sections:

1   a summary of the research team members' responses to queries regarding the case-study dimensions, which resulted in two sets of contrasts (English-speaking countries as compared to non-English-speaking countries; lower-SES schools as compared to middle-SES schools);
2   a discussion of the important effectiveness factors for each specific country context as revealed through core research team members' assessments of the case-study research;
3   a discussion of why some school effectiveness factors are *universals* and others appear to be *specific* to certain country contexts, using all the available information.

The logic for presenting the various case-study data sources and analyses in this chapter revolves around triangulation. Triangulation is the convergence of different sources of information, different views of investigators, different theories and different methodologies to support the development of themes (Cresswell, 1998; Denzin, 1978; Patton, 1990; Tashakkori and Teddlie, 1998). In this chapter, we primarily employ two types of techniques (data triangulation and investigator triangulation) to arrive at themes that give preliminary answers to ISERP research questions, especially the query, 'How many of these factors were *universals* and how many *specific* to certain countries?' The final section of this chapter provides preliminary answers to that question.

The data this chapter are based upon is taken from two questionnaires which were developed to assess the perceptions of country team members concerning the importance of case-study dimensions in successfully distinguishing between differentially effective lower-SES schools (or between differentially effective middle-SES schools) within their own country. One questionnaire asked the country team members to rate each case-study dimension on a five-point Likert scale (with five indicating very important) in terms of its capacity to distinguish between differentially effective schools. The other questionnaire asked the country team members to rank-order the case-study dimensions from 1 (the most important) to 12 (the least important) on this capacity. The country team members were asked to do this separately for their lower-SES and their middle-SES schools. (There may be some differences in the responses given to these two types of questions, since they ask for somewhat different ratings. For instance, several dimensions of contrast could be rated similarly on the Likert scale, but the rank-order protocol would force different responses.)

The responses of country team members were used because we believed we could profit from the experience that they gained conducting their case studies, and also from their intimate knowledge regarding educational processes within their specific country. The results from these analyses were used to compare:

- the overall responses of researchers from English-speaking versus non-English-speaking countries;
- the responses of the researchers to the importance of the case-study dimensions in lower-SES, as opposed to middle-SES, schools.

Responses of country team members from English-speaking and non-English-speaking countries

Several members of the cross-national intervisitation teams had expressed the opinion that elementary-grade education was more similar between almost any two English-speaking countries than between any of the English-speaking countries and any of the non-English-speaking countries. To more formally test this observation, we made English language a primary (though unanticipated) dimension for analysis.

Tables 13.1 and 13.2 contain the results from comparisons of researchers from English-speaking versus non-English-speaking countries. Previous analyses (e.g., Reynolds and Teddlie, 1995) indicated that this might be a fruitful comparison due to the different patterns that these groups of countries appeared to generate. The research teams contributing to the results found in Tables 13.1 and 13.2 were:

Table 13.1 Average ratings of the importance of case-study dimensions, by country type

Case-study dimension	Researchers from English-speaking countries	Researchers from non-English-speaking countries
General characteristics of the school	3.8	3.0
A day in the life of a child	4.0	4.5
Teachers' teaching style	3.8	4.2
The curriculum	2.5	4.0
The influence of parents	3.3	3.5
The principal	4.8	4.0
School expectations of pupils	4.6	4.0
School goals	4.3	3.5
Inter-staff relations	4.5	3.2
School resources	3.0	2.5
Relationship with local authorities	1.8	1.7
School image	3.3	3.0
Overall average	3.67	3.44

Note: The scales have five points, with 5 indicating very important. The data in this table are from six countries (the Republic of Ireland, the UK, the USA, Hong Kong, the Netherlands, Norway). Data from three countries (Australia, Canada, Taiwan) were not included because they did not have representatives attending the meetings at which the questionnaires were administered, or they had extensive missing data.

Table 13.2 Average rank orders of the importance of case-study dimensions, by country type

Case-study dimension	Researchers from English-speaking countries	Researchers from non-English-speaking countries
General characteristics of the school	7	9
A day in the life of a child	5.5	2
Teachers' teaching style	5.5	1
The curriculum	11	6.5
The influence of parents	9	8
The principal	1	3.5
School expectations of pupils	3	3.5
School goals	3	6.5
Inter-staff relations	3	5
School resources	10	10
Relationship with local authorities	12	12
School image	8	11

Note: The rank orders are from 1 to 12 with 1 indicating the most important dimension of contrast. Tied ranks (e.g., three responses tied for positions 2, 3, 4) are presented as the average of the affected ranks (e.g., a position of 3 would be given to all three respondents who tied for positions 2, 3 and 3).

- the English-speaking countries (the Republic of Ireland, the UK and USA);
- the non-English-speaking countries (Hong Kong, the Netherlands, Norway).

The other three countries (Australia, Canada, Taiwan) either did not have representatives attending the meetings at which the questionnaires were administered, or had extensive missing data.

The dimensions of contrast that were rated the most important by researchers from non-English-speaking countries (as opposed to English-speaking countries) were the child's experiences, instructional style, curriculum and parental influence. Thus researchers in non-English-speaking countries found it easier to distinguish between their differentially effective schools on the case-study dimensions associated with *traditional instructional* variables and the influence of parents.

Researchers in the English-speaking countries (in contrast to non-English-speaking countries) found it easier to distinguish among their differentially effective schools on case-study dimensions such as principal leadership, expectations for students, school goals, inter-staff relations and school image. Some of these case-study dimensions are among the most commonly described 'processes' of effective schooling found in the *school effectiveness* research literature (e.g., Levine and Lezotte, 1990; Sammons *et al.*, 1995; Reynolds and Teddlie, 2000b).

One possible explanation for these differences in responses by research-team members from different countries concerns differences in research traditions in those countries. The English-speaking countries (especially the USA and the UK) have a long tradition of research into the 'correlates' or the 'processes' of effective schooling. This research has generated lists of 'effective schools processes' that include: effective principal leadership, high expectations for students and well-articulated school goals. Thus it could be argued that researchers from English-speaking countries, where most of the effective schools research has occurred, rate these dimensions highly because they have already been associated with these findings about school effectiveness in their countries. However, the researchers from the English-speaking countries are also major examplars of a tradition of research into instructional factors and teacher effectiveness, so might have been expected to elevate these factors to high-rank like the 'school effectiveness factor' (see Teddlie and Stringfield, 1993; Muijs and Reynolds, 2001, for example). These 'personal researcher' factors are unlikely to be the explanation.

A more likely interpretation of these differences has been labelled the 'person-system' distinction. Teddlie and Reynolds (2000) explained the pattern of results reported in Tables 13.1 and 13.2 as follows:

> A plausible interpretation of these data is that in English speaking countries it is characteristics of the person that explain which institutions are effective, whereas in non-English speaking societies the system itself is so ordered, strong and well engineered/understood that individual characteristics of the principal and the relationships between the staff do not affect, and indeed are not allowed to affect, the quality of the education provided. In these non-English speaking societies, one might argue that the attention to curriculum, to instruction and to pedagogy means that there will be less of the *range* of educational quality amongst principals and staff that is characteristic of English speaking countries. For these latter, the system and the technology of schooling is so weak that it requires

unusually effective individual principals or unusually good inter-staff relations to generate effective schools.

(p. 255, italics in original)

Responses of country team members for lower-SES and middle-SES schools

Tables 13.3 and 13.4 are based on the same data set that generated Tables 13.1 and 13.2. Tables 13.3 and 13.4 summarize country team members' responses to queries regarding the case-study dimensions that best distinguished differentially effective lower-SES, as opposed to middle-SES, schools. Case studies from several countries indicated that researchers found it easier to contrast between differentially effective lower-SES schools than to contrast between differentially effective middle-SES schools.

Data shown in Table 13.3 confirms this difference: the overall Likert rating and eight out of twelve separate case-study ratings given by the country team members were higher for the lower-SES contrast than for the middle-SES contrast. Simply, there were higher perceived dimensions of contrast for the *lower-SES* schools than for the *middle-SES* schools.

Table 13.4 contains information on the rank orders of the case-study dimensions in terms of their capacity to distinguish between differentially effective schools. The country team members ranked the following case-study dimensions higher in terms of their capacity to *distinguish differentially effective lower-SES schools*: expectations for students, school goals, parental influence, image and resources. Three of these dimensions are among the effective schools correlates first publicized in the 1970s, which were from studies that were conducted in lower-SES schools (e.g., Brookover *et al.*, 1979; Edmonds, 1979a, 1979b; Venezky and Winfield, 1979; Weber, 1971).

On the other hand, the country team members ranked the following case-study dimensions higher in terms of their capacity to distinguish *differentially effective*

Table 13.3 Average ratings of the importance of case-study dimensions for discriminating among schools, broken down by SES of school

Case-study dimension	Low-SES schools	Middle-SES schools
General characteristics of the school	3.4	3.6
A day in the life of a child	4.0	4.4
Teachers' teaching style	4.0	4.0
The curriculum	3.2	2.8
The influence of parents	3.8	3.0
The principal	4.8	4.2
School expectations of pupils	4.6	4.2
School goals	4.4	3.6
Inter-staff relations	4.0	4.0
School resources	3.0	2.6
Relationship with local authorities	2.0	1.6
School image	3.8	2.6
Overall average	3.75	3.38

Note: The scales have five points, with 5 indicating very important.

Table 13.4 Average rank orders of the importance of case-study dimensions, broken down by SES of school

Case-study dimension	Low-SES schools	Middle-SES schools
General characteristics of the school	11	7
A day in the life of a child	6	3
Teachers' teaching style	4	2
The curriculum	9.5	8
The influence of parents	7	9
The principal	1	1
School expectations of pupils	2	5
School goals	3	6
Inter-staff relations	5	4
School resources	9.5	10.5
Relationship with local authorities	12	12
School image	8	10.5

Note: The rank orders are from 1 to 12 with 1 indicating the most important dimension of contrast. Tied ranks (e.g., three responses tied for positions 2, 3, 4) are presented as the average of the affected ranks (e.g., a position of 3 would be given to all three respondents who tied for positions 2, 3 and 4).

middle-SES schools: instructional style, child experiences, inter-staff relations, curriculum and school characteristics. Three of these dimensions (instructional style, child experiences, curriculum) are associated with the direct delivery of instructional services in the classroom, and a fourth (inter-staff relations) concerns how well the staff work together to produce the instruction at the schools.

Thus country team members perceive middle-SES schools to be more differentiated by instructional characteristics and delivery, while they perceive lower-SES schools to be more differentiated by the traditional 'effective schools correlates'. The contrasting perceptions of the country team members with regard to these different types of socio-economically defined schools is congruent with distinctions found in the school effectiveness research literature on 'context effects'. This literature suggests that, cross-nationally, 'effective schools correlates' are already present in many middle-SES schools at some minimal level, and that these schools can, therefore, concentrate more heavily on instructional issues. Lower-SES schools, on the other hand, must first establish these basic components of school effectiveness before concentrating on more instructional characteristics.

Teddlie, Stringfield and Teddlie and Reynolds (2000) summarized the literature (e.g., Chrispeels, 1992; Lightfoot, 1993; Teddlie and Stringfield, 1993) concerning these distinctions between the characteristics of lower- and middle-SES schools:

A common thread runs through the results from all these studies of low-SES schools on the road to improvement: the staffs at low-SES schools typically have to spend more time creating certain components of school success (e.g. high expectation levels, reward structures for academic success, safe and orderly climates) than do middle-SES schools, where the community has often already generated these components, at least in nascent form. Thus, fundamental elements in school improvement programs often differ between schools located in middle- and low-SES communities, with schools in the low-SES communities making considerable efforts to create certain baseline conditions that may already exist in more affluent communities. The effort required to create these baseline components of successful schooling in low-SES communities necessarily detracts . . . from other aspects of school improvement, such as the generation of an excellent instructional system. . . . In middle-SES schools, where these baseline conditions are often already met, resources can be marshalled with regard to the long term process change phase almost from the beginning.

(Teddlie *et al.*, 2000, p. 171)

These data from six countries' team members provide confirmatory evidence for results that had until now come primarily from USA studies. While these data are perceptual in nature, they confirm that international researchers believe that a different set of dimensions distinguish differentially effective lower-SES from differentially effective middle-SES schools. The dimensions of contrast for lower-SES schools are related to the basic *'effective schools correlates'*, while the dimensions of contrast for middle-SES schools relate more to the delivery of *classroom instructional services*.

An analysis of the important case-study dimensions for each specific country context

Members of the core research team reviewed the case studies from each country, including the tables that summarized the differences between the schools, and made determinations regarding how important each case-study dimension was in distinguishing between more and less effective schools for each country. They did this separately for the lower-SES pairs of schools and for the middle-SES pairs of schools within each country.

This process for judging the relative importance of the case-study dimensions in contrasting differentially effective schools was somewhat similar to the process described in the previous section. There are, however, two major differences in these rating procedures:

1   The ratings described in this part of the chapter were done by members of the core research team only and involved an assessment of all the countries' written case studies.
2   The rating process used by the core research team and described in this section concerns only the case-study schools described in Chapters 4–12; whereas the rating process described in the previous section concerned all schools in the sample, not just the case-study schools.

Two members from the core research team read each of the countries' case studies and assigned the ratings found in Tables 13.5 (lower-SES schools only) and 13.6 (middle-SES schools only). The ratings include the following:

1   'H' refers to a 'highly' rated dimension of contrast between the more effective and less effective schools. 'H' ratings were given a value of 5 in the calculation of the average ratings.
2   'M' refers to a 'moderately' rated dimension of contrast between the more effective and less effective schools. 'M' ratings were given a value of 3 in the calculation of the average ratings.

3   'L' refers to a 'low'-rated dimension of contrast between the more effective and less effective schools. 'L' ratings were given a value of 1 in the calculation of the average ratings.
4   'NA' means there wasn't sufficient information within a country's case-study chapter to provide a rating. These data were treated as missing values.

Not all countries had case studies with both middle-SES and lower-SES pairs of schools:

•   the case studies from Australia were designated 'mixed-SES' schools only; therefore, they could not be considered either lower-SES or middle-SES pairs of schools;
•   the case studies from Norway did not include a contrast between differentially effective lower-SES schools;
•   the case studies from Hong Kong and Taiwan did not include a contrast between differentially effective middle-SES schools.

The two core research team members agreed on 76 per cent of the ratings. For the remaining ratings on which there were disagreements, a third member of the core research team determined the final rating (H, M, L) for the case-study dimension.

Tables 13.5 and 13.6 contain information broken down by country with regard to how important each case-study dimension was in distinguishing between more and less effective schools based on the ratings of the core research team. The core research team rated the dimensions of contrast higher for the English-speaking countries (USA, Canada, the Republic of Ireland, the UK) in terms of their capacity to *distinguish between differentially effective low-SES schools*. These countries obtained an average score above 3.8 across all their case-study dimensions. On the other hand, the core research team rated the dimensions of contrast lower for the non-English-speaking countries (Taiwan, Hong Kong, the Netherlands) in terms of their capacity to *distinguish between differentially effective low-SES schools*. These countries obtained an average score below 3.3 across all their case-study dimensions. The average scores of all countries across all case-study dimensions for lower-SES schools was 3.36. (See Table 13.5.)

It is interesting that the countries receiving the highest differentiating ratings on their case-study dimensions are all English-speaking countries, while those receiving the lowest ratings are all non-English-speaking countries. These data confirm that a different pattern of results is generated by these two groups of countries and, therefore, triangulate with results discussed in the previous section of this chapter.

For middle-SES schools (see Table 13.6) the average scores of all countries across all case-study dimensions was only 2.62. This indicates that the case-study dimensions were perceived to be less powerful in distinguishing between differentially effective middle-SES schools (average score = 2.62), as opposed to lower-SES schools (average score = 3.36). These results (based on data generated by the core research team) triangulate with data reported in Tables 13.3 (generated by the country team members). (The average ratings from Table 13.3 for lower-SES schools is 3.75, while it is 3.38 for middle-SES schools.)

These results also triangulate with results reported in the school effectiveness research literature with regard to differences between lower-SES and middle-SES schools. As noted above, middle-SES schools tend to have several characteristics in common,

Table 13.5 Ratings of case-study dimensions based on analysis of each country's case-study information, lower-SES schools only (excluding Australia and Norway)

Case-study dimension	USA	Canada	Taiwan	Hong Kong	Netherlands	Republic of Ireland	UK
General characteristics of the school	M	H	M	L	L	H	M
A day in the life of a child	H	H	NA	NA	H	H	H
Teachers' teaching style	M	M	M	H	M	H	H
The curriculum	M	H	L	L	M	M	L
The influence of parents	H	H	L	H	L	M	H
The principal	H	H	L	H	M	H	M
School expectations of pupils	H	H	L	NA	H	M	H
School goals	H	M	L	NA	M	H	H
Inter-staff relations	H	H	L	H	L	H	M
School resources	H	L	L	L	L	H	M
Relationship with local authorities	L	H	NA	NA	L	M	H
School image	H	M	L	NA	M	M	M
Average rating	4.17	4.17	1.40	3.29	2.50	4.17	3.83

Note: The ratings in Tables 13.5 and 13.6 were done by members of the core research team based on all evidence presented in the case studies found in Chapters 4–12. 'NA' means there wasn't sufficient information within a country's case-study chapter to provide a rating. 'H' refers to a 'highly' rated dimension of contrast between the more effective and less effective lower-SES schools. 'M' refers to a 'moderately' rated dimension of contrast between the more effective and less effective lower-SES schools. 'L' refers to a 'low'-rated dimension of contrast between the more effective and less effective lower-SES schools. 'H' ratings were given a value of 5 in the calculation of the average ratings; 'M' ratings were given a rating of 3; and 'L' ratings were given a rating of 1. The case studies from Australia and Norway did not include a contrast between differentially effective lower-SES schools.

Table 13.6 Ratings of case-study dimensions based on analysis of each country's case-study information, middle-SES schools only (excluding Taiwan, Australia and Hong Kong)

Case-study dimension	USA	Canada	Netherlands	Norway	Republic of Ireland	UK
General characteristics of the school	M	M	M	M	H	M
A day in the life of a child	M	M	H	M	H	H
Teachers' teaching style	L	NA	M	M	M	H
The curriculum	M	L	M	L	M	L
The influence of parents	M	NA	M	L	L	M
The principal	H	L	M	M	M	M
School expectations of pupils	H	NA	M	NA	M	M
School goals	M	L	M	M	M	M
Inter-staff relations	H	NA	L	H	L	H
School resources	M	NA	L	L	M	L
Relationship with local authorities	L	NA	L	NA	L	L
School image	L	NA	NA	H	L	L
Average rating	3.00	1.80	2.64	2.80	2.67	2.83

at least in nascent form, due to the structure of and demands made by the middle-class communities in which they reside: high expectation levels, reward structures for academic success, safe and orderly climates, etc. Lower-SES schools, on the other hand, do not necessarily have these commonalities. The commonalities found among many middle-class schools on several of the case-study dimensions makes it less likely that raters would be able to distinguish between middle-SES schools on these dimensions, even if these schools were differentially effective.

Tables 13.7 and 13.8 contain further information regarding the relative importance that core research team members assigned the case-study dimensions in distinguishing between more and less effective case-study schools. Table 13.7 combines information from Tables 13.5 and 13.6. For countries with data on both the lower-SES and middle-SES pairs of schools, Table 13.7 contains an average of the two ratings. For countries with missing data on one set of schools, the data for the completed set of schools are presented here. For Australia (which had mixed-SES schools only), the ratings for those schools are contained in Table 13.7.

There are five levels of ratings in Tables 13.7 and 13.8: 'H' means that this is a 'highly' rated dimension of contrast for a particular country for both differentially effective low- and middle-SES schools; 'H/M' means that the rating is mixed between high and moderate; 'M' means that this is a 'moderately' rated dimension of contrast for a particular country for their differentially effective low- and middle-SES schools; 'M/L' means that the rating is mixed between moderate and low; 'L' means that this is a 'low'-rated dimension of contrast for a particular country for both differentially effective low- and middle-SES schools.

The information regarding countries found in Table 13.7 is very similar to that previously described in Table 13.5, in that English-speaking countries (the USA, Canada, the Republic of Ireland, the UK) have higher-rated dimensions of contrast than non-English-speaking countries (Hong Kong, Norway, the Netherlands, Taiwan). The one exception is Australia, which had some problems in sampling and data collection described previously in Chapter 2. Ratings for the country teams' ability to make differentiation across all case-study dimensions are as follows:

Table 13.7 Ratings of case-study dimensions based on analysis of each country's case-study information, averaged across all schools

Case-study dimension	USA	Canada	Taiwan	Australia	Hong Kong	Netherlands	Norway	Republic of Ireland	UK
General characteristics of the school	M	H/M	M	L	L	M/L	M	H	M
A day in the life of a child	H/M	H/M	NA	M	NA	H	M	H	H
Teachers' teaching style	M/L	M	M	H	H	M	L	H/M	H
The curriculum	M	M	L	M	L	M	L	M	L
The influence of parents	H/M	H	L	L	H	M/L	L	M/L	H/M
The principal	H	M	L	M	H	M	M	H/M	M
School expectations of pupils	H	H	L	H	NA	H/M	NA	M	H/M
School goals	H/M	M/L	L	H	NA	M	M	H/M	H/M
Inter-staff relations	H	H	L	NA	H	L	H	M	H/M
School resources	H/M	L	L	L	L	L	L	H/M	M/L
Relationship with local authorities	L	H	NA	NA	NA	L	NA	M/L	M
School image	M	M	L	L	NA	M	H	M/L	M/L
Average	3.58	3.58	1.40	2.80	3.29	2.58	2.80	3.42	3.33

Note: The ratings in Tables 13.7 and 13.8 were done by members of the core research team based on all evidence presented in the case studies found in Chapters 4–12. They summarise the ratings found in Tables 13.5 and 13.6. There are five levels of ratings: 'H' means that this is a 'highly' rated dimension of contrast for a particular country for both differentially effective low- and middle-SES schools; 'H/M' means that the rating is mixed between high and moderate; 'M' means that this is a 'moderately' rated dimension of contrast for a particular country for their differentially effective low- and middle-SES schools; 'M/L' means that the rating is mixed between moderate and low; 'L' means that this is a 'low'-rated dimension of contrast for a particular country for both differentially effective low- and middle-SES schools. For countries with missing data on one set of schools, the data for the completed set of schools are presented here. For Australia (which had 'mixed'-SES schools only), the ratings for those schools are contained in this table.

Table 13.8 Mean ratings and frequencies for importance of case-study dimensions across all schools, based on case-study information

Case-study dimension	High ratings	High/medium ratings	Medium ratings	Medium/low ratings	Low ratings	Ratings not available	Average rating
General characteristics of the school	1	1	4	1	2	0	2.78
A day in the life of a child	3	2	2	0	0	2	4.14
Teachers' teaching style	3	1	4	1	0	0	3.67
The curriculum	0	0	5	0	4	0	2.11
The influence of parents	2	2	0	2	3	0	2.78
The principal	3	1	4	0	1	0	3.56
School expectations of pupils	2	2	2	0	1	2	3.57
School goals	1	3	2	1	1	1	3.25
Inter-staff relations	4	1	1	0	2	1	3.63
School resources	0	2	0	1	6	0	1.78
Relationship with local authorities	1	0	1	1	2	4	2.40
School image	1	0	3	2	2	1	2.50

1   the USA – 3.58
2   Canada – 3.58
3   the Republic of Ireland – 3.42
4   the UK – 3.33
5   Hong Kong – 3.29 (seven dimensions only)
6 – tie   Norway and Australia – 2.80 (ten dimensions only for each country)
8   the Netherlands – 2.58
9   Taiwan – 1.40 (ten dimensions only).

Table 13.8 summarizes the core research team's ratings of the case-study dimensions in distinguishing between differentially effective schools. Ratings for the factors across all countries are as follows:

1   Child experiences – 4.14
2   Instructional style – 3.67
3   Inter-staff relations – 3.63
4   Expectations for students – 3.57
5   Principal leadership – 3.56
6   School goals – 3.25
7 – tie   School characteristics and parental influence – 2.78
9   Image – 2.50
10   Relationship with local authority – 2.40
11   Curriculum – 2.11
12   Resources – 1.78.

The higher-rated case-study dimensions (child experiences, instructional style, inter-staff relations, expectations for students, principal leadership and school goals) *are all directly related to processes ongoing at the school and classroom levels*. Most of the lower-rated dimensions (school characteristics, parental influence, image, relationship with local authority and resources) are all *much less directly related to the processes ongoing at the school and classroom levels*.

Why are some school effectiveness factors universals, while others are specific to particular country contexts?

As noted earlier, data from three sources have been presented to give preliminary answers to the question of *universals* and *specifics* concerning school effectiveness factors in: ratings given to the case-study dimensions by country team members, ratings given these same dimensions by core research team members and information gleaned from the school effectiveness research literature. This final section will be divided into three parts:

1   a discussion of three distinct trends found in the ratings of the case-study dimensions (English- versus non-English-speaking countries, lower-SES versus middle-SES schools; and lower- versus higher-rated case-study dimensions);
2   a further discussion of the case-study dimensions that appear to be *universals*;
3   a discussion of the case-study dimensions that appear to be *specifics* for certain country contexts.

Firstly, in terms of overall trends across the case-study comparisons between English-speaking and non-English-speaking countries yielded some interesting results related to the *universals–specifics* distinction:

- There were some case-study dimensions rated *universally* high by country team members from both English-speaking and non-English-speaking countries in terms of capacity to distinguish successfully between differentially effective schools. Tables 13.1 and 13.2 indicate that the following four dimensions of contrast were rated high for both groups of countries: child experiences, instructional style, principal leadership and expectations for students. There were also some case-study dimensions rated *universally* low by team members from both English-speaking and non-English-speaking countries in terms of capacity to successfully distinguish between differentially effective schools. Three dimensions of contrast were rated low for both groups of countries: relationship with local authority, resources and image.

- On the other hand, there were some dimensions that were rated much higher for one *specific* group of countries than for the other. For example, the country team members from non-English-speaking countries rated the curriculum dimension as being much more important in distinguishing between differentially effective schools in their countries. The research team members from English-speaking countries, on the other hand, rated school goals and inter-staff relations as being much more important in distinguishing between differentially effective schools in their countries. (See Tables 13.1 and 13.2.)

- Team members from the two groups of countries also generated *specific* and distinct overall patterns of responses. Researchers from non-English-speaking countries found it easier to distinguish between their differentially effective schools on the dimensions of contrast associated with traditional instruction and the influence of parents (instructional style, curriculum, child's experiences and parental influence). Researchers from the English-speaking countries, on the other hand, found it easier to distinguish among their differentially effective schools on the dimensions of contrast associated with the commonly described processes of effective schooling (e.g., principal leadership, expectations for students, school goals, inter-staff relations).

Secondly, comparisons between lower-SES and middle-SES school also yielded some interesting results related to the *universals–specifics* distinction.

- Country team members rated some of the case-study dimensions *universally* high regardless of whether the dimensions were being used to distinguish between differentially effective lower-SES schools or differentially effective middle-SES schools. Tables 13.3 and 13.4 indicate that these universal dimensions included mostly the same ones that were universals for the English-speaking/non-English-speaking comparison: instructional style, principal leadership and expectations for students. There were also some case-study dimensions rated *universally* low by research team members for both middle-SES and lower-SES schools. Tables 13.3 and 13.4 indicate that these universally low-rated dimensions were also mostly the same ones that were rated low for the English-speaking/non-English-speaking comparison: relationship with local authority, resources and image, plus curriculum and school characteristics.

- The dimensions of contrast for the differentially effective lower-SES schools generated *universally* higher ratings than the dimensions of contrast for the differentially effective middle-SES schools. Results from Table 13.3 indicated that the overall Likert rating and eight of the twelve separate case-study dimension ratings given by the country team members were higher for the lower-SES contrast than for the middle-SES contrast.
- Country team members perceived middle-SES schools to be more differentiated by instructional characteristics and delivery, while they perceived lower-SES schools to be more differentiated by the correlates of effectiveness associated with school climate and parental influence. The contrasting perceptions of the country team members with regard to these different types of socio-economically defined schools is congruent with distinctions found in the school effectiveness research literature on 'context effect'. (See Table 13.4.)
- The core research team also perceived the dimensions of contrast to be much more powerful in distinguishing between differentially effective lower-SES schools as opposed to differentially effective middle-SES schools. (See Tables 13.5–13.7.) These results triangulate with those generated by the country team members.

Thirdly, comparisons between the highest-rated case-study dimensions and the lowest-rated also yielded some interesting results related to the *universals–specifics* distinction.

- There was moderate, cross-national agreement about the most important dimensions of contrast. The country team members rated the following case-study dimensions the highest (in order) in their capacity to distinguish between differentially effective schools: principal leadership, expectations for students, child experiences, instructional style, school goals, and inter-staff relations. (See Tables 13.1 and 13.3.) The core research team members rated the following case-study dimensions the highest (in order) dimensions of contrast: child experiences, instructional style, inter-staff relations, expectations for students, principal leadership, and school goals. (See Table 13.8.) While the order of the ratings were somewhat different, the same six dimensions of contrast were rated high by both the country team members and the core research team members.
- Similarly, there was moderate, cross-national agreement about the least important dimensions of contrast. The country team members rated the following case-study dimensions the lowest (in order running to the lowest-rated dimension) in their capacity to distinguish between differentially effective schools: school characteristics, parental influence, image, curriculum, resources, and relationship with local authority. (See Tables 13.1 and 13.3.) The core research team members rated the following case-study dimensions the lowest (in order running to the lowest-rated dimension) dimensions of contrast: school characteristics, parental influence, image, relationship with local authority, curriculum, and resources. (See Table 13.8.) Again, there was triangulation of ratings for the country team members and the core research team members.
- There are *specific* differences between the patterns of results generated by the country research teams and the core research team in their assessment of the capacity of

the case-study dimensions to distinguish successfuly between differentially effective schools. With regard to the highest-rated dimensions of contrast, the country research teams preferred principal leadership and expectations for students, while the core research team preferred child experiences and instructional style. With regard to the lowest-rated dimensions of contrast, the country research teams placed relationship with local authority as one of two dimensions at the very bottom, while the core research team saw curriculum as ranking near the bottom.

A further discussion of the case-study dimensions that appear to be *universals*

A comparison of the ISERP data presented in this chapter with a summary of important process variables gleaned from the school effectiveness research literature should prove enlightening. Table 13.9 summarises the results of a recent synthesis (Reynolds and Teddlie, 2000b) of the important process variables from the school effectiveness research literature based on several other summary reports from the UK (Sammons *et al.*, 1995; Sammons, 1999), the USA (Levine and Lezotte, 1990), and the Netherlands (Scheerens and Bosker, 1997). Four of the most highly rated ISERP dimensions of contrast are similar to the effective schools processes identified in Table 13.9, which is taken from the review:

1   the ISERP dimension of 'instructional style' is similar to the 'processes of effective teaching' (process 2 from Table 13.9);
2   the ISERP dimension of 'expectations for students' is akin to 'creating high (and appropriate) expectations for all' (process 5 from Table 13.9);
3   the ISERP dimension of 'principal leadership' is similar to 'processes of effective leadership' (process 1 from Table 13.9);
4   the ISERP dimension of 'school goals' is akin to 'producing a positive school culture', sub-component 'creating a shared vision' (process 4, sub-component (a) from Table 13.9).

Similar processes for two of the ISERP highly rated dimensions of contrast (child experiences, inter-staff relations) were not listed in Table 13.9. With regard to 'child experiences', this factor was an innovative ISERP methodological component, which has seldom been used in other school effectiveness research projects. In Chapter 2, this factor was described as the 'whole school day methodology' (WSD) or 'child study' (Brigham and Gamse, 1997; Schaffer, 1994). This factor was rated by both the country teams and the core research team as one of the key dimensions of contrast that distinguished between differentially effective schools.

Inter-staff relations was another case-study characteristic that was rated highly by ISERP researchers, yet did not have an analogue on the 'processes of effective schools' found in Table 13.9. Reynolds and Teddlie (2000a, 2000c) concluded there was a need to study 'relationship patterns' in future school effectiveness research. These patterns could include: inter-staff relations, relations between the staff and the students, relations among the students, etc. Thus far, the extant research in this area has focused on inter-staff relations, and the methodology employed has been sociometric in nature (e.g., Teddlie and Kochan, 1991) or more recently network analysis (e.g., Durland, 1996; Durland and Teddlie, 1996).

Table 13.9 The processes of effective schools

Process	Components of the process
The processes of effective leadership	a. Being firm and purposeful b. Involving others in the process c. Exhibiting instructional leadership d. Frequent, personal monitoring e. Selecting and replacing staff
The processes of effective teaching	a. Maximising class time b. Successful grouping and organisation c. Exhibiting best teaching practices d. Adapting practice to particulars of classroom
Developing and maintaining a pervasive focus on learning	a. Focusing on academics b. Maximising school learning time
Producing a positive school culture	a. Creating a shared vision b. Creating an orderly environment c. Emphasising positive reinforcement
Creating high (and appropriate) expectations for all	a. For students b. For staff
Emphasising student responsibilities and rights	a. Responsibilities b. Rights
Monitoring progress at all levels	a. At the school level b. At the classroom level c. At the student level
Developing staff skills at the school site	a. Site-based b. Integrated with ongoing professional development
Involving parents in productive and appropriate ways	a. Buffering negative influences b. Encouraging productive interactions with parents

Note: Adapted from *The International Handbook of School Effectiveness* (Reynolds and Teddlie, 2000) with permission from RoutledgeFalmer.

Dimensions of contrast rated 'low'

How do the dimensions of contrast rated low from the ISERP research compare with the list of effective schools characteristics? Only one of the lower-rated ISERP dimensions of contrast is similar to an effective schools process identified in Table 13.9: parental influence. The ISERP dimension of 'parental influence' is, of course, similar to 'involving parents in productive and appropriate ways' (process 9 from Table 13.9). The school effectiveness research literature is decidedly mixed on the importance of involving parents in schools. Some research (e.g. Hallinger and Murphy, 1986; Teddlie and Stringfield, 1985, 1993) indicated that more effective schools do not involve parents and actually 'buffer' negative parental influences from their schools as these schools are going through the improvement process.

It is, perhaps, surprising that 'curriculum' was rated low by the researchers in English-speaking countries in terms of its capacity to successfully distinguish between differentially effective schools. Part of the reason for this may be methodological: the

ISERP schools were supposed to be matched on as many variables of importance as possible, and this matching may have reduced some of the natural differences in curriculum that exist within countries.

'School characteristics' was another broad category encapsulating factors such as student body size, number of teachers and staff, description of school and catchment area, public/private organisation, etc. The design of the study (controlling for SES of student body within pairs or triads of schools) reduced the variance on several of these variables. (Failure to meet the sampling requirements reintroduced some of this variance in a few of the countries.) Canada and the Republic of Ireland received some high ratings on this dimension by members of the core research team, for reasons that will be explained in the next section of this chapter.

'Image' was rated ninth in terms of capacity to distinguish between differentially effective schools for both country team members and core research team members. This case-study dimension was included partially because of the increased media attention given to the perceived failures of public education (at least in North America and Western Europe). With few exceptions, this dimension of contrast was not perceived to distinguish successfully between differentially effective schools. The exceptions included:

1   for the country team members, slightly higher ratings were given to 'image' in lower-SES schools and in English-speaking schools;
2   the core research team rated 'image' as a more important dimension of contrast for lower-SES schools.

'Resources' is rated near the bottom of the dimensions of contrast for both the country team members (tenth) and the core research team (twelfth). This result is consistent with research going back to the Coleman Report from the USA (Coleman *et al.*, 1966). We note that design made it unlikely that large differences in resource availability would be a frequent reality in the within-country samples. Hence it was unlikely to differentiate.

'Relationship with local authority' is also rated near the bottom of the dimensions of contrast for both the country team members (twelfth) and the core research team (tenth). Little variance was generated among the ratings, except that the core research-team members rated this dimension higher for lower-SES schools in Canada, the UK and Ireland.

A discussion of the case-study dimensions that appear to be *specifics* for certain country contexts

As described in the previous two sections, there are many similarities in the pattern of results generated for the ISERP countries by the research team members; on the other hand, there are also individualistic patterns of results for each of the countries. This section contains information regarding some of the dimensions of contrast that were *specifically* important in certain country contexts. For instance, despite general agreement regarding the lowest-rated dimensions of contrast, the ISERP core research team rated each of these dimensions much higher in terms of its capacity to distinguish between differentially effective schools *in at least one country*. (See Table 13.7.)

For example, core research team members rated 'school characteristics' a 'high' dimension of contrast for the Republic of Ireland. The researchers did this for both differentially effective lower-SES schools and differentially effective middle-SES schools in the Republic of Ireland. While the design of ISERP reduced the variance on several school characteristics, the nature of the school system in the Republic of Ireland resulted in some rather large differences in these characteristics between differentially effective schools.

Many of the elementary schools in the Republic of Ireland are affiliated to the major churches, Roman Catholic and Church of Ireland in particular, and there is considerable variance in the physical conditions and the faculties at these schools. For example, the comparison between characteristics of the two lower-SES schools summarized in Table 11.2 was quite striking: the more effective school (Secret Garden, a girls-only school at the relevant level) was described as 'modern, well maintained in pleasant surroundings', a 'haven' in an economically depressed area of Dublin; the less effective school (Tower View, a boys-only school) was very old, bleak, poorly maintained, 'prison-like'. While students came from the same catchment area and both schools were maintained by Catholic religious orders, the vastly contrasting school characteristics reflect the differential effectiveness of the two schools. (See Chapter 11 for more details.)

Core research team members rated 'relationship with local authority' as a 'high' dimension of contrast for the lower-SES schools in Canada: information from Table 5.1 indicates a large difference between the two schools (Inner-City School and Fly-In School) on this dimension. The relationship between Inner-City (the more effective school) and the local authority was described as following: there was a 'conventional relationship with the educational district' and there were 'close links with health, welfare, and police agencies'. On the other hand, the relationship between Fly-In (the less effective school) and the local authority was characterized as a 'complex relationship'. Fly-In School served a population on a reserve, which was politically controlled by a Band Council, composed of the chief and councillors. The school was located in a geographically remote region of Canada, where the local authorities wielded great influence. For instance, there were allegations that jobs and job security in the school were controlled by nepotism, and teachers had to be careful not to offend the Council, lest they be barred from the reserve. According to the case study, non-native teachers are there 'only to teach and . . . are never regarded as permanent community members'. (See Chapter 5 for more details.)

Parental influence was rated a high dimension of contrast for Hong Kong by the core research team. Information contained in the text in Chapter 8 and in Table 8.3 indicate at least three differences between ABC School (more effective) and XYZ School (less effective) on this dimension:

1   Parental expectations for the ABC School students were uniformly high: the students were expected to do well and go on to university. Parent expectations for the XYZ School students were more mixed: some students reported that their parents expected them to go on to university, while others reported that their parents 'only expected them to complete secondary school'.
2   There was a parents' association at the ABC School, while there was none at the XYZ School. The authors of the Hong Kong case study indicated that the XYZ principal might be responsible for the lack of a parents' association, because he

did not want the school to have to 'meet challenges from parents'. (Since parents' associations are not required in Hong Kong, this is a factor on which more variance can be expected than in the USA, where they are typically mandated by the state or district.)

3   The teacher–parent collaboration at ABC School was described as greater than that at XYZ School.

Image was rated a 'high' dimension of contrast by the core research team for the pair of differentially effective middle-SES schools located in Oslo, Norway. (See Chapter 10 and Table 10.1 for more details.) This dimension concerns how the school presents itself to the community. There is a large difference between Fjord School (less effective) and Troll School (more effective) on this dimension of contrast. Fjord School is characterized as having 'a feeling of anonymity', while Troll School projects an open and inclusive 'atmosphere to the community'. Ongoing conflicts between the principal and the parents at Fjord has led the staff at Fjord to conclude that, 'We have had enough of being focused on in the newspapers' and to feel antipathy towards 'outsiders', who are not interested in solving problems at the school. On the other hand, Troll School was working on various projects that could lead to greater networking throughout the community.

With regard to other *specific* country patterns, there are cases in which one or two countries received low ratings on dimensions of contrast that were rated highly elsewhere. For instance, the core research team rated inter-staff relations as an important dimension of contrast (moderate, moderate-high, or high) for all countries except the Netherlands and Taiwan. (See Table 13.7.) In the case of the Netherlands, there was almost no difference in the description of differentially effective schools on this dimension: the descriptions of inter-staff relations stated that there were 'good relations between staff members' at all the schools. (See Table 9.1.)

In the case of Taiwan, 'inter-staff relations' was one of eight dimensions of contrast that were rated low by core research team members (see Table 13.7), possibly reflecting the absence of variance among Taiwanese schools on any dimensions of schooling. The Taiwanese case study contends that 'the culture permits much less variance among schools than what might be expected or even accepted from schools in other countries'.

This pattern of results is, of course, radically different from those of the two ISERP countries: the USA and the UK. As indicated in Table 13.7, core research team members rated seven of the dimensions of contrast for these two countries as either 'high' or 'medium/high'. On the other hand, the core research team members rated only one of the dimensions of contrast as 'low' for these two countries.

Conclusions – our research questions reviewed

In this chapter, we used information from the case studies to provide preliminary answers to the questions posed by the ISERP study.

First, *Which* school and teacher effectiveness factors were associated with schools/teachers being effective in different countries?

The twelve a priori case-study dimensions, introduced in Chapter 2 and described for each country in Chapters 3–12, were associated with schools/teachers being more effective to a greater or lesser degree in each country. The factors appeared to work best in the USA, the UK, Canada and the Republic of Ireland and the least well in Taiwan, the Netherlands and Norway.

Second, How many of these factors were *universals* and how many *specific* to certain countries?

The *universal* dimensions of contrast were instructional style, principal leadership, child experiences, expectations for students, inter-staff relations, and school goals. These dimensions of contrast were generally rated highly by both country team members and the core research team, although there were some exceptions (e.g. Taiwan).

Third, What might explain *why* some were universal and some specific, and what were the implications of any findings for policy, for practice, and for the school effectiveness research base?

Special attention in this chapter was given to explaining two distinct overall trends found in the ratings of the case-study dimensions: lower-SES versus middle-SES schools, and English- versus non-English-speaking countries.

Our tendency is to explain lower-SES versus middle-SES schools trends using distinctions found in the school effectiveness research literature on 'context effects'. This literature suggests that 'effective schools correlates' are already present in many middle-SES schools at some minimal level, and that these schools can, therefore, concentrate more heavily on instructional issues. Lower-SES schools, on the other hand, must first establish these basic components of school effectiveness before concentrating on instructional characteristics. Therefore, the higher-rated dimensions of contrast for lower-SES schools in ISERP involved the basic 'effective schools correlates' (e.g. principal leadership, expectations for students, school goals) while those for middle-SES schools involved instructional characteristics (e.g. instructional style).

Regarding the English- versus non-English-speaking-countries distinction, a possible explanation for these differential results is the *person–system* distinction. This explanation holds that in English-speaking countries it is characteristics of the person that explain which institutions are effective, whereas in non-English-speaking societies the educational system itself is so ordered, strong and well engineered/understood that there is less variance in the individual characteristics of the principal and the relationships among the staff members. Therefore system variables are more important in non-English-speaking countries, while characteristics of individuals are more important in English-speaking countries, where systems are not so strong.

14 Creating world class schools
What have we learned?

David Reynolds, Bert Creemers,
Sam Stringfield and Gene Schaffer

Introduction – our research strategy reviewed

We have, in this book, ranged across nine countries and four continents in our search to understand issues to do with 'what works'. One of our goals has also been to attempt to answer questions as to 'why' certain things may work. When we began this study, the education debate was becoming internationalised with the possibility being increasingly realised that other countries' schooling practices might be useful in educational reform in different countries. We also noted that the school effectiveness discipline had recently neglected to further research its core – namely, 'what works' in promoting positive pupil achievement and whether 'what works' needs to be quantitatively and qualitatively different in different social settings. We also noted the criticisms of school effectiveness research and the need for the discipline therefore to move forward.

We outlined our quantitative data on school outcomes and processes both at pupil and classroom level, and studied in detail the more effective and the less effective schools we have found in the different social contexts within different societies. In Chapter 13, we summarised our findings about the classroom and school factors that appeared to be affecting multi-year outcomes. We found a large number of variables that apparently were universal and important in all countries, and some others that were specific to certain countries, and then speculated about the explanations for these findings.

In this final chapter, we move on to the question of what the educational lessons for diverse countries may be, based on the data we have gathered and analysed. In some places in this chapter, we consciously go beyond what our inevitably sometimes partial data can tell us. However, our speculations and hypotheses are not offered without support – we have, as a team, a combined experience of over 100 'person years' as school effectiveness researchers. We also, as a team, have spent some years wrestling with the themes that we now take up. Although we may go *beyond* our data, we are not *light* on data or on the *experience* involved in interpreting it.

We noted in the first two chapters the details of our research strategy and why we were adopting it. We took a cohort of pupils who moved through their schools over two years, and collected a range of data upon them, their classrooms, their schools and the societies that provided the context for their education. We explicitly reflected a mixed methodology tradition, and utilised both quantitative and qualitative data pragmatically, choosing to use the particular methods that we found appropriate for the research task in question. We developed a range of instruments that were novel in this research field, including pupil-attitude questionnaires, observation systems of classrooms and measures for obtaining data on the child's actual experience of education across an entire school day (these can be consulted in the Supplementary Information, see p. 302). We developed an innovative intervisitation system to chart the variation between societies in their contexts and cultures and the 'taken for granted' that might have gone unintentionally unreported by members of country teams. We also collected rich, intensive and high-quality data from contrasting schools of different levels of effectiveness in every one of our nine countries, with each school being described and contrasted on a common set of parameters covering their organisation, leadership, staffing, expectations and related factors that, together, represent probably all the dimensions that have historically been utilised in effectiveness research internationally (Teddlie and Reynolds, 2000).

We are confident that ISERP stands among the most conceptually advanced and methodologically sophisticated studies in our field. The multiple levels of the data collection, the multiple methods of study, the multiple outcomes on which data were collected over three cycles and two school years, and the range brought to the study by the choice of countries and contrasting schools within countries – all mark out the study design as of high quality. However, it should be clear from our discussion in this volume that the high quality of the study design was not always marked by high-quality implementation of that design. There were never the resources available to fully train and monitor country teams into fully implementing the agreed methodology in exchange for resources, and there were never the resources to monitor closely how each of the nine country teams was progressing. Like most studies in the area of international effectiveness, our study needs a health warning attached to it in several respects, although for the teams involved our studies have a considerable amount of 'face validity'.

Our confidence in our findings is confirmed by the fact that, although we were not even sampled to be a 'country versus country' study of achievement differences, such as the TIMSS project, the relative position of our nine countries on the mathematics tests utilised was quite similar to the position shown by those countries in TIMMS and in most of the international surveys to date (see Reynolds and Farrell, 1996, for a review). We note, in particular, that the comparable fourth grade TIMSS mathematics results showed students from Hong Kong scoring, on average, above those from the United States and Canada, who in turn had higher scores than those of England, Norway and Ireland, just as our results do. Findings on the influence of the social class of background of pupils in English-speaking societies also parallel the findings from a wide range of studies in this area, as do the findings on the positive relationship between pupils' attitudes and their academic achievement (see Mortimore *et al.*, 1988, for comparable findings). Although there were inevitable flaws in the implementation of the research strategy, there are enough areas of strength to draw on, enough consistency of findings with other studies and enough overlapping 'intervisitation' experience to make one certain that the results that constitute what is being reported here are not simply an artefact of variation between research teams.

Our findings reviewed

We summarise our findings as follows:

- Whatever the problems we had encountered as our research design was implemented internationally, it is clear that the great majority of schools 'played in position' in all countries, with lower-social-class schools getting lower initial maths achievement scores than middle-social-class schools, and less effective schools getting lower scores than typical or more effective schools.

- Pupils' increasing time in school weakens the relationship between pupils' achievements and their parental ethnic, educational and social-class backgrounds, in all our countries where we have usable data. These findings indicate the power of schooling to combat disadvantage. They tell us, as have many other effectiveness research studies (Teddlie and Reynolds, 2000) that schools clearly *can* make a difference (see Chapter 3).

- It is clear (see Chapter 3) that there are interesting variations between countries in the reliability of their education systems, with some evidencing 'low variance' and some, predominantly Anglo-Saxon societies, showing larger between-classroom and -school variability. We speculate later in this chapter on how this may reflect on a 'weak' system of education, one where individual headteachers and teachers of Anglo-Saxon societies are the building-blocks of schools, rather than schools being formed by 'strong' systems.

- It is clear that there is variation across the country contexts to the extent that the social background of pupils influences their progress at school, with the two Pacific Rim countries of Taiwan and Hong Kong showing the lowest background effects in two different analyses that we undertook on this issue (one from each analysis, we should make clear). Whilst it is unclear the extent to which this reflects the presence in all social strata of these countries of values derived from historic religious and cultural traditions, this finding may also reflect on the extent to which strong technologies of practice exist that are applied deliberately to the education of all children, a theme we return to later in this chapter.

- It is clear (see Chapter 3) that many of the factors that have formed the intellectual backbone of the teacher effectiveness research and practice movement internationally, to do with the quality of teachers' classroom management, their instruction and their classroom climate, *do* explain variation in pupils achievement gain in many diverse countries across the world. Indeed, at the level of the discrete behaviours exhibited by teachers, it is factors such as clarity, questioning, high expectations, a commitment to academic achievement and lesson-structuring that have formed the core constructs of the teacher effectiveness tradition that partially explain why the less effective schools of the world differ from the typical and the more effective. These amount to the *universals* that we wished our study to test out the existence of. Indeed, as one reads through the case studies of classrooms that are reported in the school case studies under the heading 'A day in the life of a child', one is struck by how similar is the experience of children in the classrooms of effective schools across the world in terms of the teachers and teacher behaviours they are encountering.

- It is also clear (see Chapter 13) that many of the concepts that have formed the intellectual backbone of the school effectiveness research and practice movement internationally, concerning the quality of the headteacher/principal, the nature of school expectations and the extent to which the school level potentiates the quality of the classroom experience, *do* travel in explaining why some schools are effective in a wide variety of different country contexts. They also travel in explaining variation between schools in their effectiveness in different socio-economic status contexts. The factors that do not travel so well (school resources, school image and school relationship with local authorities) are exactly what one would expect from this literature.

However, it is clear from the case studies reported that whilst *conceptually* factors such as 'the quality of the principal' are universal factors determining the level of a school's effectiveness in all the various countries of the world we worked in, the precise *operationalisation* of the effective principal differed according to the cultural context of individual societies. In the United States or the United Kingdom, a 'top-down' orientation was the precise method that was associated with effectiveness – in the Netherlands, it would be a more 'lateral' or collaborative orientation to one's colleagues. In marked contrast to the classroom level where the universals are more nearly the same conceptually *and* behaviourally, the school case studies show that the precise ways in which effective school factors showed themselves were somewhat different across international contexts, much more different than the teacher behaviours.

We cannot stress this too highly: *many factors that make for good schools are conceptually quite similar in countries that have widely different cultural, social and economic contexts. The factors hold true at school level, but the detail of how school level concepts play out within countries is different between countries. At the classroom level, the powerful elements of expectation, management, clarity and instructional quality transcend culture.*

The implications of the findings for policymakers

We noted at the beginning of this book that policymakers have begun to look across the globe in search of practices that might improve their schools. Reasons for this world-wide search may range from simple curiosity to, perhaps, near desperation for further increments in school quality. Much of the search may also be due to the genuine realisation that societies other than one's own may have useful educational practices, initiatives, policies and processes that might be worthy 'try-outs' in policymakers' own societies. Trying to 'cast a broad net' while seeking solutions to specific, country-level, vexing problems seems to be a generally laudable policy for policymakers to follow.

Whatever the reason for the enhanced policy internationalisation, policymakers should be reassured by the findings of our study, since it is clear that 'what is necessary for schools to work' is a conceptually very similar range of things in different countries. The classroom, the principal and the other factors that make schools 'more effective' or 'less effective' across the globe appear to be an established set of findings that should be drawn on without fear of irrelevance, or contextual irrelevance, by policymakers.

However, policymakers' ability to use studies such as ours with the confidence that the same school-level concepts discriminate between good and less good practice internationally should not be confused with the simple borrowing of the *detail* of these concepts and school practices. As an example, although the principal appears as a key factor in determining what are effective schools virtually across the globe, the precise way in which a principal is more effective in a Taiwanese context (by being rather vertical in leadership orientation) and in a Norwegian context (by often being quite horizontal or lateral) are somewhat different.

In the classroom, teaching and instructional area, by contrast, it seems that not only do the same *concepts* explain which classrooms and schools 'work', but that the precise *detail* of the effective factors themselves often look identical in different country settings. As an example, questioning techniques, giving opportunities to review and practice, and the 'learning level' factors we talked about in Chapter 13 are micro-level behaviours which appear to be identical in the classrooms of effective schools in all countries.

All this suggests that policymakers may therefore find it useful to see which interesting practices from countries other than their own might be a useful focus for experimentation and trial in their own country. One should, of course, always be aware of the dangers in 'cherry-picking' teaching and schooling practices and then proposing that they should be translated into the practices of other societies. Nevertheless, policymakers should also be made aware that effective practices do not necessarily cease to exist past the limits of their own geographic boundaries. As an illustration here are some examples of potentially useful practices as seen by the United States researchers in the ISERP team that would be available to any policymaker that would be able to visit the same countries that we did:

- A great deal of discussion has focused on increasing teacher collaboration and *community building*. Countries as diverse as Norway, Taiwan and Hong Kong provide examples of how to make this happen on a stable, ongoing basis. Existing US systems default to a teacher with her desk in a classroom, fifteen to thirty-five students with that teacher for 4.5 to 6 hours per day, with a few minutes of planning time before and after school, and perhaps two additional planning periods per week, often at her desk in her classroom. If one wanted to create a system immune to all change, one probably could not have done better.

  The non-English-speaking countries in particular had two very substantial differences in the organisation of teachers' time and space: (a) shared planning space and time, and (b) attractive teachers' work space. Teachers' desks in Hong Kong and Taiwan were not located in classrooms. Rather, they were located in central teachers' offices. The effect was that when teachers had planning periods, they were already among their peers. Seeing excellent instruction in an Asian context, one can appreciate the lesson, but also understand that the lesson did not arrive magically. It was planned, often in conjunction with an entire grade-level team (or, for a first-year teacher, with a master teacher) in the teachers' shared office and work area.

  If one wants more collaboration among teachers, and if one wants the development of more thoughtful lesson provision to our students, Asia provides a cost-achievable method for getting there. They have done this by having a substantial number of specialist teachers working with classes daily (physical education, art, music, etc.). The net effect is that even primary-grade teachers often spend less than half of their paid hours instructing. Rather, they are planning, often in teams, or grading students' papers, or meeting with parents or other adults.

  The trade off that is made for more-out-of-class time is that when teachers are teaching, they often are doing so with larger numbers of students. As an example of how this trade might work in the US, consider a school that currently has six first- and second-grade teachers, each teaching twenty-two students virtually all day (132 students total), with little planning time. Such a group might want to consider having four groups of thirty-three, with two specialist teachers in maths, science, physical education, or other areas moving among the classes so that the four remaining first- and second-grade home-room teachers all get two extra shared planning periods per day. They would have their desks in a common teachers' office that includes all of their desks, telephones, and no students. The office would have a materials storage and preparation room next door. The two office and materials rooms would be former classrooms.

The second issue to do with physical space for collaboration was made obvious in our visit to Norwegian primary schools. To visit a teachers' area in Norway was, in our experience, to visit a space with many of the comforts of home. The chairs, couches and amenities were comfortable, modern and inviting since it is obvious that the most expensive component of a school is the paid adults. A pleasant lounge would logically make those people feel more appreciated and more professional. It can also serve as a space in which collaboration is facilitated. In Norway, Taiwan and Hong Kong, we never saw a teacher's work space or lounge that included a television. The first theme in this observation is that if one wants more thoughtful, more collaborative instruction, we need to structure our schools so that teachers have the time and a place to plan, share and think.

The second suggestion in this area is that if we are to upgrade the status of teachers and teaching, we need to upgrade the quality of the environment in which they interact. Teachers' lounges should be upgraded. We were also impressed with how much the Taiwanese students seemed to take *pride in and ownership of their schools*. In the poorest neighbourhoods, we didn't see graffiti on school walls, or vandalised areas within school compounds. At first this was confusing and we thought it was simply a cultural factor that we could never match in the US. Then one morning we were observing in maths classes when the lesson ended. Vivaldi's *Four Seasons* came on the entire school's intercom, and students moved to diverse 'cleaning up' tasks. Our (language and educational) translator explained to us that this was a standard ten-minute feature of all of Taiwan's primary schools. We looked around the rooms. Every child had a job. Some put all the chairs on top of the desks, others were sweeping, others mopping, others washed windows or sills or blackboards. Some children went out and cleaned their classes' designated sections of the hallways. Students from older grades cleaned exterior walkways, and efficiently swept the paved playground. Some of the students from the highest grade went to the special education classes and helped those students with their tasks. The entire student body was organised to spend ten minutes per day looking after their own school. This taught students responsibility and respect. It gave them physical activity which their young bodies needed, it provided a very clean school at a very reasonable price, and it freed maintenance people to keep up with major repairs. These schools were teaching socially desirable traits (responsibility, cleanliness and respect) while obtaining spotlessly clean schools at low cost. All countries could learn something here.

In debriefing in Hong Kong, it became clear that in other countries we simply didn't have the sort of consistent institutionalised homework and classwork assignment books that Hong Kong's and Taiwan's students took home. These books provide a daily update on each student's work, a place for a teacher's note home to parents (Asian teachers have several hours of prep time every day), and for parents' notes back. In countries like the US, there was no equivalent of the Asian administrators' regular check of all student's assignment work. In these regular exercises a 'dean' (assistant principal) or principal looks at every child's *actual products* in a certain subject. Where is the equivalent quality control in the United States? For although there has been some discussion of 'portfolios' of students' best work in the US, there is rarely anything like the type of student accountability for all of their work, and parent and teacher accountability for being sure that all of the work is completed and corrected, that exists in Asia. If we want all children to learn, we are going to have to have measures of all children's work and progress that are much more proximate than annual achievement tests.

- Observations and interviews in *small schools* in Norway and the Netherlands left us with few doubts that smaller schools can be more 'home-like'. They can be very personal and humane. They can reduce the number of students having to get on a bus or be driven by their parents to school each day. Smaller schools can help build stronger relationships between parents and teachers, the school and the community.

At the same time, we must report that the Taipei, Taiwan schools we visited had between 3,000 and 6,000 elementary grade students, and produced a level of achievement and civility that would be the envy of most US schools. Our conclusion is that the issue isn't so much school size per se, as the posing of the question, which surrounds this entire study: 'What does the society want?' This relates back to and refines the over-all theme number 2 above: among the things that have to be taken for granted are a focused number of goals. Most days those goals can be implied, but at some point they must be specific. Our sense is that the US generally, and US educators in particular, are vexingly unable to come to a finite set of goals and say, 'these things must come first'. No one can improve everything first. We need finite priorities. School size is just one very visible repesentation of this unstated compromise.

- As a separate, perhaps quite important, example of the above general rule, we were quite impressed with the extent to which our Norwegian schools' focused on teaching *democratic values* to their students. Because our Norwegian peers had talked so much about this dimension, we discussed diverse situations with these young people. They often answered with examples of responses to potential values conflicts that focused on the importance of each of their peers' self-concept and dignity, whether an old friend or a new member of the community. As with the Taiwanese ten-minute clean-up lesson in shared responsibility, these weren't schools passively waiting for some abstracted cultural values to assert themselves. These were schools actively teaching a specific way of thinking about dilemmas and values. Democratic values are learned, and can be taught and modelled.

• Moving on to *employment policies* the Australian 'Outback' is a rural, dry, often desolate part of the world. Some of it is in Queensland, the state from which our Australian sample of schools was drawn. While our sample was in greater-Brisbane, the effect of the Outback could be seen even there. Virtually every teacher in those largely urban/suburban schools had, in the first years of their professional work, taught for two years in the Outback. This was almost never by choice. Rather, the two years of service were a state-mandated condition for long-term employment for any teacher.

Rural and inner-city school districts in the US often have a hard time obtaining adequate numbers of teachers. Australia made us wonder if states couldn't make two years of service in rural or urban areas a condition of long-term employment in, for example, Montgomery County or Baltimore County Maryland, or suburban Jefferson Parish, Louisiana.

• In *school architecture*, form should follow function. Moving around schools from Norway to Taiwan, we were struck with the extent to which facilities largely reflected the realities of their contexts, and with how often US urban and suburban elementary schools do not. Urban schools in Hong Kong and Taiwan included a brick or concrete wall surrounding the entire school and playground. The only unlocked entrance to these latter schools were inviting entryways that went directly past the school office. All persons, both desired and undesired, had to enter and exit directly past the school secretary and principal. Further, young children could not accidentally kick a ball into the street or be easily drawn into casual commerce with a drug dealer. These schools were designed for modern realities, and addressed those unfortunate elements in a way that allowed for maximum student safety while retaining space for students' physical activity.

Urban/suburban America moves by car and truck. It contains far too many highly entrepreneurial drug dealers and such. For us to continue building schools that have large outdoor spaces and inadequate barriers between children and streets (with their fast-moving cars and street-entrepreneurs) places our children and our schools at perpetual risk. There are many urban elementary schools in the US where the principal has cancelled all outdoor recess because her experience is that she cannot keep the students safely removed from the problems of the surrounding community. Hong Kong has architecturally removed that entire range of challenges to student safety. The solution saves money (e.g. the schools don't have to hire full-time police), and allows young people the safe, physical activity they need and crave.

•   Several nations (e.g. Norway, Hong Kong) guarantee *schools funding* in advance. The effect is to allow rational school-level planning. Entirely too many urban schools in the US have had the experience of having their discretionary budgets 'frozen' (e.g. removed) sometime after Christmas of a school year, due completely to a central administrator's inability to successfully manage budgets. If we really want 'rational' site-based management, we need to provide opportunities for rational site-based budget control, with budgets protected once in place.

•   There were a variety of '*little things*' in the countries' classrooms that the team suspects had a positive cumulative effect. Here are two examples from Taiwan: instead of having the speaker system sound a shrill 'bell' at the end of periods, have it sound the 'Westminster chimes' or movements from Vivaldi's *Four Seasons*. The message to students and teachers is the same (class is over), but the latter eliminates unnecessary jarring of nerves several times a day. First-grade classrooms in Taiwan have a one-step 'stage' in front of the front blackboards. The effect is that when (inherently short) young students write on the board, their peers can see the work. The Taiwanese don't ask their six-year-olds, who are just learning to write to write far above their heads when they are in front of their classes. Little things. They appeared to add up to something bigger.

The implications of the findings for researchers

For researchers, the ISERP study has validated for those of us involved in it the value of comparative study, for three reasons. Firstly, we have simply seen in other societies a variety of educational practices at classroom and school levels that would not have been seen had the core research team stayed within their own societies. In Pacific Rim societies for example, the majority of lesson time is filled with what has been called 'whole-class interactive' instruction, in which relatively short lessons of forty minutes are filled with fast, emotionally intense presentations from teachers, with accompanying very high levels of involvement with pupils. This model of teaching, which is also found within a European context in societies such as Switzerland, is now the subject of considerable debate within United Kingdom schools.

In Norway, as a contrast, there is no formal assessment of children through the entire phase of their elementary/primary education from the age of seven, a marked contrast to the English-language nations' practice of formal assessment and associated publication of results. In Pacific Rim societies again, one can see micro-level educational practices such as teachers teaching from a stage at the front of the class some six inches high (to help those at the back of the class to see), pupils marching to assembly through corridors in which loudspeakers play pleasant music (to ensure a relaxed attitude) and pupils starting the afternoon session of school with a 'sleeping' lesson (to deal with the fatigue brought about by the frantic pace of the school and the heat/humidity of the climate). Put simply, comparative investigation shows an enhanced range of what is educationally possible.

The benefits from comparative investigation are more than simply a knowledge of educational factors that might be utilised in programmes of experimentation in one's own country. They are, secondly, that one is made aware of educational philosophies that are radically different from one's own, or those of the government of one's own country. In Norway, for example, there is a strong commitment to the child as an 'active citizen', and to what are called 'democratic values' that have no British or American equivalents. In Pacific Rim societies, there is a philosophy that the role of the school is to ensure that all children learn, and that a strong 'technology' of practice should be employed to ensure that children are not dependent on their family background. Such societies are very concerned about the use of practices to improve the achievement of their trailing edge of pupils, therefore, and are therefore rather less concerned with the education of the 'gifted and talented' that appears to be the obsession of the United Kingdom and United States.

A third reason for comparative investigation is probably even more important than the two above: the possibility that within the right kind of comparative framework one can move beyond looking at the practices of other societies and actually so empathise with other societies that one can look back at one's own society with the benefit of their perspective. Such 'acculturation' is what happened to many of us in ISERP when we were confronted with, and may have identified with, Pacific Rim educational systems. Looking back at the British and other systems through their 'lens', one wonders at the utility of the combination of the very complex technology of practice that has been evidenced in British primary practice, for example, with methods of teacher education that have been premised on the importance of teachers 'discovering', or at the least playing an active role in learning about, the appropriate methods to use. To a Taiwanese educationist, this celebrates the desires of teachers for their long-term developmental needs above the needs of children to receive a reliable, consistent, predictable and competently provided experience as they pass through their schools.

The use of another culture's 'lens' adopted through the intervisitation programme to better understand the limitations and strengths of one's own educational practice also applies at the level of educational philosophy as well as educational practice. As an example, those of us involved in the British ISERP team would have historically viewed our primary education practice as loosely 'progressive', and indeed would have thought that in many senses it was the envy of the world. The encouragement of children to learn on their own rather than simply being instructed, the new sets of social outcomes that the system is widely argued to concentrate upon, and the reduced emphasis upon the testing of knowledge acquisition have been widely argued to be the hallmarks of progressive practice in the British system.

Seen from a Pacific Rim perspective, however, the characteristics of the British system would be seen as regressive, not progressive. Transferring the burden of learning to pupils would be seen as maximising both social-class influences and variation between pupils within Taiwanese educational culture, since pupils' learning gains would depend on what they brought to the learning situation in terms of achievement levels and backgrounds. Removing the 'constant' of the teacher would be seen as further maximising individual variation in knowledge gain. Avoiding the testing of basic skills could be seen as maximising the chances of children who have missed acquiring particular knowledge bases being left without them, through the absence of short-term feedback loops that alert school authorities that certain children have not learned.

For all these reasons, it remains a great pity that comparative education in general, and the international achievement surveys in particular, have not shown consistent improvement in the quality of the data gathered, and in the insights derived from that data, over the last twenty years. In the absence of an intellectually vibrant comparative education community, the increasing tendency of educational research to be cross-national or international in focus will not be resourced, and the sub-disciplines of education may make the kind of intellectual and practical errors that comparative education could have warned them about.

Within comparative education, the large-scale cross-national achievement surveys retain high public and professional interest. These surveys are well known by educational researchers and policymakers, and command attention because of the themes they address. For all their faults, they have a common dependent variable and therefore, in theory, can handle the explanation of the effects of different patterns of independent variables. They include material on the focal concerns of educational research – schools and, to a more limited extent, classrooms. From our own experience, the quality of this work would improve if it:

- utilised multiple methodologies and strategies of data collection;
- focused upon classrooms more, utilising observation of teachers and children's whole school days;
- adopted multiple outcomes;
- was sensitive to the variation between countries in their basic educational discourses;
- ensured that the factors studied were representative of the likely causal factors across all countries;
- utilised cohort studies that kept researchers in touch with the same children over time;
- utilised intervisitations across countries by qualitative researchers to understand educational phenomena better.

Current research needs to move in two directions. Firstly, the field needs a large number of small studies in which investigations focus upon the interactions between individuals, classes, schools and countries in a wide range of different locations. These may well show us the complicated nature of any search for good practice, but may, if the ISERP experience is a valid one, also show us universals that appear to matter in explaining the effectiveness of schools and teachers in different contexts. These conceptual universals may also lead to elucidation of interesting practices that might work outside the contexts that they are now found in.

Secondly, the effectiveness of these factors could be tested in programmes of planned intervention in different countries, in which the effects of the interventions are studied. Some of these interventions will have positive effects on pupil outcomes and no doubt a few will have negative effects, but this study of effectiveness in varying contexts both between and within countries will add inestimably to our knowledge. As interventions 'ripple through' to affect outcomes or are blocked by within-system, or perhaps without-system, factors we will learn much more about the complexity of the class/school/society interaction, and about the complexities of the schools and the classrooms themselves. The way to understand something is clearly to try to change it!

Some critical views

Whilst it is clear to us now that the largest single inhibitor to the evolution of truly world-class schooling in any or in all nations is our international inability to look outwards to other schools and contexts broadly, and then to have the self-confidence both to integrate and to amalgamate what we see with what we currently do, there are many who argue that one should be wary of exactly the kind of experimentation with the methods of other countries that we advocate here. Teacher behaviours and ways of administering school are, for these persons, not universals but have to be chosen specifically with the characteristics of the culture receiving the experimentation in mind. Seen from this perspective, 'what works' is not reducible to a set of behaviours or organisational processes readily transferable.

The kind of international trawl for potentially useful teaching and schooling factors, that can then be trialled in countries different from those that generated them, that we outline here is therefore not something that appeals to all comparativists or researchers alive to international educational comparison. In the United States, Stigler and Hiebert (1999) have shown in fascinating detail the very different patterns of classroom teaching exhibited by teachers in Japan, Germany and the United States, yet view these things as part of the broader cultural views of education, schools and children possessed by different country cultures. Teaching is 'cultural', they argue, and: 'the widely shared cultural beliefs and expectations that underlie teaching are so fully integrated into teachers' worldviews that they fail to see them as mutable' (p. 100). Stigler and Hiebert continue to argue that it is not the behavioural *practices* of teachers in educationally successful countries that need to be universalised, since 'what works in one classroom might not work in another' (p. 134), but that it is the methods of professional development of countries like Japan which are classroom focused that should be 'borrowed'.

In the United Kingdom the recent attacks upon the school effectiveness paradigm from numerous sources (see the Special Issue of *School Effectiveness and School Improvement*, vol. 12, no. 1) have extended to attacks upon the ISERP study and the thinking behind it. Alexander (2000), for example, criticises the focus of international school effectiveness work on teaching behaviours and school organisational forms, arguing that conceptually teaching cannot be isolated from the complex cultural, social and economic processes that it is embedded in. Lauder (2000) also criticises any 'policy importation' as potentially violating the complex interaction between 'culture' and 'educational processes', as does Broadfoot (2000) who sees the behaviours of teachers in England and France as partly reflecting national differences in the roles of teachers and students and the ways in which 'learning' is defined.

These arguments, which appear to encompass a range of persons from those who believe that effective teaching/schooling practice is culturally specific to those who believe that culture needs to be more understood, appear to be frankly non-rational to a marked degree. Firstly, there is an already extensive body of research which shows substantially reproducible findings across cultures in the 'correlates' of school effectiveness generally (Teddlie and Reynolds, 2000). If we were to look at the teacher effectiveness level, then there is substantial international agreement on the importance of such factors as expectations, high-quality review and opportunities to practice (Muijs and Reynolds, 2001). For specific subject areas like mathematics virtually all the international literature shows a positive effect of whole-class teaching, time management, pupil engagement and a negative effect of a high proportion of time for individuals working on their own.

Secondly, as well as the literature on effectiveness factors showing agreement cross-culturally there are specific programmes that are apparently effective in widely different cultures, such as *Success for All* (Slavin, 1996).

Thirdly, there are the results of this research itself which suggest a slightly more complicated position in the field than previously, but that, at the teacher level, a large number of the international teacher effectiveness behaviours still discriminate when schools of differing levels of effectiveness are compared. For countries as diverse as Hong Kong and the United Kingdom, when schools are grouped by effectiveness status, many of the teacher effectiveness factors discriminate as predicted. At school level, many conceptual characteristics are the same across countries, although the precise organisational features associated with these are different in different contexts, as the case studies showed in Chapters 4 to 12.

Quite why the critics of studies, like ISERP, in the international effectiveness tradition appear so doubtful about the possibility of creating new blends of be-haviours and organisational features independent of particular cultures is unclear. Throughout their writing is an intellectual temerity and doubt about 'what works' that probably reflects simple ignorance of the literature. Additionally, their rampant context-specificity may reflect their historical ideological commitment to teacher education and professional development that is primarily based upon loosely guided self-discovery of 'what works', a position that is conceptually and practically threatened by the existence of any universals, which should of course imply a need for countries to ensure 'core' activities independent of context. Perhaps the critics are simply taking refuge in 'context-specificity' rather than facing an intellectual challenge of determining the universality and specificity of educational factors that is simply beyond them.

However, if attention is paid to them, the critics may, wittingly or unwittingly, be damaging the prospects of educational advance, since countries that restrict the search for 'good practice' only to those educational settings within their own boundaries of necessity miss potentially valuable practices from outside those boundaries. Countries that refuse to adopt an international reach may fail to acquire innovations which certain countries have discovered and are profitably utilising, such as the highly effect-ive *Success for All* programme from the United States (Slavin, 1996) or indeed the constructivist technologies being developed in the United States and the Netherlands (see Teddlie and Reynolds, 2000, ch. 12).

Some recommendations

Since we remain certain that, on the basis of our results, there is everything to gain and nothing to lose from an international reach in the attempt to improve education systems, we clearly reject the critics' views. Indeed, it is difficult to understand them or the factors that have prompted them.

We would argue, additionally, that our experiences have made us aware not just of classroom and school factors that are in some cases conceptual and/or practical universals but have given us 'world-views' about education that we believe can facilit-ate educational advance, world-views that are couched at a level of generality above that of 'effectiveness factors' but which have clear practical utility nonetheless. It is with these 'world-views' that we conclude, couched as a series of recommendations.

1   Recommendation one: creating world-class schools requires strong systems not just people

We noted in the first section of Chapter 13 that there were differences between the English-speaking societies and others in the school characteristics that were useful to the research teams in explaining effectiveness. In English-speaking countries, *personal* factors such as the quality of the principal, or relational factors such as the nature of the relations between teachers, were relatively more associated with whether schools 'added value' or not. By contrast, in Pacific Rim societies, the factors that were most useful in explaining 'effectiveness' and 'ineffectiveness' were *systemic*, not *personal* ones, and were concerned with the degree of implementation of quality curricula, high-quality organisational structures and the like.

It is clear to us that enormous advantages accrue to those societies which possess 'strong systems', rather than rely heavily on 'strong people' or 'unusual persons' to run their schools. Strong systems minimise the variance in the quality of education provided, increase the likelihood of continuance over time and assure continuance after any key personnel leave the employment of their institution. Systems, on the other hand, that rely on persons to generate their own methods, inevitably persons of different levels of competence, will generate variance in the quality of the methods used according to how much competence persons possess initially. Strong systems can probably generate a higher proportion of educational professionals with the requisite skills to run effective schools, whereas systems that rely on personal characteristics are restricted to the number of persons who possess the requisite personal characteristics. When what is required for being successful in the occupational role of teacher is constantly being increased in quantity and difficulty, the chance of individuals already having what is required is correspondingly lessened.

What are examples of strong systems? We do have examples of strong systems that go beyond personal characteristics, yet are not as imbedded in the culture as the practices noted in our discussions of the Asian classrooms in the study. Examples from US society would be programmes such as *Success for All* (Slavin, 1996), which was externally created and is now delivered to schools through provision of curriculum, training and feedback. Over the years, continued expansion of this model incorporated not only curricular and institutional training, but developed sophisticated evaluation and assessment materials to more effectively meet the programme goals. Comprehensive systems of schooling can be found in other models such as those of the New American School Designs or High Reliability Schools. The specifics of the system employed in each programme may differ, but the provision of a coherent system is core. We believe that you cannot build educational systems on the assumption that every person working within them is exceptionally effective.

2 Recommendation two: creating world-class schools requires a taken-for-granted

In some countries that we have studied there are core beliefs held in the society regarding children, teaching and schools that form a basis for the development of a 'technology of practice' amongst educational professionals across the schools. The elements of this technology and the beliefs that support it are, however, very different from country to country. In Pacific Rim societies or Norway, for example, there are shared values that virtually all educational professionals share about 'what should happen' in a classroom or a school. In part, such cohesion reflects the very nature of the societies themselves, with their shared values of desired educational practice being derived from Confucian traditions in the case of the Pacific Rim and from a strong national community in the case of Norway.

But it is clear that educational factors can mould these cohesive values also, in addition to reflecting them. Most elementary school teachers in Taiwan, for example, receive training from nine institutions whose faculty come from the same institutions. Educational meetings to determine national policy include the major educational players, and changes can be rapidly conveyed to teachers who share the general national values about which educational values are important and which practices appropriate. There is, of course, variation among educational professionals in their practice, but it appears to be concerned with the degree of implementation of the particular practice rather than being based upon varying definitions about the purposes of teaching and the goals of the educational system in the first place.

Whereas some societies have this shared set of understandings about what schools should be doing, and particularly Norway, Taiwan and Hong Kong spring to mind here, English-speaking countries evidenced huge variation in what was seen as appropriate, or at least acceptable, practice, reflecting unresolved values debates at national level about what the purpose of education should be, and what therefore 'good practice' is. These characteristics reflect national values of individualism and local control. In such situations, children in the early-age phases of schooling may be the losers. They are exposed to variation in practice, in part because teachers have unclear or differing sets of goals, and are exposed to variation in the quality of the implementation of the practice by the different sets of teachers with the different sets of goals. This results in schools and classrooms being unpredictable and lacking in consistency, constancy and cohesion.

The creation of world-class schools clearly requires agreement upon goals amongst educationalists as educationalists, if not as individuals. There seems to be little useful purpose to be served by a continued professional debate about values present in a number of societies that we have studied until the educational system can effectively deliver any of the values. The system cannot do this at present because it has ineffective and varied 'means' that have been produced by the absence of clarity of mission and consistent delivery.

3   *Recommendation three: creating world-class schools requires technologies of practice*

We noted in Chapter 13 that there were interesting differences between countries in the extent to which children's achievements were associated with their parents' social backgrounds. In the United States and United Kingdom, children's mathematics achievement was strongly related to such factors as parental occupation and parental education. By contrast, in societies such as Taiwan and Hong Kong the relationship was less.

It is easy to explain this paradox, since the English-speaking societies have largely permitted teachers to self-determine much of their practice. In this setting, expectations of how children are influenced by their parents' lower expectations form part of the nationally based value systems about children from lower social classes that can easily be reflected in classroom practices that discriminate against such children. Put simply, if there is an absence of a shared technology of practice transmitted through programmes of professional education, then the 'hole' will be filled by practices that are determined by the personal views of teachers and principals.

The alternative, and some societies evidence this, is to ensure that professional education gives all teachers a technology that is to be applied uniformly and evenly to all children independent of any background factors that may exist. In such countries as the Netherlands and Taiwan, therefore, all teachers receive the 'technology' of their profession through instructional theory courses that bring to all trainees the world's great knowledge bases about effective instruction, intervention programmes, novel approaches such as metacognitive strategies, and the like. Undergirding this technology is the belief that effort is the basis for success rather than family or intelligence. The attempt is made to, in a structured fashion, fill the circle of professional practice that would largely be filled by a process of self-invention or 'do-it-yourself' or 'finding what works best for me' in other societies. The specification of a teaching technology is also associated with a clearly specified professional ideology that minimises the chance of children from disadvantaged homes being educated by discriminating practices. In Taiwan, for example, the belief is inculcated that all children can learn, that the school should educate all children whether their background is advantaged or disadvantaged, and that education is the right of all. Correspondingly, there is limited discussion about children's family backgrounds, since they are not seen as relevant to the job of the school, since the role of the school is to educate all children independently of their backgrounds.

Specification of a teaching technology, and its possession by all members of a teaching profession, may in the circumstances of the societies that we studied, be of value to more than only the disadvantaged. Whilst societies such as the United Kingdom have had teacher education which has been orientated towards the needs of the teacher 'artists' to be allowed to invent their own practice and therefore create potentially better practice than that they would have been given as a technology, this may result in less than good practice for those teachers who have not possessed the 'art' but could have acquired the science. The range in the quality of education provided in such societies as the United States, England, and the Republic of Ireland, as shown by the relatively high variance locatable at school level, in part reflects this lack of an agreed technology of practice.

4 Recommendation four: creating world-class schools requires societal support

At the level of the school, but even more in the level above the school, it became clear that higher-level conditions can be created for classroom teaching and the effectiveness that has to be achieved in classrooms. In the ISERP study, countries with more and less centralised educational policies were all included. We could not find much influence of the degree of centralisation (or decentralisation) on the results of students or on the way schools and teachers operate. It is the variation *within* (centralised and decentralised) systems with respect to schools and classrooms that is greater than that *between* the centralised and decentralised systems.

The differences between countries we noted above were related to the coherence and the strength of the system itself. The place of the educational system and the value that is placed on it indicates how much strength the system has. It became apparent that an effective education system level can (but not necessarily will) create effective, strong schools and classrooms, but that depends partly on the value that is placed within the society on the educational system and the importance of the teaching profession. We found in our study that the emphasis on education is different in specific countries and relates to the value that is placed upon the educational profession in different societies. In some countries, education is not regarded highly and is seen as something that only schools have to deliver. In other societies education is seen as a task for society as a whole, in which teachers and schools are important and highly respected. In the first case, one can imagine that the well-being of teachers, their own idea about their profession, and the work they are doing is affected negatively by their own position and the position of education in general in the society. In this case, it is difficult for schools and teachers to ask or to expect assistance from the family, and for the wider society to be involved and to assist in what schools are doing. For example, in the UK there is a lot of criticism of schools and education that has negatively affected the perceptions of their competence and the well-being of teachers by comparison with the societal support in Ireland. These negative attitudes again affect the functioning of schools, teachers and classrooms.

What is needed for educational effectiveness is a paradoxical, complicated set of societal features: namely, the perception that education and teachers matter and are worthy of support, but a culture that in its day-to-day functioning does the job of educating its young itself because it feels that education is not *just* a school responsibility.

5   Recommendation five: creating world-class schools requires thinking the unthinkable

Knowledge of such things as how to teach reading has advanced tremendously over the past fifty years. The content of any recent elementary text series integrates concepts from algebra, geometry and statistics into the primary grades. Reflecting the geometrically expanding knowledge base of the fields, the content of a modern science lesson is fantastically more complex than that of even forty years ago. Yet we English-speaking countries organise the provision of primary school instruction much as we did a hundred years ago: one teacher, as few students as the government can afford, and the full range of subject areas.

Perhaps because universal free public education came later in Asia, those countries have clearly adapted primary education to the realities of an increasingly complex world. For whatever reason, both Hong Kong and Taiwan (and through other studies, we are aware of the same organisational arrangements in other Asian countries) assign teachers to the specialties of mathematics and science. Because these teachers are expected to deliver those courses not in a 'drill and kill' but in an intellectually stimulating fashion, the teachers have been provided more planning time than teaching time in a school day. Teachers need time to think about and plan lessons that require active engagement and 'higher-order' thinking on the part of the students. The well-known TIMSS video series of Japanese, German and US teachers clearly presents more Japanese lessons that are more likely to demand the fullest of each child's intellect. What the videos show much less well is the amount of planning time built into all Japanese teachers' days. Here are countries that have responded to changes in the modern world by themselves innovating their practices. In our Anglo-Saxon terms, they are thinking the unthinkable. We need to do the same, or similar.

Conclusions

In virtually every field of human endeavour and achievement an increasingly inter-nationalised world is now adopting a global reach. Drugs that have been developed as effective are utilised internationally in months. New schools of thought in the humanities, such as postmodernism, spread with viral speed. In such areas as management, the practices utilised by successful companies are used by all countries within months if not years, since companies know they will simply go out of business if they do not rapidly change and improve. If in virtually every area of its existence humanity is using a world of experience to draw on to improve itself, why should we in education not do the same? Rather than being frightened by a world of educational experiences, it is surely time for us to learn from them. It is time to look broadly across the planet, and then integrate what we see with what we do, so that we may do it better. The children of the world deserve it, now.

Bibliography

Aitkin, M. and Longford, N. (1986) 'Statistical Modelling Issues in School Effectiveness Studies'. *Journal of the Royal Statistical Society, Series A*, 149(1), 1–43.

Alexander, R. (2000) *Culture and Pedagogy*. Oxford: Basil Blackwell.

Anderson, L. W., Ryan, D. W. and Shapiro, B. J. (1989) *The IEA Classroom Environment Study*. Oxford: Pergamon Press.

Bass, B. M. (ed.) (1981) *Bass and Stogdill's Handbook of Leadership: Theory, Research and Managerial Applications*. New York: The Free Press.

Bolman, L. G. and Deal, T. E. (1991) *Images of Leadership*. Occasional Paper no. 7. Boston: The National Center for Educational Leadership, Harvard Graduate School of Education.

Brandt, R. S. (1982) 'On School Improvement: A Conversation with Ron Edmonds'. *Educational Leadership*, 40(12), 13–15.

Brigham, N. and Gamse, B. (1997) 'Children's School Days'. In S. Stringfield, *et al.* (eds) *Urban and Suburban/Rural Special Strategies for Educating Disadvantaged Children: Second Year Report*. Washington, DC: US Department of Education, Planning and Evaluation Service.

Broadfoot, P. (2000) *Culture, Learning and Comparison*. Southwell: British Educational Research Association.

Bronfenbrenner, U. (1972) 'Another World of Children'. *New Society*, 10 February, 278–86.

Brookover, W. B., Beady, C., Flood, P., Schweitzer, J. and Wisenbaker, J. (1979) *Schools, Social Systems and Student Achievement: Schools Can Make a Difference*. New York: Praeger.

Bryk, A. S. and Raudenbush, S. W. (1992) *Hierarchical Linear Models: Applications and Data Analysis Methods*. Newbury Park, CA: Sage Publications.

Cammann, C. (1983) 'Assessing the Attitudes and Perceptions of Organisational Members'. In S. E. Seashore, *et al.* (eds) *Assessing Organization Change*. New York: John Wiley.

Campbell, D. and Fiske, D. W. (1959) 'Convergent and Discriminant Validation by the Multitrait-Multimethod Matrix'. *Psychological Bulletin*, 54, 297–312.

Castles, I. (1993) *Schools Australia 1992*. Canberra: Australian Bureau of Statistics.

Chan, B., Cheng, Y. C. and Hau, K. T. (1991) *A Technical Report on the Study of Principal–Teachers Relationship in Hong Kong Secondary Schools*. The Chinese University of Hong Kong.

Chan, C. C., Chan, K. Y., Cheung, W. M., Ngan, M. Y. and Yeung, V. M. (1992) 'Primary School Teacher Self-Concept: Its Relationship with Teacher Behaviours and Students' Educational Outcomes'. *Primary Education*, 3(1), 9–28.

Chan, Y. C. and Cheng, Y. C. (1993) 'A Study of Principal's Instructional Leadership in Hong Kong Secondary Schools'. *Educational Research Journal*, 8, 55–67.

Chapman, J. D. and Aspin, D. N. (1995) 'Securing the Future: An Overview of Some Problems, Issues and Trends arising from the OECD activity on "The effectiveness of schooling and of educational resource management", paper presented at the International Congress on School Effectiveness and School Improvement, Leeuwarden, the Netherlands, January 1995.

Cheng, Y. C. and Ng, K. H. (1991) 'Profile of Effective Classroom'. *Primary Education*, 2(1), 1–10.

Cheng, Y. C. (1991) 'Organizational Environment in Schools: Commitment, Control, Disengagement, and Headless'. *Educational Administration Quarterly*, 27(4), 481–505.

Cheng, Y. C. (1993a) 'The Theory and Characteristics of School-Based Management'. *International Journal of Educational Management*, 7(6), 6–17.

Cheng, Y. C. (1993b) 'Profiles of Organizational Culture and Effective Schools'. *School Effectiveness and School Improvement*, 4, 85–110.

Cheng, Y. C. (1994a) 'Classroom Environment and Student Affective Performance: an Effective Profile'. *Journal of Experimental Education*, 62(3), 221–39.

Cheng, Y. C. (1994b) 'Principal's Leadership as a Critical Factor for School Performance: Evidence From Multi-Levels of Primary Schools'. *School Effectiveness and School Improvement*, 5(3), 299–317.

Cheng, Y. C. (1994c) 'A Preliminary Analysis of Education Quality Profile of Hong Kong Primary Schools'. *Journal of Primary Education*, 5(1), 1–17.

Cheng, Y. C. (1996a) *School Effectiveness and School-Based Management: A Mechanism for Development.* London: Falmer Press.

Cheng, Y. C. (1996b) 'Relation between Teachers' Professionalism and Job Attitudes, Educational Outcomes and Organizational Factors'. *Journal of Educational Research*, 89(3), 163–71.

Cheng, Y. C. (1997) 'A Framework of Indicators of Education Quality in Hong Kong Primary Schools: Development and Application'. In H. Meng, Y. Zhou and Y. Fang (eds) *School Based Indicators of Effectiveness: Experiences and Practices in APEC Members.* China: Guangxi Normal University Press, 207–50.

Cheng, Y. C. (1999) 'The Pursuit of School Effectiveness and Educational Quality in Hong Kong'. *School Effectiveness and School Improvement*, 10(1), 10–30.

Cheng, Y. C. (2000) 'Educational Change and Development in Hong Kong: Effectiveness, Quality, and Relevance'. In T. Townsend and Y. C. Cheng (eds) *Educational Change and Development in the Asia-Pacific Region: Challenges for the Future.* The Netherlands: Swets and Zeitlinger Publisher, 17–56.

Chrispeels, J. H. (1992) *Purposeful Restructuring: Creating a Culture for Learning and Achievement in Elementary Schools.* London: The Falmer Press.

Coleman, J. S., Campbell, E., Hobson, C., McPartland, J., Mood, A., Weinfeld, R. and York, R. (1966) *Equality of Educational Opportunity.* Washington, DC: Government Printing Office.

Comber, L. C. and Keeves, P. (1973) *Science Education in Nineteen Countries.* London: John Wiley.

Crandall, V. C., Katkovsky, W. and Crandall, V. J. (1965) 'Children's Beliefs in their Own Control of Reinforcements in Intellectual-Academic Situations'. *Child Development*, 36, 91–109.

Creemers, B. (1994) *The Effective Classroom.* London: Cassell.

Creemers, B. P. M. (1994) 'The History, Value and Purpose of School Effectiveness Studies'. In D. Reynolds, B. P. M. Creemers, P. S. Nesellrodt, E. C. Schaffer, S. Stringfield and C. Teddlie (eds) *Advances in School Effectiveness Research and Practice.* Oxford: Pergamon, 9–23.

Creemers, B. P. M., Reynolds, D., Stringfield, S. and Teddlie, C. (1996) *World Class Schools: Some Further Findings*, paper presented at the Annual Meeting of the American Educational Research Association, New York.

Cresswell, J. W. (1998) *Qualitative Inquiry and Research Design.* Thousand Oaks, CA: Sage Publications, Inc.

Deming, W. E. (1993) *The New Economics for Industry, Government, Education.* Cambridge, MA: MIT.

Denzin, N. K. (1978) 'The Logic of Naturalistic Inquiry'. In N. K. Denzin (ed.) *Sociological Methods: A Sourcebook.* New York: McGraw-Hill.

Denzin, N. K. and Lincoln, Y. S. (1994) (eds) *Handbook of Qualitative Research.* Thousand Oaks, CA: Sage Publications, Inc.

Durland, M. (1996) 'The Application of Network Analysis to the Study of Differentially Effective Schools'. Unpublished doctoral dissertation, Louisiana State University, Baton Rouge, LA.

Durland, M. and Teddlie, C. (1996) 'A Network Analysis of the Structural Dimensions of Principal Leadership in Differentially Effective Schools', paper presented at the annual meeting of the American Educational Research Association, New York, NY.

Edmonds, R. R. (1979a) 'Effective Schools for the Urban Poor'. *Educational Leadership*, 37(10), 15–24.

Edmonds, R. R. (1979b) 'Some Schools Work and More Can'. *Social Policy*, 9(2), 28–32.

Education Commission (1982, 1986, 1988, 1990, 1992, 1996, 1997) reports nos 1, 2, 3, 4, 5, 6 and 7. Hong Kong: Government Printer.

Elley, W. B. (1992) *How in the World Do Students Read?* Newark, Del: IEA.

Elliott, J. (1996) 'School Effectiveness Research and its Critics: Alternative Visions of Schooling'. *Cambridge Journal of Education*, 26(2), 199–224.

Evans, L. and Teddlie, C. (1995) 'Facilitating Change in Schools: Is There One Best Style?' *School Effectiveness and School Improvement*, 6(1), 1–22.

Foxman, D. (1992) *Learning Mathematics and Science (The Second International Assessment of Educational Progress in England).* Slough: National Foundation for Educational Research.

Fraser, B. J. and Walberg, H. J. (eds) (1991) *Educational Environments: Evaluation, Antecedents and Consequences.* Oxford: Pergamon Press.

French, J. R. P. and Raven, B. (1968) 'The Bases of Social Power'. In D. Cartwright and A. Zander (eds) *Group Dynamics.* New York: Harper and Row.

Friedman, T. L. (1999) *The Lexus and the Olive Tree.* New York: Farrar, Straus and Giroux.

Fullan, M. (1991) *The New Meaning of Educational Change.* London: Cassell.

Gabbard, D. A. (ed.) (2000) *Knowledge and Power in the Global Economy.* Mahwah, NJ: Erlbaum.

Gage, N. (1989) 'The Paradigm Wars and their Aftermath: A "historical" Sketch of Research and Teaching since 1989'. *Educational Researcher*, 18, 4–10.

Geertz, C. (1973) *The Interpretation of Culture.* New York: Basic Books.

Goldstein, H. (1995) *Multilevel Models in Educational and Social Research: A Revised Edition.* London: Edward Arnold.

Good, T. L. and Brophy, J. E. (1986a) 'School Effects'. In M. Wittrock (ed.) *Third Handbook of Research on Teaching.* New York: Macmillan, 570–602.

Good, T. L. and Brophy, J. (1986b) 'Teacher Behaviour and Student Achievement'. In M. C. Wittrock (ed.) *Handbook of Research on Teaching.* New York: Macmillan, 328–775.

Guba, E. G. (1990) *The Paradigm Dialog.* Newbury Park, CA: Sage Publications, Inc.

Hage, J. and Aiken, M. (1967) 'Program Change and Organizational Properties: A Comparative Analysis'. *American Journal of Sociology*, 72, 503–19.

Hallinger, P. and Murphy, J. (1986) 'The Social Context of Effective Schools'. *American Journal of Education*, 94, 328–55.

Hallinger, P. and Murphy, J. (1987) *Instructional Leadership in the School: Issues and Controversies.* Boston: Allyn and Bacon.

Halpin, A. W. and Croft, D. B. (1963) *The Organizational Climate of Schools.* Chicago: Midwest Administration Center University of Chicago.

Hamilton, D. (1996) 'Peddling Feel Good Fictions'. *Forum*, 38(2), 54–6.

Hargreaves, A. (1994) *Changing Teachers, Changing Times. Teachers' Work and Culture in the Postmodern Age.* New York: Teachers College Press.

Harris, S., Keys, W. and Fernandes, C. (1997) *The International Mathematics and Science Study, Second National Report, Part One.* Slough: The National Foundation for Educational Research.

Hattie, J. (1993) *Did it Fall or Was it Pushed: Major trends in Australian Education.* Victoria: Australian Council for Educational Administration.

Hauge, T. E. (1982) 'Åpenhet og samarbeid i skolemiljøet' [Openness and collaboration in the school environment]. Ph.d. thesis, University of Oslo.

Hauge, T. E. (1995) 'Systemic Competence Building and Quality Development in School', paper presented at the International Congress for School Effectiveness and Improvement, Leeuwarden, the Netherlands, January.

Hebert, C. (1994) 'Teachers' Perceptions of Principal Style and Sense of Autonomy in Differentially Effective Schools'. Unpublished doctoral dissertation, Louisiana State University.

Hill, P. W. (1997) 'Shaking the Foundations: Research Driven School Reform'. *School Effectiveness and School Improvement*, 9, 419–36.

Hopkins, D. (1996) 'Towards a Theory for School Improvement'. In J. Gray, D. Reynolds and C. Fitz-Gibbon (eds) *Merging Traditions: The Future of Research on School Effectiveness and School Improvement.* London: Cassell.

Hopkins, D., Ainscow, M. and West, M. (1994) *School Improvement in an Era of Change.* London: Cassell.

Huberman, A. M. and Miles, M. B. (1994) 'Data Management and Analysis Methods'. In N. K. Denzin and Y. S. Lincoln (eds) *Handbook of Qualitative Research.* Thousand Oaks, CA: Sage Publications, Inc., 428–44.

Husen, T. (ed.) (1967) *International Study of Achievements in Mathematics, Volumes One and Two.* Stockholm: Almquist and Wiksell.

Information Office (1997) *Hong Kong 1997.* Hong Kong: Government Printer.

Keeves, J. P. (1992) *The IEA Study of Science III: Changes in Science Education and Achievement, 1970 to 1984.* Oxford: Pergamon Press.

Keys, W. and Foxman, D. (1989) *A World of Differences (A United Kingdom Perspective on an International Assessment of Mathematics and Science).* Slough: National Foundation for Educational Research.

Knight, S. L. (1990) 'The Relationship Between Classroom Learning Environment and Students' Cognitive Reading Strategies'. In H. C. Waxman and C. D. Ellett (eds) *The Study of Learning Environments.* Houston: College of Education, University of Houston, 40–7.

Kozol, J. (1991) *Savage Inequalities: Children in America's Schools.* New York: Crown.

Lapointe, A. E., Mead, N. and Phillips, G. (1989) *A World of Differences: An International Assessment of Mathematics and Science.* New Jersey: Educational Testing Services.

Lauder, H. (2000) 'The Dilemmas of Comparative Research and Policy Importation'. *British Journal of Sociology of Education*, 21(3), 465–75.

Levine, D. U. and Lezotte, L. W. (1990) *Unusually Effective Schools: A Review and Analysis of Research and Practice.* Madison, WI: The National Center for Effective Schools Research and Development.

Lezotte, L. (1989) 'School Improvement Based on the Effective Schools Research'. *International Journal of Educational Research*, 13(7), 815–25.

Lightfoot, S. L. (1993) *The Good High School: Portraits of Character and Culture.* New York: Basic Books.

Lincoln, Y. S. and Guba, E. G. (1985) *Naturalistic Inquiry.* Beverly Hills: Sage Publications, Inc.

Lynn, R. (1988) *Educational Achievement in Japan: Lessons for the West.* London: Macmillan/ Social Affairs Unit.

McHugh, B. and Spath, S. (1997) 'Carter G. Woodson Elementary School: The Success of a Private School Curriculum in an Urban Public School'. *Journal of Education for Students Placed at Risk*, 2(2), 121–36.

Mislevy, R. J. (1995) 'What Can We Learn from International Assessments?' *Educational Evaluation and Policy Analysis*, 17(4), 419–37.

Moos, R. H. and Trickett, E. J. (1974) *Classroom Environment Scale Manual.* Palo Alto: Consulting Psychologists Press.

Mortimore, P., Sammons, P., Stoll, L., Lewis, D. and Ecob, R. (1988) *School Matters. The Junior Years*. London: Open Books.

Muijs, D. and Reynolds, D. (2001) *Effective Teaching*. London: Paul Chapman.

Noah, H. J. (1987) 'Reflections'. *Comparative Education Review*, 31(1), 137–49.

Nuttall, D. (1989) 'Differential School Effectiveness'. *International Journal of Educational Research*, 13(7), 769–76.

Olden, G. R. and Hackman, J. R. (1981) 'Relationships between Organizational Structure and Employees Reactions: Comparing Alternative Frameworks'. *Administrative Science Quarterly*, 26–83.

Patton, M. Q. (1990) *Qualitative Evaluation and Research Methods*. (Second edn.) Newbury Park, CA: Sage Publications, Inc.

Peach, F. (1996) 'Attack on Bureaucratic Practices: From the D-G's desk'. *Education Views*, 5(1), 2.

Postlethwaite, T. N. and Ross, K. (1992) *Effective Schools in Reading: Implications for Educational Planners*. Newark, De: IEA.

Postlethwaite, T. M. and Wiley, D. E. (1992) *The IEA Study of Science II, Science Achievement in Twenty Three Countries*. Oxford: Pergamon Press.

Price, J. L. and Mueller, C. M. (1986) *Handbook of Organizational Measurement*. Pitman Publishing Inc.

Puma, M., Karweit, N., Price, C., Ricciuti, A., Thompson, W. and Vaden-Kiernan, M. (1997) *Prospects: Final Report on Student Outcomes*. Washington, DC: US Department of Education, Planning and Evaluation Services.

Purves, A. C. (1992) *The IEA Study of Written Composition II: Education and Performance in Fourteen Countries*. Oxford: Pergamon Press.

Reynolds, D. (1976) 'The Delinquent School'. In P. Woods (ed.) *The Process of Schooling*, London: Routledge and Kegan Paul, 217–29.

Reynolds, D. (1997) 'The East Looks West'. *Times Education Supplement*, June 27, 21.

Reynolds, D. (1998) 'School Effectiveness: Retrospect and Prospect' (the 1997 SERA lecture). *Scottish Educational Review*, 29(2), 97–113.

Reynolds, D. (1999) 'School Effectiveness: The International Dimension'. In C. Teddlie and D. Reynolds (eds) *The International Handbook of School Effectiveness Research*. London: Falmer Press, 232–56.

Reynolds, D. and Farrell, S. (1996) *Worlds Apart? – A Review of International Studies of Educational Achievement Involving England*. London: HMSO for OFSTED.

Reynolds, D. and Teddlie, C. (1995) 'World Class Schools: A Review of Data from the International School Effectiveness Research Programme', paper presented at the British Educational Research Association, Bath, United Kingdom.

Reynolds, D. and Teddlie, C. (2000a) 'The Future Agenda for School Effectiveness Research'. In C. Teddlie and D. Reynolds (eds) *The International Handbook of School Effectiveness Research*. London: Falmer Press, 322–43.

Reynolds, D. and Teddlie, C. (2000b) 'The Processes of School Effectiveness'. In C. Teddlie and D. Reynolds (eds) *The International Handbook of School Effectiveness Research*. London: Falmer Press, 134–59.

Reynolds, D. and Teddlie, C. (2000c) 'School Effectiveness and Improvement: Past, Present and Future'. In B. Moon, S. Brown and M. Ben-Peretz (eds) *Routledge International Companion to Education*. London: Routledge, 301–23.

Reynolds, D., Hopkins, D. and Stoll, L. (1993) 'Linking School Effectiveness Knowledge and School Improvement Practice: Towards a Synergy'. *School Effectiveness and School Improvement*, 4(1), 37–58.

Reynolds, D., Creemers, B., Stringfield, S. and Teddlie, C. (1998) 'Climbing an Educational Mountain: Conducting the International School Effectiveness Research Project (ISERP)'. In G. Walford (ed.) *Doing Research about Education*. London: Falmer Press, 111–24.

Reynolds, D., Creemers, B., Stringfield, S. and Teddlie, C. (2000d) 'World Class Schools: Some Preliminary Methodological Findings from The International School Effectiveness Research Project (ISERP)'. In D. Shorrocks Taylor and E. Jenkins (eds) *Learning from Others.* Dordrecht: Kluver, 115–36.

Reynolds, D., Creemers, B. P. M., Bird, J., Farrell, S. and Swint, F. (1994b) 'School Effectiveness – The Need for an International Perspective'. In D. Reynolds, B. P. M. Creemers, P. S. Nesselrodt, E. C. Schaffer, S. Stringfield and C. Teddlie (eds) *Advances in School Effectiveness Research and Practice.* Oxford: Pergamon Press, 217–37.

Reynolds, D., Sammons, P., Stoll, L., Barber, M. and Hillman, J. (1996) 'School Effectiveness and School Improvement in the United Kingdom'. *School Effectiveness and School Improvement*, 7(2), 133–58.

Reynolds, D., Creemers, B. P. M., Nesselrodt, P., Schaffer, E., Stringfield, S. and Teddlie, C. (eds) (1994c) *Advances in School Effectiveness Research and Practice.* Oxford: Pergamon Press.

Reynolds, D. *et al.* (1994a) 'School Effectiveness Research: A Review of the International Literature'. In D. Reynolds, B. P. M. Creemers, P. S. Nesellrodt, E. C. Schaffer, S. Stringfield and C. Teddlie (eds), *Advances in School Effectiveness Research and Practice.* Oxford: Pergamon, 25–51.

Robitaille, D. F. and Garden, R. A. (1989) *The IEA Study of Mathematics II: Contexts and Outcomes of School Mathematics.* Oxford: Pergamon Press.

Rosier, M. J. and Keeves, J. P. (1991) *The IEA Study of Science I – Science Education and Curricula in Twenty Three Countries.* Oxford: Pergamon Press.

Rutter, M. (1983) 'School Effects on Pupil Progress: Research Findings and Policy Implications'. In L. Shulman and G. Sykes (eds) *Handbook of Teaching and Policy.* New York: Longman, 3–41.

Rutter, M., Maughan, B., Mortimore, P. and Ouston, J. with Smith, A. (1979) *Fifteen Thousand Hours: Secondary Schools and their Effects on Children.* London: Open Books and Boston, MA: Harvard University Press.

Sammons, P., Hillman, J. and Mortimore, P. (1995) *Key Characteristics of Effective Schools: A Review of School Effectiveness Research.* London: OFSTED.

Sammons, P. (1999) *School Effectiveness: Coming of Age in the Twenty-First Century.* Lisse: Swets and Zeitlinger.

Schaffer, E. (1994) 'The Contributions of Classroom Observation to School Effectiveness Research'. In D. Reynolds, B. P. M. Creemers, P. Nesselrodt, E. Schaffer, S. Stringfield and C. Teddlie (eds) *Advances in School Effectiveness Research and Practice.* Oxford: Pergamon Press.

Schaffer, E., Clark, T. and Chen, Y. H. (1987) 'The Performance of Sixth Grade Chinese Classrooms'. *The International Review of Education*, 34(1), 115–24.

Scheerens, J. (1992) *Effective Schooling: Research Theory and Practice.* London: Cassell.

Scheerens, J. and Bosker, R. (1997) *The Foundations of Educational Effectiveness.* Oxford: Pergamon Press.

Scheerens, J. and Creemers, B. P. M. (1989) 'Conceptualising School Effectiveness'. *International Journal of Educational Research*, 13, 689–706.

Sergiovanni, T. J. (1984) 'Leadership and Excellence in Schooling'. *Educational Leadership*, 41, 4–13.

Slater, R. O. and Teddlie, C. (1992) 'Toward a Theory of School Effectiveness and Leadership'. *School Effectiveness and School Improvement*, 3(4), 247–57.

Slavin, R. (1996) *Education for All.* Lisse: Swets and Zeitlinger.

Slee, R. and Weiner, G. (1998) *School Effectiveness for Whom? Challenges to the School Effectiveness and School Improvement Movements.* London: Falmer Press.

Smith, J. K. and Heshusius, L. (1986) 'Closing Down the Conversation: The end of the Quantitative-Qualitative Debate among Educational Researchers'. *Educational Researcher*, 15, 4–12.

Stedman, L. (1999) 'Incomplete Explanations: The Case of US Performance in the International Assessments of Education'. *Educational Researchers*, 23(7), 24–32.

Stevenson, H., Azuma, H. and Hakuta, K. (1986) *Child Development and Education in Japan.* New York, NY: W. H. Freeman and Company.

Stevenson, H. (1992) 'Learning from Asian Schools'. *Scientific American*, December, 32–8.

Stevenson, H. W. and Stigler, J. W. (1992) *The Learning Gap: Why our Schools Are Failing and What We Can Learn from Japanese and Chinese Education.* New York: Summit Books.

Stigler, J. and Hiebert, J. (1999) *The Teaching Gap.* New York: Free Press.

Stringfield, S., Teddlie, C., Wimpelberg, R. K. and Kirby, P. (1992) 'A Five Year Follow-up of Schools in the Louisiana School Effectiveness Study'. In J. Bashi and Z. Sass (eds) *School Effectiveness and School Improvement: Proceedings of the Third International Congress, Jerusalem.* Jerusalem: The Magnes Press.

Stringfield, S. (1994) 'A Model of Elementary School Effects'. In D. Reynolds, B. P. M. Creemers, P. S. Nesselrodt, E. C. Schaffer, S. Stringfield and C. Teddlie (eds) *Advances in School Effectiveness Research and Practice.* Oxford: Pergamon Press, 153–87.

Stringfield, S. (1995) 'Attempting to Enhance Students' Learning through Innovative Programs: The Case for Schools Evolving into High Reliability Organisations', *School Effectiveness and School Improvement*, 6(1), 67–96.

Stringfield, S. (1996) *Fourth Year Evaluation of the Barclay/Calvert Project.* Baltimore: Johns Hopkins University.

Stringfield, S., Millsap, M. A., Herman, R., Yoder, N., Brigham, N., Nesselrodt, P., Schaffer, E., Karweit, N., Levin, M. and Stevens, R. (with Gamse, B., Puma, M., Rosenblum, S., Beaumont, J., Randall, B. and Smith, L.) (1997) *Urban and Suburban/Rural Special Strategies for Educating Disadvantaged Children. Final Report.* Washington, DC: US Department of Education.

Tashakkori, A. and Teddlie, C. (1998) *Mixed Methodology: Combining the Qualitative and Quantitative Approaches.* Thousand Oaks, CA: Sage Publications.

Teddlie, C. (1994a) 'Integrating Classroom and School Data in School Effectiveness Research'. In D. Reynolds, B. P. M. Creemers, P. S. Nesselrodt, E. C. Schaffer, S. Stringfield and C. Teddlie (eds) *Advances in School Effectiveness Research and Practice.* Oxford, UK: Pergamon, 111–32.

Teddlie, C. (1994b) 'Using Context Variables in School Effectiveness Research'. In D. Reynolds, B. P. M. Creemers, P. S. Nesselrodt, E. C. Schaffer, S. Stringfield and C. Teddlie (eds) *Advances in School Effectiveness Research and Practice.* Oxford, UK: Pergamon, 85–110.

Teddlie, C. and Kochan, S. (1991) 'Evaluation of a Troubled High School: Methods, Results and Implications', paper presented at the annual meeting of the American Education Research Association, Chicago, IL.

Teddlie, C. and Reynolds, D. (2000) *The International Handbook of School Effectiveness Research.* London: Falmer Press.

Teddlie, C. and Stringfield, S. (1985) 'A Differential Analysis of Effectiveness in Middle and Lower Socio-Economic Status Schools'. *Journal of Classroom Interaction*, 20(2), 38–44.

Teddlie, C. and Stringfield, S. (1993) *Schools Make a Difference. Lessons Learned from a 10-Year Study of School Effects.* New York: Teachers College Press.

Teddlie, C. Virgilio, I. and Oescher, J. (1990) 'Development and Validation of the Virgilio Teacher Behaviour Inventory'. *Educational and Psychological Measurement*, 50(2), 421–30.

Thomson, J. R. and Handley, H. M. (1990) 'The Relation between Classroom Learning Environment and Students' Problem-Solving Strategies in Mathematics'. In H. C. Waxman and C. D. Ellett (eds) *The Study of Learning Environments*, vol. 4, pp. 94–103. Houston: College of Education, University of Houston.

Townsend, T. (1995) 'School Effectiveness and School Improvement in Australia'. In B. Creemers and N. Osinga, *ICSEI Country Reports.* Leeuwarden, Gemeenschappelijk Centrum voor Onderwijsbegeleiding in Friesland.

Townsend, T. and Cheng, Y. C. (2000) *Educational Change and Development in the Asia Pacific Region: Challenges for the Future*. Lisse: Swets and Zeitlinger.

Travers, K. J. and Westbury, I. (1989) *The IEA Study of Mathematics I: Analysis of Mathematics Curricula*. Oxford: Pergamon Press.

Van de Grift, W. (1989) 'Self Perceptions of Educational Leadership and Mean Pupil Achievements'. In D. Reynolds, B. P. M. Creemers and T. Peters (eds) *School Effectiveness and Improvement: Selected Proceedings of the First International Congress for School Effectiveness*. Groningen, Netherlands: RION, 227–42.

Van de Grift, W. (1990) 'Educational Leadership and Academic Achievement in Secondary Education'. *School Effectiveness and School Improvement*, 1(1), 26–40.

Venezky, R. L. and Winfield, L. F. (1979) *Schools that Succeed Beyond Expectations in Reading*. Studies on Education Technical Report No. 1. Newark: University of Delaware. (ERIC Document Reproduction Services no. ED 177 484.)

Virgilio, I., Teddlie, C. and Oescher, J. (1991) 'Variance and Context Differences in Teaching at Differentially Effective Schools'. *School Effectiveness and School Improvement*, 2, 152–68.

Walberg, H. J. (1986) 'Synthesis of Research on Teaching'. In M. C. Wittrock, *Handbook of Research on Teaching*. Third edition. New York: Macmillan.

Waxman, H. C., Huang, S. Y., Knight, S. L. and Owens, E. W. (1992) 'Investigating the Effects of the Classroom Learning Environment on the Academic Achievement of At-Risk Students'. In H. C. Waxman and C. D. Ellett (eds) *The Study of Learning Environments*. Houston: College of Education, University of Houston, 92–100.

Weber, G. (1971) *Inner-City Children Can be Taught to Read: Four Successful Schools*. Washington, DC: Council for Basic Education.

Williamson, J. and Fraser, B. J. (1991) 'Elementary Education in Australia'. *The Elementary School Journal*, 92(1).

Willms, D. and Raudenbush, S. (1989) 'A Longitudinal Hierarchical Linear Model for Estimating School Effects and their Stability'. *Educational Administration Quarterly*, 25, 82–107.

Wimpelberg, R., Teddlie, C. and Stringfield, S. (1989) 'Sensitivity to Context: The Past and Future of Effective Schools Research'. *Educational Administration Quarterly*, 25(1), 82–107.

Yin, R. K. (1994) *Case Study Research Design and Methods*. (Second edition.) Newbury Park, CA: Sage Publications, Inc.

Supplementary information

The following supplementary material is available on the world wide web. For information please contact:

Professor David Reynolds
University of Exeter
School of Education
Heavitree Road
EXETER
EX1 2LU
United Kingdom

Telephone: (+44) (0) 1392 264990
Fax: (+44) (0) 1392 264998
E-mail: David.Reynolds@exeter.ac.uk

Appendix One:	Technical appendix
Appendix Two:	Methodological lessons and advances from ISERP
Appendix Three:	The educational context of ISERP participating countries
Appendix Four:	The research process in ISERP participating countries
Appendix Five:	ISERP instrumentation and its properties

Index